Irony in Action

Irony in Action

Anthropology, Practice, and the Moral Imagination

Edited by
James W. Fernandez and
Mary Taylor Huber

The University of Chicago Press
Chicago and London

James W. Fernandez is professor of anthropology at the University of Chicago. He is the author or editor of numerous works, including *Persuasions and Performances: The Play of Tropes in Culture* and *Beyond Metaphor: The Theory of Tropes in Anthropology.*

Mary Taylor Huber is a senior scholar at the Carnegie Foundation for the Advancement of Teaching. She is the author of *The Bishop's Progress: A Historical Ethnography of the Catholic Missionary Experience on the Sepik Frontier* and co-editor of *Gendered Missions: Women and Men in Missionary Discourse and Practice.*

The University of Chicago Press, Chicago 60637
The University of Chicago Press, Ltd., London
© 2001 by The University of Chicago
Printed in the United States of America
10 09 08 07 06 05 04 03 02 01   5 4 3 2 1

ISBN (cloth) : 0-226-24422-9
ISBN (paper) : 0-226-24423-7

Library of Congress Cataloging-in-Publication Data

Irony in action : anthropology, practice, and the moral imagination / edited by James W.
Fernandez and Mary Taylor Huber.
    p.   cm.
·   Includes bibliographical references and index.
    ISBN 0-226-24422-9 (cloth) — ISBN 0-226-24423-7 (pbk.)
    1. Irony in anthropology.   I. Fernandez, James W.   II. Huber, Mary Taylor, 1944 –
GN34.2 .I76   2001
301—dc21   00-011904

Contents

Preface and Acknowledgments

— • • • —

An anthropology of irony is overdue. The characteristic trope of the world-weary aristocrat and the "modern" avant-gardist alike, irony has become—many believe—the cultural signature of the *entire* postmodern condition. Artists and intellectuals no longer corner the market for heightened undercutting self-scrutiny. Popular culture now joins high culture in its playful, often subversive, stance toward the certainties, real and imagined, of former years. Things have gone so far, in fact, that there are even signs that a new generation of literati, in a "panic of influence," are reestablishing their own identity by questioning the irony of the dominant culture and taking on attitudes of sincerity instead (Scott 2000; see also Geertz 1984 on antirelativism in the academy).

Anthropologists, of course, have long been aware that volatile mixes of privilege and power in culture often invite irony, and that the ethnographic situation itself is in fact inherently ironic. Indeed, some decades ago, the editors evoked the presence of irony in their own early fieldwork (Fernandez 1964; Huber 1988). An anthropology of irony is now overdue because of the proliferation of highly ambiguous contact zones in today's more complex and globalized social worlds. But even more important as a rationale for this volume is irony's challenge to the moral imagination. In this collection of essays, twelve anthropologists and two critical friends will explore a variety of conditions that have provoked ironic expression, and survey both irony's evasions and its horizons of hope.

This volume had its origin in a session we organized at the 1996 annual meeting of the American Anthropological Association on "Irony, Practice, and the Moral Imagination." That the time had come to explore this provocative theme was borne out by our ability to entice such a distinguished group of participants, by the standing-room-only audience (highly unusual for a session scheduled for the last time slot on Sunday morning), by the overwhelmingly positive comments we received after the session, and by the willingness of every one of our busy contributors to revise their essays for publication.

We are deeply appreciative to our contributors for making this volume such a pleasure to put together, both as an intellectual project and a practical task. We would like to thank, in addition, Linda Layne for so insightfully reading a draft of our introduction, Nigel Rapport for discussions of the ironies of individualism during walks and runs in the Fife countryside, David Brent of the University of Chicago Press for his encouragement, Claudia Rex for her careful and sensitive editorial work, and the Press's two anonymous reviewers for their enthusiasm for the project, and also for their comments, suggestions, and occasional expressions of distress. Our own understandings of irony have been broadened and deepened in conversation with our students and colleagues in many settings. Irony, for example, has long been one of the tropes centrally treated in a graduate course taught by one of us on "Metaphor Theory in Anthropology" at the University of Chicago, and much of value has been learned from classroom discussions and course papers. While we cannot name all of these collaborators here, we want them to know that we are cognizant of and most grateful for their contributions.

Finally, we wish to thank Renate Fernandez and Ernest Vigdor for their un-ironic, though not unquestioning, support as we sought to take our stance on the slippery slope of this shifty trope.

James W. Fernandez
Chicago, Illinois

Mary Taylor Huber
Palo Alto, California

References

Fernandez, James W. 1964. The Sound of Bells in a Christian Country: In Quest of the Historical Schweitzer. *The Massachusetts Review* (spring): 537–62.

Geertz, Clifford. 1984. Anti Anti-Relativism. *The American Antrhopologist* 86 (2): 263–78. Reprinted in his *Available Light: Anthropological Reflections on Philosophical Topics*, 42–67. Princeton: Princeton University Press, 2000.

Huber, Mary Taylor. 1988. *The Bishops' Progress: A Historical Ethnography of Catholic Missionary Experience on the Sepik Frontier.* Washington, DC: Smithsonian Institution Press.

Scott, A. O. 2000. The Panic of Influence. Review of *Brief Interviews with Hideous Men,* by David Foster Wallace. *New York Review of Books,* 10 February, 39–43.

Introduction

JAMES W. FERNANDEZ AND MARY TAYLOR HUBER

The Anthropology of Irony

"The outer is certainly not the inner."
Søren Kierkegaard, Preface to *Either/Or*[1]

Some Introductory Observations on Irony and Social Thought

When things seem misaligned, disproportionate, unexpected, or out of place, philosophers, poets, and everyday people (including anthropologists, as we will see), often use irony to capture and comment on the pattern of contrasts they discern. By projecting an attitude of disbelief along with the "outer" meaning of their words, ironists convey a contrary, "inner," meaning to those who catch the cue.[2] But irony is far more than a simple act of speech. Because it most often is used to express skepticism toward authority, "irony" has come to describe, not just a figure of speech, but a questioning attitude and critical stance as well. As Hayden White observes, irony is the way in which "skepticism in thought and relativism in ethics are conventionally expressed" (1973: 37). In the face of uncertainty and the "unwelcome contradictions" of life, many people have found irony a valuable resource for inciting the moral and political imagination against whatever is given, assumed, or imposed.

Perhaps it is inevitable in this millennial moment, when everyone is taking stock, that anthropologists, too, should turn concerted attention to irony in their own and others' milieus. Anthropology developed as a discipline at another time when absolutes were being questioned, in the late nineteenth- and early twentieth centuries, when modernist movements in art, literature, and science were beginning to work their subversive effects on the comfortable pieties of the Victorian world (Manganaro 1990: 7). Indeed, much early anthropological

---

1. The statement, by Kierkegaard's pseudonymous editor of the purportedly found documents included in *Either/Or, Part I* (1987: 7) expresses Kierkegaard's disagreement with Hegel's position on the identity of inner (essence) and outer (being). See also note 2 to the preface.

2. For this view of irony's make-up, see the discussion of Sperber's and Wilson's "mention theory" (1981) below.

work on the lives of "others" itself acted to cast doubt on familiar certainties of metropolitan religion, culture and society (Said 1989: 222). By and large, however, while early anthropologists, like other modernists, questioned their own traditions, they still believed in objective truth and in the possibility of capturing that truth through right representation. It is only in the last several decades that anthropologists have challenged the central premises of their own practice, bringing into question the straightforwardness of anthropological inquiry, and even the possibility of traditional ethnography, the foundational activity of modern anthropology.

Irony is not only a feature of methodological concerns in today's anthropology, but it has become an object of anthropological inquiry as well, as the present collection shows. Irony certainly was not a notable feature of ethnographies devoted to exploring and expounding traditional ways of life. It has become more prevalent only as the goal of ethnography has shifted to capturing ambiguities and contradictions in the modernizing and even postmodernizing world. Perhaps most common are anthropologists' explorations of the incongruities and unintended consequences of projects undertaken by or for the presumed benefit of the people under study. But anthropologists have also begun to look at their subjects' own experience of a world at odds with the authority of received or imposed tradition, and to ask why it is so often captured indirectly by ironic tropes.

Presenting case studies from a variety of cultural and historical situations, the essays collected here survey the varieties of ironic insight and expression in anthropology and explore the politics, pragmatics, and consequences of irony's use. Geographically, the cases come from the United States, Ireland, Greece, China, Mexico, Bali, Africa, and Papua New Guinea. Historically they range from Homeric times to the present day. The ironists include poets, novelists, and essayists; villagers, peasants, and immigrants; missionaries, development workers, and anthropologists. All of our authors would probably agree with Paul Friedrich (chap. 11 in this volume) that situations inviting irony are inherent in the nature of language, the passage of time, and the structure of social life. But most would probably also agree with George Marcus (chap. 10 in this volume) that irony flourishes in certain historical conditions, and that these conditions are now especially intense and widespread.

Irony is, of course, a capricious term, notoriously difficult to pin down. Its primary academic home is in the field of rhetoric and literature, and the anthropologists writing here follow scholarly convention by treating irony, first and foremost, as a way with words. In *The Concise Oxford Dictionary of Literary Terms*, Chris Baldick adroitly defines irony as "a subtly humorous perception of inconsistency, in which an apparently straightforward statement or event is undermined by its context so as to give it a very different significance" (1990: 114). At its simplest, Baldick points out, irony involves a discrepancy between what is said and what is really meant, as in sarcasm and various other figures of speech. But he also notes that irony in literature can be more sustained and structural, for example, when the reader knows more about the situation than the protagonist (and this has a particular anthropological relevance), or when characters are portrayed as "dupes of a cruelly mocking Fate." Classics of modern criticism like D. C. Muecke's *The Compass of Irony* (1969) and Wayne Booth's *A Rhetoric of Irony* (1974) document the wide range of situations and strategies that have been embraced by the term "irony" in the West.

A glance at any critical account will demonstrate that the many varieties of irony one can identify can also encode different attitudes toward social experience or, as Alan Wilde (1981) puts it, different "horizons of assent." Still, the range of attitudes that can be captured by irony is not unlimited. As the anthropologist Dan Sperber and his colleagues have argued, irony's structure invites its use to criticize failure rather than to praise success (Sperber and Wilson 1981; Jorgenson, Miller, and Sperber 1984). It is an undercutting instrument. According to their "mention theory of irony," an ironist is not *using* a figurative meaning opposite to the literal meaning of the utterance, but is instead *mentioning* the literal meaning of the utterance and expressing an attitude toward it of ridicule, disapproval, or disbelief.[3] From this perspective, it makes sense that irony almost always has what Linda Hutcheon (1994) calls a critical "edge."

While it may be most common to use irony to criticize someone or something for not meeting expectations or cultural norms (to say, for example, "What a success!" of a failure, or "How democratic!" of an autocratic act), irony is sometimes used to question those expectations or cultural norms themselves. It is one thing to challenge the truth or adequacy of a particular performance, project, or perspective on the world. It is another to suggest that the standards of judgment in use are limited, inadequate, or inappropriate to the task. Chock (chap. 1 in this volume) suggests that irony of this type may be less a matter of perceiving disparity between practice and ideal, than "between

3. As Sperber and his colleagues point out: "Expectations of success are intrinsic to any action; culturally defined criteria of excellence and rules of behavior are invoked in most value judgments. Thus it is always possible to mention these expectations ironically when they are frustrated, or to mention these norms ironically when they are violated, and to trust that hearers will share them and so recognize them for what they are. On the other hand, expectations of failure or criticism occur only on specific occasions, and it is only on those occasions that they can be mentioned ironically and serve to bestow praise under the guise of blame. Thus, "What a failure!" could be an effective ironic reference to a success if the hearer knew or could surmise that failure had been expected" (Jorgenson, Miller, and Sperber 1984: 115).

competing, partial, and interested versions of the world, which are embedded in different discourses." As the essays in this volume show, irony can be expected in situations of unequal power when discourses, interests, or cultures clash.

Irony's association with variability and nonfixity also derives from its use in those extreme or elusive situations that are hard to grasp or master, where one struggles to find a way to say what can't be said, or do what ought to be done. This is territory that the historian Paul Fussel explores in *The Great War and Modern Memory* (1975), arguing that trench warfare in World War I was so horrific that many combatants turned to its ironic contrast with civilization's ideals (and idylls) as the best way to articulate the terror they experienced on the front. This ineffable realm, so resistant to human intention and meaning making, was also mapped by Søren Kierkegaard, although for him and many of his contemporaries, "irony is not exclusively, or even primarily, a particular kind of speech act. Rather, 'irony' indicates a particular way of engaging in public (interpersonal) activity in general; speech (or writing) is only one of the activities that may be so engaged in" (Cross 1998: 126).

With the distinctive features of verbal irony serving as a model, Kierkegaard depicts his existential ironist as one who has rejected everyday life as illusory and expresses this rejection by following convention without any real engagement in it. By only playing at practice, he (or she?) gains sufficient distance from the immediacy of the ordinary for an "'awakening of subjectivity,' that is an awakening of the conception of oneself as a subject, something separate from, and undetermined by, a certain immediately given historical entity" (ibid., 137). Interestingly, Kierkegaard (1989: 257–58) perceived an affinity between irony and "the pious mentality" in that both reject the world of immediate existence as vanity, and in so doing open themselves to some deeper, alternative, sense of the real.[4] Like irony in Socrates's hands, irony in Kierkegaard's "deceives into truth."

This capacity to bracket the quotidian world and provide perspective through what it is not, brings irony into the realm of other imaginative techniques of

---

4. Of course, Kierkegaard made a distinction between what the pious and the ironic mind was opened to. For the pious person, "all disturbing factors are set aside and the eternally existing order comes into view." For the ironist, however, "since everything is shown to be vanity, the subject becomes free" (258). Cross (1998: 140–41) argues that Kierkegaard's early view of irony, expressed in *The Concept of Irony* (published in 1841) had changed by the time he wrote his *Concluding Unscientific Postscript* (published in 1846). Cross says: "Writing [in the latter work] as Johannes Climacus, [Kierkegaard] argues that the ironist's self-contentment and sense of superiority over the ways of life he ironically engages in can only be achieved if the ironist, like the devout mentality mentioned above, relates himself not just negatively toward human existence but positively toward an absolute that is of a qualitatively different kind from the ideals that shape the ordinary person's life."

assessment and human control, such as the play of tropes (J. Fernandez 1986, 1991), paradox (States 1998), ritual (Turner 1969), art (Munn 1973), myth (Burridge 1969), folktale (Beidelman 1986), and play (Huizinga 1950).[5] Indeed, as Beidelman (1986: 2–10) has noted, imagination itself has been characterized as a form of attempted transcendence (or transgression) by thinkers as diverse as Aristotle, Wittgenstein, Simmel, and Ricoeur.[6] Unlike imagination's other servants, however, irony usually carries a negative valence of variable intensity. Deriving from the Greek *eironeia*, "feigned ignorance," from *eiron*, "dissembler," (itself from *eirein*, "to say!"), irony still carries the connotation of dissimulation. Although only rarely expressed in such charged terms as Kierkegaard's "enthusiasm for destroying" (1989: 262), irony's dark and dissimulating side is apparent in its common definition as saying the opposite of what is meant.

The politics of irony, and its ethics, arise from and depend upon this *indirection*. By stating one thing but suggesting more or less its opposite, ironists point to an alternative reading of a situation, while evading the challenge of direct dissent and protecting themselves from censorious response. To be sure, there are limiting instances of irony where no competent listener or reader could misconstrue the ironist's intent. But most frequently the ambiguity inherent to irony (does the speaker mean to be ironic or not?) allows ironists to accept or condone contradictory intentions and ambivalence about where they stand.[7] So while irony can afford political expression in circumstances where direct dissent is hard to formulate, risky, or unwise, there can also be complicity in irony (Fernandez, chap. 3 in this volume). Certainly, most of the anthropologists writing here would agree with Pocock's (1993) liberal view of irony as "the mind's weapon when dealing with multiple possibilities." But most are also aware that under conditions of uncertainty or futility, irony can serve as "a special kind of substitute for silence" (M. M. Bakhtin, quoted in Hutcheon 1994: 44).

In this introduction, we will explore this antinomy by looking at irony in anthropology's own house, and by visiting the effects of irony in today's larger culture, said by some to be an "age (or culture) of irony." First, we consider the play of irony as a component of social thought and ethnographic inquiry. We

---

5. As Beidelman says of Huizinga: "For him, play represents something yet at the same time contests that same something" (1986: 3).

6. See Beidelman (1986: 7), who cites, among others, Aristotle 1961: 76, Wittgenstein 1963: 97, Simmel 1971: xviii, and Ricoeur 1979: 152, on how imagination or fantasy "may blur or multiply choices, affording a perspective that transcends ordinary situations and perspectives."

7. This view of irony is deepened by psychoanalytic considerations—indeed, the speaker may not know his or her real intentions! What he/she denies (the "mentioned" statement) may be precisely what he/she desires or believes without being able to admit it out loud (see Stringfellow 1994).

weigh irony's consequences for a politics of complicity with the contradictions of things as they are and/or of a politics of commitment to working toward a less contradictory and, one may hope, better world. Next comes the question of what attitude might be appropriate for an anthropology aware of its own ironies. And we conclude with a discussion of ethnography attuned to other people's ironies, and a preview of how these themes intersect in the contributions to this volume.

Some Ironies of Anthropological Understanding and Inquiry

Irony is inescapable. However sober-sided men and women may seek to be in their comportment and however logical in their thinking, the contradictions of human life and the complications of thought make irony a recurrent if often unwelcome hobgoblin to everyday intentions. By the word "contradiction," we may take the simple dictionary meaning of "inconsistency or discrepancy" (*The American Heritage Dictionary* 1991). And contradictions, inconsistencies, and discrepancies, after all, are the meat upon which irony principally feeds.

Certainly, anthropology finds itself subject to unwelcome contradictions in its very method, participant observation. This method is notoriously difficult to maintain in appropriate balance. Those styling themselves observers can all too easily mock what they regard as the "mindless" involvements of the participants. And participants, in their stead, can all too easily ridicule what they regard as the observers' cloudy vision: their "poverty of theory." A closely related problem is the volatility of the subject-object relation, a kind of figure/ground effect in social science. The ready transformation of subject into object and vice versa is a core conundrum in social science theory and practice (as, indeed, it is in social life generally).[8] This volatile transformation has been particularly open to ironizing, often of a moral kind, with critics pointing on the one hand to the violation of subjectivity implicit in much objectifying social science practice, and on the other to the threat to objectivity that lies in subjective inquiry.

Indeed, it might be argued that any great theory in the human sciences is energized by a challenging contradiction that can either be ironized or resolved into a paradoxical truth. There is, for example, the Hobbesian paradox that men (and women) in their natural condition of life—'solitary, poore, nasty, brutish, and short'—can only gain their freedom by giving up their freedom. Then there

8. Cf. Mills 1994. In her article "On the Involuntary Drawing of Our Subject Matter," Mills suggests that the subject-as object conundrum (and vice versa) constitutes anthropology's "core irony" and "a reliable source of ironizing energy" (364).

is the Rousseauvian paradox, also partial to Marxism, that we are born free but everywhere find ourselves in chains. There is the Mandevillian/Adam Smithian paradox, which suggests that private vices can be public virtues and that the concentrated pursuit of individual self-interest can have public benefits. There is the more strictly Marxist paradox concerning the "creative destructiveness of capitalism"—that out of capitalism's vast profit-driven energies and organizational capacities are also produced wars, degradation, immiseration, and pollution. More recently we have the ironic insight of Gramscian hegemony—that men and women can be persuaded to support causes and accept oppressive leaders that in reality work against their best interests. And there is the Foucauldian irony that knowledge ostensibly sought for its own sake is actually self-interested and accompanied by hidden agendas related to the maintenance of place and privilege.[9]

There are, of course, many other surprising or disconcerting contradictions driving theory in the social sciences. Closer to the microethnographic involvements of anthropologists as participant observers is the ironic force of the practice of everyday life. As spelled out by de Certeau (1988), these familiar "meanderings" include the inspired improvisations and creative interludes that counter the rational ordering of the bureaucratic "iron cage" of mass society. Such creative contrarieties of everyday life are certainly ironic in implication, in view of the pretense to reason, order, and predictability of that life.[10] Beyond the contrarieties of everyday life—and even more fundamental—are the unwelcome logical contradictions that Lévi-Strauss (1966) notes characterize psychic life in all societies, contradictions which drive his structuralist theory just as surely as they drive the fabulation by which cultures struggle to cope with and even resolve them.

Inasmuch as we also might wish to begin with fundamentals in our own treatment of the contradictions that drive irony in anthropology, we might begin by

9. See, for example, Hobbes's *Leviathan;* Rousseau's *Discourse on the Origins and Foundations of Inequality among Men* and *The Social Contract;* Marx's "Philosophic manuscripts of 1844" and *Capital;* Marx's and Engels's *The Communist Manifesto;* Mandeville's *The Fable of the Bees, or Private Vices, Public Benefits;* Smith's *Theory of Moral Sentiments* and *The Wealth of Nations;* Gramsci's *Prison Notebooks;* and Foucault's *Power/Knowledge.*

10. One should be cautious of such an overarching generalization about modern life, or life generally. In respect to the creative improvisation in daily life, the challenges of a citizen of a contemporary former East Block country like Yugoslavia or Russia, undergoing tremendous economic upheaval and unpredictability, are certainly many times greater than for a citizen of a stable polity such as a Scandinavian social democracy. The irony of centrally planned economies of the East Block is that their perpetual shortages frustrated their planning and forced citizens to improvise. For the former point see Marko Zivkovic (1998) writing on everyday life in contemporary Yugoslavia and, for the latter, Dale Pesmen (1997) writing about contemporary Russia. Fernandez is grateful to these young colleagues for expanding his understanding of cultural differences as regards the practice of everyday life.

observing that of all the things anthropologists have to contemplate in ourselves and others, the most "ironogenic," to use Linda Hutcheon's useful term, is the inadequacy and partiality of that very thought. This limiting condition of "partial knowledge" has been made much of in recent years.[11] There is the fact, for example, that even though anthropologists specialize in studying the dynamics of things human, they really don't adequately understand, and probably never will understand in any fully satisfactory way, the evolutionary process that has made people "human."

Many are the efforts that have been made to postulate a scenario for our crossing the Rubicon of humanization, which is to say to our becoming the conceptualizing animal that we are (Niehoff 1998).[12] This has meant primarily the attempt to account for the development of human language, which by its nature is a conceptualizing instrument. How is it that we at some time, someplace, moved from closed language systems (mostly the call systems of other animals) to the open language systems of humans with our capacities for displacement, creativity, and abstraction? Impressively informed accounts have been written of that transition, to be sure (e.g., Hockett and Asher 1964), but since it occurred out of time and (so to speak) out of mind, no settled agreement can be reached on what actually happened. It is not surprising, and surely ironic, that despite their inveterate interest in origins, linguists and anthropologists have recurrently declared a moratorium on efforts devoted to insoluable questions of how we became human. Indeed, under the aegis of postmodern anxieties about the imposition of "grand narratives" and "final vocabularies,"[13] many anthropologists have accepted a more encompassing moratorium on any general discussion of what it is to be human. This denial of the reach of inquiry must appear ironical to anthropologists, given the fact that our specialty is, in fact, the knowing of things human.

We may speak here in this connection of "the irony of conceptualization itself," an irony addressed by Borges in his oft-referenced story, "Funes the Memorious" (1956). This is a story about a man who had the capacity (or incapacity as it turns out) of remembering everything that he experienced to

11. Most notably, by James Clifford in his critique of anthropological authority (1986). But see also the argument by Lakoff and Johnson (1980) that all intellectual devices to which thought appeals both reveal and conceal.

12. Among the most interesting and anthropologically informed of recent efforts here are Sheets-Johnstone 1991 and Noble and Davidson 1996.

13. By "grand narratives" we refer to Lyotard's *grande histoires,* which was rendered as "meta-narratives" by the translator of *The Postmodern Condition* (1984). In that work, Lyotard used the term to refer to the "big stories" about human history and destiny told by such thinkers as Kant, Hegel, and Marx. The term "final vocabulary" is used by Rorty in *Contingency, Irony, and Solidarity* (1989) to refer to the "set of words" which "all human beings carry about . . . to justify their actions, their beliefs, and their lives" (73).

the most minute detail.[14] Such prodigious capacity of memory quite inhibits thought in the conceptualizing sense since, as the author points out, such thought requires, in order to identify the necessary and the sufficient in the formulation of categories, that we be quite forgetful or neglectful of many details of our experience. The irony is that thinking demands forgetting. And it is ironic because the forgotten or the excluded may always in one way or another come back to reassert itself inadvertently or intentionally. Very often and perhaps most fundamentally, irony is a questioning of established categories of inclusion and exclusion, and the ironizer is he or she or that group who has been detrimentally categorized, and bound thereby to contest through irony the adequacy of such categories.

Now it is precisely this irony, bound up in categorizing conceptualization processes, which comes back to haunt the thoughtful and to arm those who have in one way or another been left out of or disfavored by a privileging set of conceptualizations and distinctions, a "forgetfulnesses" as it were, that some "heroic" elite have managed to impose on society. (We use "Heroic" in Vico's poetic sense of "heros of the imaginative capacity," whose talents create social and cultural worlds for others to live in.) Since we refer here to Vico's poetic science and his sense of the imaginative dynamic of world construction, it would be pertinent to review briefly his pioneering vision of the flux and reflux *(corso* and *recorso)* of history. For it is just this irony of "thoughtfulness predicated upon forgetfulness" that was addressed by Vico in his idea of the *recorso* in the "history of consciousness."[15] In Vico's grand narrative, the heroic ages pass on, and with them the reign of the tropes of metaphor and metonym that had disadvantaged the common people and confined them to "lower and servile orders." In the age of synecdoche that follows, the people begin to understand how their humanity has been denied them in the "forgetfulness" (benign or malign neglect) of antecedent heroic conceptualizations and distinctions, and they begin to see that although they were formerly subjected to a servile role they can now claim to be an integral part of the whole.

For Vico this development led (as it still leads), not only to the making of revolutionary claims for rights and privileges but is concomitant with peoples' beginning to understand the irony of social thought—its own forgetfulness and self-interestedness. A general "age of irony" follows this realization, and is

14. The relevant passage is the following: "'My memory, sir, is like a giant trash heap. Nothing is lost.' . . . I think, however, that he was not very capable of thinking. To think is to forget differences, it is to generalize, to abstract. In the indistinguishable world of Funes there are only details, almost all immediate" (translation by James Fernandez).

15. As spelled out in book 4, "The Course the Nations Run," and book 5, "The Recourse of Human Institutions," of *The New Science* ([1744] 1968). But see also Hayden White's extrapolation, "The tropics of history: The deep structure of *The New Science*" (1978).

characterized not only by a skepticism about heroes, heroism, and heroic conceptualizations as anything more than self-interested representations celebrated because of particular parochial interests, but also by a more general
skepticism about categories themselves. What is produced in Vico's scheme is
a general tendency to undercut any set of categories of differentiation as always
self-interested. This trend toward delegitimization was aided and abetted, Vico
thought, by the decline of religion as a set of unquestionable heroic myths and
sacred categories which had earlier distinguished the righteous from the unjust,
the worthy from the unworthy, the commendable from the corrupt, and those
who, by divine right, ruled from those who were ruled. The amount of effort in
recent decades devoted to categorization processes in culture would seem to be
compatible with Vico's anticipation of such ironic times.[16]

Though ironic himself about the ironic end-stage of Pagan civilizations,
Vico was interested in saving the world from such ultimate irony, and he felt
that this could be done by Christianity's sacrificed and resurrected victim-hero
leading the last to become the first—a recourse, so to speak, toward religious
transcendence that other ironists have also taken, including Kierkegaard himself (see Huber, chap. 9 in this volume). It may seem ironic to us (postmoderns)
that Vico was able to save the world, through Christianity, from the fateful
fulfillment of his philosophy of history. Indeed, the irony probably did not escape him either. But given the power of the Church at the time, he was also, no
doubt, saving himself by means of such exceptional religious sincerity. The
reader may judge whether Vico's scenario accounts for the "age of irony"
which is said to be our present condition. But we certainly esteem Vico for an
approach, the tropological one, that focuses us on the anchoring of thought in
the material experiences of the body as these rise into the mind. The mind/
body or mind/matter dichotomy has long been a source of ironic observations,
as in the familiar quotation: "What is matter? never mind. What is mind? no
matter." Vico and subsequent tropological arguments (Lakoff and Johnson
1980, Johnson 1987) give some stability to that volatile dichotomy.

The tropological approach is also one that enables us to detect other fundamental vectors of the sense of the ironic. The fact, for example, that in metaphor, the focus or target of our thought experiences displacement or substitu-
tion by some other source of attention and understanding is always possibly
ironic. Or, in the case of metonym, there is always ironic possibility when the
part is taken for the whole or vice versa, the container for the contained or vice
versa, the cause for the effect or vice versa, etc. (Durham and Fernandez 1991).

---

16. Of course, the classic statement is that of Durkheim and Mauss in *Primitive Classification*
(1967), but see also the influential series of works by Mary Douglas, including *Purity and Danger,*
Natural Symbols, and most recently a collection, edited together with David Hull, entitled *How*
Classification Works.

In these elementary thought dynamics, irony is always a possible emergent. In any event, we cannot forget the first and most fundamental irony of human thought, which the ironist might usefully keep constantly in mind: the awareness that thinking conceals as it reveals.

A second fundamental irony for anthropology, or any inquiry into human awareness and consciousness, has also to do with concealing and revealing and is, in fact, a version of the inner-outer disparity with which this introduction began. This irony arises from the tension (if not conflict) between "platitudes" and "attitudes" in communicative interaction, the tension or conflict between what one feels socially obliged to say and do and what one may "really" (at least at less public levels of awareness) think and feel and desire to do. This has often enough been seen as the tension between the desirable and the obligatory, a source of discontent in civil life often commented upon, and not only in Freud's (1989) classic statement, but also in the abundant "individual and society" literature and related "public-private" literature. It is, too, a theme in work on the efficacy of hegemony, which deals with how social order and social duties are legitimately inculcated and enforced, that is, with how something obligatory is made to seem desirable.

The tension between platitudes and attitudes is always potentially ironic, as the one perspective can always be taken to comment on the partiality or self-servingness, and therefore the inauthenticity or illegitimacy, of the other. (Indeed, we can see this in the individual-oriented phrasing of the contrast itself, which in using the negative term "platitude" is mildly biased against public obligation. Of course, in certain subcultures "attitude" is also a less than neutral term for an individual's mood or stance, designating a willful intrusion of the private upon the public.) This tension between platitudes and attitudes produces methodological problems for any social science. The challenge is to capture the dynamic of the negotiation of the public and the private, the inner and the outer, without overprivileging one or the other. In either case of overemphasis, the outcome would be ironic for any purportedly comprehensive inquiry.

In anthropology, there are those who have supposed that the discipline is particularly exposed to the dissimulation or disingenuousness or hypocrisy that accompanies the tension between public and private in social life. Especially in cross-cultural inquiry among colonized or otherwise subordinated or marginalized populations, the tension may be supposed, with some reason, to weigh heavily upon the forthcomingness of informants.[17] And anthropologists have long been cautioned that "informants may tell you anything in order to please

17. See particularly in this regard the rather contradictory counsel offered in *Notes and Queries on Anthropology* (Royal Anthropological Institute 1951: parts 1 and 2. Introduction and Methods, 27–62). This field manual takes precautions against a thoroughgoing skepticism or prejudice to-

you," a warning against an ethnography that only skims the surface of the attitudes that actually drive behavior. Indeed, a major goal of long-term participant observation is to enable access to these deeper levels of consciousness.

To be sure, the pressures of classic ethnographic inquiry, often enough conducted under the aegis of colonial or postcolonial authority structures, could result in a truncation of thoroughgoing participant observation and lead to interviews of a particularly intense and overdetermined kind (as is pointed out in Rosaldo 1986). Unless carefully modulated by the familiarities of longtime participant observation in the field, by indirection of inquiry, and by cautious use of direct questioning, such investigation could easily become selffulfilling, approaching the quality of inquisition. Indeed, the cross-cultural situation of anthropologists who themselves are products of one belief system working in another, can also be characterized and challenged by this ironic tension. Anthropologists often make an "as if" kind of inquiry, as it were, calculatedly taking at face value events or ideas or convictions that they do not really, in their heart of hearts, believe in or otherwise countenance.[18] Personal attitudes may clearly be at variance with the necessary platitudes of inquiry and participation.[19]

The ironic attitude this might suggest for anthropology would be to maintain an active awareness of the tension for both informant and anthropologist alike of the constant negotiation in the interactions of social life of platitudes versus attitudes, of social pressures versus private dispositions. Out of that tension, many ironies arise—a useful awareness, surely, for any student who would

---

ward native deception: "The idea that natives will say anything to please the investigator and will invent information is often found among Europeans who have dealt with the people mainly as their employers. Experience suggests that such views are generally much exaggerated and the investigator who establishes a sympathetic understanding with the people and develops a system for checking the materials need not be deceived by individuals of this type" (31). At the same time, as the quote indicates, such deception occurs, and methodological ways must be developed through supplementary observations and inquiries to circumvent and counter it. These pages of Notes and Queries are in part devoted to such circumventions.

18. It might be of interest to note this bit of advice, which today seems ironic, in *Notes and Queries on Anthropology:* "It is important that not even the slightest expression of amusement or disapproval should ever be displayed at the description of ridiculous, impossible or disgusting features in custom, cult or legend" (Royal Anthropological Institute 1951: 32).

19. As Geertz noted in his essay, "Thinking as a Moral Act" (1968), "fiction . . . lies at the very heart of successful anthropological fieldwork," and makes fieldwork ironic because the necessary fictions are never completely convincing for either the anthropologist or those among whom he or she works. These would include the formal fictions of social placement. For example, taking her cue from Geertz, Lutkehaus (1995: 16) describes her own fieldwork in the mid-1970s on Manam Island in Papua New Guinea as "doubly" ironic: "Not only was I made a fictive member of a particular clan, as anthropologists who work in kinship-based societies often are, and thereby acquired a set of fictive kin with whom to interact; I was also given a fictive relationship with Camilla Wedgewood [an anthropologist who studied the Manam some forty years before]: people considered me to be her 'granddaughter.'"

seek to avoid being misled and who would hope to fully understand the fabric of meaning and intentionality both in society and in the methods for studying it. At the very least one is made hesitant about privileging one's own inquiry and attributing the possibility of disingenuousness to informants and subalterns only.

But here let us highlight two special ironies of anthropological inquiry: the irony of privileged understanding and the irony of privileged categorization. In both cases ironic questions of inadvertent complicity arise. One may well argue for a mindfulness in fieldwork of the tension between "surface" and "deep" layers of awareness lest one be misled in the contextualizations of one's materials (Fabian 1995). But one must also be aware of the possible irony in one's own claims to privileged understanding of deeper levels of meaning and to the privileged deployment of conceptualizing categories as its sign.

On the face of it, anthropology or any social science confronts the irony of privileged understanding—the irony patent in the fact that it proposes to know more objectively about a population subject to inquiry than that subject population knows about itself. It is not easy to decide whether this situation is to be considered ironic or not or if it is so only from certain perspectives. One person's irony is always possibly another person's sincerity. Still the question of privileged and self-arrogating understanding bears reflection insofar as the question goes to the heart of what a discipline like anthropology is about, in what spirit it is to be conducted, and, indeed, what attitudes accompany such aboutness. Based on the answer given one might confidently decide whether or not anthropology is in essence an ironic discipline and whether the lot of the anthropologist is, in final judgment, inevitably ironic.

In respect to the related problem of privileged categorization, the question arises of the right to apply categories to an "other," with which they may well be uncomfortable and by which they may also be disadvantaged. As was mentioned above, it is very often the uncomfortable and disadvantaged of the world who ironize and contest categories that the privileged impose. The right to "heroic categorization," to recall Vico (for whom it is the role of heroes of the imagination to categorize the world), has long been central and normal to social science inquiry and understanding. But it has been a characteristic of the ironic age in which we live to question that right and to suggest the inadvertence or hidden agendas that may be present in it.[20]

In the United States in recent years, this has been particularly the case as

20. To the point of the offering of a "categorical imperative" in this regard: "Assign categories to others only insofar as you would be willing to have such categories assigned to yourself" (Fernandez 1984: 224). This ironic imperative, if practiced it would be, to say the least, inhibiting to social science, is a version of Groucho Marx's renowned ultra ironic observation, as regards the hierarchy always present in social categorization processes, that he "would not want to be a member of a club that would have him as a member"!

regards the racial and ethnic categories that have been the objects of affirmative action. The unambiguous benevolence of this action has been questioned by those supposedly the beneficiaries of it. The argument is that what has platitudinously been put forth to be affirmative and beneficial has turned out to be detrimental at a deeper level (let us say, attitudinally), and serves ironically a hidden agenda. It serves inadvertently or complicitly, so the argument goes, to maintain disadvantageous differences in society (see Dominguez 1994). The whole issue of complicity in social action, that is to say the issue of social thought that conceals more than it reveals, and of platitudinous actions that actually serve hidden agendas and unexpressed and/or unexpressible attitudes, is laden with the possibilities of ironic awareness. The condition of participating in the perpetuation of that which one professes to abhor is a quintessential irony of the human condition, and surely not alien to social thought, or so it would seem.[21] These issues of intentionality and inadvertence raise questions about the politics of irony and of the moral imagination to which we now turn.

Ironic Times, the Politics of Irony, and the Moral Imagination of Better Times

Vico's argument for an eventual evolution of human consciousness or poetic wisdom into a general state of ironic apprehension leads to the eventuality of an age of irony. For anthropology, very likely, the idea of "cultures of irony" is more pertinent than the idea of "ages of irony," lodged as the latter is in thinking about the "history of consciousness," an overarching interest in the academy which many anthropologists find uncomfortably panoramic. Nevertheless, given the propensity to think of today's postmodern condition as especially ironic, some periodization of ironic times might be assayed. Perhaps the problem is best phrased in terms of the irony's moving targets, for clearly irony itself is an occupational hazard of being human, present in every age.

Vico's "ironic times" are, in our view, quite modern in spirit, the target being those traditional categorizations and authority structures of heroic times. Indeed, it is quite common to define the modern, in the Enlightenment sense at any rate, by its concepts of autonomy and freedom, abandoning support from tradition, authority, religion, or metaphysics. Vico clearly recognized the potential instability in the eventuality of "modern" irony, and offered as a brake a religious solution that could easily be regarded as a premodern stance. In religious representations, the world's contradictions, disparities, and inconsistencies are ironically subsumed in the ineffable, which encompasses and uses

---

21. A case that has been made effectively for terrorism discourse in Zulaika and Douglas 1996.

them to launch us into what lies beyond the reach of direct communication, conjuring, thereby, a realm more really real. In some ways, it seems, the step from premodern to postmodern irony, in respect to the playing with contradictions, is not very long. For once modern irony breaks down the acceptance of the ineffable, on the one hand, and the Enlightenment's signature belief in progress through reason, on the other, the mourning period for lost certainties may be quite brief. But curiously, though the postmodern spirit views reason (categorization) with suspicion, it claims (with religious echo) to see *something* positive in the disorder, or pastiche of contradictions, that are left behind.

The possibility has occurred to more than a few students of social life that anthropology itself, while a product of and contributor to the modern age of irony, has contributed to the shift to a postmodern suspension of commitment and belief. Consider, for example, a recent essay on the disappearance of Satan as an assertive presence in human moral judgment and moral action—as a presence, that is, in the moral imagination. The author, Andrew Delbanco (1995), associates this loss of the sense of the possibility of evil in modern life with anthropological relativism, an important player in what he calls the contemporary "culture of irony" (190, 209–10). It is not that Delbanco, who styles himself a secular liberal, wishes to return to the exaltation of local practices and local values as universals or any similar monolithic and authoritarian judgmentalism with its associated arrogance of righteousness. Rather, his wish is for a continuation of an active moral imagination attuned to and openly acknowledging the human capacity for radical evil, and not only the other's capacity for evil but also one's own. Certainly much happened in the twentieth century, a century of holocausts, to make this argument for the continuing awareness of the presence of evil convincing. And much has happened to shame those ironists who would corrode any attribution of evil whatsoever. As Kierkegaard argued, the ironist gains a degree of subjective freedom from personal responsibility for the woes of the world. But Delbanco's view is that irony should not free us from the need to make judgments and do something about the recurrent fact of radical evil.

If there is merit to the charge that anthropology has contributed to this situation, the irony is striking. Is it possible that in all its sincerity, in all its eagerness to understand the world's variety of lifeways and byways, anthropologists' work has had ironic consequences for the sincere engagement of others with that world? And might this be true, one could suggest, even for the anthropologists' own engagement with their subjects? If anthropologists have been a part of the twentieth century's crisis of legitimation, might not that crisis very likely have had ironic consequences, quite independently of anthropological pluralism, for anthropology itself (Krupat 1990; Rapport 2000)? In light of these possibilities, it is not surprising that overviews by some of the most prestigious anthropologists of recent decades have been distinctly ironic in tone (Gellner 1991; Geertz 1995; Sahlins 1995).[22]

The ironic consequences of anthropological work, in any event, have been particularly palpable, and objectionable, to those who take their cultural commitments and social obligations as so serious and so uniquely dignifying as to justify devoting some significant part of their lives to carrying one or another version of the Civilizing Mission to others. In the Pan-Christian West and its colonial and neocolonial outposts where until recently most anthropologists worked and engaged protectively in a pluralistic spirit with local cultures, anthropologists' relativizing work has been ironic in its implications for those engaged directly in projects designed to civilize or in some way "better" local lives. Indeed, there has long been a minor literature in anthropology that explores the ironies involved in the civilizing mission and its various missionizing enterprises—a literature which now joins forces with the larger interdisciplinary field of colonial studies. See, for example, Fernandez 1964, Beidelman 1982, Huber 1988, Cooper and Stoler 1997, and Huber and Lutkehaus 1999.

By spotlighting the ironies involved in imagining better and worse times in human affairs, this literature raises the most serious question in the politics of irony, which is to say irony's practical consequences in either encouraging people to change the world, or, in being so corrosive to commitment as to lead to the abandonment of any serious hope or work toward change. Although this issue cannot be resolved here, we may note, first, that even if an ironic awareness of the contradictions entailed in missions of a humanitarian or improving kind has perhaps discouraged some from these engagements, there surely re-

---

22. Each of these three anthropologists is associated with a distinctly ironic stance and register revealed in the titles of the books referenced here—Gellner's *Spectacles and Predicaments: Essays in Social Theory;* Geertz's *After the Fact: Two Cultures, Four Decades, One Anthropologist;* and Sahlins's *How "Natives" Think: About Captain Cook, for Example.* To take Gellner for an example, he was persistently an ironic spectator of the "spectacles and predicaments" that drove humans (and social scientists in particular) away from reason and rationality, whether that be patronage needs, populism, postmodernism, nativism, relativism, or religious nationalism. Every ironist tends toward his bête noire, or "pet peeve." Whereas Gellner's ironies are directed against those who, in his view, violate the rules of reason, Geertz's ironies are directed against the "fact-finders" of this world who neglect the complexities of meaning in culture and Sahlins's against those who "too easily universalize human nature."

Marilyn Strathern surely belongs on the list of eminent anthropologists taking an ironic stance, although hers is a case of inclusive and self-referential irony, for she is particularly attentive to the ironies in her own arguments, in her own attempts to be persuasive. See, for example, "Nostalgia and the New Genetics," where she tells the reader at the outset that, ironically, she has failed in her persuasive task. "It will become clear that I arrive at a rhetorical impasse. One could say I succumb to my own resistence to my argument. The only comfort, of course, is that had I succeeded, the success of the effect would indeed have belonged to the rhetoric" (Strathern 1995: 98). This last sentence makes these observations doubly ironic. See Fernandez (chap. 3 in this volume) for further comment on Strathern's awareness of irony in anthropology.

mains (in the United States, at least) a convincingly strong flow of energy for "reform" both abroad and at home.[23] Certainly, too, we may remark that irony has often enough been regarded as a "weapon of the weak," [24] providing space for subordinated persons to voice resistance, imagine alternatives, build community, and mobilize for better times. No doubt, too, an ironic perspective gives relief to difficult human situations by recognizing humourous contradictions in these situations and in those who seem to be in control (see, for example, the chapters by Chock, Scoggin, and Taylor in this volume).

But the practical consequences of such irony, its place in effective action in the world, can well be questioned. A recent ethnography on Mexican tomato workers entitled *The Force of Irony* (Torres 1997) documents the presence of the parodic in the experience of these impoverished laborers in the global vineyard, and their ironizing about all those who appear to manage their lives (including anthropologists, let it be said). Surely, irony in this kind of situation is psychologically assuaging to the discomfort and suffering of subordinates. But does this "weapon," in the end, wield any effective power in changing workers' objective conditions as measured, say, by the United Nations Development Index? These workers' ironies are exercises of the moral imagination, without question, but the pragmatics may be questioned. The politics involved may ultimately turn out to be a politics of accommodation and cooptation and not real-world resistance tending toward ameliorating disease rates, caloric intake, or disposable income. From this perspective, one may ironize about the complacent and possibly complicitous use of such terms as "weapons," "force," and "power," when they are applied to irony (Fernandez, in this volume).

No doubt irony plays different roles at—and on—different stages of the political process, whether one means by "politics" the play of plural perspectives in most contemporary polities, the heavy-handed regimes of oppressive elites, the subtly subversive hegemonies discussed by Gramsci, the pervasive powers perceived by Foucault, or the subversive powers extolled by Machiavelli.[25] After all, in the politics extolled by Machiavelli, that Master of Politicians, there is the deceitful play of the inner against the outer, platitudes against attitudes, which is to say the least ironogenic. At the present juncture in American

23. We have in mind, for example, continuing domestic support for this country's international human rights initiatives and official efforts to spread democracy and other aspects of American culture, as well as—at home—the widespread interest of high school and college students in community service, the steady drumbeat for civic virtue, and the like.

24. The phrase is from James Scott's *Weapons of the Weak: Everyday Peasant Forms of Resistance* (1985), the first of a series of works designed to document the ways that subordinate groups manage their subordination and offer alleviation for it as well as resistence to dominating forces generally. For a brief account of this work in anthropology, see Spencer 1996.

25. See Gramsci's *Prison Notebooks,* Foucault's *Power/Knowledge,* and Machiavelli's *The Prince.*

politics, we cannot forget Machiavelli's key injunction that in a politician "a reputation for virtue" is far better than the actual article.

In all these political processes, irony's capacity to reveal the deceitfulness of a leader's proclamations or the contingency of an opposing truth, thus opening eyes to the possibility of alternatives, can have consequences in the real world. Thanks to its oft-mentioned capacity to create or strengthen an in-group of those in the know, irony can contribute to solidarity among the weak, although it can also elicit countermoves of irony, ridicule, and worse from the strong. Whether irony can lead to effective action depends ultimately, of course, on such particularities as the nature of the grievance, the complexity of its causes, the distances among the parties involved, and whether or not irony is the only "weapon" the aggrieved can or will use. Indeed, as Marcus (in this volume) reminds us through his evocation of Ulrich Beck's notion of "reflexive modernization," modernity today is characterized by living with constant risk that challenges the traditional capacities of even the most advantaged people to act effectively to improve conditions in the first and second worlds (Beck 1992; Beck, Giddens, and Lash 1994).

The deeper concern here, in any event, is with the role of irony in activating or assuaging the moral imagination and the relationship of this activation and/ or assuagement to effective action in the world. On the one hand, we might take the case of Nietzsche, the most ironic of philosophers, indeed a philosopher who used his impressively imaginative powers of argument to weigh in against all traditional moral commitments. But one would be hard pressed to talk about effectiveness in regard to any positive political program of Nietzschean moral nihilism, even though the philosopher styled himself "the redeemer of culture."[26] On the other hand, if one regards ideological overcommitment and overconfidence—or all the arrogant self-satisfactions characteristic of partisanship—as the source of some of the principal political evils in the world, then the fallibilism,[27] and the sense of human frailty induced by much irony, is to be highly valued as a particularly effective kind of politics or, perhaps better, antipolitics.

26. On Nietzsche's conflicted, self-betraying "redemptive program," laid out in *The Genealogy of Morals,* see Daniel Conway's article, "Comedians of the Ascetic Ideal: The Performance of Genealogy," in a collection edited by Conway and Seery entitled *The Politics of Irony: Essays in Self Betrayal* (1992: 73–95). The subtitle of this collection is to be noted in respect to the relation of ironic perspectives and effective political commitment.

27. The concept "fallibilism" was explored by Ricoeur in *Fallible Man* (1986). Ricoeur concludes: "To say that man is fallible is to say that the limitation peculiar to a being who does not coincide with himself is the primordial weakness from which evil arises" (146).

Poste and Riposte: Anthropology as the Creator and the Object of Irony

We come now to a more awkward subject, the ironic views of the efforts and results of anthropological work taken both within and without the discipline. We have suggested above that it is quite reasonable to see anthropology as an ironic discipline. As participant observers, anthropologists cannot help but dance on irony's sharp edge. And as "writers of cultures," anthropologists' relativizing inevitably has destabilizing and ironic consequences for the sincere engagements of others (and quite possibly themselves). It is not surprising, then, to find irony used in counterpart, as a natural riposte taken toward such destabilization by those who find their sincerities impugned.

There are, after all, people who in all sincerity value occupying a stable position, talking straight, and being taken seriously and straightforwardly without the complication of alternate or undercutting perspectives. We have noted such sincerity in "the civilizing mission," for example. For people committed to this mission there is, so to speak, only one world: it is not a question of a turtle standing on yet another turtle standing on "turtles all the way down," as in the ironic story that Clifford Geertz tells (1973: 28–29). But anthropologists, in contrast to missionaries, have always offered alternative perspectives, or, we might say, other turtles to rest worldviews upon. At the very least, good anthropological work has offered *estrangement* because anthropologists have long sought to make "the strange familiar and the familiar strange." From Frazer to Lévi-Strauss, they have fashioned work to show either the savage in the civilized or the civilized in the savage.[28] In this way anthropologists, as "purveyors of estrangement," have indeed been part of the twentieth century's crisis of legitimation.

If one main object/victim of anthropological irony has been the civilizing mission, it is not at all surprising that the favor has been returned from those imbued with that sense of mission.[29] For "missionaries," in the broadest sense of the term, do not hesitate to universalize their values and understandings, and, indeed, such universalization and its accompanying sincerities provide crucial

28. The phrase derives from Frazer, whose project sought to explain certain puzzling aspects of contemporary culture as "survivals" from a previous age. According to Frazer: "The instrument for the detection of savagery under civilisation is the comparative method, which, applied to the human mind, enables us to trace man's intellectual and moral evolution" (1918, 1: viii, quoted in Strathern 1990: 90). In anthropology, however, Frazer's project was soon made obsolete. As Strathern points out: "Malinowski put forward the same proposition but in reverse: the detection of civilisation under savagery"—a project that dominated most anthropology for the next half century and more (90–91).

29. See, for example, the literature on relations between Christian missionaries and anthropologists, including Salamone 1977; Burridge 1978, 1991; Stipe 1980; Stocking 1983; Huber 1988, 1996.

energy to that mission. Of course, anthropologists have not escaped their own identification with that "mission" and its preferential positioning vis-à-vis those whom anthropologists have typically studied. And more indirectly, independent of any "missionary" interests, much ethnography of the third (and fourth) worlds in the last hundred years has been accompanied by an undercurrent of irony arising out of anthropology's implicit, sometimes complicit, comparisons on one or another evolutionary scale of higher or lower, better or worse, saner or sicker cultures and civilizations. It is the irony of superiors, in some way more "civilized," contemplating in supposed objectivity the fate of inferiors. It is the irony of the West contemplating the Rest, as the ironic phrasing goes.

Anthropologists are aware that the Rest have long, in riposte, been making undercutting observations about anthropology and anthropologists—observations that are sardonic or ironic in tone or implication. Perhaps this began with anthropology's political subservience to the colonialist and imperialist contexts of the Victorian world, but it has continued in postcolonial times with ironic commentary and protest about the ubiquitousness and prejudgment that local peoples and minorities have felt in the anthropological presence. It is an irony that continues to be brought to our attention by third-world or minority intellectuals in their work.[30] The most celebrated, perhaps, is the work of the Standing Rock Sioux, Vine Deloria Jr., in *Custer Died for Your Sins: An Indian Manifesto* (1969). The notorious chapter 4, titled ironically "Anthropologists and Other Friends," begins by listing the various misfortunes of mankind and then observes, "But Indians have been cursed above all other people in history. Indians have anthropologists" (78). This chapter is a virtuoso display at the expense of anthropologists and their students of what we can call the entire continuum of ironic reactions—parody, mockery, satire, and ridicule—all the distancing and downputting and undercutting modes of expression by which subalterns detect and suggest the discrepancies in any judgmental "final vocabulary," such as anthropology, between the outer and the inner, between platitudes and attitudes.[31]

But we should make some distinctions with respect to this continuum from parody to ridicule, particularly as we subsequently turn to focus upon *anthropological* irony (as opposed to irony about anthropologists). Certainly it is doubtful that any anthropologist, however ironic, would purposefully cast a professional ethnography or serious theoretical interpretation in the form of a parody, much less of sarcasm or ridicule. This is not to deny that there have

30. The list of works by minorities or third-world intellectuals commenting ironically on anthropologists and anthropology's relation to the politics of imperialism would certainly include Talal Asad, Jose Limon, Americo Paredes, Edward Said, and Valentin Mudimbe.

31. It also ought to be said, however, that chapter 7, "Indian Humor," is plentifully supplied with "inclusive irony" in which the Indian himself is the brunt of his own humor.

been intentional efforts at parody by anthropologists, like Horace Miner's well-known esssay "Body Ritual among the Nacirema" (1956), an "ethnographic study" of American ritual habits of hygiene and body culture which, as in the title itself, is coded in an ironic way so as to *estrange* and make these habits seem excessive and ritualistic. Indeed, it must be said that the effect is bound to be ironic whenever anthropologists use analytical tools associated with the study of third- or fourth-world others to gain perspective on first- and second-world people positioned similarly to or above themselves.[32] J. McIver Weatherford's semiserious but intentionally distancing book *Tribes on the Hill: The U.S. Congress, Rituals and Realities* (1985) is an apt example of how studying "up" by speaking "down" cannot help but have an undercutting (and in this case humorous) effect.[33]

However, for most of this century, and certainly since Malinowski, anthropologists' principal effort has been directed the other way. In their own special version of the civilizing mission—discovering for their own colleagues and countrymen that there is a kind of "civilization" in "savagery"—most anthropologists directed their irony only to those who might not expect such a discovery to be possible. By contrast, in regard to the people studied, anthropologists have generally proceeded with great sincerity, even though, often enough, peoples in rapid transition to a sense of modernity have felt themselves ridiculed or parodied in what are, from an ethnographer's perspective, quite responsible and professional presentations of traditional lifeways. And this difference of interpretation has been a source of tension between anthropologists and anthropological work and the local peoples it addresses. It has been a source of proactive and reactive irony.

In any event, let us distinguish "true irony" and, more particularly, true anthropological irony from these other expressions of discrepancy. We may do so by noting the absence of militancy and malice. Indeed, satire and parody have been described as militant forms of irony that, like sarcasm, are positioned confidently as to what is right and wrong in the world. Militant or malicious ironists use parody or satire of the other to express their self-confidence

---

32. Micaela di Leonardo (1998: 57) notes that this "anthropological gambit has both an intellectual and an affective component. The intellectual point is that 'we' are like primitives; the emotional layering is whimsical and pseudo-profound—primitives 'R' us." Relatively common in Americanist anthropology, there are limits on how this relatively light-hearted strategy can be effectively used. As di Leonardo points out, "the anthropological gambit is only usable on relatively privileged Americans, never on those who are in some way stigmatized" (63–64).

33. The effect is also ironic when "timeless" traditions, which people take to be emblematic of their own identity, are shown to be a relatively recent inventions and not even their own. Thus there is a debunking thrust to the literature on the "invention of tradition," whether undertaken innocently or not. See, especially, Trevor-Roper's essay on the origins of the kilt in Scotland, in the collection edited by Hobsbawm and Ranger (1983) that fired the imagination of many anthropologists as well as historians.

and mock the others' lack of knowledge, and/or values and accomplishments. These expressions pretend to possess a sense of how the world works and what the causes and solutions are, and they use the tools of discrepancy positively or negatively, benignly or maliciously, to favor that confident worldview. "True irony" on the other hand may be said to dwell in uncertainty, with a kind of cosmic sense of the finitude and impermanence of all things human. While it shares the generic sense of the discrepant it sees no easy solutions or definitive causes of the kind that can confidently, even maliciously, energize ridicule and sarcasm.[34]

True anthropological irony in the best sense, then, contains both the sense of the discrepant and the sense of the uncertain which derive from the nature of work across cultural boundaries. But it pulls up well short of malice and parody of the other. Indeed, such attitudes arising from a self-confident or pretendedly self-confident worldview are hardly compatible with that openness to the worldview of the other that is of the essence in the anthropological attitude and method. Thus anthropological ethnography may be undertaken fully mindful of those various senses of the discrepancies of method and presence which compromise inquiry in various ways. The irony of this undertaking may express itself in the ethnography. But it is hardly to be expected that the ethnographer's sense of the discrepant is ultimately referable to the kind of self-confidence that may lead to militancy or maliciousness.

What is true anthropological irony then? And how is it to be distinguished from the more usually distinguished ironies: Socratic, historic, and dramatic? Several contributions in this collection address these questions more or less directly (see especially the essays by Boon and by Losche, chaps. 5 and 4). From what we have said in an introductory way, however, true anthropological irony emerges out of the conditions of ethnographic work and the acquisition of ethnographic knowledge. They are conditions of participant observation in cross-cultural, not to say contradictory, cultural circumstances. They are conditions of work which elicit both revelatory statements and actions but are, as well, faced with much concealment. It is work faced with the tension between platitudes and attitudes. It is, in short, work undertaken in the presence of the partiality of knowledge and the tendentiousness of categorical understanding. All of this makes any statement of anthropological understanding subject to counterstatements, undercutting, and second-guessing, all of which have ironic dimensions. And it is such conditions of work that sooner or later cause

34. This concept, "true irony," bears a family resemblance to Burke's (1969) "classic irony" which is "not superior . . . [but] is based upon a sense of fundamental kinship with the enemy, as one needs him, is indebted, is not merely outside him as an observer but contains him within, being consubstantial with him" (514). For application of Burke's formulation to anthropology, see also Boon (chap. 5 in this volume) and Huber 1988.

anthropologists to reexamine, by self-reference, the position from which their knowledge is acquired! The cautions inculcated by such self-reference, or sometimes self-reverence[35] (with its ironic implications), we would argue to be central, to true anthropological irony.

Irony in the Field

Many ironies of anthropological inquiry and understanding have been present to anthropological awareness for a long time now. Indeed, an exemplary discussion of anthropological irony penned by Clifford Geertz, a prime reference in the argument of several of our contributors, has been with us since 1968. And we have mentioned the historical argument, also available for some time, that a deeply ironic tenor can be found in the work of the founding fathers of both American anthropology, Franz Boas (Krupat 1990), and of British anthropology, Frazer and Malinowski (Strathern 1990).

Anthropologists' application of this awareness of irony to the collection of field materials has been more spotty, especially with regard to recognizing the presence, place, and persuasiveness of irony in the daily life of those they study, and hence the importance to the adequacy of fieldwork of taking ironic registers into account.[36] It is true that there we have long had work that documents ironic commentary on the presumptions of the civilizing mission from the colonized point of view, for example, *The Savage Hits Back* (Lips 1937). More recently, Basso (1979) has given us a pioneering study of Apache humor that includes many ironizing observations by Apache on the presence and presumptions of the "Whiteman."[37] Indeed, there is now anthropological work that documents ironic commentary on the civilizing mission from the colonizers' own perspective, as in Huber's (1988) study of Catholic missionaries in Papua New Guinea, which took up as a central theme these missionaries' use of irony in representing the detours they experienced in their evangelical work (see also Huber's essay in this volume).

Anthropologists' awareness of irony, even when not explicitly called so by name, has been especially acute in recent ethnographies focusing on colonial situations, postcolonial predicaments, and other globalized entanglements.

35. A point made by Conway (1992: 74).

36. This is not to deny that, though they do not explicitly explore "irony," many of the finest ethnographies highlight or even foreground contradictions and complexities of situation that readers may recognize as "ironic." See Friedrich (chap. 11 in this volume).

37. The northern Plains humor in Deloria's *Custer Died For Your Sins*, with its pungent mocking ironies about anthropological parasitism upon Indians, remarked upon above, can be seen in Basso's work to have its resonances in the Southwest—an indication of how widespread this reservoir of undercutting attitudes must be among native Americans and what a rich resource for both their and our understanding.

Mary Margaret Steedly's *Hanging Without a Rope: Narrative Experience in Colonial and Postcolonial Karoland* (1993) notes that Karo tellings of "singular experiences" and "marvelous encounters," though sometimes "enmeshed in a colonial discourse of otherness, therein signifying Duplicity . . . still testif[y] to the occasionally subversive power of strangeness: of the inappropriate word, the obtuse word, the word spoken out of place" (239). Another recent Indonesian ethnography, Anna Tsing's *In the Realm of the Diamond Queen: Marginality in an Out of the Way Place* (1993) also examines the use of "spiritual notions as a counterdiscourse against the demands of [state] authority," while noting that "such rural protests are interpreted by national elites and foreign travelers as timeless spirituality" (300).

The ironies of mutual misapprehension and prefabricated "authenticity" generated through global tourism have received increasing attention from anthropologists in recent years—from brief encounters in new tourist destinations like Papua New Guinea (Gewertz and Errington 1991; Lutkehaus 1989; see also Bruner and Kirshenblatt-Gimblett 1994, Bruner 1996, Handler and Gable 1997) to the more extended and mutually defining experience of Sherpas and foreign mountaineers in the Himalayan region of Nepal (Adams 1996; Ortner 1997, 1999). Ortner acknowledges the economic, political, and cultural power that the touring "sahibs" have wielded in shaping the situations in which Sherpas and sahibs interact, and documents Sherpa efforts both to please and control the sahibs. Yet Ortner does not embrace Adams's (1996) ironic interpretation of contemporary Sherpa culture as a "virtual" construction of these encounters. Ortner argues instead that sahibs and Sherpas are each playing their own set of "serious games" and that "sahib construction of Sherpas, and something like Sherpa self-fashioning, take place simultaneously, in a complex and unpredictable dialectic" (1999: 58), which in the end, however, is often ironic in its multilayered implications!

Accepting the indeterminacy and contingency of such situations is key to Keith Brown's (1999) call for a truly "ironic ethnography." While the tendency of global elites to essentialize local forms of spiritual expression and to under-interpret its political force is well-known, Brown emphasizes the other side of "Orientalism." As he notes, occupying authorities in Macedonia typically over-interpret their subjects' ambiguous actions, producing the idea of the "shifty native," whose straightforwardness and loyalty are always in question. Yet Brown gently criticizes anthropologists who, though trying to tell a different story, unwittingly "resemble the state" in their "determination to delve behind one account of the past to reveal another," anchoring themselves thus irrefutably in the supposed veracity of insider knowledge. Like outsiders in Macedonia for the past century, anthropologists have "sought to document 'the truth' in order to represent people in straightforward ways," missing in the process the indeterminacy and contingency of the experience of people "constructed as marginal by the expansive states." Brown suggests instead an "ironic ethnography," attuned not only to the political context in which people's shifts in allegiance make sense, but also to the people's recognition of the ambiguities of their past and present and to the humor they derive from "the certainties of others." In other words, as Brown argues, ethnographers should be aware that the people they study may be Rortyan ironists: "never quite able to take themselves seriously because always aware that the terms in which they describe themselves are subject to change" (Rorty 1989: 73–74, quoted in Brown 1999: 16)

Something of an "ironic ethnography" is achieved by Daniel Bradburd in his "Being There: The Necessity of Fieldwork." (1998). This work is thoroughly infused with "a slight tone of irony and self deprecation" (xv) about the various aspects of his fieldwork among the Komachi Nomads of South Persia. The title of the ethnography is itself an ironic commentary on all the talk about doing fieldwork that never actually gets the fieldwork done.[38] But the ethnography, too, is infused with the author's awareness of his ironic positioning vis-à-vis his informants and especially various levels of Iranian officialdom. Bradburd is also sensitive to the ironic views taken of him by his Komachi informants.

Quite apart from the ironies of colonization, military occupation, Western domination, and globalization, Johannes Fabian (1995) has emphasized how important it is to take account of ironic registers in informants' statements lest our work be betrayed by literal-mindedness. Two recent ethnographers of Oceanic societies have, in fact, taken special note of irony in local discursive practices. Lamont Lindstrom (1990, chap. 5) looks specifically at how irony and ridicule serve as "editorial devices" in the "knowledge universe" or "information market" on Tanna, an island of southern Vanuatu (New Hebrides). Interestingly, Lindstrom notes that Tannese orators are less likely to question the "truth" of an opponent's message (directly or indirectly) than the opponent's

38. A relevant subinterest to our focus here would be a study of the titling of books in anthropology whose register is predominantly ironic or at least subject to double entendre. An example would be Marshall Sahlins, *How "Natives" Think: About Captain Cook for Example* (1995), which evokes at once a traditional and outmoded style of reference to local thought in anthropology as it also evokes the "native anthropologist," Gananath Obeyesekere, with whose "mistaken thought" Sahlins is contending. Obeyesekere's own book, *The Apotheosis of Captain Cook: European Mythmaking in the Pacific* (1992), itself makes plentiful ironic comment on anthropological self-inflation and mistakenness. Another example of an ironic title would be Renate Fernandez's *A Simple Matter of Salt: An Ethnography of Nutritional Deficiency in Spain* (1991), which is a study primarily of endemic goiter which, in the end, as the book fully demonstrates and for a whole host of historical, political, and economic reasons, is not simply a matter of iodizing salt.

commitment to that message or qualifications to be its spokesman at all. From Samoa, Brad Shore (1995) shows how understudied the ironic register has been in Samoan ethnography. Indeed, he tells us, "the Samoans have a wonderful sense of irony which often expresses itself in teasing, mockery and often quite sophisticated political satire." Irony is "contradiction's sweetest fruit," Shore says, and adds (in a vein similar to Lindstrom's on Tannese irony) that "in Samoa it is fueled by the unresolved tension between contradictory cultural models of authority relations" (223).

Bitter ironies that test the human spirit, rather than sweet ones that affirm it, are the subject of Linda Layne's work on miscarriage and stillbirth among white middle-class families in the United States. Many of the stories and poems that appear in the newsletters of pregnancy-loss support groups use irony to convey an experience completely at odds with their authors' strongly held beliefs about the nature of things. For these sufferers (like many others), irony, while it has its powers of assuagement, "undermines clarities" and "opens up vistas of chaos" (Booth 1974: ix). But many would-have-been parents avoid the more extreme positions of doubt and dismay to which irony might lead by turning to Christianity or a secularized version of redemptive nature. "Christian dogma," Layne points out,

> presents ready-made a framework for dealing with discrepancies between our cultural models of nature, of science, of a normal life-course, and the harsh reality of lived experience. As Sontag has observed, there is no Christian tragedy. "In a world envisaged by . . . Christianity, there are no free-standing arbitrary events . . . every crucifixion must be topped by a resurrection. Every disaster or calamity must be seen . . . as leading to a greater good" (Sontag 1966: 137, quoted in Layne 1996: 143)

Layne thus explores, in the parlous precinct of human reproduction, the difficult relation between irony and the moral imagination that is one of the challenging themes of the collection of articles here offered to the reader.

Sequence and Coherence of the Volume

While this collection hopes to provide a deeper understanding of the ironies anthropologists confront in their own inquiry, we also wish to stimulate awareness of the energy of the ironies of everyday life in the field and the importance of paying ethnographic attention to irony as a local resource of insight into local lifeways. With this dual purpose in mind, we have divided the essays into two groups of five, each with commentary by a scholar well known for critical work on rhetoric and representation. Each section begins with two essays that focus on irony's articulation of political tensions within a larger social world, moves on to an essay foregrounding the antinomies of classic contact-zone cultures, and ends with two essays that bring irony "home" to ethnography. This is not to say, of course, that many of these essays do not bear on several themes at once.

The collection begins in a dark mood with contributions on "internal" ironies by Chock on congressional hearings on immigration in the United States, and by Herzfeld on mockery in the political contestation of Greek identity. Chock's essay examines the limits of irony in the high seriousness of legal discourse. The ideology of speech in this context sets up a model of disinterested, univocal, affectless, unmarked speech, against which witnesses at immigration law hearings have attempted to use irony to clear space for new meanings. But irony is not necessarily liberating: as her cases show, those in power can counter with irony to make retorts, silence speakers, and rule out competing meanings.

Herzfeld's study of the politics of mockery in Greece also involves the interaction of official and subaltern subcultures, but his assessment of irony's liberatory force is even darker than that of Chock. Contrary to their reputation for humorless self-seriousness, Herzfeld suggests that Greeks of all levels of sophistication use irony to bridge the gap between the intimacy of everyday experience and the formalism of official practice. When Greeks ironize their relationship with powerful Western nations or when marginalized citizens use it to confront the bureaucratic and clientilistic state, irony can be a confirmation of unequal power rather than effective resistance to it. Irony may give a brief sense of mastery over forms intended as a means of control, but, because it does not have to be acknowledged, it can contribute to the perpetuation rather than to the eradication of a sense of victimization.

The third essay, by Fernandez, takes up the "colossal irony" of the developing disparities of affluence and influence in the world, despite four decades of the Development enterprise. In examining some of the ironies generated in the energetic but often counterproductive work of International Development, Fernandez raises the question of how commitment to humanitarian action can be maintained against this history's corrosive ironic effects. He notes that the disparity between haves and have-nots, inherently ironic, has aroused the moral imagination of some anthropologists, but is also ripe for the politics of irony, a residual politics which is often expressed in the meditative inaction, the quiet complicity, that is the final resting place of so much irony. In search of stable irony, Fernandez makes use of a distinction between inclusiveness and exclusiveness in ironic register.

The essays that follow by Losche and Boon explore ironic attitudes in anthropology. Losche begins with an ethnographic question, and ends with reflections on the hubris of anthropologists' irony in the field. Can words and ideas like irony travel and illuminate life in a distant culture? Indeed, in reconsidering her field experience among the Abelam of Papua New Guinea, Losche finds in the play of names and of secrecy and revelation in the men's yam cult an ironic view of knowledge in which 'truth,' for the Abelam, is constructed via falsity. The narrative seduction of these institutions, with each layer of meaning promising one secret yet ahead, works on expatriates as well as on the Abelam, but while true believers are vulnerable to the bitter truth that in the end there is no ultimate secret at all, the anthropologist, protected from disappointment by her ironic, distancing stance, is left forever on the outside of belief, and open to the undecidability of truth.

Boon focuses on humility rather than hubris in anthropological irony. Kenneth Burke's concept of "true irony" as humble, not superior to the enemy, but based upon a fundamental kinship with the enemy, Boon suggests, can illuminate ethnographic exchange and intercultural interpretation. Exploring his own "seriocomic" encounters over a decade with a Balinese informant and friend, Boon notes how they are connected by the mutual incongruities of their lives. Indeed, without a Burkean sensitivity to 'as-if' kinship, to resemblance through a difference, it would be very difficult to recognize "plural cultures, histories, and critiques," or to see the ways in which they become like "footnotes and marginalia" to each other.

The second section opens with pieces that treat the seriocomic side of irony within large, divided polities. Scoggin examines tropes in China that associate wine with escape from and commentary upon social, political, and moral problems and argues that this usage is primarily ironic, masking the desire to engage with precisely those problems from which people seem to want to escape. She draws examples primarily from the "miscellaneous essay" *(zawen)*, which is especially suited to exploring the relationship between the complexities of the individual writer's imagination and literary, moral, and political currents. Scoggin argues that the three kinds of irony in *zawen* writing are ultimately intended to bring the most worrisome human problems into better focus, discussing, changing, if not actually resolving, problems such as hierarchy, moral criticism, political struggle, and loneliness. Irony is a mask that in many ways might not hide or protect, but rather emphasize, or accent an expression. And yet irony, like wine, may also offer the opportunity to dismiss what is said as arrogant, foolish, or simply crazy.

Taylor, too, attends to the comic in his exploration of the Irish use of irony to construct the individual and collective self, particularly vis-à-vis the English and Americans. These definitive contrasts are examined as they appear in songs, jokes, and typical comments, where they are often characterized by an irony that envelops subject, speaker, and listener. In fact, Taylor argues, the subtle power of irony may lie precisely in its ambiguity with regard to the true position of the speaker, marking an ambivalence about the self which is a key feature of the postcolonial condition. Self-ironic jokes, in particular, can function as a "preemptive strike" on powerful others. As Taylor notes, the message of the performance is a warning: "I can do a better job on myself than you, . . . and I could easily do a job on you."

In this part's third essay, Huber takes up the irony that was used by colonials—patrol officers, travelers, anthropologists, and missionaries—in Papua New Guinea to convey the contradictory qualities of colonial life. Placing Catholic missionaries' irony in this general context of colonial commentary, Huber argues that their use of irony was tempered by the narrative tradition of biblical paradox, in which a seemingly contradictory statement nevertheless conveys a sacred truth. Although they admitted that their work sometimes appeared to depart from conventional expectations, missionaries' ironic expressions implicitly argued that they were nonetheless adapting to local circumstances so that real missionary work could progress. This indirection was important, Huber suggests, because of the potentially subversive implications of this situation for the applicability of distant standards to the emerging local church. For good reasons, these missionaries turned ironies into paradoxes: while their practice appeared to point out the shortcomings of certain expectations, their imagery made these seeming contradictions reveal deeper truths.

In the two essays that follow, Marcus and Friedrich engage the question of whether certain times or situations are especially prone to irony. Marcus sees the ironic predicament of our times as enhanced by the reach of nonlocal agencies into the local, so that conventional ideas of the social no longer have authority and actors are confronted with the same kind of impasse that academics experience in the face of postmodern anxieties about knowledge. These impasses often appear as pragmatic problems requiring responses for everyday life to proceed at all—evasions, displacements, halfhearted investments in old theories or exotic constructions, and idiosyncratic theories of the way the world works. Marcus suggests that contemporary conspiracy theories are one of these ad hoc and embedded responses to massive changes in the world for which there is no one authoritative macronarrative, and proposes that the interview/dialogue format, with its associated writing challenges, is an appropriately ironic strategy for an ethnography of the contemporary predicament of irony in the academy and beyond.

Friedrich approaches the varieties of ironic experience through literature as well as ethnography. Indeed, many ethnographies have been insensitive to irony, although much of cultural anthropology and sociolinguistics centers on experience marked by the kinds of flux and gaps and discontinuities that are so often called "ironic." Drawing on Homer's *Odyssey,* Tolstoy's *Anna Karenina,* and the author's own ethnography of the Mexican peasantry *Princes of Naranja,* Friedrich develops the theme that irony is always with us, inevitably implicated in the nature of time and power, culture and language, tropes and tragedy. "All is irony," Friedrich argues, even those transient moments of "zero irony," which are empowered and given meaning by the ironies of life which precede and follow them. Irony should not be treated in terms of isolated cases and events, but in terms of how cases and events encapsulate and depend on each other—a pattern that informs not only the best literature but the most interesting ethnographies whether or not it bears "irony's" name.

The two sections conclude with commentary by Arnold Krupat (part 1) and James Clifford (part 2), who take respectively, as Clifford points out, an "Apollonian" approach to irony, clarifying its formal qualities, and a "Dionysian" approach, celebrating the transformative potential of irony as process, rather than form. Along the way, each questions some of the guiding premises of our work. Krupat wishes to rein in our general tendency to attribute too much to irony. For example, he does not agree that "visions of disparity" should automatically be productive of irony, nor that it is appropriate to think of every ambiguity or plural meaning as ironic, nor that it makes sense to focus so much on the liberating or destructive capacity of irony, when so often they simply affirm culturally agreed upon truth. Still, he agrees with the larger point made in this introduction and by many of our contributors: that irony's potential to undercut all positions motivates a search for stability, and that as long as one's irony remains humble, a recuperation of humanism may be possible.

Clifford returns to irony's creative side, warning that ironic paradigms never lead quite where one wants them to, and that stability (if not humility) may be hoped for in vain. Yet perhaps there is transformative potential in irony's drive toward perpetual displacement. Of course, irony is often used ideologically to express and to contain complexity, wrestle with dissonance and disorder, and critique innovation and deviance. But irony can also help achieve historical openness and self-location if, as Clifford says, the Holy Spirit you put your faith in is enough of a trickster, or if, like Taylor's Irish singers, you drink enough to get "drunk, singing, and blissfully delusional in the face of history." Indeed, Clifford is inclined to see virtue in the "all is irony" view. For if we restore to the agenda the question of temporality, we place at center stage (as in Frazer's *Golden Bough*) the irony—or is it a paradox?—of "disintegration: death as a transformative source for more life."

These essays, as we seek to reveal and as the reader will find, shed much light on the presence and absence of the "force of irony" in human relations—in our relations to each other and to the world. They also raise complex problems for our ethnographic work, for our ethnographic interpretations, and for the positioning of our discipline, in the academy and in the world. We will return for brief final comment on this complex of problems and possibilities in our "coda" to the collection.

References

Adams, Vincanne. 1996. *Tigers of the Snow (and Other Virtual Sherpas): An Ethnography of Himalayan Encounters*. Princeton: Princeton University Press.
Aristotle. 1961. *Aristotle's Poetics*. Ed. Francis Ferguson. New York: Hill and Wang.
Asad, Talal, ed. 1973. *Anthropology and the Colonial Encounter*. New York: Humanities Press.
Bakhtin, M. M. 1986. *Speech Genres and Other Late Essays*. Trans. Vern W. McGee; ed. Caryl Emerson and Michael Holquist. Austin: University of Texas Press.
Baldick, Chris. 1990. *The Concise Oxford Dictionary of Literary Terms*. New York: Oxford University Press.
Basso, Keith. 1979. *Portraits of "The Whiteman": Linguistic Play and Cultural Symbols among the Western Apache*. Cambridge: Cambridge University Press.
Beck, Ulrich. 1992. *Risk Society: Towards a New Modernity*. London: Sage Publications.
Beck, Ulrich, Anthony Giddens, and Scott Lash. 1994. *Reflexive Modernization: Politics, Tradition and Aesthetics in the Modern Social Order*. Stanford: Stanford University Press.
Beidelman, T. O. 1982. *Colonial Evangelism: A Socio-Historical Study of an East African Mission at the Grassroots*. Bloomington: Indiana University Press.
———. 1986. *Moral Imagination in Kaguru Modes of Thought*. Bloomington: Indiana University Press.
Booth, Wayne C. 1974. *A Rhetoric of Irony*. Chicago: University of Chicago Press.
Borges, Jorge Luis. 1956. *Ficciones*. Buenos Aires: Emcee Editores, S.A.
Bradburd, Daniel. 1998. *Being There: The Necessity of Fieldwork*. Washington, D.C.: Smithsonian Institution Press.
Brown, K. S. 1999. Marginal Narratives and Shifty Natives: Ironic Ethnography as Antinationalist Discourse. *Anthropology Today* 15(1): 13–16.
Bruner, Edward M. 1996. Tourism in the Balinese Borderzone. In *Displacement, Diaspora, and Geographies of Identity*, ed. Smadar Lavie and Ted Swedenburg, 157–79. Durham, NC: Duke University Press.
Bruner, Edward M., and Barbara Kirshenblatt-Gimblett. 1994. Maasai on the Lawn: Tourist Realism in East Africa. *Cultural Anthropology* 9(4): 435–70.
Burke, Kenneth. 1969. *A Grammar of Motives*. Berkeley: University of California Press.
Burridge, Kenelm O. 1969. *Tangu Traditions*. Oxford: Clarendon.
———. 1978. Missionary Occasions. In *Mission, Church, and Sect in Oceania*, ed. James A. Boutilier, Daniel T. Hughes, and Sharon W. Tiffany, 1–30. Ann Arbor: University of Michigan Press.
———. 1991. *In the Way: A Study of Christian Missionary Endeavours*. Vancouver: UBC Press.
Certeau, Michel de. 1988. *The Practice of Everyday Life*. Berkeley: University of California Press.

Clifford, James. 1986. Partial Truths. Introduction to *Writing Cultures: The Poetics and Politics of Ethnography*, ed. James Clifford and George E. Marcus, 1–26. Berkeley: University of California Press.

Conway, Daniel W. 1992. Comedians of the Ascetic Ideal: The Performance of Genealogy. In *The Politics of Irony: Essays in Self Betrayal*, ed. Daniel W. Conway and John E. Seery, 73–95. New York: St. Martin's Press.

Cooper, Frederick, and Stoler, Ann Laura, eds. 1997. *Tensions of Empire: Colonial Cultures in a Bourgeois World*. Berkeley: University of California Press.

Cross, Andrew. 1998. Neither Either nor Or: The Perils of Reflexive Irony. In *The Cambridge Companion to Kierkegaard*, ed. Alastair Hannay and Gordon D. Marino, 125–53. Cambridge: Cambridge University Press.

Delbanco, Andrew. 1995. *The Death of Satan: How Americans have Lost the Sense of Evil*. New York: Ferrar, Straus and Giroux.

Deloria, Vine, Jr. [1969] 1998. *Custer Died for Your Sins: An Indian Manifesto*. Norman: University of Oklahoma Press.

di Leonardo, Micaela. 1998. *Exotics at Home: Anthropologies, Others, American Modernity*. Chicago: University of Chicago Press.

Dominguez, Virginia. 1994. A Taste for the Other: Intellectual Complicity in Racializing Practices. *Current Anthropology* 35(4): 333–48.

Douglas, Mary. [1966] 1993. *Purity and Danger: An Analysis of Conceptions of Pollution and Taboo*. London: Routledge.

———. [1970] 1995. *Natural Symbols: Explorations in Cosmology*. London: Routledge.

Douglas, Mary, and David Hull, eds. 1992. *How Classification Works: Nelson Goodman among the Social Sciences*. Edinburgh: Edinburgh University Press.

Durham, Deborah, and James W. Fernandez. 1991. Tropical Dominions: The Figurative Struggle over Domains of Belonging and Apartness in Africa. In *Beyond Metaphor: The Theory of Tropes in Anthropology*, ed. James W. Fernandez, 179–208. Stanford: Stanford University Press.

Durkheim, Emile, and Marcel Mauss. 1967. *Primitive Classification*. Chicago: University of Chicago Press.

Fabian, Johannes. 1995. Ethnographic Misunderstanding and the Perils of Context. *American Anthropologist* 97(1): 41–50.

Fernandez, James W. 1964. The Sound of Bells in a Christian Country: In quest of the historical Schweitzer. *The Massachusetts Review* (spring): 537–62.

———. 1984. Moving Up in the World: Transcendence in Symbolic Anthropology. *Stanford Literature Review* 1(2): 201–26.

———. 1986. *Persuasions and Performances: The Play of Tropes in Culture*. Bloomington: Indiana University Press.

Fernandez, James W., ed. 1991. *Beyond Metaphor: The Theory of Tropes in Anthropology*. Stanford: Stanford University Press.

Fernandez, Renate Lellep. 1991. *A Simple Matter of Salt: An Ethnography of Nutritional Deficiency in Spain*. Berkeley: University of California Press.

Foucault, Michel. 1981. *Power/Knowledge: Selected Interviews and Other Writings, 1972–1977*. New York: Pantheon Books.

Frazer, James G. 1918. *Folk-lore in the Old Testament: Studies in Comparative Religion, Legend and Law*. 3 vols. London: Macmillan.

Friedrich, Paul. 1986. *The Princes of Naranja*. Austin: University of Texas Press.

Freud, Sigmund. [1930] 1989. *Civilization and Its Discontents*, ed. James Strachey. New York: W.W. Norton.

Fussel, Paul. 1975. *The Great War and Modern Memory*. London: Oxford University Press.

Geertz, Clifford. 1968. Thinking as a Moral Act: Ethical Dimensions of Anthropological Fieldwork in the New States. *The Antioch Review* 28: 139–58.

———. 1973. Thick Description: Toward an Interpretive Theory of Culture. In *The Interpretation of Cultures*, 3–30. New York: Basic Books.

———. 1995. *After the Fact: Two Countries, Four Decades, One Anthropologist*. Cambridge: Harvard University Press.

Gellner, Ernest. [1979] 1991. *Spectacles and Predicaments: Essays in Social Theory*. Oxford: Blackwell Publishers.

Gewertz, Deborah, and Frederick Errington. 1991. *Twisted Histories, Altered Contexts: Representing the Chambri in a World System*. Cambridge: Cambridge University Press.

Gramsci, Antonio. 1971. *Selections from the Prison Notebooks of Antonio Gramsci*. Ed. and trans. Quintin Hoare and Geoffrey Nowell Smith. New York: International Publishers.

Handler, Richard, and Eric Gable. 1997. *The New History in an Old Museum: Creating the Past at Colonial Williamsburg*. Durham, NC: Duke University Press.

Hobbes, Thomas. [1651] 1996. *Leviathan*. Ed. Richard Tuck. Cambridge: Cambridge University Press.

Hobsbawm, Eric and Terence Ranger, eds. 1983. *The Invention of Tradition*. Cambridge: Cambridge University Press.

Hockett, Charles F., and Robert Ascher. 1964. The Human Revolution. *Current Anthropology* 5(3): 135–47.

Huber, Mary Taylor. 1988. *The Bishops' Progress: A Historical Ethnography of Catholic Missionary Experience on the Sepik Frontier*. Washington, DC: The Smithsonian Institution Press.

———. 1996. Missionaries. In *Encyclopedia of Social and Cultural Anthropology*, ed. Alan Barnard and Jonathan Spencer, 373–75. London: Routledge.

Huber, Mary Taylor, and Nancy Lutkehaus. 1999. Gendered Missions at Home and Abroad. Introduction to *Gendered Missions: Women and Men in Missionary Discourse and Practice*. Ann Arbor: University of Michigan Press.

Huizinga, Johan. [1938] 1950. *Homo Ludens*. Boston: Beacon Press.

Hutcheon, Linda. 1994. *Irony's Edge: The Theory and Politics of Irony*. London: Routledge.

Johnson, Mark. 1987. *The Body in the Mind: The Bodily Basis of Meaning, Imagination, and Reason*. Chicago: University of Chicago Press.

Jorgensen, Julia, George Miller, and Dan Sperber. 1984. Test of the Mention Theory of Irony. *Journal of Experimental Psychology: General*, 113(1): 112–20.

Kierkegaard, Søren. [1841] 1989. *The Concept of Irony with Constant Reference to Socrates*. Ed. and trans. Howard V. Hong and Edna H. Hong. Princeton: Princeton University Press.

———. [1843] 1987. *Either/Or, Part I*. Ed. and trans. Howard V. Hong and Edna H. Hong. Princeton: Princeton University Press.

————. [1846] 1992. *Concluding Unscientific Postscript to Philosophical Fragments.* Vol. 1: Text. Ed. and trans. Howard V. Hong and Edna H. Hong. Princeton: Princeton University Press.

Krupat, Arnold. 1990. Irony in Anthropology: The Work of Franz Boas. In *Modernist Anthropology: From Fieldwork to Text,* ed. Marc Manganaro, 133–45. Princeton: Princeton University Press.

Lakoff, George, and Mark Johnson. 1980. *Metaphors We Live By.* Chicago: University of Chicago Press.

Layne, Linda L. 1996. "Never Such Innocence Again": Irony, Nature and Technoscience in Narratives of Pregnancy Loss. In *Comparative Studies in Pregnancy Loss,* ed. Rosanne Cecil, 131–52. Oxford: Berg Publishers.

Lévi-Strauss, Claude. 1966. *The Savage Mind.* Chicago: University of Chicago Press.

Limon, Jose. 1994. *Dancing with the Devil: Society and Cultural Poetics in Mexican American South Texas.* Madison: University of Wisconsin Press.

Lindstrom, Lamont. 1990. *Knowledge and Power in a South Pacific Society.* Washington: Smithsonian Institution Press.

Lips, Julius E. [1937] 1966. *The Savage Hits Back; or The White Man Through Native Eyes.* New ed., with an introduction by B. Malinowski. New Hyde Park: University Books.

Lutkehaus, Nancy. 1989. "Excuse Me, Everything Is Not Alright": On Film, Ethnography and Representation—An Interview with Filmmaker Dennis O'Rourke. *Cultural Anthropology* 4(4): 422–37.

————. 1995. *Zaria's Fire: Engendered Moments in Manam Ethnography.* Durham, NC: Carolina Academic Press.

Lyotard, Jean-François. 1984. *The Postmodern Condition: A Report on Knowledge.* Trans. Geoff Bennington and Brian Massumi. Theory and History of Literature, vol. 10. Minneapolis: University of Minnesota Press.

Machiavelli, Niccolò. [1513] 1984. *The Prince.* Ed. Daniel Donno. New York: Bantam Classics.

Mandeville, Bernard de. [1723] 1989. *The Fable of the Bees, or Private Vices, Public Benefits.* Ed. Phillip Harth. New York: Penguin USA.

Manganaro, Marc. 1990. Textual Play, Power, and Cultural Critique: An Orientation to Modernist Anthropology. Introduction to *Modernist Anthropology: From Fieldwork to Text,* ed. Marc Manganaro, 3–47. Princeton: Princeton University Press.

Marx, Karl. 1978. Economic and Philosophic Manuscripts of 1844. In *The Marx-Engels Reader.* 2d ed., ed. Robert C. Tucker, 66–125. New York: W.W. Norton.

————. [1867] 1992. *Capital: A Critique of Political Economy,* vol. 1. Trans. Ben Fowkes. New York: Penguin USA.

Marx, Karl, and Friedrich Engels. 1978. Manifesto of the Communist Party. In *The Marx-Engels Reader.* 2d ed., ed. Robert C. Tucker, 469–500. New York: W.W. Norton.

Mills, Margaret. 1994. On the Involuntary Drawing of Our Subject Matter. *Cultural Anthropology* 9(3): 364.

Miner, Horace. 1956. Body Ritual among the Nacirema. *American Anthropologist* 58: 503–7. Reprinted in *The Nacirema: Readings on American Culture,* ed. James P. Spradley and Michael A. Rynkiewich, 10–13. Boston: Little, Brown, 1975.

Mudimbe, Valentin Y. 1988. *The Invention of Africa: Gnosis, Philosophy and the Order of Knowledge.* Bloomington: Indiana University Press.

Muecke, D. C. 1969. *The Compass of Irony.* London: Methuen.

Munn, Nancy D. 1973. *Walbiri Iconography: Graphic Representation and Cultural Symbolism in a Central Australian Society.* Ithaca: Cornell University Press.

Niehoff, Arthur H. 1998. *On Being a Conceptual Animal.* Bonsall, CA: Hominid Press.

Noble, William, and Iain Davidson. 1996. *Human Evolution, Language, and Mind: A Psychological and Archaeological Inquiry.* Cambridge: Cambridge University Press.

Obeyesekere, Gananath. 1992. *The Apotheosis of Captain Cook: European Mythmaking in the Pacific.* Princeton: Princeton University Press.

Ortner, Sherry B. 1997. Thick Resistance: Death and the Cultural Construction of Agency in Himalayan Mountaineering. *Representations* 59 (summer): 135–62.

———. 1999. *Life and Death on Mt. Everest: Sherpas and Himalayan Mountaineering.* Princeton: Princeton University Press.

Paredes, Americo, ed. 1992. *Folklore and Culture on the Texas-Mexican Border.* Edited and with an introduction by Richard Bauman. Austin: CMAS Books.

Pesmen, Dale. 1997. The Russian Soul: Ethnography and Metaphysics. Ph.D. diss., the University of Chicago.

Pocock, J. G. A. 1993. Notes of an Occidental Tourist, I. *Common Knowledge* 2(2): 1–5.

Rapport, Nigel. 2000. Irony. In *Social and Cultural Anthropology: Key Concepts.* Routledge: London and New York.

Ricoeur, Paul. 1979. The Metaphysical Process as Cognition, Imagination and Feeling. In *On Metaphor,* ed. Sheldon Sacks, 141–57. Chicago: University of Chicago Press.

———. 1986. *Fallibile Man.* Trans. Charles A. Kelley. New York: Fordham University Press.

Rorty, Richard. 1989. *Contingency, Irony, and Solidarity.* New York: Cambridge University Press.

Rosaldo, Renate. 1986. From the Door of His Tent: The Fieldworker and the Inquisitor. In James Clifford and George E. Marcus, eds., *Writing Culture: The Poetics and Politics of Ethnography,* ed. James Clifford and George E. Marcus, 77–97. Berkeley: University of California Press.

Rousseau, Jean-Jacques. 1973. *"The Social Contract" and "Discourses."* London: Everyman, J.M. Dent.

Royal Anthropological Institute of Great Britain and Ireland. 1951. *Notes and Queries on Anthropology.* London: Routledge and Kegan Paul.

Sahlins, Marshall. 1995. *How "Natives" Think: About Captain Cook for Example.* Chicago: University of Chicago Press.

Said, Edward. 1989. Representing the Colonized: Anthropology's Interlocutors. *Critical Inquiry* 15(2): 205–25.

Salamone, Frank A. 1977. Anthropologists and Missionaries: Competition or Reciprocity? *Human Organization* 36: 407–12.

Scott, James. 1985. *Weapons of the Weak: Everyday Peasant Forms of Resistance.* New Haven: Yale University Press.

Sheets-Johnstone, Maxine. 1991. *The Roots of Thinking.* Reprint. Philadelphia: Temple University Press.

Shore, Brad. 1995. *Culture in Mind: Cognition, Culture, and the Problem of Meaning.* New York: Oxford University Press.

Simmel, Georg. 1971. *Georg Simmel on Individuality and Social Forms.* Ed. Donald N. Levine. Chicago: University of Chicago Press.

Smith, Adam. [1759] 1984. *The Theory of Moral Sentiments*. Indianapolis: Liberty Fund.
———. [1776] 1998. *An Inquiry into the Nature and Causes of the Wealth of Nations*. Oxford: Oxford University Press.
Sontag, Susan. 1966. The Death of Tragedy. In *Against Interpretation and Other Essays*, 132–39. New York: Anchor Books.
Spencer, Jonathan. 1996. Resistance. *Encyclopedia of Social and Cultural Anthropology*, ed. Alan Barnard and Jonathan Spencer, 488–89. London: Routledge.
Sperber, Dan, and Deirdre Wilson. 1981. Irony and the Use-Mention Distinction. In *Radical Pragmatics*, ed. Peter Cole, 295–318. New York: Academic Press.
States, Bert O. 1998. Of Paradoxes and Tautologies. *The American Scholar* 67(1): 51–66.
Steedly, Mary Margaret. 1993. *Hanging without a Rope: Narrative Experience in Colonial and Postcolonial Karoland*. Princeton: Princeton University Press.
Stocking, George W., Jr. 1983. The Ethnographer's Magic: Fieldwork in British Anthropology from Tylor to Malinowski. In *Observers Observed: Essays on Ethnographic Fieldwork*, ed. George W. Stocking Jr., 70–120. Madison: University of Wisconsin Press.
Stringfellow, Frank. 1994. *The Meaning of Irony: A Psychoanalytic Investigation*. Albany: State University of New York Press.
Stipe, Claude E. 1980. Anthropologists versus Missionaries: The Influence of Presuppositions. *Current Anthropology* 21: 165–79.
Strathern, Marilyn. 1990. Out of Context: The Persuasive Fictions of Anthropology. In *Modernist Anthropology: From Fieldwork to Text*, ed. Marc Manganaro, 80–122. Princeton: Princeton University Press.
———. 1995. Nostalgia and the New Genetics. In *Rhetorics of Self-Making*, ed. Debbora Battaglia, 97–120. Berkeley: University of California Press.
Tolstoy, Leo. [1873–76] 1995. *Anna Karenina*. Trans. Louise and Aylmer Maude; rev. and ed. George Gibian. New York: W.W. Norton.
Torres, Gabriel. 1997. *The Force of Irony: Power in the Everyday Life of Mexican Tomato Workers*. Oxford: Berg Publishers.
Trevor-Roper, Hugh. 1983. The Invention of Tradition: The Highland Tradition of Scotland. In *The Invention of Tradition*, ed. Eric Hobsbawm and Terence Ranger, 15–41. Cambridge: Cambridge University Press.
Tsing, Anna Lowenhaupt. 1993. *In the Realm of the Diamond Queen: Marginality in an Out-of-the-Way Place*. Princeton: Princeton University Press.
Turner, Victor. 1969. *The Ritual Process*. Harmondsworth: Penguin.
Vico, Giambattista. [1744] 1968. *The New Science of Giambattista Vico*. Trans. Thomas Goddard Bergin and Max Harold Fisch. Ithaca: Cornell University Press.
Weatherford, J. McIver. [1981] 1985. *Tribes on the Hill: The U.S. Congress, Rituals and Realities*. South Hadley, MA: Bergin and Garvey.
White, Hayden. 1973. *Metahistory: The Historical Imagination in Nineteenth Century Europe*. Baltimore: Johns Hopkins University Press.
———. 1978. The Tropics of History: The Deep Structure of *The New Science*. In *Tropics of Discourse: Essays in Cultural Criticism*. Baltimore: Johns Hopkins University Press.
Wilde, Alan. 1981. *Horizons of Assent: Modernism, Postmodernism, and the Ironic Imagination*. Baltimore: Johns Hopkins University Press.

Wittgenstein, Ludwig. 1963. *Philosophical Investigations*. Oxford: Blackwell.

Zivkovic, Marko. 1998. Why Vote for Milosevic: Bewilderment, Tactics of Survival and the Non-synoptic View. Manuscript.

Zulaika, Joseba, and William Douglas. 1996. *Terror and Taboo: The Follies, Fables, and Faces of Terrorism*. London: Routledge.

Part One

Chapter One

———————— PHYLLIS PEASE CHOCK ————————

The Constrained Use of Irony
In U.S. Congressional Hearings
on Immigration

When Irony Is Rare

Irony is a pervasive condition of social life. As Paul Friedrich points out
(chap. 11 in this volume), irony is always implicated in time or power, where
there is "some slippage or lack of fit" in temporal sequences or disparities of
resources, between intentions and understandings, anticipations and events, or
within structures of feeling. As humans make meanings and social relations
in the face of ambiguities and ambivalences, they sometimes are able to call attention to, or at least to point to, the gaps between their categories and realities
that the categories can not encompass.

Legal categories partake of this condition. Carol Greenhouse (1996) argues
in her analysis of concepts of time in law and politics:

> Law has a mythic dimension in the West, in its self-totalization, its quality of
> being in time (in that it is a human product) but also out of time (where did it
> or does it begin and end?), and in its promise of systematic yet permutable
> meanings. (183)

Greenhouse argues that understandings of law that are based in dominant institutions are nevertheless objects of relentless struggle, as bureaucrats, legislators, and jurists—as well as those less powerful or well-placed—speak and
act. Elites apply themselves to "the constant work of maintaining the cultural
legitimacy of the state against a host of forces that make legitimacy provisional,
even in the systems that have seemed most durable or intransigent, even in our
own time" (13). Univocality is thus a claim that elites make for law. Even in

democratic states, people whose lives are materially affected by law are not always able to contest directly what legislators or jurists make legal categories mean. But they regularly try to draw attention to disparities between those meanings and others with which they shape their existences.

One means that they have to do so is to use ironical tropes. I examine below some of the ways that they do this even in circumstances that greatly constrain what can be said or done. My cases come from congressional hearings about immigration reform spanning almost three decades. Some of the participants in these hearings used irony as a strategy for sustaining understandings of personhood, social structures, and relations between them that a view of the law as univocal elides. Doing so, these participants played roles, albeit modest ones, in the political processes of defining immigrants as "persons," of making amnesty a conceivable policy towards immigrants, and sometimes of stopping or delaying anti-immigrant measures.

I use *irony* to refer to "visions of disparity," a phrase that I have taken from Alan Wilde (1981), and also to ways in which people call attention to such disparities. The disparity of their visions is not that between the real and the ideal, but rather between the competing, partial, and interested versions of the world embedded in different discourses. Speakers using irony call attention to the frame of interpretation in place by stipulating a competing one. That is, they introduce new terms that come from the competing framework. They do not so much give a phenomenon a new name as set up a framework in which to present a different reality. By doing so, they point to both frames as frames, neither of which they can dismiss. As active interpreters, they try to "rearticulate" (LaCapra 1983: 334–35) a frame of interpretation. Their interpretive practices are efforts to negotiate new understandings that resemble the "assent" that Wilde calls a complement to irony, in that these speakers are self-consciously trying to compose another version of the world.

What can be accomplished with irony affects and is affected by its specific contexts of use. As Susan Gal (1995) has pointed out,

> Any linguistic form—such as euphemisms, metaphor, indirection, trickster tale, or anonymous speaking—gains different meanings and has different social and political effects within specific institutional and ideological contexts. (419)

Speakers bring different resources to settings where meanings are being negotiated (Bourdieu 1991). The power lodged in institutions is not available to everyone. Also, particular settings of speech may be defined as limiting what some people can do to contest frames of understanding that have been put in place by others who can speak first or more authoritatively. Speech may also be constrained by an ideology of neutrality or impartiality. Consequently in such settings, speakers' abilities to use irony and what they can possibly accomplish with it may be very restricted.

Take the case of journalists, who by no means are powerless, but whose ability to use ironical tropes is still limited. When journalists write accounts of events or situations, their ability to comment on what they are writing about, as well as their use of irony in particular, are constrained by their ideology of impartiality and their positioning themselves as "balanced" reporters. Balance, in their view, consists of reporting "both sides" of a dispute. But sometimes journalists *do* point to contradictions and paradoxes in the stories that they write. One means that they have available is to use "inductive ironies," that is, ironical juxtapositions of details that purport to "enable the world to speak for itself," rather than placing the journalists as active interpreters of the story (Manoff 1987: 227–28). In an analysis of reporting on the implications and effects of the Immigration Reform and Control Act of 1986, Susan Coutin and I (1995: 137–38) found such a use of irony in stories about immigrants who were ineligible for the legalization provided for by IRCA. One story contained, for example, the words of a ditty sung by a homeless Salvadoran immigrant. He implied that, despite the neighborhood residents' belief that he and his friends were undesirables, it was he and his companions who were "perfect" and the residents who were "ugly" (Greene 1987: B1). The man's song inverted the residents' opinions and thereby made the terms of those opinions appear constructed rather than natural or matter-of-fact. The journalist's embedding this story within a story enabled her to cast doubt on the frame of interpretation used by the man's neighbors, but also by her readers. Over all, we found that journalists did on occasion use irony within the constraints of reporting. They composed stories that contained "conflicting meanings, inversions of definitions, ambiguous images, ironical juxtapositions, self-contradiction, and the like" (139). With these interpretive practices, they were able to point to the constructedness of social/legal categories like "immigrant" and "citizen."

Speech by witnesses in criminal trials is even more constrained than that of journalists. For example, Matoesian (1993, 1997) argues that both attorneys and witnesses in rape trials participate in creating meaning. He writes that

> . . . although the resources with which to direct the course and outcome of interaction are asymmetrically distributed between the [defense attorney] and [victim], both must struggle to negotiate meaning, to make their accounts count, and to reproduce their systematic courtroom relationship as a micromode of domination. (1993: 170)

He describes, for example, how defense attorneys (DAs) may try to assign blame to a victim. In one strategy to do this, a defense attorney's questions may be ironic, in that s/he says one thing but means another (81). For example, in his analysis of the William Kennedy Smith rape trial, Matoesian finds that DA Roy Black played on the sexual and nonsexual meanings of the word "interest" ("interested in him [sexually]" vs. "interested in the house" or "interested in him as a person"). Black used both irony and such devices as repetition to "hyperamplify" (88) its poetic effects. On the other hand, certain poetic devices are also available to witnesses, though their ability to use these devices is more constrained—often much more constrained—than the attorney's (87). In the Smith trial, for example, the witness's resistance to these devices in her answers served to "further escalate and expand the ironic force of the questions" (88), because the double meaning of "interest" created a double bind for her. To assent to its sexual meanings would mean that she concurred in the blame assigned to her; to hold to its nonsexual meanings would suggest that she was "polishing her testimony." This questioning strategy made the witness appear irrational because her answers did not conform to an implicit "patriarchal logic of sexual rationality."[1]

In contrast to these cases of rather limited and limiting uses of irony, consider its prominent, if not pervasive and encompassing role in other kinds of speech events. The use of ethnic labels and categories is an activity fraught with contention of a kind related to that of immigration debates, to which I will turn for my central cases later. In some settings these labels are often freely used in highly ironical ways. To mention just a few of these settings, Strong and Van Winkle (1996) have described how "Indian blood," a term from a powerful bureaucratic discourse, and tribal identity categories have been used by Native Americans in expressive-artistic settings. Artists, poets, museum exhibit creators, audiences, and others infused their works with an irony that is biting, pain-filled, humorous, or playful. Such uses point to disparities between discourses that make such terms fixed and essential and those that make them fluid

1. Sally Merry (1990: 112–115) identifies three competing discourses in use in lower level courts—namely, legal, moral, and therapeutic—and describes how participants struggled to define a situation in terms of one or the other of these frames. Court clerks sometimes pressured disputants not to use legal discourse, but instead to frame their problem as a moral or therapeutic one. Some disputants resisted this pressure in order to try to use the legal discourse. Disputants radically contested these frames not through irony, but by "becoming emotional" (147). Emotion introduced "the most chaotic element into mediation and court hearings" (ibid.).

In contrast, Collins (1996) and Mertz (1996) analyze cases of situations where "highly regimented discourse styles" (Mertz 1996: 246) pertained—grade-school classrooms that were grouped by reading ability and law-school classrooms, respectively. Mehan (1996) describes conferences in which students are labeled "learning disabled." The school psychologist's technical framework with its arcane language dominated in the process of defining a particular youngster as "LD" over his classroom teacher's situational frame and his mother's historical/personal frame. In this case neither the teacher nor the mother used irony to resist the psychologist's framework. In none of these cases was use of irony by those who might wish to contest a frame of interpretation noted. In each case institutional versions of definitions were imposed. None of these studies, however, explicitly looked for cases of use of ironical tropes in these settings.

and multidimensional (558).[2] Another instance is the ironical use of ethnic categories by Greek-Americans in banal talk with and about these categories in such relatively informal settings as ethnographic interviews (Chock 1987). Their talk pointed to the ambiguity of the categories and the ambivalence with which they used them.

Now I turn to situations such as legislative hearings in which use of irony by some participants is very constrained.

The Case of Congressional Hearings

Congressional hearings are settings of public speech in which legislators variously seek information, affirm ideologies, and position themselves as authoritative voices. In hearings, legislators usually move meanings of legal categories toward "finalization" (Hanks 1996: 243), so that the meanings of the categories are "inscribed" in law.[3] That is, hearings are part of the process in which legislators seek to make the terms of law univocal. As well, legislators in hearings "officialize" (244) the terms of law so that their meanings get adjusted to dominant structures and become authoritative. In these settings, legislators must transform often inconsistent, even contradictory, meanings that are parts of diverse discourses. They do so in the face of uncertainties, both of the institutional surround and of public careers, constrained by audiences inside and outside of the institution and by a record. Nevertheless, legislators also have many sources of power, including the institution and its practices.

In legislative hearings, some participants, especially those who contest meanings of law, are caught in a dilemma. The law may offer remedies for ills that can be translated into its terms, an outcome that these participants themselves seek; but its terms cannot reflect the multifarious nature of personhood and social context without the active contention of participants. These participants often resist the efforts of legislators to regularize speech in hearings and try with a range of strategies to challenge understandings of categories of law. With bemusement, defiance, hope, or despair, they point to the difficulty of the task.

2. Think also of irony that is rife in the theater performances of Guillermo Gómez-Peña concerning the U.S.–Mexico borderland. On irony in museum exhibits "which undermines, unsettles, or engages through unexpected juxtapositions," and which may be "the work of irreverent audiences, but increasingly . . . also part an exhibition's design," see Strong (1997: 43). Such exhibits, she writes, purport to "engage their audiences in a more open, dialogical process of interpretation" rather than to "construe themselves as factual and authoritative endpoints of inquiry" (45).

3. Alternatively, legislators may sometimes try to keep meanings open to interpretation. Susan Coutin (pers. comm.) pointed out to me, for example, the case of the work of immigrant advocates to get particular language inserted into a bill by its sponsors. Their object was to be able after the bill's passage to interpret the language in ways that they wanted and to quote this language in appeals for their clients.

One perspective on law in which hearings are carried out takes language to
be transparent and nearly tautological. As more than one legislator in various
immigration bill hearings put it, "Illegal is illegal." This view of the univocality of legal categories, Peter Goodrich (1987) writes, is facilitated by

> the semantic preconditions of legal discourse, the legal world view, [which
> transposes] existent human beings and groups—the diffuse, complex and
> changing biographical and social entities of motivated interaction—into the
> ethical and political—rhetorical—subjects of legal rationality and formal
> justice. (Quoted in Wagner-Pacifici 1994: 118)

In the case of legislative hearings, differences between the view of social life
assumed by some legislators and views that hold elsewhere make participation
problematic for some witnesses. This is true both in the hearings in which legal terms are being defined and in other social scenes in which the terms are
deployed and participants are subjected to and respond to the terms. Everyday
situations in which social identities are claimed, ascribed, or disclaimed, do not
resemble the autonomous, rational ("individualized and generalized") categories that elites can claim for legal discourse (cf. Darwin 1996). Rather, actors
are regularly constrained by processes that produce inequalities. They confront
and deploy codes of cultural marking and social evaluation—"stereotypes"
(see Chock 1987, 1995a), which are practices of which the law takes only partial account. As participants in hearings, witnesses may be defined as both
simpler and more passive beings than the complex social actors presumed
by other discourses, including commonsense discourses of everyday life. Witnesses may be seen merely as providers of "facts" in speech that is already
scripted (Wagner-Pacifici 1994: 111, 120; Molotch and Boden 1985), rather
than as active interpreters of experiences (Wagner-Pacifici 1994: 121) or participants in the negotiation of meaning (Matoesian 1993). On the other hand,
participants bring various, often contradictory frames of interpretation (for
example, those of science, religion, bureaucracy, personhood, and natural history, some of which are described in Wagner-Pacifici 1994 and in Chock 1991,
1995b, and 1998) to hearings. There, they use them to inform, persuade, or ed-
ify their audiences as to the meanings of legal categories in contexts outside the
hearings. They point out, moreover, that these meanings are ambiguous, unstable, and context-dependent.

Legislators themselves frame congressional hearings variously as searches
for information, arenas of democratic participation by parties who air differing
interests and views, occasions to obtain consensus on policies, or as part of
their mandated oversight of the bureaucracy (Aberbach 1990; Smith and Deering 1984; Morris 1985; Wolpe and Levine 1996). Analysts, though, have called
legislative committee hearings "rituals" that leave real decision-making behind
the scenes out of public view (Weatherford 1985), or at least occasions that are

"stage manage[d]" by legislators' staffs (Whiteman 1995: 97) with "large element[s] of performance" (Scheier and Gross 1993: 170–72). Legislators may
use hearings to "blow off steam" and to avoid taking action (160; see also
Wolpe and Levine 1996: 55–57). Nevertheless, the occasion may also provide
a "point of direct contact" between policy advocates and legislators; "and for
the member of the House or Senate, it is one of the principal means of learning
the bases of conflict and compromise" (Scheier and Gross 1993: 171).

Though not always in an adversarial relation with witnesses, in practice legislators are able to adjudicate the participation of witnesses because they and
their staffs decide who will be heard, issue invitations to them to appear as witnesses, rehearse witnesses (and even themselves), and set agendas (Whiteman
1995; Scheier and Gross 1993). As well, legislators try to maintain the "linguistic premises upon which the legitimacy of accounts will be judged" (Molotch and Boden 1985: 273). Legislators accomplish this control not only by
defining what kind of participant a witness can be, but also by imposing a variety of sanctions on witnesses whose participation does not conform to this
definition. For example, legislators can cut speakers off, they can reprimand
them for being uncooperative, or they can declare speakers' views to be wrong,
irrelevant, or incomprehensible.

Despite legislators' power to maintain frames of interpretation, witnesses
sometimes struggle to challenge the frames and their meanings. The problem
for these witnesses is how to accomplish a shift from one frame of interpretation to another. There are formidable obstacles to such a shift. These witnesses'
authority to speak is constrained by procedures and by codes of speaking. Testimony normally has three parts: the first two are a witness' prepared oral statement and the written version of this statement. The third part is providing answers in a question-and-answer session, in which legislators direct specific
questions to witnesses. This last form constrains witnesses' speech, but it also
may afford an occasion when a witness, at some risk to his continued participation in the interaction, may move out of an "information" mode of speech by
employing various poetic devices.

In their analysis of portions of the Iran-Contra hearings in Congress,
Molotch and Boden (1985) have described how the question-and-answer form
of hearings makes a presumed, commonsense requirement for the delivery of
"facts" from a witness, without regard to the context of interaction from which
the facts may be taken. Against this presumption a witness may deploy one of
several counterstrategies (276). These include providing details of the missing
context or engaging in "metatalk" (talk about talk) to give his/her theories
about how the meaning and legitimacy of accounts is constructed.

Wagner-Pacifici (1994: 121) adds that a witness in hearings may sometimes flexibly cross domains of meaning, for example, by inserting a personal

narrative into an account, or may combine his or her own narrative with signs
of deference to the questioner (122).[4] Another possible, but very risky counterstrategy is aggressive reaction to a frame established by a questioner. In this
case the witness renarrates his or her own account, then uses metatalk explicitly to question the legitimacy of the authority of the questioner. Wagner-
Pacifici quotes one such witness in the MOVE Commission hearings:

> ... I have explained to you. I don't talk in hieroglyphics here. I speak perfectly
> good English, and you understand it. For you to sit there and listen to what I
> have just said and come back and ask me were we concerned is complete in-
> sanity. (124)

Finally, a witness may use irony as a counterstrategy—though evidence
of the use of irony by witnesses is understandably uncommon in hearings.
Wagner-Pacifici mentions three or four times in her book that there is "no
irony" in the particular passages of hearings transcripts that she is analyzing.
Similarly, I have not found many instances in the few thousand pages of transcripts that I have read.[5]

In what follows, I examine cases from three congressional hearings on immigration in which witnesses used irony as part of a counterstrategy to make
themselves heard. These witnesses were not simply engaged in acts of imagination or play; their interpretive practices were complex, contestatory political
practices in the world. With them, these witnesses tried to open discursive
spaces in structures that materially shape people's lives—affecting where they
may reside and whether they may work.

Legislative History: Defining the "Illegal Alien Problem"

For a period of more than a decade, spanning the 1970s and 80s, the U.S. Congress tried to write and pass legislation to deal with what became known as an
"illegal alien crisis." The goals of hearings changed over the years as understandings of the problem changed. Early on, in 1975, participants in hearings

---

4. Crossing domains may, however, be more generally a characteristic of speech and not limited
to a particular strategy of response to questions. Susan Coutin (1995: 525) notes that "many, if not
most, social positions [are] contradictory" and they allow speakers to cross discursive boundaries.

5. Our two cases are different in some respects. The MOVE Commission hearings that Wagner-
Pacifici analyzes were adversarial, investigative hearings that followed a tragic event, while the
legislative hearings that I analyze were inquiries to define and resolve public policy problems. But
despite the differences, the similarities of form are significant. Both were constructed as settings
of speech in a formal register, organized by a dominant discourse, and comprised statement and
question-and-answer forms, all of which shape and are shaped by the information that is their goal.
In such settings, irony "punctuates" speech in that it shifts the mood to the subjunctive and threatens the legislators' goal of univocality.

struggled for a definition. Much testimony focused on the questions of how many illegal aliens there were and whether they were taking jobs away from Americans. Some called for further efforts to find out the exact number of illegal aliens, and for increased enforcement of immigration law. In 1975 there was also a provisional, if contested, attempt to make connections between some illegal aliens and visions of immigrant "opportunity." The American bicentennial was approaching, and tales about ancestral immigrants were being retold and sometimes revised in the public domain. In response, there were charges, often from districts where unemployment was high, that the opportunities that belonged to Americans were being stolen by "illegal" migrants. The real "crisis," though, was still viewed from Washington as mainly a regional one for the Southwest U.S.

By the 1980s there were complex immigration bills before congressional subcommittees, to which the bills' proponents had by then made substantial, politically risky investments. There was a greater diversity of groups being heard from than was the case earlier. Consequently, legislators sought witnesses' support for the specific provisions of their bills in which they tried to mediate opposing, even contradictory conceptions of the problem the legislation was to solve. Legislators, that is, sought to transform the dispute by narrowing it (Mather and Yngvesson 1980–81). Doing so, legislators viewed themselves as accomplishing a consensus among groups, so that witnesses who still challenged the terms of the provisions—often witnesses from Latino organizations who took oppositional stances—were likely to be cajoled, scolded, or dismissed by the legislators.

In the 1990s legislators found themselves continuing to be confronted by immigration issues. Among these issues were what to do about the many migrants from Central America who did not qualify for amnesty provisions of earlier legislation, whether the numbers of undocumented migrants had been significantly reduced by the measures taken in the 1980s, whether categories of "guest workers" or "temporary workers" ought to be created, whether the relation between immigration and citizenship ought to be reexamined and altered, and whether the very definition of "citizen" should be changed. That is, the dispute, in Mather and Yngvesson's view, had been transformed again, this time to broaden it. Actions that took place largely outside of hearings contributed to this broadening. These actions included steps taken by advocates on behalf of particular immigrants and campaigns by community and national organizations. As well, there was a significant change in the composition of Congress. Whereas previously much advocacy in hearings on behalf of immigrants had come from various Latino organizations, in the 1990s a larger number of Hispanic members of Congress were positioned on subcommittees where these issues would be aired. The practices of opposition, resistance, accommodation, or concurrence of these new participants were new ingredients of the hearings as well.

The Irony of Stereotypes

I turn first to a case from the middle period of this legislative history. The following two passages are from 1982 joint Senate and House hearings (USSHR 1982). The witness is Tony Bonilla, National President of the League of United Latin American Citizens (LULAC), the Representative is Roman Mazzoli (D) of Kentucky, the Senator, Alan Simpson (R) of Wyoming. The topic is "employer sanctions" provisions of bills.

> Mr. BONILLA. . . . It is [Hispanic community members'] feeling that employer sanctions will open the door for employers to throw up their hands and say, "We will not hire any short, fat Hispanic with a receding hairline who has a big mustache."
> Mr. MAZZOLI. Is there such a person in this room? I am trying to find him.
> Mr. BONILLA. I would like to plead guilty, Mr. Chairman. *[Laughter.]* It is a lot easier for them to say, "We will not hire any Hispanic-looking character so that we will not have the Federal Government on our back" (188).

> Mr. BONILLA. . . . the fact that the handsome, debonair Senator Simpson from the great State of Wyoming walks in there [to apply for a job] with little old fat Tony Bonilla from South Texas—
> Senator SIMPSON. Well, we will both wear our hair pieces. *[Laughter]*
> Mr. BONILLA. I will wear my hat.
> Senator SIMPSON. All right.
> Mr. BONILLA. We both walk in and the employer is going to find it very simple to check your name off, he has[n't] asked you for your ID card because you look so good. You look like an "All American" citizen.
> On the other hand, I walk in next to you and they are going to ask me to show mine. That is when the door to discrimination starts opening.
> Sure, you say, "Well, he is required to ask it of everyone," but our point is that he will never get to the point of ever asking you, or having to ask you because you do not have the foreign look. (277)

One vexing issue in immigration legislation was the so-called employer sanction provisions. One of these called for employers to ask that all prospective employees show some document of legal residence and to keep records showing that they had done so. Such provisions would ostensibly have made employers liable for criminal and civil penalties for hiring undocumented workers. But some witnesses, particularly those representing immigrants, immigrants' advocates, and Hispanic community groups, like Bonilla, pointed out that the bills shifted the burden of enforcing immigration laws from the government to employers. Employers, they argued, would assume that they could tell by an applicant's appearance whether s/he were likely to be illegally present and ineligible for employment.

Simpson, Mazzoli, and other legislators were advocates of employer sanction provisions. Their views of these provisions, however, assumed that applying a legal category is a simple, straightforward task; that is, they assumed that law has transparent univocal meanings.

These two exchanges—between Mazzoli and Bonilla and between Simpson and Bonilla—tackle what had become a persistent problem of meaning in legislators' efforts to enact immigration "reform." The contention was over the meaning of the term "everyone." "Everyone" for legislators like Simpson denoted a collective unit composed of individuals, each of whom, for purposes of the law, was like every other individual; differences among individuals were presumed to be trivial and personal, and therefore outside the purview of the law.[6] For example, throughout the years of hearings, Simpson repeatedly referred to himself in a self-deprecating way as a "bald, skinny Anglo" (for a newspaper account, see Thornton 1986: A8, A9). With this expression, Simpson was claiming that the law and its agents overlooked such minor shortcomings in himself, something that after all "everyone" has, and that if an immigration law were properly crafted, he implied, it would apply only to uniform, rights-bearing individuals.

Bonilla's stories were attempts to shift the frame of interpretation away from the discourse in which "everyone" is a univocal, neutral term, to a discourse of personhood, in which social meanings of "person" are multivocal, complex, and for some people, hazardous (see, for example, Urciuoli 1996). Hispanic community advocates and others who testified in various hearings, presumed that, in procedures under employer sanction provisions, the meaning of a job applicant's appearance was not a simple matter. Rather, they presumed that such situations are fraught with multiple social evaluations and their consequences. In their view, employers' practices would be based on racialized and other meanings that are routinely assigned to aspects of appearance or stereotypes. (They further implied that the law would make employers in this capacity into participants in a new surveillance of the population.)

Bonilla's is one of the rare instances in which a witness inserted a performance into the question-and-answer form of talk of the testimony. Bonilla was using a form of jesting play in which usually only the legislators engaged among themselves (or sometimes invited a witness to join). In the 1982 joint hearings, Simpson and Mazzoli occasionally used a bantering routine with each other in which they exchanged mock insults or compliments. For example,

---

6. The Immigration Reform and Control Act of 1986 (IRCA) that eventually was passed did indeed contain antidiscrimination provisions. That is, that law took note of some kinds of differences.

Mr. MAZZOLI. . . . Let me yield to my friend from Wisconsin—I mean
Wyoming. It begins with a "W," so I got confused.
Senator SIMPSON. I thank the Congressman from Kansas for his—
Mr. MAZZOLI. It begins with "K" yes. *[Laughter.]* This guy really knows
how to hurt a person, I must say; he knows how to do it. (274)

As in this example, the play always depended upon each participant's knowing that the other's words were not to be taken literally or seriously, that is, that
a play frame was being established. One of the effects of their play was to make
it impossible for others to speak. Another effect was to signal their solidarity
with each other and their distance from others. In their performances they held
the stage jointly in front of other legislators, the witnesses, and the public view-
ers, in time periods they had the power informally to set aside for themselves.
The play also validated their own authority to establish frames of talk; they decided when a play frame would be in force and when they would revert to the
testimony frame.

Both of Bonilla's performances used the form of Simpson's and Mazzoli's
jesting routine. In them, he first set up a racialized ethnic stereotype (stipula-
tion), then played on the meanings of this stereotype ("Hispanic") and Simpson's inversion of the stereotype ("Anglo"). In both exchanges Bonilla moved
from talking about making judgments based on appearance (stereotypes) to en-
acting a scene in which such judgments were (playfully) being made (using
stereotypes). In both, Mazzoli and Simpson participated by taking roles in the
drama that Bonilla was putting on. In the first story, Bonilla took the role of an
employer making a judgment about an applicant's appearance (ironically, his
own). Mazzoli then joined Bonilla, "the employer," by denying that he (Mazzoli) was able to find the applicant (also Bonilla) that Bonilla was referring to.
("I am trying to find him.") Bonilla replied by stating the obvious, that he was
referring to himself, by making the mock "confession" that he fit the description of the stereotype. ("I . . . plead guilty.")

The second story makes unlikely or even absurd claims that common sense
says are not true. For one, Bonilla asserted that Simpson is "good looking" and
he himself is not. But far more important, he claimed that it is good looks or
homely looks that make a person "all American," or clearly a person who "belongs" here, or not. His irony points to the unstated possibility that neither is
the case: (1) that Simpson's self-deprecating assessment of his appearance is
right after all, and (2) that the difference between his and Simpson's receptions
is based on some other aspect of their appearances, for example, race or class.
He implied, but did not say, that Simpson is judged all-American because his
appearance says that he is white or well-off, while Bonilla is not because his
says neither.

His irony pointed to yet other distrust. If meanings of legal categories are ambiguous, unstable, and context-dependent, then they may be an integral part of the processes that create and maintain social hierarchies. The categories "citizen" and "alien" then would not distinguish simply between who belonged (was employable) and who did not (was not employable), but would accommodate and perpetuate these hierarchies. Distrust of legal categories also suggests distrust of protections and remedies that law affords. "Discrimination," for example, is one such category out of which legal remedies are built, but in which some witnesses, not unlike Bonilla, had maybe some hope, a little confidence, and considerable wariness. It was also a weapon that could be used by legislators against witnesses like Bonilla, a matter to which I will return later.

Bonilla's strategy of indirection saved him from having to say what other meanings were possible: that Simpson enjoyed the privilege of being less subjected to surveillance by the law and employers because, for example, he is white or well-off, while not having to admit to having the privilege. (That is, Bonilla did not have to say that Simpson was safely playing at self-deprecation.) If he had said it, he would have been directly calling the legitimacy of Simpson's authority into question.

But more important, in these two exchanges Bonilla was renegotiating an understanding of the setting. He was redefining himself as not merely a recorder and conduit of information, but as an active interpreter of the events. For the hearings setting itself, he was redefining its other participants, two of whom were talking inside a frame that he had set up; the form of his participation as a jesting performance; and the frames of interpretation in which to provide meanings for categories of law.

The Irony of Remedies

Now I turn to the second case, which is from the 1970s. The following excerpts come from hearings of the House of Representatives on "Illegal Aliens" (USHR 1975), early in the legislative history. The witness is Manuel Fierro, President of the National Congress of Hispanic-American Citizens. Legislators include Elizabeth Holtzman (D) of New York, Martin Russo (D) of Illinois, and Joshua Eilberg (D) of Pennsylvania:

> Mr. FIERRO. Let me say this: I think illegal aliens are good for the United States; it's good for business . . . , you know, and they have encouraged it. Administration after administration. (324)

This instance was one of the few uses of irony in the testimony at these hearings. Up to this point, these hearings had been devoted to clarifying what kind of a problem "illegal aliens" were for the country. Then Fierro said the unsayable: "Illegal aliens are good for the United States." His reframing took apart all the terms of the frame of interpretation in which the hearings were being conducted. It opened up the possibility that none of the terms would hold: that rather than transparently describing the world, these terms were interested and partial ("business" and "administration") and authorized but unstable and historically specific ("administration after administration"). He ironically posited an equation between the United States, the whole, on the one hand, and business and administrations, only parts of the whole, on the other. Finally, he queried, who are illegal aliens? who are the United States?

Fierro's strategy, then, was not just to reverse the terms of an originary narrative. "The United States is good for immigrants" was doubly reversed to "illegal aliens are good for the United States." Nor did he simply reverse the terms of law ("illegal alien" was reversed to "like an immigrant or citizen") and of evaluation ("problem" was reversed to "good"). Rather, Fierro tried to rearticulate a frame of understanding. He was trying to talk of political and economic structures which immigration narratives and legal categories elide. Finally, like Bonilla, Fierro was renegotiating the form of hearings as a setting of speech and himself as a participant who was an active interpreter of events.

Liberal legislators responded to Fierro's irony by restating the problem in order to provide a remedy. The restatement steered the talk back into legal discourse:

> Ms. HOLTZMAN. What troubles me, though, is [inadequate nondiscrimination provisions]. . . .
> Mr. FIERRO. Our community today, is very devisive [*sic*] about [immigration reform]. It has split our community wide open because there are a lot of relationships, a lot of blood lines that are affected by this. . . . "Do I get a job or do I continue to sit here and allow this preposterous problem to continue and live in poverty?" . . . Let me tell you: Discrimination is nothing new to us at all. (325)

Fierro responded by trying to tell a story that registered the anguish ("preposterous [and unsayable?] problem") of communities "split . . . wide open" across "a lot of blood lines." He stipulated that communities are bleeding, as they are slashed by legal categories like illegal and legal. His story also articulated "community" and "kin" as relationships and their dilemmas as class contradictions that are exacerbated, not remedied, by law. They are experienced, he says, as painful dilemmas—do I get a job or do I let my kinsman stay while I live in poverty?

The language of legal remedy, "(non)discrimination," about which Holtzman had expressed concern, paradoxically provided other legislators with the means to silence Fierro. Fierro responded to her query with his claim to the floor, "Let me say this. . . ," "Let me tell you. . . ," that is, for speech authorized by experience. He also responded with a term from the legal frame of interpretation—*discrimination.* That term allowed two legislators arrogantly to reassert the legal frame and the authority of the committee:

> Mr. RUSSO. I think it's a system [employer sanctions] that we have to use to knock out the discrimination that we're all faced with up here. . . .
> Mr. EILBERG. Mr. Fierro, would you check your records to see how many of your people have been discriminated against? How many [charges] have been filed and how much delay has there been? What are the charges? (326, 328)

Russo and Eilberg turned the language of legal remedies against Fierro by requiring him to account for the dilemmas of communities in legal terms. First Russo took the preposterous problem away from Fierro and asserted committee ownership of it ("we up here"); he transformed painful dilemmas into a legislative problem to be "knocked out." Then Eilberg used the bureaucratic voice and transformed contradictions into discrete and orderly files; he required Fierro to count the cases.

The Irony of Legal Categories

My third case comes from the most recent period of immigration legislation, when the dispute was again broadened. In 1995 two House subcommittees considered a bill that would deny U.S. citizenship to children who were born in the United States if their parents were "illegal aliens" (USHR 1996). In the first excerpt below, Lamar Smith (R, TX) and Elton Gallegly (R, CA) are legislators who were subcommittee members, and Brian Bilbray (R, CA) and Luis Gutierrez (D, IL) are legislators who had been designated as witnesses at these hearings. Gutierrez was testifying on behalf of the congressional Hispanic Caucus.

Smith, who was chairing the hearings, asked Bilbray, "[D]o you feel that individuals are enticed to come to our country illegally because of the promise of the easy availability of benefits and the easy access to jobs?" (53). Bilbray replied,

> . . . anyone who wants to come to the emergency rooms and the hospitals of San Diego and see what we see going firsthand, see what we see in the parking lot waiting for a young lady to dilate, just so she can deliver her baby in a U.S. hospital. . . . I would ask them to look at the documents that we have from Mexico that advises women on how to cross the border, how to get into the United States, how to present themselves for delivery for an American child, and then to be able to access the welfare system because they are parents of a U.S. citizen.

A few minutes later Gallegly asked Gutierrez whether "that is an incentive for people to illegally come to the country" (57). Gutierrez replied,

> It has not been my experience. Nor do I believe that people sit on one side of the border, sit down, make love, procreate, wait 8 months and I don't know how many days, and then decide to skip over the border to have [a baby].

Like the witnesses in the earlier hearings, Gutierrez was responding within a frame already established—that women willfully violate U.S. laws by having babies in the U.S.[7] He tried to renegotiate meaning by denying that this is so. But also he used ridicule by conjoining two incompatible interpretive frames—on the one hand, rational, intentional behavior (a calculated "wait," "decide") and on the other, irrational, emotive behavior ("making love"). He also mixed formal, colloquial, and slang registers—"procreate," "make love," "skip over the border," respectively—perhaps to ridicule Bilbray's demeaning mixture of terms—"dilate," "deliver," "present themselves" (formal, distant terms) in contrast to "young lady" (mock formal and patronizing).

What was unlike previous hearings is that such inversions of terms were begun early in these most recent hearings. Xavier Becerra (D, Representative from California), a member of one of the subcommittees holding the hearings, interrupted the beginning rounds of comments in order to insert his reframing of the hearings:

> I find it interesting that last week we had a hearing on the issue of immigration, in this case dealing with the issue of allowing people to come into this country who are immigrants, but only for a temporary period to do work and then leave. There is a proposal these days to provide a guest worker program. . . . [As in the days of the Bracero program] American citizens who are unemployed could [not] do the work. . . , so it was necessary for us to import people from other countries, temporarily of course, to do the work. I find that very fascinating, that today now we're discussing just the opposite.
>
> Today, not only do we wish to exclude, but we wish to exclude people who by birth become U.S. citizens. I am very interested in seeing the distinction. (19, 20)

Becerra's irony suggests that his audience can explain how these two contradictory premises—that there are not enough citizens and that there are too many—are both true and compatible with each other. He included himself among those who work within this frame ("we"). He amplifies his ironical reframing of this framework, finding it first "interesting" and then "fascinating."

José Serrano (D, Representative from New York), who, like Becerra, was a member of one of the subcommittees, did his own reframing later in the proceedings: "This . . . [is] . . . misguided immigrant bashing" (62). Shortly thereafter he added, "It is also ironic that we discuss this issue when the country was founded by illegal aliens who had no right to be here, just showed up at Plymouth Rock and at other places" (63). Twice he inverted the terms that were

---

7. Gender was a persistent problem in congressional talk about immigration. In the 1970s, immigrants in this talk were gendered implicitly as masculine. But by the 1980s, women immigrants had entered this talk as signs of fertility and social disorder that could not be regulated by the market. In contrast, by the 1990s a small number of women, who were speaking on behalf of various organizations, had become participants as witnesses in these hearings. See Chock 1996.

framing the discussion. First, he claimed that "well-intentioned people" concerned about immigration are in fact engaging in "immigrant bashing," and then that, rather than "illegal aliens" being a problem for the U.S., the country after all had been "founded by illegal aliens." The latter was an extraordinary reversal in that it undid the "nation of immigrants" originary story of U.S. history. He was implying that even (white, English-speaking) European immigrants and their descendants do not count as legal immigrants and citizens.

Serrano continued in this vein, attacking with irony the specific provisions of the bills to deny citizenship to children of undocumented migrants:

> . . . We're going to say if you are born here from undocumented parents, you are not a citizen. . . . How the heck do you enforce this? Lincoln Hospital in the South Bronx has more births than anywhere in New York City. "Dr. Smith, this one looks dark. Check him out." "Yes, but his mother is speaking English. He doesn't speak Spanish." "Well, where is she coming from? From a British colony?" Who makes that determination? "This one is light-skinned. He's probably ok, he's probably a citizen." Boy, are Puerto Ricans going to be in trouble, because we come in all colors, and citizenship is not the issue. (63)

He gave here a mock performance of reading citizenship from appearance and language. In a way that recalls to us Bonilla's playing with racial, class, and citizenship categories in his exchanges with Mazzoli and Simpson, we see Serrano set up a situation that is false. Doctors and nurses do not make citizenship decisions. But it is a situation that also is true, in that racial and linguistic categories do figure in everyday judgments and practices, and even in committee deliberations about citizenship. He stipulated that a particular world, one in which citizenship is denied to some children, one that the bills being considered would help to create, exists. Then he played on its ambiguities and contradictions. Like Bonilla's play, Serrano's is reflexive. He spoke with others' voices—those of the doctor and the interlocuter. But he also placed himself on the scene. First, it was set in his district. Second, he figured as a "Puerto Rican" who is thereby a citizen but one who nevertheless is, for sure ("Boy, . . ."), "going to be in trouble" in that world.

•   •   •

What did these speakers accomplish with their insertions of irony into these hearings? The question of whether irony in the hearings was liberatory or not is equivocal. On the one hand, in a setting that so constrained speech these witnesses used irony to suspend for a while a dominant discourse and to suggest what frames, as yet unarticulated, might otherwise be put in place. Although irony by itself contributed only momentary pauses in these proceedings, hearings are only one stage of the legislative process. They are followed by yet other settings—floor speeches, conference committees, backstage communications, and eventually the cases in which law is applied—in which the meanings of law continue to be defined. Meanings may be taken from hearings to these other forums and further revised (see, for example, Coutin 1999, 2000, on how immigration law is used by immigrant advocates and communities).

As well, as the hearings on immigration continued over the next few years, representatives from more groups who, like Fierro, had something else to say, became participants, largely because of their activism in arenas outside of the hearings. The provisions for legalization for some immigrants, which were part of the 1986 law (IRCA), became thinkable as frames other than the law were inserted into the hearings. The personhood frame that Bonilla ironically performed in 1982 was predominant among the new frames that shaped the amnesty provisions in IRCA. Some speakers also tried, like Fierro as well as Bonilla, to articulate other frames. In later years, some like Serrano, Becerra, and Gutierrez, who were now legislators and therefore had new positions as speakers, were able to continue Fierro's inversions of national myths and to pursue his and Bonilla's uses of the personhood framework. Both strategies contributed provisionally to redefining legislative agendas. Serrano, Becerra, Gutierrez, and others were also better situated than earlier speakers to stop or at least deflect action on bills they opposed, such as those to limit birthright citizenship. As Wolpe and Levine (1996: 55) point out, in legislative processes "[i]t is much easier to stop something than to start something."

On the other hand, one would have to say that the use of irony was not necessarily liberatory. In the first cases I examined here, the frames established by the witnesses' irony were only temporary breaks. Legal discourse was quickly put back in place because the legislators were able to sanction speakers who left its terms. Furthermore, witnesses by participating in the hearings took up positions offered by the frame that the legislators set up. In later hearings, resistance to frames of interpretation could be inserted more readily into the proceedings because of changes that had taken place in institutional contexts. There were new members of Congress, like Serrano and his colleagues, whose constituencies included some whose voices had been excluded from earlier hearings, and who could now not only speak to answer questions but also to ask the questions. These changes in resources for speaking originated both outside Congress (through, for example, the activism of immigrant advocates or electoral politics) and inside it (placement in key committee memberships or formation of the Congressional Hispanic Caucus). As well, IRCA's provisions themselves helped to stimulate the growth of organizations that supported immigrants' rights (Coutin 1999).

Overall, though, the use of irony in hearings had little long-term effect on some very important future legislation, for example, the 1996 Illegal Immigration Reform and Immigrant Responsibility Act and its anti-immigrant provisions. Some people perceived that the 1986 amnesty resulted in greatly increased numbers of immigrants, as those who were amnestied became eligible to bring family members to the U.S. (Branigin 1996: A1; cf. Coutin 1999). Public concerns about levels of immigration contributed to renewed efforts to impose limits and to reverse liberalized immigration measures through legislation such as the 1996 Act (among other things, this act made it more difficult for people to sponsor the immigration of their relatives).[8] New bills, new hearings, new participants, and new demands from constituencies thus continuously alter the contexts in which irony may be used, if it is used. In this new climate, the discourse frame of personhood—and irony—nearly disappeared from hearings on immigration bills, for example, one on birthright citizenship in 1997 (USHR 1997).

What the irony did in the hearings I have analyzed was to create a pause—a discursive semicolon, perhaps—that draws our attention to the power that is not so much in the discourse as around it (Bourdieu 1991). These pauses identify realities that are otherwise denied or delegitimized by those who claim to speak with authority. And they create spaces of continuing struggle to define nationhood and citizenship.[9] Using the different resources that they had, participants brought them to bear in their speaking, and stipulated, hedged, and contested hierarchies of social value—uniform or different legal subjects, legislators or witnesses, racialized or non-racialized citizens, citizens or aliens.

Acknowledgments

I wish to thank Jon Anderson, Susan Coutin, Jean-Paul Dumont, Mary Huber, and the readers for the University of Chicago Press for their critical readings and helpful suggestions on previous versions of this paper.

References

Aberbach, Joel D. 1990. *Keeping a Watchful Eye: The Politics of Congressional Oversight.* Washington, DC: The Brookings Institution.
Bourdieu, Pierre. 1991. *Language and Symbolic Power.* Ed. and intro. by John B. Thompson. Trans. by Gino Raymond and Matthew Adamson. Cambridge: Harvard University Press.
Branigin, William. 1996. Immigration Issues Await New Congress. *Washington Post,* 18 November, pp. A1, A12.
Chock, Phyllis Pease. 1987. The Irony of Stereotypes: Toward an Anthropology of Ethnicity. *Cultural Anthropology* 2: 347–68.

8. For the views of an immigrant advocate of the 1996 law on how sweeping, and adverse its changes were, see Coutin 1999. There, Susan Alva states that that law "*really* wiped out immigration law as we know it. . . . It was like *years* of practice and experience was out the door. . . . That's how major the revamping of immigration laws [was]" (112).
9. I thank Susan Coutin for helping me to clarify this point.

————. 1991. "Illegal Alien" and "Opportunity": Myth-making in Congressional Testimony. *American Ethnologist* 17(2): 279–94.

————. 1995a. The Self-made Woman: The Success Story and Gender in Greek-American Family Histories. In *Naturalizing Power*, ed. Sylvia Yanagisako and Carol Delaney, 239–55. New York: Routledge.

————. 1995b. Ambiguity in Policy Discourse: Congressional Talk About Immigration. *Policy Sciences* 28: 165–84.

————. 1996. No New Women: Gender, "Alien," and "Citizen" in Congressional Debate on Immigration Reform. *PoLAR: Political and Legal Anthropology Review* 19(1): 1–10.

————. 1998. Porous Borders: Discourses of Difference in Congressional Hearings on Immigration. In *Democracy and Ethnography: Constructing Identities in Multicultural Liberal States,* ed. Carol J. Greenhouse with Roshanak Kheshti, 143–62. Albany, NY: SUNY Press.

Collins, James. 1996. Socialization to Text: Structure and Contradiction in Schooled Literacy. In *Natural Histories of Discourse*, ed. Michael Silverstein and Greg Urban, 203–28. Chicago: University of Chicago Press.

Coutin, Susan. 1995. Ethnographies of Violence: Law, Dissidence, and the State. *Law and Society Review* 29(3): 517–39.

————. 1999. Advocating for Immigrants' Rights: An Interview with Susan Alva. *PoLAR: Political and Legal Anthropology Review* 22(2): 110–119.

————. 2000. *Legalizing Moves: Salvadoran Immigrants' Struggle for U.S. Residency.* Ann Arbor: University of Michigan Press.

Coutin, Susan Bibler, and Phyllis Pease Chock. 1995. "Your Friend, the Illegal": Definition and Paradox in Newspaper Accounts of Immigration Reform. *Identities* 2(1–2): 123–48.

Darwin, Thomas J. 1996. Telling the Truth: The Rhetoric of Consistency and Credibility in the Hill-Thomas Hearings. In *The Lynching of Language: Gender, Politics, and Power in the Hill-Thomas Hearings*, ed. Sandra L. Ragan, Dianne G. Bystrom, Lynda Lee Kaid, and Christina S. Beck, 190–211. Urbana: University of Illinois Press.

Gal, Susan. 1995. Language and the "Arts of Resistance." *Cultural Anthropology* 10(3): 407–24.

Goodrich, Peter. 1987. *Legal Discourse: Studies in Linguistics, Rhetoric, and Legal Analysis.* New York: St. Martin's Press.

Greene, Mary Slocum. 1987. Homeless Immigrants Camp Out in Mount Pleasant Alleys. *Washington Post,* 22 July, p. B1.

Greenhouse, Carol J. 1996. *A Moment's Notice: Time Politics Across Cultures.* Ithaca: Cornell University Press.

Hanks, William F. 1996. *Language and Communicative Practices.* Boulder, CO: Westview Press.

LaCapra, Dominick. 1983. *Rethinking Intellectual History: Texts, Contexts, Language.* Ithaca: Cornell University Press.

Manoff, Robert K. 1987. Writing the News. In *Reading the News,* ed. R. K. Manoff and M. Schudson, 197–229. New York: Pantheon.

Mather, Lynn and Barbara Yngvesson. 1980–81. Language, Audience, and the Transformation of Disputes. *Law and Society Review* 15(3–4): 775–821.

Matoesian, Gregory M. 1993. *Reproducing Rape: Domination Through Talk in the Courtroom.* Chicago: University of Chicago Press.

————. 1997. "You Were Interested in Him as a Person?": Rhythms of Domination in the Kennedy Smith Rape Trial. *Law and Social Inquiry* 22(1): 55–91.

Mehan, Hugh. 1996. The Construction of an LD Student: A Case Study in the Politics of Representation. In *Natural Histories of Discourse*, ed. Michael Silverstein and Greg Urban, 253–76. Chicago: University of Chicago Press.

Merry, Sally Engle. 1990. *Getting Justice and Getting Even: Legal Consciousness Among Working-Class Americans.* Chicago: University of Chicago Press.

Mertz, Elizabeth. 1996. Recontextualization as Socialization: Text and Pragmatics in the Law School Classroom. In *Natural Histories of Discourse*, ed. Michael Silverstein and Greg Urban, 229–49. Chicago: University of Chicago Press.

Molotch, Harvey and Deirdre Boden. 1985. Talking Social Structure: Discourse, Domination, and the Watergate Hearings. *American Sociological Review* 50: 273–88.

Morris, Milton D. 1985. *Immigration: The Beleaguered Bureaucracy.* Washington, DC: The Brookings Institution.

Scheier, Edward V. and Bertram Gross. 1993. *Legislative Strategy: Shaping Public Policy.* New York: St. Martin's Press.

Smith, Steven S. and Christopher J. Deering. 1984. *Committees in Congress: Members, Staff, and the Search for Information.* Washington, DC: Congressional Quarterly Press.

Strong, Pauline Turner. 1997. Exclusive Labels: Indexing the National "We" in Commemorative and Oppositional Exhibitions. *Museum Anthropology* 21(1): 42–56.

Strong, Pauline Turner and Barrik Van Winkle. 1996. "Indian Blood": Reflections on the Reckoning and Refiguring of Native North American Identity. *Cultural Anthropology* 11(4): 547–76.

Thornton, Mary. 1986. Simpson, the "Anglo" Behind the Immigration Bill. *Washington Post,* 19 October, pp. A8, A9.

U.S. Congress, House of Representatives [USHR]. 1975. *Illegal Aliens.* Hearings before the Subcommittee on Immigration, Citizenship, and International Law of the Committee on the Judiciary. 94th Congress, First Session, on H.R. 982 and Related Bills. Washington, DC: U.S. Government Printing Office.

————. 1996. *Societal and Legal Issues Surrounding Children Born in the United States to Illegal Alien Parents.* Joint Hearing before the Subcommittee on Immigration and Claims and the Subcommittee on the Constitution of the Committee on the Judiciary. 104th Congress, First Session, 13 December 1995. Washington, DC: U.S. Government Printing Office.

————. 1997. *Citizenship Reform Act of 1997; and Voter Eligibility Verification Act.* Hearing before the Subcommittee on Immigration and Claims of the Committee on the Judiciary. 105th Congress, First Session, 25 June 1997. http: //commdocs.house .gov/committees/judiciary/hju43144.000/hju43144_0.htm.

U.S. Congress, Senate and House of Representatives [USSHR]. 1982. *Immigration Reform and Control Act of 1982.* Joint Hearings before the Subcommittee on Immigration and Refugee Policy of the Senate Committee on the Judiciary and Subcommittee on Immigration, Refugees, and International Law of the House Committee on the Judiciary. 97th Congress, Second Session. Washington, DC: U.S. Government Printing Office.

————. 1986. *Anti-Discrimination Provision of H.R.3080.* Joint Hearings of the Subcommittee on Immigration, Refugees, and International Law of the House Committee on the Judiciary and Subcommittee on Immigration and Refugee Policy of the

Senate Committee on the Judiciary. 99th Congress, First Session. 9 October 1985. Washington, DC: U.S. Government Printing Office.

Urciuoli, Bonnie. 1996. *Exposing Prejudice: Puerto Rican Experiences of Language, Race, and Class.* Boulder, CO: Westview Press.

Wagner-Pacifici, Robin. 1994. *Discourse and Destruction: The City of Philadelphia vs. MOVE.* Chicago: University of Chicago Press.

Weatherford, J. McIver. 1985. *Tribes on the Hill: The U.S. Congress, Rituals and Reality.* Rev. ed. South Hadley, MA: Bergin and Garvey.

Whiteman, David. 1995. *Communication in Congress: Members, Staff, and the Search for Information.* Lawrence, KS: University Press of Kansas.

Wilde, Alan. 1981. *Horizons of Assent: Modernism, Postmodernism, and the Ironic Imagination.* Baltimore, MD: Johns Hopkins University Press.

Wolpe, Bruce C. and Bertram J. Levine. 1996. *Lobbying Congress: How the System Works, Second Edition.* Washington, DC: Congressional Quarterly.

Chapter Two

————— MICHAEL HERZFELD —————

Irony and Power: Toward a Politics of Mockery in Greece

The Elusiveness of Irony

The description of irony in social relations poses a basic problem of method: it presupposes the possibility of recognizing intentionality—if not in psychological terms, then at least in terms acknowledged in the ethnopsychology of the culture in question. The very idea of irony entails a high degree of uncertainty, and cultures in which social status is seen less in structural terms than as dependent on a willingness to take risks (see, e.g., Oxfeld 1993, Malaby 1999) may be more amenable to the production of ironic discourse. Similarly, those cultures in which an awareness of the postmodern condition is cultivated (see Hutcheon 1995) may be more amenable than those in which authority has successfully imposed a legalistic understanding of the past.

But the difficulty here is one of recognition. The ability to discern even a potentially ironic implication depends on a thorough knowledge of the language—not only of the standard forms, but sometimes of local dialects, official usages, and punning and syntactic play. The older ethnographic tradition of focusing on a single community encouraged an equally localized form of language competence, so that ethnographers were not necessarily attuned in the field to the ironic echoes of media, legal, or even academic language—forms of discourse the use of which signaled resistance to, and perhaps contempt for, what they represented politically. The ironic incorporation into leftist rhetoric of the fascist-supported neoclassical *katharévousa* register, abolished after the fall of the colonels' regime in 1974, would be invisible to an anthropologist who had no knowledge of the ancient language and no memories of the colonels' appalling misuse of the neoclassical forms. Yet such irony is rampant in

public political speeches (Herzfeld 1997b), whence we should expect it to surface again in the everyday conversation of politically engaged Greek citizens.

The separation of cultural from linguistic anthropology was never part of the
Boasian or Malinowskian visions. It is presumably a consequence of the professionalization of the discipline and the need for ever narrower forms of competence to meet its demands. It has especially inhibited the recognition of parallels between the role of indeterminacy in social life and the play of irony in
the semantic domain. Successive phases of anthropological scientism, averse to
engaging with the imponderables of meaning, hardly helped. Yet, as Vico has
taught us, there are always important parallels between the dominant forms of
trope and the distribution of power: an excess of literalism generally accompanies political authoritarianism, while irony—the trope most directly associated
with critical reflection—threatens absolute power through its evocation of the
absurdity of all claims to total transparency, certainty, and referentiality. Certain knowledge, once ironized, can never return to its pristine immunity; absolute power, once challenged, is forever at risk. These parallels between semantics and politics are not coincidental: the authority of authoritarianism rests
on the premise of pure referentiality, so that word games and puns usually represent the threat of subversion or at least of ridicule.

Moreover, irony is not always purely linguistic, or even linguistic at all. Linguistic irony is hard to repress because to do so requires the potentially dam-
aging acknowledgment of its capacity for mischief. Ironic acts beyond language are all the more treacherous: the ironist can always deny any intention to
satirize. A speaker of the modern dialect of Rome *(romanesco),* for example,
can neutralize the effects of a witticism that inadvertently causes offense by
denying any intent to wound—but must do so in standard Italian, thereby implicitly excluding the other person from the space of social intimacy. And that
exclusion may remain ironic for other listeners, their understanding—never
enturely reducible to the certainty of words—maintained through the use of
"in-group" gesture and stance. Again, a polite gesture accompanying criticism
may be highly expressive of discomfort with an unclear status relationship, or
even contempt for the failures of a superior. Irony can express disaffection
when more direct means either are too dangerous or require a greater degree of
political awareness than is currently available. And the less reducible to words
the ironic stance becomes, the harder it is to refute. Taking offense exposes the
speaker to even greater risks of ridicule, because ironic intentions are so easily
denied.

Finally, the great earnestness with which we currently approach such themes
as resistance makes the recognition of irony extremely difficult. When our own
discourse brooks no humor, we are unlikely to recognize it in other places. Yet
it is precisely because the everyday acts of resistance may be so delicately

ironic (Comaroff 1985, Scott 1985) that we may wonder whether in fact we only imagined them.

The key issue, then, is one of methodology. If irony does not play much of a role in the literature, that may largely be because anthropologists have found it descriptively as elusive as the sense of smell. Indeed, perhaps more than any other trope, irony has generally been all but invisible in anthropological description, despite the efforts of Chock (1987) and Norman (1994) to document its significance for the politics of resistance and insubordination. Both these authors, be it noted, were working in their native languages—although many of the English-language devices used by Chock's Greek-Americans are quite recognizable, indeed ironically so, as direct translations of phrases used with equal irony in Greek. It is impossible to know how aware her informants were of that transference, but it is at least conceivable that some of them were quite aware of it and that this awareness enhanced the ironic stance that they adopted toward, especially, non-Greeks who had married into their families.

One key to interpretation is the recognition that one's informants are capable of ironic, even theoretical, reflection on their own predicaments. While flashes of such understanding often do light up the pages of the most persuasive ethnographies, the intractable issue of intentionality impedes the development of a more general theoretical approach on this point as well. If we cannot be sure that irony is intended, we surely cannot be confident that conscious ratiocination has led to the effect that we are interpreting as irony. That, at least, is the usual assumption.

I want to argue against that position, not by reverting to psychological inference, but by pointing out that there is a source that satisfies the most stringent empiricism: the existence of an expressed consensus about what certain *types* of utterance imply, a consensus that brings even the most personal evaluations into direct calibration with familiar collective representations. This implicit recognition of a theoretical disposition on the part of informants, recoverable through their more or less casual commentaries on the social order, is an argument that in a rather different guise has long been advanced to justify the study of gossip as an entrée into the moral universe of a community—that what people gossip about reveals the criteria they are applying. (The functionalists added that it also served to reinforce the collective version of order, strengthening it against change, but that is a logically unnecessary step.) The moral order is a collective resource—"moral imagination." That term is not necessarily a psychologistic retreat to methodological individualism—as witness such analyses of collective representation as T. O. Beidelman's work on the Kaguru trickster (1986), James W. Fernandez's magisterial *Bwiti* (1982), or Charles Stewart's historically and textually grounded ethnography of Greek ideas about moral boundaries (1991). But the further we move from the field site to larger encompassments such as the nation-state, the greater the risk of returning to that kind of reductionist reading—a lurking weakness in, for example, Benedict Anderson's otherwise persuasive analysis of the nation-state as an "imagined community" (1983). Our concern is with the *social* dimensions of imagination—of imaging, as it might perhaps be better expressed—of the politics of belonging-as-resemblance. In that context, it is irony that offers the most effective challenge not only to state authority but also to such conformities as populist egalitarianism, racism, and the kind of friendship that calls for enforcers and a law of *omertà* (the stony silence of mafiosi).

Now, resemblances are quite contingent, both politically and culturally—a huge literature on "iconicity" makes that clear (Bouissac et al. 1986). But whereas (say) metaphor usually foregrounds the nature of the "tensile" (Richards 1936) relationship between similarity and difference that the *speaker/ writer* wishes to convey, irony makes it problematic. "Now we have become socialists," jested the member of a Cretan village lineage who found himself compelled by kinship bloc voting to support a candidate whose party his co-villagers had never even heard of in earlier years (see Herzfeld 1985: 117). But how do I know this was ironic? Prosodic and gestural clues abounded, to be sure, suggesting that ethnographers' usual inattention to such matters commits them to an interpretive literalism that they would surely reject in the abstract.

Greek Voices: Ambiguities in a Contested National Space

I have already made several allusions to Greek material. These data are especially suitable for a consideration of irony for a number of reasons: the juxtaposition of fierce local loyalties with equally fierce nationalism and a large diaspora, making simplistic assumptions about boundaries problematic for the Greeks themselves; a complex language history in which heightened awareness of the politics of syntax and lexicon offers innumerable opportunities for ironic word play; the ambiguous status of Greece itself as both the hearth of Western civilization and the exotic margin of Europe; and the prejudice, which I often encounter even among colleagues who work in Greece, that Greeks are not particularly interested in irony (and, as some have solemnly assured me, that they are incapable of understanding its subtleties). We can recognize the peculiar predicaments of being Greek as fertile ground for irony that may even turn out to be at our professional expense—a rather disconcerting reminder of the importance of at least recognizing irony when it occurs.

I propose to use the Greek case (in its national entirety, not simply the situation in one village), and the peculiar irony of the Greek "take" on intentionality, also as a means of opening up the issue of indeterminacy and insubordination. (I prefer the less question-begging term "insubordination" to the more

fashionable "resistance.") The strategy of taking a country as a whole is deliberately ironic in itself: for while ethnography is an intimate enterprise, even the
denizens of a small village *also* inhabit a country, a religious community, and
so on. The premise of hermetic village discourse is thus no less silly than that
of a uniform national culture, and this way of talking about the whole country
as though it were a single field site should serve to highlight both absurdities
with—appropriately—equal irony.

There is another circumstance that makes Greece very suitable for a study
of the aleatory character of attributions of intent. Most Greeks generally deny
the *generic* possibility of knowing the innermost thoughts of another person
and therefore that person's intentions, yet this has never prevented them either
from trying to fathom such matters in *specific* cases or from attributing motives
without any obvious sense of contradiction. To recognize someone's speech as
ironic is to attribute to that person quite mischievous motives as well as a certain capacity for dissembling. It presupposes a recognition of similar proclivi-
ties in oneself; Greeks stereotype their own society as one in which evasiveness
and secrecy permit a high level of deception, conventionalized to form the basis of a rueful collective self-recognition. So it is by imagining a common sensibility, not a very flattering one by the ostensible values of church and state,
that Greeks overcome the dilemma of combining a generic agnosticism about
motives with a desire to attribute the worst possible intentions to everyone except themselves as individuals and—sometimes—their nearest and dearest.

Greeks inhabit a highly bureaucratized nation-state, but that state is
grounded—much like the United States—in an ideological distrust of authority. Both countries count rebels as the glorious predecessors of their national
sense of order; both regard resistance to official authority—especially fiscal
authority—as a socially amiable trait; and both have for significant periods of
time upheld the view that doctrines of collective identity such as communism
are quintessentially opposed to the national self-image. In Greece, however, bureaucratic academicism is much more clearly the result of the imposition of
foreign models, many of them imported from the German-speaking world and
all of them supported by the various Great Powers that have taken it upon themselves to manage Greece's destiny. As a result everyday life is richly coded in
the terms of a constant tussle between extreme formalism and a virtual caricature of anarchist chaos. The very notion of an independent Greek nation-state
is widely—but surreptitiously—felt to be something of an oxymoron: the insubordination that gave strength to Greek resistance to foreign domination ren-
ders the country divided, and therefore weak, before more powerful patrons
and enemies. Every failure is attributed to *to ellinikó dhemónio* ("the Greek genius")—a perfect template for irony at the expense of the collectivity.

Perhaps the clearest expression of this attitude comes in the proverbial self-deprecation, *éna mialó ki aftó roméïko* ("[I have] one brain, and that one's Greek!"). This saying is especially interesting in that it identifies the self-critical person of the speaker with a national identity—a national identity, however, that is very explicitly coded in terms of the Byzantine- and Turkish-influenced heritage of everyday life and the vernacular culture rather than the Hellenic *(ellinikó)* culture promulgated by a state bureaucracy greatly beholden to the West's vision of Hellas reborn. This, the so-called Romeic culture, comprises the interior things of the culture, the familiar forms of the intimate zone to which foreigners are rarely admitted—a source of weakness in the global cultural economy if breached, but a fortress of familiarity as long as it is adequately guarded. Since irony demands some degree of opacity, it flourishes in this rueful interior.

Such tensions exist in many nation-states; they are sustained by a common disjunction between national ideals of formalism and homogeneity on the one hand and the local insistence on difference and unpredictability on the other. But Greece experiences these tensions with particular force because of the role it plays in the larger European context, where the spiritual ancestors' modern representatives can be chastised by more powerful partners for their failure to emulate their ancient ancestors. Here it is especially before Western European (and North American) observers that Greeks are prone to conceal personal or local features that could be construed as reflecting badly on the nation as a whole—as betrayals of *cultural intimacy* through the careless sharing of *social intimacy,* the ethnographer's point of entry (Herzfeld 1997a: 90).

Language Games

Irony serves this purpose admirably: it implies that whoever is able to understand it is already an "insider." Greeks often deal with the awkwardness posed for their sense of cultural privacy by my fluency in Greek, which upsets their comforting biogenetic model of the inheritance of linguistic competence through the blood, by acting as though I represented a freak situation that had, in effect, resulted in my cooptation into the gene pool. Such cooptation may extend to other domains of symbolic identity as well. When someone amicably clapped me about the shoulders and addressed me as *Khristiané mou* ("my Christian")—an endearment that conjures up the fellowship of sinners rather than attributes of saintly virtue—and I objected on the literal-minded grounds of not being a Christian, he rather crossly said that this was not meant as a religious inclusion at all. Interlopers who give the lie to the assumption of biological kinship among all fluent speakers of Greek must be firmly put in their place, the enabling fictive kinship being, in effect, a demand for tactful cooperation.

The alternative, as every fieldworker knows, is to be accused of being a spy—the only conceivable alternative to full acceptance, and the exclusionary version of turning one into a virtual native. The spy version, moreover, rests on the defensive view that no other reason could exist for learning such an obscure language as Greek; in the prevailing politics of culture, the flip side—that of the inclusionary, absorptive strategy toward outsiders perceived as fundamentally friendly—is that they must share in the logic that only insiders could possibly speak Greek at all and that it was too difficult for anyone else to learn unless they had motives at once powerful and nefarious for doing so. Here the endearment "my Christian" takes on added significance: most Greeks share the view, for which there is some historical justification, that the church played a major role in preserving the language—especially its difficult archaic forms, which also come closer to some dialects for which, again, a higher exclusionary power is claimed. It is no coincidence that on Rhodes, where my attempts at gaining intimate access to an endogamous village ultimately failed, I was actively discouraged from learning the local dialect through the double device of calling my Greek better than theirs because it was more formal and simultaneously explaining the impenetrability of theirs by ironically calling it *katharévousa*. On Crete, by contrast, my search for access was much more richly rewarded, and there too I was actively taught a dialect I had gained the right to know—in a village of animal-thieves—by "stealing" words, as the villagers put it.

Language is indeed a topic about which virtually all Greeks have had to become social analysts in order to survive. There is a discourse about language that, transcending ideological differences and a vast educational disparity, unites the most illiterate peasant with the intellectuals of the metropolis. The abolition of the neo-Classical *katharévousa* diglossic register after the fall of the military dictatorship of 1967–74 did not remove the shadow of a language that had until that moment been the official and constitutional language of government, instruction, and media usage for most of the country's history—a language so arcane that occasionally interpreters were needed for official legal transactions, and that pitted generations of "educated" schoolchildren against their "ignorant" parents. On the contrary, it now—because officially nonexistent—became the ideal tool of political irony. The socialist Papandreou, for example, taunted his conservative rival Mitsotakis with it in the 1984 elections, raising the specter of stuffy formality backed by the still-fresh incubus of the military dictatorship—and it mattered not a jot that Mitsotakis was extremely careful not to use a single phrase of *katharévousa* in his own speeches (see Herzfeld 1997b).

But although the major battle was fought in the domain of language, the ideological tension that undergirded it also infuses an enormous range of other cultural domains—music, architecture, ethics, and even social relations. As I have argued extensively elsewhere (Herzfeld 1997a), this situation allowed considerable play to the tensions between the cherished values of sociability and the puritanical moralism—the concern with international respectability as a "European" nation—that has so often marked the official face of the national culture. What I have not done, and what I would like to begin addressing here, is the role of irony in the political contestation of Greek identity at all levels from the interpersonal to public debates about national culture. Because the anthropologist's contribution can bridge the gap between the intimacy of everyday experience and the formalism of official practice, ironic reflections of that tension can prove equally revealing.

Let me also state what may be obvious to analysts of some other European societies but in Greece seems to have escaped much comment until now. It may be that for most of the history of anthropological work in Greece the major preoccupation was with poorly educated rural dwellers. That is no longer always the case, and anthropologists (notably Faubion 1993) have begun to work closely with intellectuals as well, seeing continuities as well as discontinuities with "traditional ethnography." While this move is long overdue, it should not be allowed to obscure the fact that the Greek countryside was *never* completely isolated from the city (see Hirschon 1989); the unlettered peasants have long been able to do a passable imitation of educated speech, and the media have been a major conduit between populations that are in any case historically inseparable. To the extent that we accept Anderson's (1983) thesis about print capitalism and its role in fostering nationalism, we should not expect matters to be otherwise: even though the authorities did use formal language as a tool of exclusion, that language could never have existed as long as it did without some vernacular involvement in its use. Yes, there is a village style of speech (or, rather, there are many such styles); but the fact that the Rhodian villagers who mocked my educated language as *katharévousa* could also—surely with irony aforethought!—claim that *their own speech* was also *katharévousa,* because it contained so many archaisms as to be incomprehensible to outsiders, suggests that even in 1974, when I heard those comments, villagers knew quite a lot about linguistic politics at the national level. The comment is especially significant because it was made in a preponderantly right-wing village during the period of the fascist dictatorship, in a place designated as lying within the frontier regions that faced—and genuinely feared invasion by—the Turkish foe. In describing my speech pattern in terms of the then official language, the villagers were engaging in a particularly subtle form of irony: any attempt on my part to disagree would have left me looking extremely foolish—they were, after all, paying me a compliment—or like a probable spy who was trying to cover his traces.

To speak as a villager thus arguably means knowing more about the complex language situation, not less, than urban sophisticates, because the latter—from their position of power—actually have less need to know about village dialect than the villagers do about official forms. Greek villagers' mockery of the learned is not anti-intellectualism of the kind we encounter in the United States, for example, but reflects a grim realization that those who lack power have a greater need of certain forms of knowledge and face greater barriers to access. Insubordination is not always resistance: it can lock one into the structures of power more firmly than ever—a considerable price for the momentary satisfaction of symbolically inverting the prevailing order. Those who mock the educated and powerful, for example, may nonetheless play the game of clientilism because it is pragmatically stupid not to do so. They have a morally inflected historiography that absolves them from effective social censure and indeed enfolds them in the warmth of a sociality defined by its resistance to power: the Turks are to blame for all our shortcomings (including clientilism!), the West and its agents at home block our access to the good things of life, and so on—and this is an ideology that the Greek state, diplomatically marginalized on the international stage, itself often cultivates. It is implicit in the nation's own ideology of national genesis: cheeky heroism in defense of an independence that, even today, is hardly unconditional. Those who have castigated "the Greeks" as collectively incapable of self-criticism or self-restraint are simply not hearing the multiplicity of dissonant and dissenting Greek voices—the poet Nikos Dimou writing of *The Misery of Being Greek* (1976) in an aphoristic rehearsal of some of the most painful aspects of that self-knowledge, for example—and perhaps sometimes, despite careful formal training, lack the experience of everyday language use, an ironic reflection indeed on the ignorance of the educated.

One source of popular awareness of the world of the professional intellect has been through music. Composers like Mikis Theodorakis and Manos Hadjidakis set the words of some of Greece's leading poets to their enormously popular music. Some of the more cerebral Greek poets—Cavafy, for example—may not enter the popular imagination in this way, but the throngs of poets who attend national conferences handing out enormous quantities of their privately printed output suggest that in a more general sense poetry is no arcane mystery to most Greeks. Plato, fortunately, did not get his way, and the proliferation of poets may indeed be a sign that the intimate spaces of Greek life are flourishing. Be that as it may, there is a continuum of not only language but imagery, style, and rhetoric that embraces both ordinary speech and literary works. Irony is strongly present at both extremes—indeed, travels easily along the continuum. Poets and peasants alike, and especially those who are both, entertain theories of meaning in which irony must play a major part.

Irony and the Commonality of Discourse

It is for this reason that I feel justified, if justification is needed, in combining the insights of literary scholar Gregory Jusdanis (1987) into the poetics of Cavafy with my own perception of theoretical capacities in the exegetical framework of my informants in the highland Cretan village I have called "Glendi" (Herzfeld 1985).

Western intellectuals are fond of distinguishing between practical and discursive forms of consciousness (see Bourdieu 1977: 109, Comaroff 1985: 232, Giddens 1984). But this strikes me as a form of special pleading. We can certainly say that the professionalization of social science requires us to formalize our theories, so that their discursive organization and comparative reach may be very different from those of a shepherd or a potter. To say, however, that these intellectual positions are *not* expressions of "practical consciousness" is to deny the point that theory itself, as Eco (1976: 29) has remarked (and see also Crick 1976), is a form of social practice. We *use* theories—admittedly in a verbal domain, for the most part—and in this our awareness of their significance is as embedded in the social dimensions of our professional lives as the constructions of the shepherds and potters are in theirs.

This adjustment to the underlying separation of the world into theorizing ethnographers and theorized informants has been a long time in the making: it is part of the intellectual world's elaboration of its own social privileges. Yet it has been under challenge at least since Labov (1972) discerned a capacity for abstract logic in youthful speakers of inner-city dialects. Even that insight presupposes a high valuation of abstract thought, just as my own concern to treat highland Cretan shepherds' views of meaning as reflecting a theoretical stance (Herzfeld 1985: xi–xv) might legitimately be criticized as reductive in the sense that it places a high valuation on the notion of theory. If, however, we simply see such devices as means of comparison that permit us to calibrate local understandings to our own without privileging either, we can at least begin to interpret specific actions—including ironic ones—as "motivated" by an underlying set of shared assumptions about the way in which social relations work. That, in turn, permits us to avoid making assumptions about intentionality: we can instead read specific instances of what appears to be meant as irony in terms of local actors' own generic (that is, theoretical) assumptions, rather than either presupposing our own ability to fathom others' intentions or ignoring the basis on which they are interpreting each other. In this way we avoid the objectivist stand of Lévi-Strauss (1963), who argued that unconscious models were always more reliable than conscious ones because they represented a structure on which self-aware reflection had not exercised any distorting effects—a position that implies an omniscient observer capable of separating the unconscious wheat from the conscious chaff.

The approach developed by Jusdanis is especially apt for my present purposes. First, quite simply, the fact that he is dealing with a poet who wrote in Greek, but whose mastery of irony seems to survive translation into English very well, makes his analysis directly comparable to what I have said about the theoretical assumptions of Cretan shepherds. Second, Jusdanis shows how to disembed the writer's theory of poetics from the texts themselves, given that Cavafy's theoretical writings are very sparse. In this way Jusdanis avoids the pitfalls of Lévi-Straussian objectivism: there is evidence in the poems that the writer entertained certain theories of poetics, but it is not necessary to make any prior assumptions about whether he did so consciously or not (or, indeed, about what this distinction might mean in analytic terms). Jusdanis shows instead that an intellectually alert individual, one who also knew how to express the most intense sensuality, might not verbalize what were nonetheless a set of evolving principles of composition. No judgment is made as to whether the poet was "aware" of applying these principles (and we might want to recall that Lévi-Strauss joined Roman Jakobson in a similarly constructed exercise around Baudelaire's "Les chats" before he went on to his more tendentious exercises in discriminating between "hot" and "cold" societies (Jakobson and Lévi-Strauss 1962, Lévi-Strauss [1960] 1976: 28–30; [1962] 1966: 233–34]). Jusdanis's achievement is to show how the poet speaks in his poetry, sometimes quite directly, of the principles he has applied in the construction of the poems themselves. Yet if we are to recognize such a theorizing capacity in what may be theoretically unreflexive artistic productions, we can certainly also recognize a theoretical orientation in the ironic observations of displaced or marginal individuals, however illiterate they may be.

Ordinary language often conveys implicit theory of this kind. Because ironic commentary foregrounds the features that help others to recognize it as ironic, fulfilling Jakobson's (1960) criteria for the "poetic function" by emphasizing the deliberate distortion of conventional form, it testifies to a socially accepted pattern of portraying intention as ultimately unfathomable as well as to an individual's mastery of the technique. Indeed, the Greek expression *mi m'iro-névese,* "don't make fun of me," has at its core the concept of irony *(ironía)* as potential insult: the aleatory character of Greek social interaction (Malaby 1999) is heightened, reproduced, and—in a distinctly Jakobsonian sense— "diagrammed" in the use of phrases that could be construed as complimentary but were probably not intended that way.

When a low-status resident of Glendi constantly addressed me as "Mister Michael" *(kírie Mikháli),* emphasizing the *Mister* in an exaggerated manner that turned a normal mode of address from inferior to superior (or between two people who do not know each other very well) into a challenge, he was playing on the ambiguities of my position as a stranger: in the community, I might nevertheless have had access to enormously desirable resources. His use of a simple mode of address turned it into a vivid commentary on the uncertainty of our relative positions and, inasmuch as it usually made me feel quite uncomfortable, was—*if* my reading of his intentions was right—therefore successful in temporarily putting me in my place before those who were locally his superiors.

Another villager, to whom I had expressed discomfort with the inequality implied by this form of address, almost never used between villagers, constantly addressed me with a heavy emphasis on the *kírie,* albeit pronounced—deliberately?—in what sounded like an exaggeration of the Cretan accent. He then pretended to catch himself, so turning my egalitarian conceit into a true weapon of someone who, in this situation, turned out not to be very weak at all.

It is this ambiguity as to intention that makes irony the ideal vehicle for gossip in the Greek mode. If one cannot truly know another's mind—*pou na kséro ton álo?* ("how should I know another person?")—one can imagine all kinds of evil in that person's character. The question itself is ironic. It is almost always used in conjunction with the intention of hurting the other person's reputation (du Boulay 1974). Here, too, irony is barbed. When a young woman confided to one of her peers that she was pregnant and swore the other woman to secrecy, the latter did not tell anyone directly—but kept making pointed remarks to the effect that the first woman must have eaten too many beans lately. Because there could hardly be any doubt about what was meant, and because in fact the villagers collectively interpreted it correctly (as the ethnographer's confident report makes clear), we may infer, if not the actual motivation of the gossip, then at least the motive that others attributed to her. And again, the great beauty of the ironic commentary, at least from the perpetrator's vantage point, was that it could not be directly challenged without bringing further ridicule on its victim. Indeed, the remark about beans *could* have been innocent of malice.

This kind of irony occurs in a world of nominal equals where, because of that egalitarian ethos, small increments of power count for a great deal. Observers have often noted the fragility of status in such communities: irony, which in situations of clear hierarchy can become the expression of power (Rosaldo 1986), contributes to the tense fragility of social relations among those for whom status differences are rarely stable and easily displaced. In such situations, anyone may use irony about anyone else. But this does not invalidate the point that irony often serves to express a desire for much greater degrees of power.

Cretan mountain villagers, for example, inhabit a world in which fragile local differences barely threaten both the illusion of horizontal egalitarianism and the experience of virtually indestructible vertical ties of patron-client hierarchy. If irony constantly infuses the brittle bickering that organizes villagers' perceptions of each other, it may also provide a socially internal mode of addressing external political inequalities.

In this less manipulable external world a familiar form of irony, which rests on claims to moral superiority over those who are one's political superiors, is encapsulated in another trope. This is the metonymic relationship in which mockery at the entirely hypothetical expense of the target creates an illusion of doing battle in an intimate setting and on a level playing field. Because the experienced reality is in fact so much more unequal, irony of this kind may bring enormous moral satisfaction to a speaker, but it has virtually no practical effect on the balance of actual power, and is one of the least satisfactory aspects of the various models of "resistance" that have been proposed (see especially Abu-Lughod 1990, Reed-Danahay 1993).

Ironies of the Ironic: Cooptation by License

Note, however, that the problem of whether we can speak of resistance where no obvious, lasting effects are evident is precisely that of irony: its uncertain presence, the recognition of which depends on a willingness to suspend agnostic doubts in favor of recognizing some form of intention. The critiques of resistance theory have been extremely useful in disinterring the assumptions—the folk theory, as it were—that underlie our own use of the term. Comaroff (1985), in a basically Gramscian mode of argument, retains it even though she fully recognizes that it becomes one of the means whereby inequality is maintained: whether by absorbing Tshidi anger or by confirming the contempt of the powerful apartheid regime, the Zionist churches both mocked (and ironized) the symbols of the dominant secular and ecclesiastical establishments and yet contributed to the ongoing structures of domination. Because her own interpretations often seem arbitrary, however appealing they may be to those of us who share her outrage at the conditions under which Tshidi were forced to live, they rescue intentionality—whether as resistance or as irony—at the expense of falsifiability. While this dilemma serves to highlight the mutual engagement of positivist theory and structures of power, by its very nature it can only preach to the already converted.

Moreover, the Gramscian trap applies as much to irony as it does to resistance. When we write that Greeks ironize their relationship with powerful Western nations, or when we encounter apparent irony in the way in which marginalized citizens confront the bureaucratic and clientistic state, we may be seeing a confirmation of unequal power rather than effective resistance to it.

The use of irony may actually serve to remind both sides of a fundamental *inequity* in such situations. Irony that is heard clearly, like that of the village gossip, is understood to aim at the creation of a practical advantage. Irony that remains unheard—"What a joke it was! . . . a government minister, now, with the shepherds. With the thieves!," remarked one particularly talented animal-thief of my acquaintance, commenting on deals in which the politician pledged to help the thief if the latter was ever caught by the police (Herzfeld 1985: 107)—offers one the sense of a solidary moral advantage. That animal-thief was speaking about his own political patron. He knew that by the official standards expressed by the political establishment, animal-theft was a grave blot on the Cretan escutcheon. That very same deputy has repeatedly introduced ferocious-sounding legislation in the national parliament against what he and others piously dub the "scourge" of their home island. But the thief also knows that many politicians, especially those of right-wing and centrist persuasion, have been willing to deploy their good offices on the thieves' behalf in exchange for significantly sized clan bloc votes. This—as Scott (1985: 288–89) has also noted—is the one source of the power of the weak: their presence, especially in large numbers, secures their patrons' authority. But it also locks them into a self-reproducing inequality, which is why the sheep-thieves, small-scale shepherds who have much to gain collectively from the successful abolition of animal-theft, vote for these particular politicians. In effect they vote for short-term advantage against long-term freedom from economic constraint. And so it is they, rather than the even poorer shepherds who became farmers because they were inadequate thieves and protectors of their own flocks and who now most commonly vote for socialist candidates, who ironize the actions of the politicians on whom they depend—and thereby perpetuate that dependence.

The left-wing farmers (and a few shepherds who have broken free of the system in recent years, or who have followed their political principles rather than pragmatic considerations) occasionally mock these patron-politicians for their affectations of local dress and speech or for their addiction to power, but they can also more openly express direct anger because they have much less to lose. One communist directly addressed a visiting "liberal" in verse, pointing out that promises before elections never translated into deeds afterward. This was not irony, but direct criticism. If in this community irony is, in Scott's sense, a "weapon of the weak," direct criticism is made possible by the freedom from any degree of dependency that marks the extreme limit of the masculine code that, for most of its adherents, locks them in the very nexus of mutual obligation and hierarchical prestation on which the whole patronage system depends.

I now return to gossip, where some of the same concerns operate on a more intimate scale. Here the possibilities for a more active use of irony are greater because there are few major discriminations of class or economic status: irony can actually "do things" in the Austinian sense. Social actors here know each other all too well, so they can engage in the subtle undermining of reputations that relies on their being both intimates and outsiders at one and the same time.

Such is the fundamentally segmentary nature of Greek social interactions: we are all divided against one another, but we feel morally superior *together* in the face of those who exercise political control over us. And since, as it were, it takes one to know one, my deep knowledge of *your* evil character is based on my own equally evil personality, which I can also generalize to the community as a whole. This is why social life is only possible among real human beings—flawed, divided, and sinful—rather than saints: Christians in the sense I mentioned earlier.

Here the irony of gossip iconically reproduces the dilemma of exceptionalism—a view of the world in which Greeks generally acknowledge a common humanity from which they then tactically exclude themselves. In such a world, flawed as it is, all women (say the men) are immoral and polluting—but don't you dare say specifically that my wife and daughters are whores, even though I know that yours are (and am prepared to say so if challenged). In other words, *my* women are the sole exceptions to the rule, the only women who even partially approach the goodness of the Virgin Mary rather than the seductiveness of Eve.

Transposed onto asymmetrical relationships such as those that obtain between client and patron (behind the significantly reciprocal protestations of friendship, *filía*, that at once mask the inequality and render it viable and useful to both parties), irony provides both the means of retaining a measure of self-respect and—because it *is* always ambiguous and thus not readily contested—the greatest impediment to escaping the unequal relationship. The recipient of favors and the Greek citizen contemplating his country's dependence on "Europe" can resort to irony as a protectively ambiguous idiom for attacking the friend who is also oppressor, enemy, and rival. But precisely because irony does not have to be acknowledged—because, indeed, its acknowledgment can be an admission of weakness by the target—it may contribute more to the perpetuation than to the eradication of a sense of grievance and victimage: Greeks often argue that they stood up for the Allies in World War II and made great sacrifices, and wonder why the Allies treat them so shabbily now. Is this the tactical irony of the critical agent? Or is it the passive recognition of an ironic condition imposed from outside?

Indeed, the concept of *filía*—of friendship—provides rich grounds for irony precisely because it is (a) of ambiguous disinterestedness; (b) both horizontal and vertical; and (c) caught between models alleged to be local and "Western," respectively. These three aspects are closely intertwined. Social scientists (e.g., Loizos 1975: 89–92) have been especially interested in the play of instrumentality versus affect, and many who have written about Greece have suggested that friendship in the Western sense is rare because in Greece *filía* always seems to entail expectations of material reciprocity, the strenuous denial of which itself affords rich grounds for irony inasmuch as everyone "knows" just how much faith to place in such claims of disinterestedness.

Irony Reflected and Reflexive: Language Games Again

The language of irony plays crucially with aspects of linguistic organization—hierarchies of dialect and standard forms, diglossia, honorifics, grammatical stratifications along gender lines (as in the contrasted uses of active and passive voice, for example), and so on. In Greece, irony often utilizes the resources of diglossia, which was long a major educational issue and continues to cast a shadow made even more effective as a source of irony by its newly marginal status. Since the abolition of the neo-Classical register, its creeping presence in everything from political speeches to advertising and satire has, if anything, grown ever more evident.

Thus, for example, a wide gamut of Greek-speakers from villagers to urban sophisticates will use such forms as *tas Evrópas* (acc. fem. plu.) for "Europe" or *ta Parísia* (nom./acc. n. pl.) for "Paris." The more educated users can doubtless explain in more technical terms just why these are ironic forms: the first is modeled on the Classical/*katharévousa* form *tas Athínas*, "Athens," while the latter is actually correct but almost never used in spoken Greek today. To the less educated these forms sound pretentious, but also perhaps a little threatening: they reproduce that odd set of grammatical markers that only affected members of the urban elite ever use, but which can serve to mark the presence of a harsh authority. And yet a quick inquiry will quickly establish that even rural illiterates are aware that these forms have something to do with neo-Classical pretensions—a universal education system has long since assured at least that level of recognition and, as I have already noted, the poor have considerable incentives to be able to decode the language of the rich and powerful.

Are the rustics mocking or not? The impossibility of calling them on it marks the limits of their power to resist, because an insult that cannot be surely tagged as such also has only limited power to injure—and can easily be dismissed as the product of mere envy, or simply beneath the dignity of a response. This is the irony of the artist, as Jusdanis (1987: 45–46) points out in his study of a Cavafy poem, who hides his best pieces because he does not wish to sell them—an irony that Jusdanis takes as an allegory of the poet's unwillingness to share his best work with an insufficiently sensitive public—but persuades the customers that the second-rate pieces he shows are the best he can do. When a villager remarks that "God wants things covered up," this, too, expresses an underlying theory of social relations that the story about the pregnant woman who "must have" eaten too many beans then recasts as an account of *why* secrecy is desirable. The irony exposes the impossibility of concealment without committing the treacherous friend to a literal—and therefore accountable—act of betrayal. In thus exposing her friend, the gossip has exposed herself as well; if another's motives are unknowable, those of the people we betray reveal them as morally consubstantial with ourselves: segmentation again.

Especially interesting here is the contrast this subtlety offers in relation to the heavy-handed literalism of the Greek written word, not only in bureaucratic documents (where one would expect it), but also in journalism and even literature. Peter Mackridge, a literary and linguistic specialist, has noted that Greeks writing "fact" demonstrate a kind of nervousness about the use of metaphor, underlining it to the point where irony becomes impossible—where, oddly, the metaphor itself becomes the object of an attempt at pure reference. Such a concern, which Mackridge rightly attributes to the effects of a German-derived philological tradition (1985: 348), also has roots in the history of the nation-state and its attempt to create "scientific" underpinnings.

It would be impossible for the villagers to gossip in this ironic mode unless they already possessed a confident sense of how irony worked. Like the poet in Jusdanis's analysis, who displays his underlying ideas about the way in which poetry achieves its effects by letting his characters express these ideas through a constant ironic reflection on language, these villagers display their understanding of the techniques of innuendo and social competition by the ironic introduction of phrases marking the explicit goals of illocution: "not that I want to suggest anything," "not that I wish to praise myself," "how do you know what another person is thinking?" In a rather different arena, a waiter's emphatic "I have arrived," said as he rather ostentatiously walks away, conventional though it is, acquires a disdainfully ironic tone when offered in response to an excessively demanding customer's request for service. In numerous such devices, the tension between what is declared and what actually happens can destabilize and reorient the perception of social relations on the part of both observers and participants.

All these usages depend on a knowledge of conventional speech and a willingness to deploy aggressively literal remarks in situations where they are unlikely to be true. Most people do not discuss these devices in such theoretical terms; there is no need to do so. But the uses to which they put stock phrases of this sort indicate a comprehensive understanding which *can* be rendered in discursive form if this becomes necessary or advantageous. Much of the time, however, irony is an evasively insubordinate idiom. To specify its properties not only has the deadening effects that one sometimes encounters in philological analyses of ancient humor, for example, but also exposes the user to greater political or social risk. Depriving irony of the aleatory conditions offered for its interpretation—since the "reader" is a vital participant in its construction *as irony*—is to ensure that it will not appear ironic at all.

While this condition of what we might call "suspended theorizing" applies to everyday speech, it is probably easier to make the case if we observe parallels in literary usage. Here Jusdanis's reading of Cavafy is especially helpful. Cavafy was a consummate ironist; he also had a whimsical understanding of history, one that respected the Hellenistic antecedents of his native Alexandria but was more concerned with its hedonism than its glory—and had few illusions about the latter.

Let me therefore end with one of his poems, in which a minor Syrian princeling was taken to be a measured, wise man because he spoke only rarely. In fact, we discover, his self-restraint arose from his fear of exposing his poor command of Greek:

> So he confined himself to a few words,
> watching with religious care his declensions and his accent,
> and he was more than a little bored having
> conversations stacked up within himself.

> (Savvidis 1963:68)

The ultimate irony is this: the princeling's most successful achievement of Greekness lay in his carefully sustained concealment, which cost him dearly. The tyranny of language and of an officializing culture was so overwhelming that only silence—the negation of his access to the accoutrements of power—could guarantee him at least the illusion of authority.

The most illiterate villagers of Greece would understand this poem because they, too, know the consequences of using incorrect forms and hypercorrections, and they also insist on the importance of concealment. Hence their defensive comments to me, so much like Chock's Greek-American responses to in-marrying spouses: "You speak Greek better than we do." Hence, too, their eventual willingness to admit me to the role of (inadequate) speaker of a highly intimate dialect associated with animal-theft and sundry other delicious illegalities. And hence their constant concern with etymology—with dismissing some words as "Turkish" while claiming deep antiquity for their own speech in general and especially for local toponyms. (This is the logic of chastity: our own village is Greek and our women are chaste; but not so the rest of the district, the province, the country—which, in the final analysis, also allows them to call the representatives of the bureaucratic state "Turks" and to view the American and perhaps other Western "protectors" of the country as "first cousins to the Turks.")

Not being princelings, however, and therefore having less to lose, the villagers have a great deal more fun than Cavafy's petrified Syrian in commenting on the absurdity of linguistic tyranny. Cavafy here gives us real insight into the motivations that produce deception: again, he knows the other because he knows himself, and it is this entailment in an experienced social world of competitiveness and deception that informs his ironic depiction of that world. It is a world in which reputations are easily lost and hard to recover, because the difference between acceptance and exclusion may quite literally hang on a single misspoken word or the irony that it evokes.

But it is also a world in which language easily becomes self-referential to a degree that might surprise educated native speakers of English. Greeks often objectify language: as often as a tough young man home on leave from military service may express his attachment to place by plucking some familiar flower and ostentatiously, pleasurably breathing in its scent, so others may arrest their own speech in mid-sentence in order to savor a word, the pure sound of which, rather than its meaning (in such moments they are thoroughly Jakobsonian), has excited their senses. Such sensual appreciations of language, gloriously celebrated by Cavafy, are far from rare among speakers of Greek: Cavafy intensifies his readers' focus on what they already experience. In Jusdanis's (1987: xiv–xv) explicitly Jakobsonian treatment of Cavafy we see features that the poet shares both with the Cretan villagers of whom I have written and with Jakobson's understanding of how language works. "In this labyrinth of books," Jusdanis writes of Cavafy's interest in literary themes, "the concept of written language prevails as a literary language, which having repudiated its communicative function, partakes in the drama of its own being" (120)—a condition that also applies, as Jakobson's own perspective would lead us to expect, to all self-consciousness about language.

Their political history, and especially the long struggle between demoticism and neo-Classicism, has made most Greeks acutely aware of the formal dimensions of language. To some extent this also applies to other domains in which the tension between self-presentation and the intimate spaces of the familiar, everyday culture are expressed aesthetically and spatially. The peculiar effect of this deeply idiosyncratic self-consciousness is to produce a constant concern with form over content—not in the sense that Greeks engage in intentional deceit, although this is socially sanctioned in defense of intimacy (Hirschon 1992), but because they know from direct experience that referentiality is always an illusion to some extent.

In such a context, when officialdom clings to ideals of literal meaning and attempts to link it indissolubly with the external trappings of syntactic and lexical formalism, ordinary citizens—forever suspicious of the state and all its ways—find in irony an inexhaustible source of alternative explanation and representation. It discommodes the obvious, producing new insights that are as precious as they are evanescent—the brief mastery over forms intended as a means of control over the hearts and minds of the speakers. The latter know, as

I have noted, that the inner workings of those hearts and minds are radically unfathomable, so the entire gamut of official semantics is available for creative reversal—for irony. And while social actors could in principle spell out the theoretical properties on which this reversibility rests, some things, as Cavafy also seems to have decided, wilt under excessive attention, and so are best left unsaid.

References

Abu-Lughod, Lila. 1990. The Romance of Resistance: Tracing Transformations of Power through Bedouin Women. *American Ethnologist* 17: 41–55.

Anderson, Benedict R. 1983. *Imagined Communities: Reflections on the Origin and Spread of Nationalism.* London: Verso.

Beidelman, T. O. 1986. *Moral Imagination in Kaguru Modes of Thought.* Bloomington: Indiana University Press.

Bouissac, Paul, Michael Herzfeld, and Roland Posner, eds. 1986. *Iconicity: Essays on the Nature of Culture.* Tubingen: Stauffenburg.

Bourdieu, Pierre. 1997. *Outline of a Theory of Practice.* Trans. Richard Nice. Cambridge: Cambridge University Press.

Chock, Phyllis Pease. 1987. The Irony of Stereotypes: Toward an Anthropology of Ethnicity. *Cultural Anthropology* 2: 347–68.

Comaroff, Jean. 1985. *Body of Power, Spirit of Resistance: The Culture and History of a South African People.* Chicago: University of Chicago Press.

Crick, Malcolm. 1976. *Explorations in Language and Meaning: Towards a Semantic Anthropology.* New York: John Wiley.

Dimou, Nikos. 1976. *I dhistikhía tou na íse Éllinas* [The Misery of Being Greek]. 5th printing. Athens: Ikaros.

du Boulay, Juliet. 1974. *Portrait of a Greek Mountain Village.* Oxford: Clarendon Press.

Eco, Umberto. 1976. *A Theory of Semiotics.* Bloomington: Indiana University Press.

Faubion, James D. 1993. *Modern Greek Lessons: A Primer in Historical Constructivism.* Princeton: Princeton University Press.

Fernandez, James W. 1982. *Bwiti: An Ethnography of the Religious Imagination in Africa.* Princeton: Princeton University Press.

Giddens, Anthony. 1984. *The Constitution of Society: Outline of the Theory of Structuration.* Cambridge: Polity Press.

Herzfeld, Michael. 1985. *The Poetics of Manhood: Contest and Identity in a Cretan Mountain Village.* Princeton: Princeton University Press.

———. 1997a. *Cultural Intimacy: Social Poetics in the Nation-State.* New York: Routledge.

———. 1997b. Political Philology: Everyday Consequences of Grandiose Grammars. *Anthropological Linguistics* 39: 351–75.

Hirschon, Renée. 1989. *Heirs of the Greek Catastrophe: The Social Life of Asia Minor Refugees in Piraeus.* Oxford: Clarendon Press.

———. 1992. Greek Adults' Play, or, How to Train for Caution. *Journal of Modern Greek Studies* 10: 35–56.

Hutcheon, Linda. 1995. *Irony's Edge: The Theory and Politics of Irony.* New York: Routledge.

Jakobson, Roman. 1960. Linguistics and Poetics. In *Style in Language*, ed. Thomas A. Sebeok, 350–77. Cambridge, MA: MIT Press.

Jakobson, Roman and Claude Lévi-Strauss. 1962. "Les Chats" de Charles Baudelaire. *L'Homme* 2: 5–21.

Jusdanis, Gregory. 1987. *The Poetics of Cavafy: Textuality, Eroticism, History.* Princeton: Princeton University Press.

Labov, William. 1972. *Language in the Inner City: Studies in the Black English Vernacular.* Philadelphia: University of Pennsylvania Press.

Lévi-Strauss, Claude. [1962] 1966. *The Savage Mind*, trans. John Weightman and Doreen Weightman. Chicago: University of Chicago Press.

———. 1963. *Structural Anthropology*, trans. Claire Jacobson and Brooke Grundfest Schoepf. New York: Basic Books.

———. [1960] 1976. The Scope of Anthropology. In *Structural Anthropology, Volume 2*, trans. Monique Layton, 3–32. Chicago: University of Chicago Press.

Loizos, Peter. 1975. *The Greek Gift: Politics in a Cypriot Village.* Oxford: Basil Blackwell.

Mackridge, Peter A. 1985. *The Modern Greek Language: A Descriptive Analysis of Standard Modern Greek.* Oxford: Clarendon Press.

Malaby, Thomas Michael. 1999. Fateful Misconceptions: Rethinking Paradigms of Chance among Gamblers in Crete. *Social Analysis* 43: 141–64.

Norman, Karin. 1994. Ironic Body: Obscene Joking among Swedish Working-Class Women. *Ethnos* 59: 187–211.

Oxfeld, Ellen. 1993. *Blood, Sweat, and Mahjong: Family and Enterprise in an Overseas Chinese Community.* Ithaca: Cornell University Press.

Reed-Danahay, Deborah. 1993. Talking about Resistance: Ethnography and Theory in Rural France. *Anthropological Quarterly* 66: 221–29.

Richards, I. A. 1936. *The Philosophy of Rhetoric.* Oxford: Oxford University Press.

Rosaldo, Renato. 1986. From the Door of His Tent: The Fieldworker and the Inquisitor. In *Writing Culture: The Poetics and Politics of Ethnography*, ed. James Clifford and George E. Marcus, 77–97. Berkeley: University of California Press.

Savidis, G. P., ed. 1968. *K.P. Kavafi Piimata.* Vol. 1: *1919–1933.* Athens: Ikaros.

Scott, James C. 1985. *Weapons of the Weak: Everyday Forms of Peasant Resistance.* New Haven: Yale University Press.

Stewart, Charles. 1991. *Demons and the Devil: Moral Imagination in Modern Greek Culture.* Princeton: Princeton University Press.

Chapter Three

The Irony of Complicity
and the Complicity of Irony
in Development Discourse

"Nobody smiled at these colossal ironies!"
Mark Twain, *Life on the Mississippi* (1990: 8)

Colossal Ironies and Their Correction

Early on in his *Life on the Mississippi,* a historical and anecdotal account full of the flow of Mark Twain's sardonic and dissolving humor,[1] the author recounts the "colossal irony" of how, for mere trinkets, millenarian religious promises, and by catering to and trading in on Indian credulity and weakness for drink, Europeans got unto themselves the vast lands drained and watered by the Great River. By this "robbery" they gained untold riches. Indeed, one might add that in a government (in its first 150 years) so circumspect and reserved in collecting taxes, the major source of wealth was the sale of these cheaply bartered Indian lands;[2] this is a fact which Americans, as Twain relates—and even unto this day—have great difficulty in recognizing, along, of course, with the requirements of fair compensation. A hundred years later, at the turn of the twenty-first century, Twain surely would be interested to observe the fate of the great river boats whose churning progress lay at the heart of river life as he

1. Twain's thoroughgoing ironic stance about American, indeed human, character has not always been easy to grasp, witness the recent attempt to suppress *The Adventures of Huckleberry Finn* in the schools because of the figure of Nigger Jim. Yet Jim, it can be argued, is the only true person of character and honor in the novel in comparison with the parade of white reprobates, liars, frauds, swindlers, lynchers and murderers he and Huck encounter. Unless that irony is grasped, the "Adventure" seems satirical at best and ridiculing at worst! (See Baker 1982: A23).

2. My colleague Raymond Fogelson, as knowledgeable about Native American history and culture as anyone I know, argues this case: that the appropriation of Indian lands was one of the chief sources of American wealth in the first hundred or more years of the Republic (pers. comm.).

knew it, and which were central to his own account. Up and down the Mississippi, these are now cabled more or less permanently to the shore, transmogrified into casinos catering to American "credulity and weakness." Twain would also appreciate the irony of how the descendants of the original "innocent inhabitants," through their participation in flourishing Indian casino operations, are themselves catering to and trading in on the "credulity and weakness" of their dispossessors.

In this essay I will focus on the kinds of historical ironies, colossal in their way, that Twain contemplated, ironies having to do with contacts between peoples greatly unequal in power and wherewithal: people in the center and on the margins of history.[3] This has been a contact attended by the production of very unequal, not to say colossal, accumulations of values on the one hand and appalling deprivation, on the other, in good part as a consequence of that contact. It is a contact that also has been attended by various attempts to alleviate these inequalities, an "alleviation" that will be central to our concerns.

These are all matters productive of ironies well known to anthropologists, whose discipline, perhaps more than any other, has explored the frontiers of these contacts between the possessors and the dispossessed, the "haves" and the "have nots." In particular, I will focus on "the Development Project"—a notable attempt undertaken by nations privileged in power and wherewithal to correct the gross, not to say colossal, inequalities that have developed in world history.

"Making the World Safe for Democracy":
The Development Project, A Short and Sincere History of its Trajectory

Let me preface my account with two bits of evidence for my argument: some ironic verses and an ironic account, both of which have arisen out of the development project. The first is a bit of doggerel, "The Development Set," which appeared in mimeographed form and was widely circulated on bulletin boards of the Agency of International Development in the late 1970s and early 80s. The second is a semifictional account by Leonard Frank of a development project in South Asia.

The Development Set
The Development Set is bright and noble.
Our thoughts are deep and our vision global.
Although we move with the better classes,
Our thoughts are always with the masses.

---

3. On this contact, see the work of Eric Wolf, particularly his magnum opus with the ironic title (it plays on dispossession), *Europe and the People without History* (1982).

In Holiday Inns in scattered nations
We damm multinational corporations
Injustice seems easy to protest
In such seething hotbeds of social rest.

We discuss malnutrition over steaks
And plan hunger talks during coffee breaks, *etc.*

The Development Game

This Dutch girl [on the Development Team] is a Nuisance. . . . What are they
doing sending a young woman to a Moslem country anyway? For her it is an
important discovery that the official world does not match the real one. She
visits villages and reports back to us at dinner that the irrigation schemes are
not working the way the government says they are, or that the veterinary employees are selling drugs they should give away . . . or that money for building primary schools has gone into the pockets of contractors and politicians. . . . We make non-committal replies and try and change the subject. The
older Japanese member says nothing and finds an excuse to leave the table
early.

You have to make a choice about the world you live in—the real world or
the official world. Nowadays I live in the official world. . . . When you discover
that the official world does not correspond to the real world, you can either accept the official version or make your own judgement. It's always best to take
the government figures. That way you save yourself work and don't tread on
toes. We are here, after all, as guests." (Frank 1986)

These subtle and not-so-subtle parodies of a very large investment of time
and resources going on, as it is said, in the First World as regards the Third over
the last half century, requires some brief contextualization. Americans, at least,
will recall those euphoric and confident years after World War II and the unconditional victory by the more-or-less egalitarian democracies allied against
the fascist, authoritarian, and racist regimes of the axis. After this victory, the
disparity between the rich (mostly white) and the poor (mostly black, brown,
and yellow) parts of the world was noted as an embarrassment and an authentic challenge to the recently victorious egalitarian ethic and to the compassionate religious principles of most of the victorious nations. It was a challenge to
the authenticity, that is, to the truly representative nature of the newly founded
United Nations. After all, fighting for egalitarian values and a world united under their aegis was an earnest commitment that had been important to the war
effort.

Thus came into being, in some mix of sincerity and geopolitical self-interest,
the Development Project which has forever after and in many affluent nations
been one of the major vehicles for conveying commitment to egalitarian values in the world and for the dispersal, with distributive justice in mind, of
a modicum of first-world surplus monies, technologies, and "know-how" into

second- and third-world polities and economies. The defeat of fascism made no worldly task seem too great, and the success of the Marshall Plan in Europe— the first (re)Development Project—confirmed that confidence. Entering into a worldwide development project was simply a continuation by other means of the wartime effort to make the world safe for democracy, and, as a prevalent irony would have it (an irony undercutting to the grandeur of the democratic vision) safe for industrial capitalism.

The Disillusions of Development

But, as is well known, and for a host of reasons, half a century later we find a continuing but much less confident Development Project ripe for the whole escalating continuum of expressions belonging to the *trope of indirection:* irony, sarcasm, satire, mockery, ridicule, parody, and caricature, which it has, indeed, received. The inflated hopes of the 1940s, 50s, and early 60s have been deflated by a series of limiting factors, and, while one cannot say that development at the present time is in a pervasively dispirited condition, it is certainly not the inspired, world-encompassing task it was first felt to be. The real world has caught up with it in too many ways, deriding the too simple and too optimistic postwar views of the rich/poor world and its problems and their solutions that energized the Development Project in its first decades.

There are many explanations for this state of affairs, and we may list them: *inertia,* passivity, fatalism, disinterest, often enough the downright contrariness or "cussedness" of "other worlds"; *corruption,* the subversion or malversation of the public development monies into the private hands of local kleptocratic elites and the politically powerful; *reaction formations,* the production of repressive (often brutally so) governments seeking to control or counter the unwanted effect of development on existing and privileging hierarchies of domination-subordination; *subservience,* the alienated loyalty of local elites to international or multinational interests rather than to their own populace; and *counterproductivity,* because of the exponential flourishing of the rich world, in part exploitative of the poor, the increase in relative deprivation as between the "haves" and the "have nots" remains despite some absolute or arithmetic improvement among the poor (i.e., poor economies may be better off than they were fifty years ago in absolute terms, but compared to the progress in well-being of the rich they are relatively poorer). These factors and others have tested what was bound to be a less thoroughgoing, not to say less compassionate, identification of First Worlders (Europeans and Americans, largely) with the distinctly "other" peoples of the poor world, compared to the easier American identifications with European devastation that energized the Marshall Plan. And these factors have produced the ironic indirections in discourse and expressive culture represented by our evidential texts and which are the focus of our analytic interest here. Terms loaded with sardonic assessment (e.g., "banana republic," "tropical kleptocracy," "devspeak," and "devthink") have been coined in the crucible of that development frustration, and novels from *The Quiet American* on down, and novelists from E. M. Forster to Saul Bellow, have found that contact zone between the developed and the undeveloped rich in ironic insight into the contrary dynamics of human character in the cross-cultural milieus of colonials and postcolonials, that is, "the developing and development world."

The Irony of the Successful Failure (and vice versa) and Other Types of Subversion (and Self-subversion) of "Sincere" Commitment?

"The Development Set" doggerel and "The Development Game," quoted above—both apparently instances of self-mockery—are representative of the ironic or derisory literature that has circulated widely in the last several decades. The verses seem to have appeared first on the bulletin boards and in office memoranda of the Agency of International Development in the late 70s or early 80s, possibly coming from the hand of an A.I.D. officer or employee. The second piece, "The Development Game," was written by an international development professional based in Paris with a decade and a half of development experience at the time of writing. And though Frank states that "none of the people and events described bear any relation to real people or events" (1986: 256), his account of leading a mission to the northwest frontier of Pakistan—of the types of team members involved and their struggle for reality—is tinged with jaded professionalism and mission fatigue, and seems particularly informed, making his disclaimer itself ironic.

Little more need be said about "The Development Set" except to note that, like much recent work in the academy (see, e.g., Escobar 1995), it also treats of the real-world effect of the discourse of development though, perhaps, unlike this recent work, it goes on to undercut and disclaim its constitutive power to create the very object whose life quality conditions it presupposes to be in need of development:

> The language of the Development Set
> Stretches the English Alphabet
> We use swell words like "epigenetic,"
> "Micro," "Macro" and "logarithmetic."
>
> It pleasures us to be so esoteric—
> It's so intellectually atmospheric
> And though local establishments may be unmoved
> Our vocabularies are much improved.

Clearly what is being ridiculed here is the inflated professional rhetoric laid beside the self-serving quality of development work. It is a point made with pungency in the final verse:

> Enough with these verses—on with the mission!
> Our work is as broad as the human condition
> Just Pray God the biblical promise is true,
> The poor ye shall always have with you!

The major thrust of "The Development Game," on the other hand, is rather more that of portraying the jaded acceptance, for self-interested purposes to be sure, of official definitions of situation—of playing the official game without regard to emerging realities. It limns what all that acceptance implies for the truncation or perversion of effective, on-the-ground, development. It is really about the closed, or sui generis world of developers' lifeways frequently noted by those critical of the Development Project. Within or alongside worlds of need, there is the irony (and the ironic unreality) of a project world whose greatest pressures very often concern moving monies efficiently and quickly so that unspent funds do not flow over into subsequent fiscal periods.

But since these pieces tend rather more to the caricature pole on the continuum of the trope of critical indirection, it is more illuminating to consider the energizing ironies in recent books by two central figures in the scholarship of development: James Ferguson's ethnography of development in Southern Africa, *The Anti-Politics Machine* (1994), and Albert Hirschman's collected reflections on a life dedicated to development economics, *A Propensity to Self-Subversion* (1995).[4] Up to a point, these two figures may be read as representing the two main ideological camps in the literature on development: the first is a neo-Marxist, fundamentally antipathetic to development as being part of the problem of the capitalist strategy of domination of markets and creation of inequality, and not part of the solution; the second is a liberal academic, critical but fundamentally supportive of the development project as a force and practical tool for beneficial change in an unjust world. But it would be unfair to the awareness and experience of either thinker to so easily and ideologically type their work.

Of course, both of our prefatory quotes illustrate a widespread propensity to "self-subversion" in the development enterprise, but Hirschman's ironies,

---

4. This essay was completed before the publication of James C. Scott's important work on The Development Project: *Seeing Like a State: How Certain Schemes to Improve the Human Condition Have Failed* (1998). Scott's preeminence in subaltern studies in relation to development would make him an excellent subject for the kind of discussion directed here toward the work of Ferguson and Hirschman. Not only does he combine, like Hirschman, a commitment to the Development Project in general terms with a wry, even skeptical, awareness of its particular failings, but his argument about "everyday resistance" summed up in the oxymoron "weapons of the weak" has been subject to ironic critique as a form of complicity; cf. Gutmann 1993.

summed up in the very title of his collected reflections, are much gentler and, while skeptical, hardly mocking or satirical of the development enterprise itself—to the formulation of which he has over the many decades patiently, and in the face of many frustrations, made a major contribution. It was he, after all, who pointed out most clearly the painful political irony of the development project: that the first several decades of development in the third world had been accompanied by the appearance of many harshly repressive political regimes mainly stimulated to repressiveness by the development project itself. The notion of redistributive justice built into the agenda of the project in effect inspired much reaction, overt and covert, on the part of local hierarchies, aimed at subverting that agenda. It was to these repressive regimes that the development industry was, in Hirschman's view, all too accommodating.

And not only in this political way, but also in the more strictly economic workings of development, Hirschman has long recognized the ever-present possibility and ironic outcome for an effort aimed at greater economic equality; of, in fact, the developing of increasing income inequality as a consequence of development.[5] But Hirschman has maintained throughout enough confidence that significant advances were taking place through the work of development and that while the problem of world poverty was and is far from resolved that work has made enough encouraging inroads upon it all along the way so as to continue to recommend support of it in principle if not always in specific fact. Thus, while certain ironies were present in his thinking on development, they never exceeded themselves or became so satiric or mocking of economic development as to suggest simple self-servingness in anyone who would continue to support it or to lead to utter denunciation or denial of it. His self-subversion, while cultivating skepticism toward too easy or acquiescent claims for development,[6] never passes to subversiveness of the development effort itself. He consistently maintains "a bias for hope."[7] It is a sympathetic bias with shadings of self-inclusive irony however, and with a certain sense of finding oneself in the middle, betwixt and between bitterly contending camps."[8]

5. Albert O. Hirschman, "The Rise and Decline of Development Economics," chapter 1 in *Essays in Trespassing: Economics to Politics and Beyond* (1981).

6. Hirschman says, "I do admit to having frequently a reaction, perhaps something approaching a reflex, to other people's theories, of the 'it ain't necessarily so' variety. Skepticism toward other people's claims to spectacular theoretical discoveries is, of course, not a particularly noteworthy trait. It is, however, more unusual to develop this sort of reaction to one's own generalizations or theoretical constructs. And this has become increasingly the characteristic of my writings that I wish to look at here" (1995: 87).

7. Hirschman made this the title of an earlier collection of essays (1971).

8. Development economics, as Hirschman (1981) points out, has been attacked with the intent of nullification from two sides—by Marxists and neo-Marxists on the one side, and from neoclassical quantitative noninstitutional monoeconomics on the other: "The strange alliance of neo marxism and monoeconomics against development economics" (sec. 4, 14–19).

In the same way that the combination of economic and social and cultural reasoning and the betwixtness of his positioning would make it difficult to typologize Hirschman, so Ferguson's espousal, in respect to the Development Project, of the deeply skeptical social critique of Foucault makes it difficult to place him unreservedly in the neo-Marxist camp. There is a complex of ironies involved in Foucault's work, as in Ferguson's,[9] all more-or-less present in Foucault's 1979 study (highly influential in *The Anti-Politics Machine*) of the institution of the prison. Over the last several centuries this institution seems a persistent failure which yet, in its way, succeeds. It is the irony of the "successful failure" one might say. For just as the institution of the prison has mostly failed in its stated goal of redeeming miscreants and returning them redeemed to society, it has "succeeded," although not in an obvious and "intentional" way, in creating a class of miscreants and delinquents more easily managed by bureaucrats in the "service" of a more "efficient" and more privileging society, and more easily put out of mind as a social issue by society itself. It is this "surprising and ironic process"[10] by which structures of power are inadvertently created and reproduced in the interests of a particular group that both Foucault, in respect to the prison, and Ferguson in respect to development (more particularly the World Bank), analyze. It is the irony of structural reproduction. For although development has so frequently failed in the third world to fulfill the "quality of life" goals of greater local productivity and distributive justice, less poverty and hunger, it has succeeded in reproducing, if not bringing into being, an "infestation," as Ferguson calls it, of ever more controlling, often enough repressive and self-serving, bureaucratic structures. It is this counterintentionality, this contradictoriness of structural reproduction, that is so very ripe for irony.

There are many other attendant ironies in this intellectual project: the irony of the fallacy of equivocation,[11] the irony of the incompatibility of the development of capitalism with a thoroughgoing redistribution and the across-the-board improvement of quality of life, the irony of self-serving generalization, the irony of unconscious selection of the elements of definition or

9. I concentrate attention here on the irony of agrarian development projects in Lesotho that Ferguson exposes and explores in *The Anti-Politics Machine*. But his more recent work (e.g., 1993: 78–92) is also, in different ways, grist for any mill that wishes to grind out the ironies involved in the Western Development Project. Ferguson's *Anthropology and Its Evil Twin: Development in the Constitution of a Discipline* (1997) is particularly relevant to the problem of complicity.

10. Ferguson (1994: 13). The quote is taken from Ferguson's discussion of Paul Willis's *Learning to Labor: How Working Class Kids get Working Class Jobs* (1981), and is one of the few places—perhaps the only place—that the word "irony" appears in the text. This, however, does not make his trenchant critique any less pertinent to someone interested in the ironies of the development project!

11. Which is to say, the irony of changing the meaning of the terms of reference in the process of syllogistic argumentation (Ferguson 1994: 55).

representation of situation, and, above all, the irony of instrumental effects to which Ferguson's book is devoted and which is contained in its very title, *The Anti-Politics Machine*. This is the irony of a project, the Development Project, ostensibly and explicitly apolitical, having as a consequence significant political results in terms of the reproduction, indeed development, of a political apparatus: local self-serving bureaucracies determined to restrain, control, or suppress political protest about pervasive poverty. The ironic effect in a project aimed at the amelioration of world poverty is the depoliticization of that very poverty, making it the more difficult to deal with it in any explicit contestatory way.

Of course, there is also the "Foucauldian" irony, as we might call it, of an analysis so revelatory of the counterproductivity and subversiveness of human intentionality in the world, of the inevitable subversive relation of power to knowledge, as to itself be incapacitated to offer any tactical advice, or any relatively straightforward uncomplicated knowledge, on how to deal with the pervasive poverty, hunger, and sickness in the world. There is always the possibility of an undertone of irrelevance, in the practical, real-world-manipulating sense, of what has been intellectually grasped by the analyses of structural reproduction.[12] And it is the presence of this subversive possibility of irrelevance and its complicitous implications to which we may now turn. For the irrelevance of any action or declaration is always possibly ironic in implication, and irony is always possibly complicitous with the situation it ironizes.

"Radical Asymmetry" and Other Sources of a "Culture of Irony" in Anthropology

In recent decades there have been several notable contributions to the detection of irony in anthropology and as a particular condition of the discipline. Indeed the thrust of these arguments would make out something very akin to a "culture of irony" in anthropology. The first is that of Clifford Geertz in his late 60s paper, "Thinking as a Moral Act" (1968), which interestingly, perhaps ironically in view of our focus here, has only recently been included in Geertz' subsequent collections of essays and articles. The second is that of Marilyn Strathern (1990), in her Frazer lecture on "persuasive fictions of anthropology" which reflects upon the irony implicit in the postmodern view of a social science like anthropology resting its case, not on observable facts and verifiable

---

12. Ferguson in his "Epilogue: What is to be Done" does endeavor to offer counsel and a bill of particulars on the responsibilities of intellectuals interested in greater equality in the world and less suffering—interested, that is, in "popular empowerment." But he ends on a Foucaultian note, remarking the possible irrelevance of intellectual inquiry to the movers and shakers who can bring about significant changes in that world!

generalizations, but on "persuasive fictions." And the third is that of Arnold Krupat (1990), who is not an anthropologist, so that his observations on ironies in our discipline partake a bit of dramatic (or perhaps literary) irony; that is, there is a contrast between what we characters in the drama of anthropology conceive our situation to be, or to have been, and what astute members of the audience, Krupat among them, know it to be, and about which Krupat can conspire with other literary persons to portray it ironically to be. So we have here three formulations of the ironies of our anthropological fate: two that view from within and one from without.

The Geertz work is of particular relevance to our topic because he argues that *anthropological irony* is not quite like the classical ironies, dramatic, literary, Socratic, or historical, in that it involves a crucial difference, a "radical asymmetry," between the situation and privileges and quality of life of the anthropologist as fieldworker and the situation of those he or she studies. It is the kind of pervasive difference in the contemporary world, as we have noted above, that has energized the development project. Says Geertz,

> It is this radical asymmetry in view of what the informant's (and beyond him his country's) life chances really are, especially when it is combined with an agreement on what they should be, which colors the field-work situation with that very special moral tone I think of as ironic. (1968: 149)

We may feel the need to remark here that the anthropological irony which arises from "radical asymmetry" is perhaps more particularly the irony of fieldwork after World War II, undertaken either during the period of decolonization or in the period of the postcolonial world of rising expectations in the contemporary third world and of frustrated, if not dashed, expectations of rapid development and accession to first-world status. As I have indicated, it has been increasingly a world of "relative deprivation," where the sense of straightforward and unalloyed commitment in fieldwork is more difficult to maintain and live by than was the case in the colonial world. The asymmetries of the colonial period were indeed radical, but there was usually a paternalistic confidence and assumption that there was, despite the obvious exploitation, a fundamental benevolence in colonialism, a "civilizing mission," as it was called, that would eventually bring enlightenment and well-being, if not at the levels of the metropolitan powers, at least at a long remove from the perceived backwardness of the colonial peoples.

Also during much of the colonial period many colonized peoples were still living in relatively integrated, inward-looking cultures that shielded them from the angering or vitiating knowledge of their "relative deprivation." In any event, the irony portrayed would seem to be more the characteristic irony of that period in which the predominant narrative (Bruner 1986) was that of, if not full assimilation to civilization, at least of expected rapid modernization. The

ironies, or what Beidelman (1986) has called the "pathetic tensions" of a subsequent anthropology, including contemporary anthropology, involve a deeper
deception and more bitter unrequitement. And they have produced more poignant and penetrating challenges, such as that of Ferguson, to the confident
base-narrative of the Development Project.

Perhaps this anthropological irony, which is a complex combination of
abashment—the persistent unmitigated juxtaposition of the advantaged and
the disadvantaged—with the sense of relative helplessness to influence the
world system so as to be able to do anything very effective about it (to level the
global playing field, as it were) which Geertz portrays, has always, at least implicitly, existed. It has existed, one might suppose, as an inevitable "condition
of being" when anthropologists from more affluent and more powerful societies
work among people deprived in one way or another. This is especially the
case when, influenced by a core set of benevolent and ameliorating (civilizing)
Western values, such fieldworkers come to feel themselves accountable to, or
at least interdependent with (if not actively involved in), seeking the benefit of
the less privileged and dependent peoples they study—and, of course, upon
whom they themselves, in their career performance, ultimately depend.

Arnold Krupat (1990) departs, not from the radical asymmetry of most
twentieth-century fieldwork and the "pathetic tension" it produces in the anthropologist, but from the radical "epistemological crisis" of the late nineteenth
century—"the shift away from apparently absolute certainties . . . in religion,
linguistics, mathematics, physics and so on—in the direction of relativity."
This epistemological shift was bound to effect Franz Boas, American anthropology's "founding father," as it would any other European intellectual. Combined with psychoanalysis, another of the late-ninteenth-century wounds to intellectual narcissism, the resulting atmosphere of intellectual uncertainty was
compounded in a trained physicist like Boas by a significantly relativizing career shift—from physics first to geography, less quantitative but surely still
more measurable than the contingencies of inquiry bound up in his final shift
to an anthropological method based on interpersonal dialogue. As I read Krupat's argument, the shift to a career based on the much greater contingency of
interpersonal cross-cultural relations could only produce in a former physicist
ironic attitudes toward the possibility of scientific certainty in his new and final
profession.

Taking account of Boas's well-known resistance to generalizations, Krupat
detects in Boas at least the irony of aporia, that is, endemic doubt about the possibility of generalization. But, perhaps, one might even detect in Boas the irony
of catachresis *(abusio)* or mischievous undermining of any pervasive certainty
to the point of impeding the effective engagement of self and others in fulfilling real-world projects of any kind. At moments, and perhaps mainly, Krupat

argues, Boas's attitude seemed aporitic, expressing a robust doubt about the validity and verifiability of then-current generalizations in the discipline, but with the intention of preparing the way for a more securely grounded science of anthropology. At times, however, his attitudes toward the meaning of his own work and that of his students seemed catachrestic in that his sense of the contradictions of the discipline led him to set impossible conditions for a science of anthropology, resting his case and his contribution on his famous five-foot shelf of detailed but starkly undertheorized native ethnography: an "immense celebratory record of randomness," as Krupat puts it in hyperbole, as if Boas's career spun around like a roulette wheel.

While Krupat would locate irony of various kinds in the epistemological crisis present in Europe at the time of anthropology's origins and continuing henceforth in the prevailing uncertainty of modernism and only partial understandings of postmodernism, Marilyn Strathern (1990) places her concern in the irony—no doubt congruent with epistemological crisis—that is contained in the postmodern view, the view that, in the final analysis, cultures, including the culture of anthropology, are and depend upon "persuasive fictions" for their legitimizing real-world effects.

In fact, this view of the narrative framing of cultural and intellectual realities is already implied in the epistemological crisis of the late nineteenth century. It is perhaps true to say that the very active awareness of this narrative framing involved in the work of culture and of the ethnographic work of the anthropologist contrasts the postmodernist present with the subliminal or, at best, half-realized awareness of such as Darwin, Frazer, or Boas—a half-realized awareness which literary critics like Krupat feel confident in teasing out of ambiguous texts as explanatory of Boasian resistances to full scientific generalization and full reductionist scientific commitment. In any event, it is in that awareness—most often a strong self-awareness of the inescapability of narrative framing of ethnographic and ethnologic argument and interpretation/presentation—that, in Strathern's view, our present ironic condition is expressed and realized.

For our present purposes however, it is important to remark that Strathern saves her argument from the ultimate instability and uncertainty of endless narrative reframings; saves it, that is, from the infinite regress, de-legitimizing, in effect, that can lurk in the recognition of the conditions of irony.[13] She saves herself, in other words, from that oceanic possibility of endless undercutting, the condition that all is irony and irony about irony, by pointing, in the end, to the fact that the human condition is characterized by *human relationships* that

13. Indeed, the de-legitimizing effect is the critique of Strathern's lecture advanced by Jarvie (1990: 124), who asks, "If we discover that social science argument is persuasive fiction, who is to believe in it?"

do, indeed, function for better or for worse, to greater pain or greater pleasure, and about whose better or worse functioning anthropologists do have something relevant to say. It is to the study of those relationships wherein lies, although Strathern might not quite put it this way, our enduring obligations as anthropologists. "We shall not be able to return to a pre-fictionalized consciousness," she observes to end her essay, "but we might be persuaded that there are still significant relationships to be studied" (1990: 122). And, indeed, although the word "significant" remains undefined, she and her colleagues and students have been persistent in their commitment to studying them.

Conclusion: Complicitous Irony and the Possibilities of a "Higher Irony"

I should like to end on that note of finding stability of commitment in what has been called our contemporary "culture of irony."[14] This must, I suppose, mean the maintaining of, or the finding of, some kind of commitment that, while given the epistemological crises and awareness of paradox of the times, is itself inevitably susceptible to ironic assessment, yet not defeated by it (aporectic) nor complicit with it (catechrestic). The idea of stable irony is suggested in Wayne Booth's *The Rhetoric of Irony*, though the definition here offered is somewhat different.[15] I would like to define this stability, in the context of the discussion of development, as the kind of irony that is stabilized by resting finally, however buffeted, on an overriding commitment to the age-old task of alleviating poverty, sickness, and hunger in the world.

It may be contrasted with what we might call the "irony of complicity"— something that we can identify in our two satirical quotations. Both pieces, as we recall, suggest complicity with the condition of the development work they satirize. While they satirize the self-serving indulgences and the self-evidently willful "definitions of situation" of development work, they yet choose to remain, for all we know, unaffectedly engaged and complaisant with these

---

14. Noted in many places recently, but most particularly for my argument in Andrew Del Banco, *The Death of Satan: How Americans Have Lost the Sense of Evil* (1995). While this culture is more broadly defined by Del Banco than the "culture of irony" to be found in anthropology, anthropological relativism is still implicated in the more general culture of irony. For subsequent, more recent observations on this "culture," see Purdy 1999.

15. Cf. Wayne C. Booth, *A Rhetoric of Irony* (1974), chapter 1, "The Ways of Stable Irony," and, in respect to unstable irony, part 3, "Instabilities." As I understand Booth, "stable irony" is irony whose meaning is more-or-less easily (or at least systematically) interpretable. That is, we know that the author *intends* to mean the opposite or something different from what he or she says, and, knowing that, we are thus invited to interpret what he or she is saying *covertly*. Once made, this interpretation is not endlessly undermined with further "demolitions and reconstructions" (10–13). This is to say that our interpretation of the covert meaning of an ironic utterance does not lead on

conditions. "On with the Mission!" the doggerel concludes. These are, or at least can be read as, complicitous satires.

This irony of complicity (or complaisance), with the contradictions identified in its undercuttings, may be contrasted with the ironies present in the work of Hirschman and Ferguson, both of whom, in the presence of the ironies noted, yet use these ironies as motivating instruments for a more perfected development task vis-à-vis, in their different ways, the encouragement of popular empowerment and the alleviation of the pervasive poverty, disease, and hunger in the world. They are ironies, one might say, that arise from those situated *within* the world as a moral community of mutual obligation. They are the ironies of those in some way constrained by that obligation and not somehow *without* it and independent of it. They are, in short, ironies in action, and not ironies complacent or complicit with inaction. They call upon us to work toward better times.

Since irony is always a form of dissimulation—a feigning or dissembling, an indirection, in speech or other communication—complicity or complaisance in or with the situation being ironized can all too easily obfuscate what is centrally motivating in the dissembling, and the directionlessness to be found out in the ironic indirection. No doubt here we are putting our finger into a great wound in the human condition, the ever-present difference between the *platitudes* of human life and human relationships and persistent underlying social *attitudes* toward the place of self and others in the social order. And in the space opened up by the recognition of this difference, complicity can all too easily work its way in: complicity, that is, in league with the ironic fact that our best conscious intentions (platitudes of a kind) are subverted by "the way things actually work out," because "the way things actually work out" is, whatever the platitudes, still congruent with our deeper lying attitudes and interests.

---

to mock all our commitments and knowledge, leaving us in an endlessly ironic universe where we cannot really know or commit to anything. The argument put forth in this chapter, correspondingly, assumes that we do know something for sure: that there are unacceptable ("colossal" in Mark Twain's view) differences in quality of life in the world, and we should do something about these differences between the West and the Rest. Furthermore, it assumes that we should not allow justified ironies about how we are or are not going about doing that from disarming us in that commitment and that task, which is ultimately the Development Project. In the best sense, as Booth points out, irony is a communal achievement—a sharing of some insight or truth about the universe and the human condition that can constitute a bond of friendship or of mutual comprehension by kindred spirits: a mutuality of engagement, if only that engagement be something of the kind of "Alas what fools we mortals be!"

Evoking this "higher irony" is very much what this chapter is about and it has very much to do, therefore, with the building of the stable moral community founded in inclusive understandings. Needless to say, perhaps, the engagement with the development project implies active engagement in the world and not just passive observation upon it.

In the Development Project discussed here, this would be complicity with the fact that many development programs do not significantly alleviate poverty, sickness, and hunger but do, in fact, strengthen the control of local bureaucratic elites and international political economic structures in the lives of the impoverished, the sick, and the hungry. . . elites and controls which, in point of fact and on the ground, espouse our complacent attitudes and serve our status-quo interests. Inclusive irony, I would argue, is motivated irony aware of the impediments in self and other of contradiction and inconsistency and yet so conditioned by their presence as not to be defeated in the mutuality of its commitment to better times.

The problem of complicity, it may be mentioned and not simply in passing, has arisen not only in respect to the international development project but also in respect to the ironies of affirmative action in our own society, one of the more generous attempts in America to move toward better times and to alleviate situations of deprivation and historical disadvantage. In this case it has been pointed out that the platitudes of affirmative action, which propose favoring by special enactments and set-asides the advancement of classified ethnic groups, may in fact, and ironically, actually harden the lines of racial separation and confirm underlying attitudinal feelings about the categorized social reality being contested.[16] But that awareness of the ironic aspect of affirmative action can, when the irony is mutual, only humanize such action and not defeat it!

Another way of addressing this issue, therefore, is to contrast two kinds of irony: a gentler *inclusive* irony with a harsher aggressive and *exclusive* irony.[17] We might speak, also, of irony that is "humanizing," which acts to include the folly of otherness in humanness, and irony that is "dehumanizing" in the sense that in its ironizing it addresses, even creates, unreasonable "otherness" and puts at risk the humanness of that other.[18] Phrasing it this way suggests the old

16. See Dominguez 1994 and Skrentny 1996. The latter work is an interesting analysis of the way the platitudes of politics, that is to say the proclamatory politics of racial equality, actually worked to bring about affirmative-action programs in the 1960s, although, when such attitudes were later probed, as many as 80 percent of Americans were attitudinally unfavorable to affirmative action. What is implied is some latent function or hidden agenda in affirmative action more compatible with these underlying attitudes.

17. This distinction can be found in several of my previous papers: see, in particular, "Convivial Attitudes: The Ironic Play of Tropes in an International Kayak Festival in Northern Spain" (1984) and "Emergencias Etnográficas: Tiempos Heroicos, Tiempos Irónicos y la Tarea Etnográfica" (1993). The distinction is, of course, similar to the idea of "self-irony" found in the work of Kenneth Burke and others examined elsewhere in this volume.

18. Relevant here is the recent discussion of "insider humor," a smug form of exclusive irony, as practiced by, among others, talk show hosts like David Letterman and Jay Leno, and by the comedian Jerry Seinfeld. See the review of various discussions of this kind of humor in the *Utne Reader* (March–April 1997, 12–13). The *Reader* contrasts this recent cynical and world-weary humor with that of the Marx Brothers, who always included themselves in their variegated mockery of the human condition.

humanistic notion, associated with Erasmus in *The Praise of Folly,* of "the higher irony."[19]

This notion has been recently evoked again by Hayden White in writing about Vico, who conceived of the age of irony, such as ours, as a transitory phase in the cyclical course of history preparatory to a return to the sincerity and authenticity of true literal belief and unambiguous commitment . . . the beginning phase of every recurrent historical cycle.[20] While such phenomena are well known to anthropologists as revivalism, fundamentalism, moral rearmament, and revitalization movements of all kinds—expressing the desire for or achievement of such returns to sincerity and authenticity[21]—one cannot very easily in the modern world espouse the Vichian idea of the circular course of history—passing through phases of sincere commitment, followed by phases of ironic apprehension of the contradictory and inauthentic in commitment, followed by a revived true commitment—any more than one can easily espouse a contemporary fundamentalism where sincerity and authenticity are unaccompanied by irony. What one *can* espouse, following the ironists we favor here, is the humanist notion of *folly*—in our case, development held up to ironic scrutiny in the various works here considered—*not* as the opposite of reason and the reasonable, but as the very condition of its existence, with which the Development Project must constantly wrestle and out of

19. Erasmus [1509] 1925. This curious "Humanistic" document, full of *Erasmian Irony,* has been repeatedly debated ever since its composition. It seems to have been composed as a response to the gross humor but intense, literal high-mindedness (and single-mindedness) of such reformers as Luther. It is especially relevant to the perspective of this chapter. This is so if only because, like Erasmus, I am struggling with the problem of the relation between virtue and knowledge, and not primarily with the Foucaultian problem of the relation between power and knowledge, which is very much the contemporary agenda. Erasmian irony, I might define as "that state of mind produced by a manifold appreciation of the complex contradictions and paradoxes of the human condition in this life, ignorance of which inevitably produces many follies." The perspective Erasmus seeks is one that encompasses these contradictions and paradoxes and thus contains a "higher truth" and a higher commitment. That perspective is still necessarily an ironic one, because it arises from a sense of contradiction.

Leonard F. Dean (1965: 349) contrasts Erasmian irony with the classical and medieval (Lucian) "Ship of Fools" type of irony, forever forensic and jesting, which ends up by mocking all human endeavor and pretense in favor of, if anything, the more serious religious engagements aimed at the afterlife. "Erasmian irony," on the other hand, produces a meaning comparable to that derived from a play or from any piece of literature conceived as drama. The irony resides in the simultaneous expression of several points of view, just as a play is composed of speeches by many different characters, and the meaning of the irony and of the play is not that of any point of view or of any one character, but of all of them interacting upon each other. The result is not paralysis or abject relativism, but a larger communal truth and mutual engagement which is greater than that presented by any one of the characters alone. It is larger, that is to say, than any sum of its parts.

20. Vico's historical cycle *(recorso)* is detailed in White 1976: 216.

21. I evoke here Lionel Trilling's well-known essay, *Sincerity and Authenticity* (1972) to a purpose: Trilling's is a classic argument against the transparency of these terms and the ironies, lodged in the complexities of culture, attendant on their transparent, i.e., unreflective use.

which wrestling insight into a greater perfection in its projects in the world is produced.

At the heart of the Higher Irony, then, is this "inclusiveness" or this "mutuality"[22] that derives from the humanistic recognition of that inevitable, existential gap between human intention and human effects and which is the product of the pervasiveness of "human inexperience"[23] and of human forgetfulness. These defects are no less present and reproduced over and over again in the Development Project as a constant challenge to its realization in the world. But it is one thing to withdraw from these challenges and simply ironize about them, and quite another to recognize in them a binding commonality that conditions as it humanizes commitment. The difference, to return to the title of this volume, is between inactive irony and irony in action.

References

Baker, Russell. 1982. Observer: The Only Gentleman. *The New York Times,* 14 April 1982, p. A23.
Del Banco, Andrew. 1995. *The Death of Satan: How Americans Have Lost the Sense of Evil.* New York: Farrar, Straus, and Giroux.
Beidelman, Thomas O. 1986. *Moral Imagination in Kaguru Modes of Thought.* Bloomington: Indiana University Press.
Bennett, Jane. 1992. Kundera, Coetzee and the Politics of Anonymity. In *The Politics of Irony: Essays in Self-Betrayal,* ed. Daniel W. Conway and John E. Seery, 151–70. New York: St. Martins Press.
Booth, Wayne C. 1974. *A Rhetoric of Irony.* Chicago: University of Chicago Press.
Bruner, Edward. 1986. Ethnography As Narrative. In *The Anthropology of Experience,* ed. Victor Turner and Edward Bruner, 138–55. Champaign: University of Illinois Press.
Dean, Leonard F. 1965. Introduction to *The Praise of Folly.* In *Essential Works of Erasmus,* ed. W. T. H. Jackson, 349. New York: Bantam Books.
Dominguez, Virginia. 1994. A Taste for the Other: Intellectual Complicity in Racializing Practices. *Current Anthropology* 35(4): 333–48.
Erasmus, Desiderius. [1509] 1925. *Erasmus in Praise of Folly.* New York: Brentanos.
Escobar, Arturo. 1995. *Encountering Development: The Making and Unmaking of the Third World.* Princeton: Princeton University Press.
Ferguson, James. 1993. De-moralizing Economies: African Socialism, Scientific Cap-

22. In respect to the development project, see Nef (1994) for a particularly trenchant call to "mutuality" of perspective, carrying an underlying ironic comment on the inability of any one part of the earth to escape self-contradiction in its attempts to solve all the earth's problems (and therefore on the need for other complementary or contrastive perspectives).

23. These points are made by the Czech novelist, Milan Kundera, in *The Unbearable Lightness of Being* (1984), addressed to the existential dilemmas of resistance to the oppressive power of the state. Kundera defines the ironies ever-present in his account, and indeed all irony, as the result of "human inexperience," the inevitable, existential, gap between human intentions and human effects (Bennett 1992).

italism and the Moral Politics of Structural Adjustment. In *Moralizing States and the Ethnography of the Present,* ed. Sally Falk Moore, 78–92. AES Monograph Series, no. 5. Washington, DC: American Anthropological Association.

————. 1994. *The Anti-Politics Machine: Development, Depolitization and Bureaucratic Power in Lesotho.* Minneapolis: University of Minnesota Press.

————. 1997. Anthropology and Its Evil Twin: Development in the Constitution of a Discipline. In *International Development and the Social Sciences: Essays on the History and Politics of Knowledge,* ed. Frederick Cooper and Randall Packard, 150–175. Berkeley: University of California Press.

Fernandez, James W. 1984. Convivial Attitudes: The Ironic Play of Tropes in an International Kayak Festival in Northern Spain. In *Text, Play, and Story: The Construction and Reconstruction of Self and Society,* ed. Edward M. Bruner, 199–229. Proceedings of the American Ethnological Society, 1983. Washington, DC: American Ethnological Society.

————. 1993. "Emergencias Etnográficas: Tiempos Heroicos, Tiempos Irónicos y la Tarea Etnográfica," Joan Bestard i Camps (Coord). *Despues de Malinowski,* 33–67. La Laguna: Dirección General de Patrimonio Histórico.

Foucault, Michel. 1979. *Discipline and Punish: The Birth of the Prison.* New York: Vintage.

Frank, Leonard. 1986. The Development Game. *Granta* 20: 229–43.

Geertz, Clifford. 1968. Thinking as a Moral Act: Ethical Dimensions of Fieldwork in the New States. *The Antioch Review* 28(3): 139–58.

Gutmann, Matthew C. 1993. Rituals of Resistance: A Critique of the Theory of Everyday Forms of Resistance. *Latin American Perspectives* 20(2): 74–92.

Hirschman, Albert O. 1971. *A Bias for Hope: Essays on Development in Latin America.* New Haven: Yale University Press.

————. 1981. *Essays in Trespassing: Economics to Politics and Beyond.* Cambridge: Harvard University Press.

————. 1995. *A Propensity to Self-Subversion.* Cambridge: Harvard University Press.

Jarvie, I. C. 1990. Comments on Persuasive Fictions in Anthropology. In *Modernist Anthropology: From Fieldwork to Text,* ed. Marc Manganaro, 122–25. Princeton: Princeton University Press.

Krupat, Arnold. 1990. Irony in Anthropology: The Work of Franz Boas. In *Modernist Anthropology: From Fieldwork to Text,* ed. Marc Manganaro, 132–45. Princeton: Princeton University Press.

Kundera, Milan. 1984, *The Unbearable Lightness of Being.* Trans. M. H. Hein. New York: Harper and Row.

Manganaro, Marc, ed. 1990. *Modernist Anthropology: From Fieldwork to Text.* Princeton: Princeton University Press.

Nef, Jorge. 1994. *Human Security and Mutual Vulnerability: Some Conceptual and Empirical Observations about Global Issues.* Kingston, Ontario: National Defense College.

Purdy, Jedediah. 1999. *For Common Things: Irony, Trust and Commitment in America Today.* New York: Knopf.

Scott, James C. 1998. *Seeing Like a State: How Certain Schemes to Improve the Human Condition Have Failed.* New Haven: Yale University Press.

Skrentny, John D. 1996. *The Ironies of Affirmative Action: Politics, Culture, and Justice in America.* Chicago: University of Chicago Press.

Strathern, Marilyn. 1990. Out of Context: The Persuasive Fictions of Anthropology. In *Modernist Anthropology: From Fieldwork to Text,* ed. Marc Manganaro, 80–122. Princeton: Princeton University Press.

Trilling, Lionel. 1972. *Sincerity and Authenticity.* Cambridge: Harvard University Press.

Twain, Mark. 1990. *Life on the Mississippi.* New York: Bantam Books.

White, Hayden. 1976. *Tropics of Discourse.* Baltimore: Johns Hopkins University Press.

Willis, Paul. 1981. *Learning to Labor: How Working Class Kids Get Working Class Jobs.* New York: Columbia University Press.

Wolf, Eric. 1982. *Europe and the People without History.* Berkeley: University of California Press.

Chapter Four

── DIANE LOSCHE ──

What Makes the Anthropologist Laugh?: The Abelam, Irony, and Me

Before being invited to write this essay I had given little thought to applying the concept of irony to the Sepik region of Papua New Guinea. I was intrigued by the topic, as it presented a difficult task for translation into a very different region from its own circulation, into the cultural and linguistic arena of the Abelam area of Papua New Guinea.[1] In this chapter I will suggest that in this culture, despite difficulties in translation, irony is a seductive and crucial dimension of language play that turns everyday life into theater. Finally, however, irony has another, less obvious, characteristic. It surrounds its creators in a trap that they have, unwittingly, made for themselves. The topic of Abelam irony has turned out to provide a rich, though somewhat unsettling, vein of insight for me, as self-interrogation in the face of irony became an intrinsic part of the research. In the end this essay is as much about looking at myself looking at, or, to be more precise, looking *for* irony, as it is about Abelam irony itself.

Learning the Language of Irony

I confess a certain ambivalence about irony, but ambivalence seems a natural accompaniment to the subject. Although I myself often use it, irony seems too clever and distant and, in the postmodern world, so much used as to risk being boring, surely a shameful thing for ironists. The more it is used, the more crit-

---

1. The word "Abelam" designates a population of approximately forty to fifty thousand people living to the north of the middle Sepik region. They speak a number of mutually intelligible dialects. Abelam clans cluster into villages surrounded by gardens which are cultivated by slash and burn horticulture. The main staples of these gardens are many varieties of yams. The Abelam are known throughout the world for their spectacular carving and painting produced in men's cults. There has been quite extensive research and publication about the Abelam. For more information relevant to the topic of this chapter see Forge 1962, 1966, 1967, 1970a, 1970b, 1973, 1979; Hauser-Schaublin 1989, 1994; Losche 1995, 1996, 1997.

ics decry its overuse.[2] I became even more worried about entering irony's kingdom, never mind carrying it to foreign places, when I read:

> Getting to grips with irony seems to have something in common with gathering the mist; there is plenty to take hold of if only one could. To attempt a taxonomy of a phenomenon so nebulous that it disappears as one approaches is an even more desperate adventure. Yet, if, upon examination, irony becomes less nebulous, as it does, it remains exclusively Protean. Its forms and functions are so diverse as to seem scarcely amenable to a single definition. (Muecke 1969: 3)

After an enormously long paragraph describing only a few of the most significant uses of irony, this learned critic ends his list on a phrase of double negatives that smacks of a delicately controlled, dare I say it, *ironic* hysteria ". . . we may find nothing on earth and quite certainly nothing in heaven that is not ironic" (ibid.)!

This aspect of irony's contagion worries me, since it involves the issue of how irony will travel to another region, to a place far from its Greek origins, for I certainly do not want the ironic to become a kind of cross-cultural cliché. In his volume on Proust, Alain de Botton pinpoints the philosophical problem of the cliché, a problem which, I suggest, lies at the heart of the anthropological project. Here is De Botton's comment on Proust's dismay at a gentleman who seems to continually confuse Proust with another contemporary writer, a Monsieur Prevost:

> Using a single word to describe two different things . . . suggests a disregard for the world's real diversity that bears comparison with that shown by the cliché user. A person who invariably describes heavy rain with the phrase "il pleut des cordes" can be accused of neglecting the real diversity of rain showers, much as the person who calls every writer whose name begins with *P* and ends in *t* Monsieur Prevost can be accused of neglecting the real diversity of literature. . . . So if speaking in clichés is problematic, it is because the world itself contains a far broader range of rainfalls, moons, sunshines and emotions than stock expressions either capture or teach us to expect. (De Botton 1997: 105–6)

If I take this quote seriously, and I want to do that here, the greatest risk in taking irony to another place is the risk of discovering something which is not

2. In his book *The End of Science* (1996), John Horgan characterizes certain contemporary scientists as practicing ironic science, that is, science in a speculative, postempirical mode. Horgan suggests that "Ironic science resembles literary criticism in that it offers points of view, opinions which are, at best, interesting, which provoke further comment. But it does not converge on the truth. It cannot achieve empirically verifiable surprises that force scientists to make substantial revisions in their basic description of reality" (7). Horgan's book relies a bit too heavily on a simplistic taxonomy of irony. Apparently there are ironic physicists, ironic cosmologists and, would you believe?, ironic social scientists. An interesting discussion of contemporary irony can be found in Michael Roth's *The Ironist's Cage* (1995).

there, or alternatively, of missing something that is an intrinsic part of a particular place and time. This excursion must be sensitive not only to the protean
and elusive quality of irony in the arena where it circulates freely, but also to
the question of its existence, or absence, in a place where the word, as such, is
certainly not recognized: where there is no obvious word that stands out as a
concise translation and where, I suspect, no one, including myself, has given
much thought to whether "irony" can be translated usefully. On the other hand,
this project, of looking for Abelam irony, is enticing, since it appears to go to
the core of the cross-cultural project. Can words and ideas travel? How much
do they illuminate, or obscure, when they do? In order to cope with this problem of whether irony can usefully travel to the Abelam, I decided that this chapter must be an enquiry into my own knowledge, a revelation of the process of
"coming to perhaps know something about irony."

Despite Mr. Muecke's earlier despair at locating irony at all, he gives me
hope that perhaps I might find irony in a place where it is not named:

> . . . irony, both as something we see and respond to and as something we prac-
> tice, has to be distinguished from the word irony and the concept of irony. For
> the phenomenon existed before it was named and consequently before there
> could have been a concept of it; and the word existed before it was applied to
> the phenomenon. If Homer had a word for the suitor's mockery it was neither
> *sarkasmos* nor *eironeia;* the former did not acquire its modern meaning until
> very late and the latter did not mean verbal irony until the time of Aristotle.
> As for situational irony, the irony of the suitor's saying in Odysseus' presence
> that Odysseus would never come home, though it has been the staple irony of
> drama from Aeschylus to the present, no one called it irony until, at the earli-
> est, the late eighteenth century. (Muecke 1970: 14)

In a further note, he gives me some confidence in finding a form of irony
among the Abelam. This is not because of any sudden illumination on my part
that Abelam irony exists, but rather because of the chaos of irony studies. Lis-
ten to Muecke once again; this is a long quote, but one worth reading, since its
very length brings home this chaos:

> In seeking to define irony or distinguish its several kinds one can quite legit-
> imately look at it from many different angles. But it is precisely this that
> explains the chaos that the terminology of irony presents. One has only to
> reflect for a moment upon the various names that have been given to "kinds"
> of irony—tragic irony, comic irony, irony of manner, irony of situation,
> philosophical irony, practical irony, dramatic irony, verbal irony, ingenu
> irony, double irony, rhetorical irony, self-irony, Socratic irony, Romantic
> irony, cosmic irony, sentimental irony, irony of fate, irony of chance, irony
> of character, etc.—to see that some have been named from the effect, oth-
> ers from the medium, others again from the technique, or the function, or the
> object, or the practitioner, or the tone or the attitude. Clearly there could be

several mutually independent (and separately inadequate) classifications of
the kinds of irony, each based on a different point of view. (Muecke 1969: 4)

The question, of course, once one determines that one will risk forging into
the wilderness to create a path of translation—and why not?, given the jumble
outlined in the above quote—is to decide which ironies one is going to take
on one's journey. Here I ran into a common problem of translation, the multi-
tudes I uncovered when I started what turned out to be a voluminous reading
project. One important question in all travel is which baggage to take—literary irony, dramatic irony, everyday irony, situational irony, and philosophical
irony, just to begin with. There is Flaubertian, Austinian, and Burkean irony to
choose from: a veritable cornucopia. How to choose? In what I suspect might
be a well-trodden path (but not one always confessed to) I continued my journey carrying a few ideas chosen via a simple criterion—they appealed to me
most. One of these I'll share with you now. One book told me that "*eironeia* is
first recorded in Plato's *Republic*. Applied to Socrates by one of his victims it
appears to have meant something like a 'smooth, low down way of taking
people in'" (Muecke 1970: 14). I could relate to Muecke's idea of a smooth,
low down way of talking. It struck a chord in my memories of learning the
Abelam language.

Skin is the surface of things, the outside and surface of the body, the membrane that separates the inside from the outside. Names are like skin, at least
this is how I envision my introduction to Abelam words. In retrospect I realize
that irony was brought home to me quite early on in my research in a village
called Apangai. This occurred during a period that I call my window of opportunity, when I began to understand their language, Samukundi. I knew I was
beginning to understand this language, after some painful months of being unable to discern even sounds, never mind words and meanings, when, as I ap-
proached two *nemandu,* older men of high status, I heard one of them say to
the other: *"nematagwa ndiou."* At that moment I simultaneously realized two
things: first, that I could understand something; and second, the ironic dimensions of the language I was now involved in.

This instantaneous learning curve centered on my understanding of the word
nema, a word used in Samukundi to describe two qualities, physical size, and
status or importance. My first reaction, on overhearing the two men call me *nematagwa* was to be very pleased with myself, flattered. I thought: "I'm a person of status." Then the clouds of uncertainty descended—or did the two men
mean simply that I was big, like a big tomato, or a big tree? I was certainly
aware that in this village I was tall, the size of most adult men, and I towered
over women. How could I tell which of the two meanings they meant? Perhaps the speaker did mean to indicate my status? Perhaps there was no ironic

inflection in his voice? Perhaps I was paranoid, a common enough condition in fieldwork. How would I ever know? I never did find out what the *nemandu* meant in that instance, but I learned something more important, that words can be, and often are, like a skin or surface. The course of learning to speak Samukundi involves crucially the ability to understand words, in particular names, as a surface which conceals layers of meanings.

To demonstrate my idea of language being like a surface or skin, let me give some examples of the way that names function. People generally receive more than one name during their lifetime, although only one of these names may be used in everyday speech. Everyone receives a name at birth. Later in life people sometimes take other names to indicate an important change which they want to signify to others. One can be given a name that reveals something embarrassing and shameful. One man had the name Kwamikitnya, which means literally "vulva meat." How does one get the name Vulva Meat? This man was a failure at producing the special yams raised only by adult men. It was presumed that the reason for this was his inability to obey stringent sex taboos when raising yams. Hence his name refers to his love for meat and the vulva, his preference for women and meat over raising yams! In general, women have only two names throughout their lifetimes, but men, through the course of an elaborate cult system that will concern us later in this chapter, may receive as many as three or four names.

My neighbor, a man of some power and esteem, was often called "Gilenang." *Gile* means black and *nang* means sago. Thus his name is Black Sago, referring to the oxidized leaves of the sago plant. People are often given the names of plants and flowers, however in his case this name, Gilenang or Black Sago, refers to his important role as the sponsor of a particular secret and sacred ceremony, where these black sago leaves are used as part of the wall which separates a visible section of the initiation display from a hidden section. Gilenang's name is the signifier of particular secret information but this name also signifies the power of secrecy in general since, even if one knows that Gilenang's name refers to the *giletapu,* that wall which hides a secret recess, one may not know what is behind the wall. Thus this man's name refers to specific multiple pieces of secret information but also signifies secrecy, and its power, in general. There are many layers to the way in which Gilenang's name functions. One may have no idea at all that the name is anything other than a description of an important plant. One may know that the name has multiple references but not know what the other references are. One may know that it refers to the activities of the *korombo,* but not know what. A further layer of knowledge is that the name refers to a particular initiation. Going deeper into these hidden layers of secrecy, the name refers to this membrane-like interior wall. A further piece of information is that this wall hides yet another, secret space. One may know what is inside the space and, finally, one may know that Gilenang was given this name because he came up with the idea for this particular form of wall. These levels of secrecy serve to divide people by age, gender, status, power, and techno/magical prowess.

The ultimate effect of these layers of meaning is to produce the potential for an ironic effect in discourse. This language usage provides a theater in which irony can be performed. By this I mean that in learning how to use language one becomes aware that things can have two or more meanings, some of which one has access to and others which are forbidden. The meaning may or may not be known, and very often the listener is not entirely sure which meaning is being referred to. Not all speakers of this language engage in irony, indeed, some seem not to have any sense of irony at all; instead they are fatuous, innocent, and even, in some cases, paranoid. These may also be rhetorical stances, and one person may be able to signal to another that they know some particular secret that they are pretending ignorance about. Women may pretend to know less than they actually do, but it is also a fact that women do not want to know much about this *maira* because of its association with magic and sorcery which can harm them. Nevertheless this language play, based on widespread knowledge of multiple and hidden meanings, sets the stage for theatrical effects in language. I will experiment with translating this potential as an ironic effect.

The getting of wisdom in Abelam is a long, slow, sometimes painful, often hilarious process, not simply for me, but for all persons. The only innocents in this may be children. Teenagers, of both sexes nowadays, are aware that there is another life, another set of meanings behind the façade of the names that they learn. Some young teenage men may have already learned aspects of this secret life. Others know nothing at all, except that they know nothing about that something. Some men who have been away from the village for education or work become, on their return to the village, completely terrified about reading the symbols and signs of their adult male relatives. They may see sorcery everywhere, since the sorcery techniques known by big men are the most powerful agents in illness and even death. Communication about sorcery encodes hidden meaning par excellence, or so it is thought.

Eventually in this slow and painful getting of wisdom, there might be, in theory, someone who knows everything. This person is, by definition, old and male. Can I, should I, find this person, the epitome of the getting of wisdom? Something in the logic of the practice of anthropology causes one to seek those individuals who are at the peak of the system. After all, anthropology is an enlightenment project, the point is to know, isn't it? But I take what I can only call an ironic stance in relation to this getting of wisdom. I am compelled by the premises of fieldwork to know everything related to my chosen topic of investigation. Given the logic of anthropological holism I thus seem to be committed to knowing everything. However, I hesitated in pursuing this path of commitment to total knowledge because I met, in the course of my stay in the village of Apangai, a few white men who were also very interested in this culture. My stance toward these men was ambivalent. I liked them, and we shared an interest in the culture around us. From my perspective, however, they appeared to be totally seduced by the culture of masculine secrecy that they had chosen to live in for a few years.[3] They went as often as they could to initiations. They talked to old men and seemed convinced that one man somewhere possessed the key to the mystery of Abelam cult life.

I pause at the sight of such true believers. My own understanding of Abelam culture is of an acephalous political system of big men. The endless invention of secrets is a structurally necessary outcome of the competitive gift-giving of initiations and yams by which *nemandu* vie with one another for status. Thus there is unlikely to be, given the logic of this decentralized political system, one central man, or group of men, with a total, panopticonic knowledge of the men's cults. I am not suggesting that there were no ritual experts. Indeed there certainly were such, but I sometimes wondered if the fascinated white men were drawn to secret cults precisely because they were bastions of masculine power, and because they excluded women. My own stance, on the other hand, became one of irony in the face of these masculine secrets, partly as the result of a sense of multiple outsiderness—as anthropologist and woman—watching the true believers and judging them naive. I now will examine the structure of this secret masculine life to which I brought my ironic gaze.

Hubris

Hubris, a noun, is derived from Greek. In tragedy the word signifies arrogant pride toward the gods, leading to nemesis. This blind self-confidence, this hubris, characterizes Oedipus. In this section I want to take a different notion of irony out of my tool kit and contemplate dramatic and philosophical irony, the

---

3. I should note here that my attitude toward and opinions about the other outsiders, those few white men I am discussing here, has changed considerably as I have given the issue thought over the years. Much of the research I discuss here took place between 1976 and 1980. Although I was often exempted from the rules excluding women from the men's cult, especially in Apangai and neighboring villages, I nevertheless often suspected that Abelam men would have been happier to share their information with a man. I have wondered over the years if I was simply feeling competitive with these often kind and helpful white men. And I have some doubts as to whether they were as naive as I thought at the time: or was this simply a youthful professional arrogance? Nevertheless, my reaction, and the protective irony it led to, is what I want to emphasize here.

bitter irony of Sophocles' Oedipus cycle. We move from a kind of funny, if naughty irony, to a much more sombre dark space of the tragedy of hubris. The hubris of Oedipus is contained in the phrase in which he unwittingly curses himself at the very moment when he makes himself king:

> And it is my solemn prayer
> That the unknown murderer, and his accomplices,
> If such there be, may wear the brand of shame
> For their shameful act, unfriended, to their life's end.
>
> (*King Oedipus,* lines 244–47)

In this drama the irony lies in the fact that the audience has been given information and knows what Oedipus cannot know. The point, of course, is that in life we don't have the knowledge of hindsight provided to the audience by the dramatist. When we begin projects and create particular structures, we have only hope; it is the beginning of the journey. Lacking foresight, we see only the positives, only the power. Given his desire and ambition, how could Oedipus have turned down the chance to be king, to wed and bed Jocasta? How could she not bear him children, given the desires and rules of marriage?

In Samukundi it is not only language use that encodes secrecy. The entire structure of the masculine cult circulates around one word, which can signify many particular pieces of information but always refers to one central concept—*maira*—which I would translate, at its simplest, most powerful and embracing, as "secret." *Maira* can be used as a noun or an adjective and it always encapsulates the notion that beneath the surface there is another reality that may or may not become known. The word *maira* also has very strong spatial connotations, primarily attached to the participation of men in the activities of the *korombo,* a magnificent building, a temple which is the site of the creation and display of spectacular tableaus at particular times. *Maira* also refers to other activities of men, who grow very large varieties of yams in gardens that only certain categories of individuals may enter. These yams, called *wapinyen* (literally, "yam children"), are reciprocally exchanged between partners in a system of competitive, restricted exchange. Many of the activities that take place in the *korombo* and in yam gardens are referred to as *maira,* and *maira* also refers to the powers, abilities and techniques that allow men to produce the spectacular products of these two spaces—the garden and the *korombo.* Included in *maira* are such specifics as recipes for paint, carving techniques, the plaiting and making of headdresses, magical formulas, chants, and spells, and sources for particular items used in the cult. Some people say that women have parallel *maira* in the birth they give to children; however, the act of giving birth is not a particularly secret or restricted activity. When people say that women's *maira* is giving birth, they seem to be referring to the fact that women's bodies have a space which has the capacity, within itself, to produce children. Others suggest that women's *maira* is not giving birth but becoming a witch. Whatever people's opinions about the *maira* of women, the force and power of the secret devolves primarily onto the men's cults.

The institution of *maira* is an act of power, for it is primarily via the functioning of secret activities that adult men control the fate and destiny of their villages. The implied narrative contained in the concept of *maira* is, like the story of Oedipus, about taboos and rules, and the dire consequences of breaking such rules. It is the possession of the secret that turns senior men of Abelam clans into *nemandu,* big men of status and power, and which causes the subsequent subjection of others in the village: women, younger men, and children. Another word for *maira* might be "taboo," for, in the life of the *maira,* secret activities are hedged by many restrictions on food and sex. Senior men refrain from sexual activities during the growth of their *wapinyen,* and there are stringent food and sex taboos obeyed during the activities of the *korombo.*[4] According to some, *maira* requires a sacrifice, a form of hard work, which are these taboos. Thus from one point of view a *maira* is a taboo, a rule that creates a boundary between an external space and an internal one. A taboo is like a membrane dividing these two spaces. There is a dark side to this power, one which enforces obedience and conformity, for at the heart of the *maira* are specific techniques for using paint, not only to make things beautiful, but also to hurt, to create illness, and even to kill.[5] The secret weapon of sorcery is the final, if seldom used, threat by which this patriarchy rules.

It is in the *korombo* that the *maira* becomes a system structuring not only space but time, as specific secret information is acquired in a series of sequential stages of initiations throughout the life cycle of men. Commonly used names for these stages are *ulketagwa, kutagwa, puti* and *lunggwallndu.* (There are, of course, other names by which the stages may be referred to, depending on who one asks.) These sequential stages of acquiring secret knowledge are constructed as initiations in which one group of men creates a series of carved and painted tableaus inside the *korombo,* for others who are the initiates. The initiates are secluded, and go through a series of ordeals that may include beatings, being force-fed water, and penis incisions. They are also much pampered with special foods, and finally the spectacular *korombo* tableaus are revealed to them. After this period of tender care, which is thought to make them beautiful, and ferocious terrorization, which hopefully reveals and enhances their masculine strength and ensures their obedience to older men, there is an all-night dance involving some very fancy costumes and then a return to everyday life.

4. For more information about Abelam food and sex taboos, see Losche 1982: 137–81.
5. See Forge 1962 for interesting observations on the Abelam use of paint in magic and sorcery.

The entire system of initiations constructs time and space as a nest of secrets within secrets. The spectacular displays inside the *korombo,* for example, hide secret rooms and compartments that contain musical instruments and other paraphernalia. Thus the spatial structure of the *korombo* is a series of nested secrets. Time through the life cycle is structured in a similar fashion. At each stage of initiation one is told that this is the true manifestation of *nggwal,* or spirits, whose substance always remains sufficiently vague as to be adaptable to any number of manifestations, and that whatever other tableaus one has seen before were only hiding the real version of a particular carving or painting. Names, those verbal forms by which I first got to know about doubleness, the play of Samukundi language, and the need to read behind the surface of words, reach their peak of articulation in this onion-like structuring of space and time into one of secrecy and revelation.

What one learns in this cultural system, both in everyday language and in the structures of initiation, with its parallel visual and verbal effects, is that truth is constructed via falsity. From this viewpoint truth itself is a theatrical effect, the result of an idea that any image can hide another image; any name or word, another word. A potential effect of this theater of revelation is to produce an expectation that something which is true may turn out to be false and, inversely, that something which is false may turn out to be true. The entire structure of Abelam life, with constant reminders in language, and written into the body via taboo, draws in everyone, including women and children, but to greater or lesser degrees. Anyone can become a victim of sorcery, and, of course, the most potent sorcerers are the most powerful men of the *korombo.* Such men are referred to as *kwusmairndu,* which literally translated means "secret paint man." In using this word, the speaker may either be describing a man as a sorcerer or simply referring to his status and skill in *korombo* activities. The speaker may imply both meanings at the same time. The greatest magicians de facto make the greatest sorcerers, and all Abelam must learn to read beneath the surface of language and behavior and be alert to multiple meanings. Children learn early to discern that there are interiors, spatial and linguistic, which they must skirt carefully.

This *maira* is a brilliant structure. It confers the power of knowledge on a select group. And the process inspires a compulsion to know often associated with narrative: like a good detective story, it draws one to seek what lies ahead. Thus this institution compels adherence to its rules, less by rules—although it has many—than by the power of seduction, each stage enticing one to go on to the next, each layer promising one secret yet ahead. This narrative seduction also compels the anthropologist to keep seeking more information, since its seductive nature blends with the logic of the anthropologist's own practice of knowledge: the idea that one must explore a system completely, must bring hidden passages and obscure meanings to light. Isn't that what we're here for, enlightenment?

Irony and Hubris: The Heart of the Thing

. . . Oedipus uncovered the hideous secret of his unwitting sins. The man whom he had, in an angry moment, slain on the road between Corinth and Thebes was no other than his father Laius, and the wife whom he had married on his elevation to the throne of Thebes and who had borne him now two sons and two daughters, was his own mother Jocasta. In his horror at this discovery, and at the self-inflicted death of Jocasta, he destroyed the sight of his own eyes. (Watling 1986: 69)

At first there may seem to be few parallels to draw between an ancient Greek story and a modern culture, but, in my search for the Abelam ironic, I find such parallels at the heart of the matter. As I continued fieldwork I marveled at the brilliant structure of this *korombo*. I was seduced, as were the men who constructed its secrets. But finally the *korombo* contains a twist which you, reader, may have already detected since you have been given clues and hindsight. The structure of the *maira* is, like the act by which Oedipus becomes king, an act of power, but it is also one that unwittingly condemns itself to an unforeseen fate. The bite of the *korombo,* its greatest strength, is also its great weakness. This minotaur, buried skillfully in the heart of the structure, is the fact that, at its center, the *maira* has no secret. Through many everyday events, through constant repetitions, and tiny movements, eventually everyone colludes in revealing and concealing many specific pieces of information and knowledge. However, the secret, of course, is that there is no secret. I, the outsider, the audience in this theater, call this tragic irony. It bites hardest on those who have worked hardest to create its structure and who have gained the most power and status from it. For others in the village, for women, for example, who have been only marginally involved in the *korombo,* there always lies the possibility that the *maira* may hide some secret force or power, something special that will explain the world as it is. But what about the most influential big men—the priests who have devoted their lives to the maintenance of this structure? If they have survived, they have seen many initiations and been involved in the creation and maintenance of many specific secrets. There is no one left to tell them that there are secrets that lie ahead. For many of these men, a decrease in their physical abilities coincides with this particular revelation, a revelation which is only possible, ironically, at the peak of their magical powers, at the pinnacle of the knowledge system. There is nothing else. It is important to realize the way in which some men serve the *korombo* in order to taste the bitterness of their realization. *Nemandu* have invested years of abstinence from sex and food in order to be skilled at the *korombo.* As Kangwemba, one of the men I introduced in the beginning of this story, said: "I cannot see well any more, my yams are not growing well, my bones are tired. This, this rubbish *korombo* goes on and on, but what is it? Nothing. I just sit by the fire now, I have no work anymore."

The irony, and a bitter one, for these exalted practitioners, is that behind the glittering façade there is nothing but the concept of the secret. The structure is labyrinthine, but at the center lies not that mythical minotaur, that at least might be a sign from the universe that something special is going on here, but rather only the knowledge that one has created one's own imprisonment. Finally the problem is that irony is contagious. The sting of irony, the barb hidden in its seductive structure is revealed. As Kierkegaard (1841) thought, I now think ". . . whoever has essential irony has it all day long; he is not ironical from time to time or in this or that direction but considers the totality of existence *sub speciae ironiae*" (quoted in in Muecke 1970: 23).

What Makes an Anthropologist Laugh?

What of anthropologists? Do we not follow a similar quest for enlightenment? I, the anthropologist, have my own hubris. Like many other foreigners, I love this magnificent system, because of its seductive nature and mysterious intellectual power, and because I am often exempt from the taboos and rules that surround its secrets. Like the *nemandu,* I have spent time and effort understanding this system. Is an ironic stance a useful attitude for an anthropologist? How should I react to my final revelation, that the secret of the *maira* is that there is no secret? Kenneth Burke suggests:

> The progress of humane enlightenment can go no further than in picturing people not as vicious, but as mistaken. When you add that people are necessarily mistaken, that all people are exposed to situations in which they must act as fools, that every insight contains its own special kind of blindness, you complete the comic circle, returning again to the lesson of humility that underlies great tragedy. The audience, from its vantage point, see the operation of errors that the characters of the play cannot see; thus seeing two angles at once, it is chastened by dramatic irony; it is admonished to remember that when intelligence means wisdom . . . it requires fear, resignation, the sense of limits as an important ingredient. (1961: 41–42)

There is a final step necessary to the completion of Burke's ironic enlightenment. This is the specification of what one's own particular hubris is, and the particular form that my own hubris takes is, in fact, an ironic stance. From the beginning of this project I suspected that there was no spectacular, world-altering secret. I looked with amusement on those true believers as they fervently scoured the area for the road to the wizard of this Oz. But I also realized that I had made my own pact with the devil, trading in desire, the desire to believe in a spectacular secret, for the protection of irony.

Perhaps, as an anthropologist, mine is the road of Flaubert, who is often characterized as the most ironic of novelists. At times he was criticized for his irony being a form of cold detachment (Nadeau 1972: 250). Toward the end of his life he wrote a story, one of my favorites, called "A Simple Heart." This is the story of a poor woman, named Felicity, who devoted her life to people, places, and things that abandoned her. Finally Felicity ends her life in complete devotion to a stuffed parrot. As she breathes her last, Flaubert describes the state that the parrot is in:

> Although the parrot was not a corpse, the worms were eating him up. One of his wings was broken, and the stuffing was coming out of his stomach. But she was blind by now, and she kissed him on the forehead and pressed him against her cheek. (Flaubert 1961: 54)

Finally, as Felicity breathes her last:

> A blue cloud of incense was wafted up into Felicité's room. She opened her nostrils wide and breathed it in with a mystical, sensuous fervour. Then she closed her eyes, her lips smiled. Her heart beats grew slower and slower, each a little fainter and gentler, like a fountain running dry, an echo fading away. And as she breathed her last, she thought she could see, in the opening heavens a gigantic parrot hovering above her head. (56)

These phrases seem to reach the heights, and depths, of irony. We smile as we feel for Felicity. Via Flaubert's implacable, crystalline prose we picture her surrendering her fate, with great faith, to a moth-eaten, decaying stuffed bird.

What did Flaubert think of this? From the evidence of a letter he wrote, one might surmise that Flaubert, like the Abelam men, and this anthropologist herself, was caught in the trap of his own irony. At the end of his life Flaubert suffered many terrible losses. Beloved people died and he became bankrupt. The story of Felicity was one of his last writings. In a letter to a friend, who reproached him for his cold, distant and irrefutably ironic stance in "A Simple Heart," it becomes clear that Flaubert no longer has any use for irony. Flaubert writes in response to the accusation:

> The story *Un Simple Coeur* is just an account of an obscure life, the life of a poor country girl who is pious but mystical, fanciful without fuss, and tender as new bread. She loves in turn a man, her mistress's children, her nephew, an old man and then her parrot. When the parrot dies she has it stuffed, and when she too dies she confuses the parrot with the Holy Ghost. . . . this is not at all ironical, as you suppose, on the contrary it is very serious and very sad. (Nadeau 1972: 252–53)

I wonder if, despite Flaubert's protest, he can escape his irony? Flaubert's situation may seem a far cry from that of an anthropologist among Abelam priests but it speaks to the stance that I brought to the *maira*. Was I not caught in the same entanglement as Flaubert? The detached eye can record the faith of others but it cannot participate in such faith, even when such a faith would be most helpful. But one must suspect that for Flaubert to devote his life's energies to writing about faith, even with detachment, and for an anthropologist to expend so much energy on describing the *maira,* a faith in something must sustain those energies. What is the anthropologist's parrot? What is my mystical stuffed bird? Where is the anthropologist's *korombo?* What is my *maira,* and in what lies the twist of my fate? The unspoken question in this paper, is that of the anthropologist's, this writer's hubris, since she seems so aware of everyone else's folly. The anthropologist's parrot is irony itself, the distanced eye, so powerful, so seductive, but, in the end, its own trap. Yet, if I am absolutely true to my own faith in irony, how can I know for certain that Felicity is mistaken or that the secret at the center of the *maira* does not exist? Perhaps the heavens did open to reveal her parrot to the dying Felicity. By its own logic, the ironist's cage must open to the undecidability of truth.

References

Burke, Kenneth. 1961. *Attitudes toward History.* Boston: Beacon Press.
De Botton, Alain. 1997. *How Proust Can Change Your Life.* London: Picador.
Flaubert, Gustave. 1961. A Simple Heart. In *Three Tales.* London: Penguin.
Forge, Anthony. 1962. Paint—A Magical Substance. *Palette* 9 (Switzerland): 9–16.
———. 1966. Art and Environment in the Sepik. *Proceedings of the Royal Anthropological Institute of Great Britain and Ireland for 1965,* 23–31.
———. 1967. The Abelam Artist. In *Social Organisation: Essays Presented to Raymond Firth,* ed. M. Freedman, 65–84. London: Frank Cass.
———. 1970a. Prestige, Influence and Sorcery: A New Guinea Example. In *Witchcraft Confessions and Accusations,* ed. M. Douglas, 257–75. London: Tavistock.
———. 1970b. Learning to See in New Guinea. In *Socialisation: The Approach from Social Anthropology,* ed. Philip Mayer, 269–91. London: Tavistock.
———. 1973. Style and Meaning in Sepik Art. In *Primitive Art and Society,* ed. A. Forge, 170–192. London: Oxford University Press for the Wenner-Gren Foundation.
———. 1979. The Problem of Meaning in Art. In *Exploring the Visual Art of Oceania,* ed. Sidney Mead, 278–86. Honolulu: University Press of Hawaii.
Hauser-Schaublin, Brigitta. 1989. *Kulthauser in Nordneuguinea.* 2 vols. Berlin: Akademie-Verlag.
———. 1994. The Track of the Triangle: Form and Meaning in the Sepik, Papua New Guinea. *Pacific Studies* 17(3): 133–70.
Horgan, John. [1996] 1998. *The End of Science: Facing the Limits of Knowledge in the Twilight of the Scientific Age.* London: Abacus.
Kierkegaard, Søren. [1841] 1989. *The Concept of Irony with Constant Reference to Socrates.* Ed. and trans. Howard V. Hong and Edna H. Hong. Princeton: Princeton University Press.
Losche, Diane. 1982. Male and Female in Abelam Society: Opposition and Complementarity. Ph.D. dissertation, Columbia University. University Microfilms International.

————. 1995. The Sepik Gaze: Iconographic Interpretation of Abelam Form. *Social Analysis* 38: 47–60.

————. 1996. The Impossible Aesthetic: The Abelam, the Moa Bird and Me. In *Articulation of Memory: Politics of Embodiment, Locality and the Contingent*, ed. Andrew Lattas. *Oceania* 66(4): 305–11.

————. 1997. What Do Abelam Images Want From Us?: Plato's Cave and Kwatbil's Belly. In *Anthro/aesthetics: The Cultural Construction of Aesthetic Objects*, ed. D. Losche. *The Australian Journal of Anthropology* 8(1): 35–49.

Muecke, D. C. 1970. *Irony: The Critical Idiom*. London: Methuen & Co.

————. 1969. *The Compass of Irony*. London: Methuen & Co.

Nadeau, Maurice. 1972. *The Greatness of Flaubert*. London: The Alcove Press.

Roth, Michael. 1995. *The Ironist's Cage*. New York: Columbia University Press.

Watling, E. F., trans. [1974] 1986. Sophocles, *The Theban Plays*. Harmondsworth: Penguin.

Chapter Five

— JAMES A. BOON —

Kenneth Burke's "True Irony": One Model for Ethnography, Still

Kenneth Burke (1897–1993), when widowed, had married the sister of his deceased wife.[1] This independent-minded practitioner of the sororate also liked to demonstrate unlikely "coincidences" among incongruous theories—those of Marx and Carlyle, for example. Indeed, Burke seems to have preferred reading-together (and perhaps living) contrary-seeming discourses and disciplines. His intellectual and existential eclecticism helped this polymath critic intensify comparative perspectives. Customarily, Burke's endeavors both explored and enacted rhetorical "effects" produced when diverse factions imagine themselves as each other's audience, ritually and/or politically.

The ungainly *corpus* of Kenneth Burke may be as ageless as those interpretive processes it emphasized. Hoping so, I have devised this compressed chapter in two parts: first, a *general* salute to Burke's theme of ironic practice; second, a *specific* bit of fieldwork-recollection from research in Bali. After confessing, not unsheepishly, my works' manifold debts to Burke, I try to show how circumstantial uncertainties may prevail on every side of ethnographic exchange, contestation, and translation-through-time. Burke teaches us that social life and its interpretation are alike riddled with diverse ironies—worth bearing in mind whenever cultures and anthropologies are experienced, written, and read.

---

1. Burke's obituary in the press mentioned his second marriage without designating it "sororate." Materials in this essay, differently arranged, appear in Boon (1999: "Rehearsals" and chap. 13). There the accent falls more on capitalist commodification mediating fieldwork; here I try to isolate Burkean irony in relatively "purer" fashion, as if irony could ever be so assayed.

I thank Mary Huber in particular for encouraging this paper, and I appreciate responses by others at the AAA panel (which ill health prevented my attending)—particularly Arnold Krupat who sent me his study of Thoreau.

Humbly Ironic, and Proud of It: Burke's Paradoxical Position

With a nod to I. M. Richards, Kenneth Burke tied a keynote "attitude" designated *ironic* to sundry antecedent formations: Socratic argumentation, Jane Austen's novels, early Romantic philosophy, modernist fiction, etc. ("postmodernist" irony postdates Burke's prime). His preferred brand of irony, while irremediably hard to pin down, was neither holier-than-thou nor self-sure—and it was never, never glib. Or so Burke, about to footnote Falstaff, implied in his *Grammar of Motives:*

> True irony, however, irony that really does justify the attribute of "humility," is not "superior" to the enemy. True irony, humble irony, is based upon a sense of fundamental kinship with the enemy, as one . . . is indebted to him. . . . This is the irony of Flaubert, when he recognizes that Madame Bovary is himself. . . . Folly and villainy are integral motives, necessary to wisdom or virtue." (1962: 514–15)

Burke also appreciated Thomas Mann's "highly ironical traditionalism"—a style, as Erich Heller once indicated, that "modeled itself on the classical products of literary history but at the same time could not help 'parodying' them." [2] (I cite Heller from his afterword to an English version of Mann's *Der Tod in Venedig* translated by none other than Kenneth Burke, in a somewhat stilted fashion—intentionally, perhaps, to make us aware of its "translatedness.").

Burke himself elsewhere addressed "Greek love" (relevant to the Mann novella he had stiltedly translated) along with classical Socratic ironies—a sticky pedagogical flashpoint recently rekindled ("The metaphors, may they mix!") in the work (and life) of Michel Foucault, with its aftermath of disciples and detractors.[3] Here's how Burke, before Foucault, began:

> Biologically, Greek love was an offence, since its fruitfulness would not be that of tribal progeny. It was thus the "representative crime" of the Athenian enlightenment, the practice that corresponded in the realm of transgression to the pedagogy of Socratic intercourse in the realm of the transcendent and ideal.
>
> Socrates was thus accused of the "representative" transgression. And whatever may have been the realities of the case in the literal sense, the structure of the Phaedrus shows that he was a "corruptor of youth" in the transcendental sense. He was thus resigned to the hemlock. . . .
>
> Ironically, then, this theorist of transcendence was the victim of a transcendence transcended. (1962: 426–28)

2. Heller in Mann 1970: 127. On Mann's irony, Schopenhauer's "double-bottomed philosophy," and Wittgenstein, see Safranski 1991: 338–44.

3. One helpful source on Foucault's corpus is O'Farrell 1989; see also Roth 1992 and sources cited in Boon 1999.

"The victim of a transcendence transcended!" Similar twists and twirls in dialectics, subsequent to those dialectics scapegoating Socrates, advanced rhetoric to the historical stage of Burke's own "counterstatements" marshaled against many foes: Hitler, fascism, the Cold War, and triumphal dichotomies of any stripe. These were critical battles Burke tirelessly and passionately waged.[4]

Barely underway, my chapter may already have conveyed that Burkean irony is nonstop. Burke's works doom or privilege his readers to encounter him rather as he did Freud:

> The reading of Freud I find suggestive almost to the point of bewilderment. Accordingly, what I should like most to do would be simply to take representative excerpts from his work, copy them out, and write glosses upon them.
>
> Very often these glosses would be straight extensions of his own thinking. . . . Such a desire to write an article on Freud in the margin of his books must for practical reasons here remain a frustrated desire. . . .
>
> Freud's terminology is a dictionary, a lexicon for charting a vastly complex and hitherto largely uncharted field. You can't refute a dictionary. The only profitable answer to a dictionary is another one.[5]

As the "later" Freud to the late Burke, so Burke (and Freud) to also belated me: intent on Burke, as Burke was on Freud.[6] Yes, we readers (whether ethnographers or literateurs, moderns or postmoderns) may find our every experience pre-Post-It-ed "in the margins of [Burke's] books." Again, I dutifully draw the notion of margins from Burke himself, dutifully embroiled in Freud, Mann, Socrates, and more.

In 1965, gratefully subjected to undergraduate assignments by James Peacock (a wonderful teacher and wildly interdisciplinary scholar destined to became president of the American Anthropological Association thirty years later), I suffered a "first contact" with Burke. Burke himself was destined to receive spotty canonization in symbolic anthropology according to Peacock (1975) and Fernandez (1991); in philosophy according to Sills and Jensen (1992); and in further critical circles, both literary and extra-that.[7]

My little corpus, too, stands (dwarfishly) on the shoulders of Burke-as-giant. (For an aptly devious guide to misreadings of the "dwarves on shoulders of giants" *topos,* see the vintage Menippean satire by Robert Merton, a giant among

---

4. A considerable literature on Burke includes Rueckert 1982. Donoghue (1987: 265–80, 275) links "perspectives by incongruity" to Thoreau; he also counters both Lentricchia's (1983) appropriation of Burke and Jameson's scoldings of his work; for more about Jameson, see Boon 1982a, 1998. On Burke and "modernism," see Lorrigio 1990. The Thoreau connection in Burke is stressed in Boon 1999.

5. Burke 1957: 221; one could compare Burke's desire of copying-out to Benjamin's writing "arcades" (see Boon 1999).

6. For a keen transvaluation of Freud's theme of "belatedness," which condition everyone (particularly Americans) might as well acknowledge in him- or herself, see Cavell 1990, 1994.

7. See Peacock 1975; Fernandez 1991; Sills and Jensen 1992, vol. 1.

ironic sociologists).[8] *From Symbolism to Structuralism* (Boon 1972) poached Burke's pastiches of Marxian slogans against "critiques of critical criticism" to explicate a fin-de-siècle poetics in Lévi-Strauss's artful ethnology. *The Anthropological Romance of Bali* (Boon 1977) framed its history of Balinese research with Burke's metaphors about perspectives through incongruity; that book's fieldwork covered dynamics of Balinese ancestral ideology—what Burke calls "socio-anagogic" dimensions of culture.[9]

Later, *Other Tribes, Other Scribes* (Boon 1982) synoptically matched Burke's dramatism with the interpretive anthropology of Clifford Geertz; eventually in his *Works and Lives,* Geertz (1987) wink-and-nodded toward Burke as his "governing inspiration at almost every point."[10] Back in 1984, rumors reached me that *Other Tribes* had annoyed Marxists—particularly its commentary on Marx (and Mauss, plus Durkheim) opening with cloth coats. I then wondered (not undefensively) if oversensitive Marxists had forgotten what Burke remembered: "Marx says that the modern division of labor began in earnest with the manufacture of Cloth"?[11] Or did Marxists frown on juxtaposing scholars whom they needed to believe diametrically (dialectically?) sundered? Again, my inspiration had been Burke, who tactically conjoined Marx on cloth with an apparent antithesis, Thomas Carlyle; in *Sartor Resartus* Carlyle "is not writing a book on the clothing industry":

> He is writing a book about symbols, which demand reverence because, in the last analysis, the images of nature are the Symbols of God. He uses Clothes as a surrogate for the symbolic in general. Examining his book to see what they are symbolic of, you find how Carlyle resembles Marx: Both are talking about the kind of hierarchy that arose in the world with the division of labor. (Burke 1962: 642–43)

Indeed, Burke's *Grammar of Motives* seemed almost to coin a contrary-trio of Marx, Carlyle, and the Lévi-Strauss of *Tristes tropiques* (as yet, when Burke wrote, unwritten):

> Reading *The German Ideology* and *Sartor Resartus* together, with the perhaps somewhat perverse pleasure of seeing how they can be brought to share the light that each throws upon the other, we might begin with the proposition that

8. Merton 1985.
9. Boon 1972: vii, 49; 1977: 9, 213.
10. Boon 1982a: 144–47; Geertz 1987: preface.
11. Burke 1962: 643; on coats, see Boon 1982a: 85–87; on cloth across cultures, see Weiner and Schnieder 1989. Lentricchia (1983) also makes a "case for the work of Kenneth Burke as a native alternative to Marxism," according to Simpson (1995: 164). To savor Burke's artful embrace of Marx, consider these insights: "*Identity itself is a 'mystification.'* . . . Unless Marxists are ready to deny Marx by attacking his term 'alienation' itself, they must permit of research into the nature of alienation and into the nature of attempts, adequate and inadequate, to combat alienation" (1957: 265).

mystery arises at that point where different kinds of beings are in communication. In mystery there must be Strangeness; but the estranged must also be
thought of as in some way capable of communion. There is mystery in an animal's eyes at those moments when a man feels that he and the animal understand each other in some inexpressible fashion. (639)

Such a-chronism—as-if reading the concluding cat-winks of *Tristes tropiques*
before the fact—can occur because the world's shifting genres and rhetorical
transformations might—just might—form a closed book.[12]

Affinities and Extremes (Boon 1990) adapted to different ends Burke's foxy
way (he called it "logology") of countering dichotomous dogma. I "deployed"
Burke to reopen Dutch and British colonialist representations of Indonesia; to
reconsider Bali's oft-interpreted ritual-rhetorics; and to rescrutinize Margaret
Mead's controversial *Lebenswerk*—among other panoramic discourses entan-
gling Bali, the East Indies, Europe, India, and the World in each other's flows.
Likely going too far, I even heeded Burke's advice to apply Alexander Pope to
devious interpretive aims, "if one were feeling ironical."[13]

Spiritually obsessed with Burke, I find his irony—nevertheless and therefore—forever elusive. Readers of Burke can but go on beginning again—repli-
cating the experience that Burke (1962: 406) designated "the ambiguity of
starting points . . . either as inaugurating moment . . . or as the point abandoned." For that very reason I cannot shake off a perhaps unwholesome hunch:
Burke's "attitude toward history" suits cultural anthropology *cum* critical theory; it also seems tailored to fit cultural studies. "Humble irony" may offer few
answers; still, without it, the palpable doubt that admits recognition of plural
cultures, histories, *and critiques* would be difficult to imagine and impossible
to enact.

How, then, did and do what Burke deemed "terministic screens" operate? In
a word, they operate ironically. His *Grammar of Motives* plots "antinomies of
definition" of any term, including "motive." "As soon as we encounter, verbally
or thematically, a motivational simplicity," Burke advises, "we must assume as
a matter of course that it contains a diversity" (1962: 101). Motives of "motive"
lead Burke into oscillations with Wagnerian *Leitmotiven*—by way of eros/
thanatos in *Tristan und Isolde*'s "Liebestod," which Burke accurately declares
already "implicit Tannhäuser." (More precisely, *Tannhäuser* became explicitly
Tristanian when Wagner reworked its final version [1861] into his ripened style
of endless transitioning.) Burke (1966: 390) calls *Tristan*'s plot a "'perfect par-
adigm' for a 'myth' so equating Eros and Thanatos that any 'combat' between
them becomes transformed into a species of 'concerted action' . . . (in the idea

---

12. The cat-winks in *Tristes tropiques* appear in the final paragraphs of Lévi-Strauss 1955. On
Carlyle and Lévi-Strauss, see Morris 1979, reviewed in Boon 1982b.
13. Quoted in Boon 1990: 91.

of a musical concerto . . .)." Burke considers mythic "language" harmonic rather than melodic, counter-*chronologique* (my term), and subversive of manifest plot; these insights recall and/or anticipate another (imperfect) Wagnerite: Lévi-Strauss.[14]

Yes, Burke dared to broach highest art—if *höchste* is the apt term for Wagnerian music drama. But he was no mere Mandarin; an earthy chap, Burke addressed popular amusement as well—which he considered "basic" to capitalism (rather like production). Furthermore, like Marcel Mauss—another ironist of sorts, I have wagered—Burke cross-read motives of "the gift," "magic," and "money." Burke even pegs money as the "capitalist psychosis" (a gloss reminiscent of Ruth Benedict's manner of labeling configurations, this time pinned on the right donkey).[15] Like Georg Simmel, and Max Weber's reading of him, Burke lodges money's "profit motive" in renunciatory reinvestment.[16] In short, Burke took *seriocomically,* I'd say, something that Marx mysteriously neglected (as pointed out by several theorists associated with the Frankfurt school).[17] Burke's artfully casual way of talking through his arguments about ultra-conspicuous consumption was all his own. His style here—vintage Burkean "conversationalese"—is worth rereading "dramatistically" (Burke 1968); try delivering it out loud:

> In sum, if you have an unpleasant piece of work to be done, and don't want to do it yourself, in a slave culture you may get this done by force . . . or in a pious culture you may get it done "religiously." . . . But in a capitalist labor market, all that is necessary is for you to say, "Who'll do this for five dollars?"— and men press forward "independently," of their "own free will," under orders from no one, to "voluntarily" enlist for the work. . . . And though the work might "in itself" be drudgery, in time this shortcoming was rectified by the growth of the "amusement industry" to the point where it formed one of the biggest investments in our entire culture. And by going where one chose to be amused, one could enjoy for almost nothing such a wealth of performers, avid to entertain, as was never available to the most jaded of Oriental potentates, however vast his revenues. Under . . . "market law," . . . men could be "substantially" free in willing to obey the necessities of monetary wage and monetary tax (or "price"), wanting to do what they had to do, uniting "I must," "I ought," and "I will." The noun for this union of necessity, duty, and volition was "ambition." Another such was "enterprise." (1962: 93)

Burke thus credits phantasmagoric consumption with important consequences; and he invokes an antecedent man of letters, Henry Adams, who a century

---

14. For his discussion of the harmonic/melodic, see Burke 1970: 258. On Lévi-Strauss and Wagner, see Boon 1972, 1989; Backès-Clément 1970; Nattiez 1993; and Žižek 1993.

15. Burke 1962: 113; pp. 566–68 seem compatible with Mauss (see Boon 1999: chap. 6). On Benedict's controversial characterizations of Dobu and Kwakiutl econo-ritual practices, see Boon 1999: chap. 1.

16. Weber's reading of Simmel is mentioned by Gerth and Mills in Weber 1946: 4.

17. Helpful sources on the Frankfurt school include Jay 1973, and Hohendahl 1982.

ago showed that ritual extravaganzas are key to the "education" of *homo capitalismus:*

> Henry Adams' pairing of Virgin and Dynamo clearly suggests two contrast-
> ing orders of power.... his Education seems to be a rebirth ritual whereby the
> author would finally bring himself to see himself in terms of impersonal
> "force," while renouncing the strongly familial sense of his identity (the
> "eighteenth-century" self) with which his life began. His book traces a kind
> of attenuated self-immolation.... It is at the successive world's fairs and in-
> ternational expositions that Adams gets his "education." Of the Chicago Ex-
> position in 1893, we are told that "education ran riot" there.... And it is
> in the "great gallery of machines" at the Paris Exposition of 1900, that he
> found "his historical neck broken by the sudden irruption of forces totally
> new," forces which he compares and contrasts with the forces of the Christian
> Cross, on the grounds that both kinds, in their way, have been revolutionary.
> (1962: 121)

As was noted in my "Prelude" to *Affinities and Extremes* (1990), Henry Adams (intricate, yet American) carefully crossed such cultures as Ceylon and Tahiti; into his comparative history Adams factored world exhibitions, anticipating Walter Benjamin, among others.[18] Adams, moreover, proved a fitting contemporary of William James, who also felt "called" to witness excess ironically. As Stephen Webb cogently remarks:

> James is attracted to religious excess precisely because it is difficult to con-
> cretize or define, and his blend of fascination and frustration is a key element
> of his success in crafting [*The Varieties of Religious Experience*] ..., a trea-
> tise about excess, that is, about the trope of hyperbole.... James's own rhe-
> torical style articulates the excessive religious experiences that he recounts
> and ... his book tells us about excess itself and magic and the danger of this
> troubling but much neglected figure of speech....
>
>   Exaggeration, or hyperbole, is a species ... of both praxis and language; in
> either arena, excess is that which goes too far for a reason ... ; it is held in
> suspicion. Indeed, the rhetorical tradition, following Aristotle's connection of
> exaggeration with adolescence ... frequently maligned hyperbole as the trope
> that lies.
>
>   ... James was drawn toward the full range and drama of religious ex-
> cess.... James's own rhetoric both responds to and helps delimit the trope of
> extravagance.[19]

It is hardly surprising that William James's attraction to exaggeration (an ironic mode) attracted Kenneth Burke *en suite.* Indeed, Burke (1962: 854) saluted

18. On Henry Adams, see Samuels 1989; Rowe 1976, 1996. Benjamin's relevance to "popular culture" is conveyed in Charney and Swartz 1995: see chap. 5. For one anthropologist's sense of Benjamin, see Taussig 1992, 1993; sensing Benjamin is a multitudinous task of translation (Boon 1982a: chap. 7; 1999: chap. 6).

19. Webb 1995: 27–28. On William James, see H. Feinstein 1984, G. Allen 1967, and G. Cotkin (1990: 115), who, stressing habit and *Hamlet,* clarifies James's deepest dislikes—monism, determinism, and absolutism. On the anthropology of religion framed by William James's figurative sense of polytheism, see Boon 1987. On Thoreau's related idea of extra-vagance, see Boon 1999.

James's insights about Dionysius in a fashion itself Dionysian: "It is super-lucent, super-splendent, super-essential, super-sublime, super everything that can be named." *Via* William James (and Henry), Burke elaborated both revolutionary moments and the "mystic moment" (which might also be called "magical"): "the stage of revelation after which all is felt to be different" (305).

Finally, Burke—again, neither Mandarin (nor anti-Mandarin!) and always earthy—includes among such momentary and momentous *sacra* experiences of politics, literature, and popular culture. For example, anecdotes about elevator riding and Jimmy Durante movies "prelude" a commentary on Proust:

> In *The Past Recovered,* where Proust is writing of the various moments in his life that all had the same quality (being all in effect *one* moment, in deriving from the same principle) he says that these many occasions in essence one were like a peacock's tail spread out. (307)

In resolutely "democratic" fashion Burke's work kept right on transgressing *back toward* its theoretic goal: motives of ironic-dialectic. Yes, Kenneth Burke just couldn't stop back-pedaling (or back-peddling); such was *his* "enterprise," as cited above—his "ambition," his ironic "union of necessity, duty, and volition" over a lifetime of scholarly-capitalist enactment.

"True Irony" and Contingencies: A Fieldwork Incidence

To suggest possible saliences to ethnography of the foregoing synopsis of Burke's ironies (and my debts to them), I now continue back-pedaling (still emulating Burke, through my personal field encounters. Our theme remains what Burke called "true irony": humble irony that does not assume superiority to the enemy (i.e., the rhetorical antagonist) but rather suffers a fellow feeling. One could, I suppose, oppose Burke's trademark irony to postmodern varieties; but even in doing so, humble irony would wind up sensing its kinship with that "other irony" from which it only *seems* to want to dissociate itself. Distinctions of ironies remain ironic. This is not a war I'm fighting.

Consider then, one Balinese life (and work) in which this Burke-reader's work (and life) became entangled over decades of episodic, not to say picaresque, encounter. The "informant" in question, a friend, deserves sheltering with pseudonymity. It is a worthy anthropological usage (one lost on our discipline's detractors), to obfuscate sources; this is for *their* benfit, given that no academic enterprise can control policing powers or legal accountability abroad or at home.) In Balinese custom, where personal names are lacking anyway, witness-protection is a piece of cake.[20] Let us call the hero of our case study "I Gde" (loosely "Mr. Big," a stock status-title that slightly distinguishes so many Balinese "natives" that nobody much gains distinction).

20. On naming, titles, etc. in Bali, see Geertz 1973: chap. 14.

I Gde, a truly fine fellow, figured vitally in several studies I consecrated in whole or in part to his island. Instantly profiled, he is an eldest son in a subline of an ancestor group of enormous consequence in the history of western Bali. He was (and is) about my age, had recently married (as had I, when we first met in 1972), but was not yet (then) a parent (as I already was). His wife, unlike mine, is his *mindon*—second patriparallel cousin (i.e., these spouses are the grandchildren of brothers). His favorite uncle was the charismatic force behind the fragile coherence of a fractious kin group and marriage-alliance network. I Gde's sense of humor and mine matched (unless he fooled me into feeling so). Reminiscence still finds me laughing at jokes he could crack (in Indonesian and Balinese) as we whiled away night-long vigils at temple ceremonies with undercurrent tensions and complications that I "ethnographed." In 1972, preparing to depart after a year's stay, I bequeathed to I Gde a motorbike, as a token of gratitude for all he had given. So culturally entangled are Balinese rivalries that my meant-to-be-generous gesture inadvertently incurred the severe displeasure of his wife's sister-in-law (translation here is particularly difficult, and necessarily stilted). This sensitive woman had hoped, I later learned, that one of I Gde's cousins (her son: a likable guy too, but younger, and neither as funny nor in certain respects as sharp) would be so favored. No amount of cash could compensate her for this disappointment: she took it all as something like a snub.

In 1982, I was back in Bali; I Gde helped catch me up on island-wide political-*cum*-kinship *événements* and/or *habitus*. Attentive to aftermaths of subtle status movements that were the subject of my earlier research, he had become an *informal* observer of ethnohistory as it happened. *Formally,* on the other hand, I Gde had secured coveted employment with a travel bureau—a fact known to me from letters. That knowledge had prompted my return-gift *(oleh):* the latest English-Indonesian dictionary in a strongly bound American edition, highly preferable to flimsy local reproductions. Alas, my well-intentioned *cadeau*—accepted by I Gde with glassy-eyed grace—flopped. Because of his recent reassignment by the firm's boss, intent on tapping into more animated tourist sectors, I Gde was professionally now drilling (and exclusively) Indonesian-Italian.

Meanwhile, his family had expanded by two children (the same total as mine), beautiful as only Balinese can be (I intend no invidious comparison with our—my wife's and my—also, but differently, attractive offspring). That cousin of I Gde who had previously lost out (his mother felt) on the motor bike had subsequently (for unconnected reasons) bailed out of Bali to Australia. Indeed he had married there—a fact desperately regretted by his parents, I was led to surmise.

By 1992, when I Gde and I met again, his sister-in-law (the aforementioned cousin's mother: she who had been disgruntled twenty years before) had just "left the world" *(meninggal dunia)*. The two of us—I Gde and I—remained close enough in spirit (as I interpreted these things) for him to recommend not revisiting her houseyard. The apparent reasons were complex. Her mourning husband (a warm and compassionate man whose nostalgia rivals my own) had a history of depression. I Gde seemed to be implying—with subtle discretion and agile indirection (even in Indonesian, which is performatively more abrupt than Balinese)—that my arrival might provoke despair, triggered by the widower's memories of twenty-long-years-ago, when their children were young, our infant daughter had been their plaything, and conditions in Bali were far happier than now. *Tempo dulu* ("Ou sont les neiges d'antan?"), truly. I, of course, abided by I Gde's implicit and very much appreciated counsel.

As for I Gde himself, much also had changed. Risen in the ranks of his tourist business, he proudly (and, I suspect, not without irony, perhaps "humble irony") apprised me that he had earlier been awarded by Japan Airlines a trip via Tokyo to Alaska. I must confess that his exciting news precipitated between us what I can only call a Twainian moment:

"Alaska?" said I, pointing.
"Alaska, " said he.[21]

I Gde fied in my utterly blank look (less graceful than his glassy-eyed stare of yore) by explaining that his professional *spécialité* had again switched (causing me earnestly to hope he hadn't discarded that previous dictionary-gift). Having bid *arrivederci* to globe-trotting Romans, he was now lubricating tour groups being busily shunted to Bali from Juneau.

I report this blatantly global fact with some trepidation. Many modernist and/or postmodernist friends (with whom I sometimes sympathize and even feel related to) could hardly resist spotlighting and trumpeting this ultra-transnational flow: Bali-Juneau (what a hoot!). But before readers (including this author as his own reader) titter or sigh—or smirk or rue—it may be worth wondering what further prospects of and for Burke's true-and-humble irony—exist at this juncture of my fieldwork example. One slim possibility glistens, as I understand these intricate affairs.

The incongruities of I Gde's life are really no more ludicrous than those of mine—details of which readers deserve to be spared—nor those of my father, whose life bridged cotton farm to national insurance agency; nor his father before him: ex-cotton farmer (*his* enterprise fell victim to boll weevils) demoted to stockings-peddler, killed crossing a street in the town where indigence had forced him to relocate . . . and so on. And, as elsewhere confessed (Boon 1999:

chap. 13), our distaff sides (I Gde's and mine), like those of so many, are her-stories of repeated displacements, inequality, and gender-based prejudices.

Burkean irony might just detect in such circumstances an as-if kinship (*wahl-verwandshaft*—Kenneth Burke, I should note, often commented on Goethe).[22] Yes Burke (practitioner of the sororate, remember) might well have found figuratively fraternal (such are rhetoric's "effects") two unlikely "Balinists" (among so many): good old I Gde and good old I—one "foreigner" engaged on Bali academically, one "native" engaged on Bali *parawisata*ly (Indonesian for tourism).[23]

In positing this conceivable resemblance "through a difference" I seek to provoke no titter (or tsk-tsking) about nonstop inauthenticity or antiauthority. What's more, I intend to tender no proclamation or insinuation (postmodernist, modernist, or pre-them) of triumph or defeat. Indeed, I desire to promote no critical edge or theoretic fixity of any kind. Instead, I would acknowledge in-terlinking recognitions of overlapping disparities—not identical, not equal, but still *comparable* (susceptible of comparison). *Lui:* A Balinese tourbroker arisen from semitraditional courtliness; *Moi:* an American scholar arisen from boll-weevil rurality—both occasionally worldly and, after a fashion or two, cosmopolitan (kind of); but for all that, both local (kind of) as well. Our tran-sitory bonds—like anything politically fence-leaping—were enmeshed in dis-ciplines of research and commodification (requiring passports, visas, tickets, permits, licensing, and worse). But the poetics and rhetorics of seriocomic encounter do not reduce to official policies of border-patrolling or surrepti-tious palm-greasing. Nor have any attributes of power-knowledge ostensibly separating "I Gde and I" ever worked only in one direction. It may be through mutual "incongruities" (a favorite term of Burke's) that irony—a two-way street—truly (humbly) obtains, and cross-culturally as well.

Irony unter Alles

The serious sport of Kenneth Burke's *Lebenswerk*—together with such ethno-graphic encounters as here evoked—reinforces my anthropological skepticism regarding tendencies to claim postmodern critique (which I, obviously, value) is more ironic (or perhaps parodic) than yesterday's. It is not just Burke and I Gde, but strands of irony in Franz Boas, James Frazer, Friedrich Schlegel, Jean Paul (to name four of hundreds)—along with long-term Menippean sat-ire and pervasive carnivalizings enacted in and as polyglot cultures through

22. On "elective affinities" in Goethe, Weber, and elsewhere, see Boon 1990: x; a place to begin again on this endless topic is S. Corngold's translation of Benjamin's essay on Goethe's *Wahlver-wandshaften* in M. Bullock and M. Jennings's edition of his collected works (Benjamin 1996).

23. For more on this episode, including plays of commodity life across generations on both the Balinese and the American side of this encounter, see Boon 1999: chaps. 13, 4.

time (heteroglossic chronotopes!)—that sustain my interdisciplinary doubts (ironic ones) about higher/lower degrees of irony.[24] Indeed, to congratulate oneself—or the -isms one favors, or the era one inhabits or straddles, or the friends one makes—for exceeding another's irony seems a singularly unironic thing to do. That flaw afflicts some "postmodern irony," I suspect . . . *Oops!* (By "Oops!" I mean to imply that I just committed against "postmodern irony" what I was accusing it of: assuming that one's "own irony" [in this case mine] was more ironic [about irony] than "that other irony" was. By that "Oops!" I acknowledge, in Burkean fashion, that I am thus guilty of my accusation: i.e., kin with "the enemy," rather than its superior [see Boon 1990: xiv–xv].)

And after all, irony doesn't exactly grow, does it? Nor can discourse quite "progress" into irony—and out of belief, credulity, sincerity, naïveté, or even positivism. Irony, to be sure, is routinely repressed in "official" regimentation (rhetorics of *énoncé*); yet it remains intrinsically implicit even in those institutional sectors and frames of discourse designed to suppress ambiguity: courts of law, disciplinary dogma, ideologies of identity. For, irony obtains from human negativities and multiplicities. Such seems to be the case "in Bali, at least," plus everywhere "else," I suspect. Hence, the world's overlapping and interleaved cultures (variously construed) become, as Burke might have phrased it, "like footnotes and marginalia," each to each. Whence a final enigmatic certainty: any assumed *absence* of irony is (was) also ironic. Call it all dynamically *paradoxical*—which is how cultures *are,* relative to one another.[25] "I" like to think that "I Gde" would concur—not to mention good old "Kenneth Burke" (1897–1993).

References

Ackerman, Robert. 1987. *J. G. Frazer: His Life and Work.* New York: Cambridge University Press.
Allen, Gay Wilson. 1967. *William James.* New York: Viking Press.
Babcock, Barbara. 1978. *The Reversible World: Essays in Symbolic Inversion.* Ithaca: Cornell University Press.
Backès-Clément, C. 1970. *Lévi-Strauss.* Paris: Seghers.

24. On Boas and irony, see Krupat 1990. On Frazer as a (romantic) ironist, see sources cited in Boon 1982a: chap. 1; see also Manganaro 1990, Ackerman 1987, and especially Fraser 1990. On Schlegel's *Lucinda,* see Hohendahl 1988; I thank Jay Geller for inspiration in this matter. Menippean Satire and cross-cultural research is discussed in Boon 1982a: 264, 278–79; 1990: 67–68, 88–91. On carnivalizing, see Babcock 1978, Bruner 1984, and abundant literature on Bakhtin—for example, Holquist 1990 and Emerson 1996.

25. How can one list sources on irony other than ironically? A few are Kierkegaard 1989, Booth 1974, De Man 1979, Chai 1987 (on irony and comedy), Hutcheson 1994 . . . : it's hopeless. For an ironic shaking-off of the fashionable attitude of irony, see Cavell 1988: 195ff. On "cultures" as paradoxical rather than paradigmatic, see Boon 1973.

Benjamin, Walter. 1996. *Selected Writings*. Vol. 1, *1913–1926*. Ed. Marcus Bullock and Michael W. Jennings. Cambridge: Harvard University Press.

Boon, James A. 1972. *From Symbolism to Structuralism: Lévi-Strauss in a Literary Tradition*. New York: Harper and Row.

———. 1973. Further Operations of "Culture": A Synthesis of and for Debate. In *The Idea of Culture in the Social Sciences*, ed. Louis Schneider and Charles M. Bonjean, 221–52. New York: Cambridge University Press.

———. 1977. *The Anthropological Romance of Bali, 1597–1972: Dynamic Perspectives in Marriage and Caste, Politics and Religion*. New York: Cambridge University Press.

———. 1982a. *Other Tribes, Other Scribes: Symbolic Anthropology in the Comparative Study of Cultures, Histories, Religions, and Texts*. New York: Cambridge University Press.

———. 1982b. Review of W. Morris (1979). *Novel* 15(3): 260–62.

———. 1987a. Anthropology, Ethnology, and Religion. In *Encyclopedia of Religion*, ed. Mircea Eliade, 1: 308–16. New York: Macmillan.

———. 1988. Among the Golden Boughs. Review of Ackerman (1987). *New York Times, Sunday Book Review*. 6 March 1988, pp. 16–17.

———. 1989 Lévi-Strauss, Wagner, Romanticism: A Reading Back. In *Romantic Motives: Essays on Anthropological Sensitivity*, ed. George W. Stocking, 124–68. Madison: University of Wisconsin Press.

———. 1990. *Affinities and Extremes: Crisscrossing the Bittersweet Ethnology of East Indies History, Hindu-Balinese Culture, and Indo-European Allure*. Chicago: University of Chicago Press.

———. 1998. Accenting Hybridity: Postcolonial Cultural Theory, a Boasian Anthropologist, and I. In *Culture and the Problems of the Disciplines*, ed. John Carlos Rowe, 141–69. New York: Columbia University Press.

———. 1999. *Verging on Extra-Vagance: Anthropology, History, Religion, Literature, Arts . . . Showbiz*. Princeton: Princeton University Press.

Booth, Wayne C. 1974. *A Rhetoric of Irony*. Chicago: University of Chicago Press.

Bruner, Edward, ed. 1984. *Text, Play and Story: The Construction and Reconstruction of Self and Society*. Prospect Heights: Waveland Press.

Burke, Kenneth. 1937. *Attitudes toward History*. New York: The New Republic.

———. [1941] 1957. *The Philosophy of Literary Form: Studies in Symbolic Action*. New York: Vintage Books.

———. 1962. *A Grammar of Motives* [1945] and *A Rhetoric of Motives* [1950]. Cleveland: Meridian Books.

———. 1966. *Language as Symbolic Action*. Berkeley: University of California Press.

———. 1968. Interaction: Dramatism. *International Encyclopedia of the Social Sciences*, 7: 445–52. New York: Macmillan.

———. 1970. *Rhetoric of Religion*. Berkeley: University of California Press.

———. 1984. *Attitudes Toward History*. 3d ed. Berkeley: University of California Press.

Cavell, Stanley. 1988. *Themes Out of School: Effects and Causes*. Chicago: University of Chicago Press.

———. 1990. *Conditions Handsome and Unhandsome: The Constitutions of Emersonian Perfectionism*. Chicago: University of Chicago Press.

———. 1994. *In Quest of the Ordinary: Lines of Skepticism and Romanticism*. Chicago: University of Chicago Press.

Chai, Leon. 1987. *The Romantic Foundations of the American Renaissance.* Ithaca: Cornell University Press.

Charney, Leo and Vanessa Schwartz, eds. 1995. *Cinema and the Invention of Modern Life.* Berkeley: University of California Press.

Cotkin, George. 1990. *William James: Public Philosopher.* Baltimore: Johns Hopkins University Press.

De Man, Paul. 1979. *Allegories of Reading: Figural Language in Rousseau, Nietzsche, Rilke, and Proust.* New Haven: Yale University Press.

Donoghue, Denis. 1987. *Reading America: Essays on American Literature.* New York: Knopf.

Emerson, Caryl. 1996. *Bakhtin's First One Hundred Years.* Princeton: Princeton University Press.

Feinstein, Howard M. 1984. *Becoming William James.* Ithaca: Cornell University Press.

Fernandez, James, ed. 1991. *Beyond Metaphor: The Theory of Tropes in Anthropology.* Stanford: Stanford University Press.

Fraser, Robert. 1990. *The Making of "The Golden Bough": The Origins and Growth of an Argument.* New York: St. Martin's Press.

Geertz, Clifford. 1973. *The Interpretation of Cultures.* New York: Basic Books.

———. 1987 *Works and Lives: The Anthropologist as Author.* Stanford: Stanford University Press.

Hohendahl, Peter Uwe. 1982. *The Institution of Criticism.* Ithaca: Cornell University Press.

———, ed. 1988. *A History of German Literary Criticism.* Lincoln: University of Nebraska Press.

Holquist, Michael. 1990. *Dialogism: Bakhtin and his World.* New York: Routledge.

Hutcheon, Linda. 1994. *Irony's Edge: The Theory and Politics of Irony.* New York: Routledge.

Jay, Martin. 1973. *The Dialectical Imagination: A History of the Frankfurt School and the Institute of Social Research, 1923–1950.* Boston: Little Brown.

Kierkegaard, Søren. 1989. *The Concept of Irony.* Trans. Howard V. Hong and Edna H. Hong. Princeton: Princeton University Press.

Krupat, Arnold. 1979. *Woodsmen, or, Thoreau and the Indians.* New York: The Letter Press.

———. 1990. Irony in Anthropology: The Work of Franz Boas. In *Modernist Anthropology: From Fieldwork to Text,* ed. Marc Manganaro, 133–45. Princeton: Princeton University Press.

Lentricchia, Frank. 1883. *Criticism and Social Change.* Chicago: University of Chicago Press.

Lévi-Strauss, Claude. 1955. *Tristes tropiques.* Paris: Plon.

Lorrigio, Francesco. 1990. Anthropology, Literary Theory, and the Traditions of Modernism. In *Modernist Anthropology: From Fieldwork to Text,* ed. Marc Manganaro, 215–42. Princeton: Princeton University Press.

Manganaro, Marc, ed. 1990. *Modernist Anthropology: From Fieldwork to Text.* Princeton: Princeton University Press.

Mann, Thomas. [1912] 1970. *Death in Venice.* Trans. Kenneth Burke (1924). New York: Random House.

Merton, Robert K. 1985. *On the Shoulders of Giants: A Shandean Postscript.* 2d ed. New York: Harcourt Brace Jovanovich.

Morris, Wesley. 1979. *Friday's Footprint: Structuralism and the Articulated Text.* Ohio State University Press.

Nattiez, Jean-Jacques. 1990. *Music and Discourse: Toward a Semiology of Music.* Trans. Carolyn Abbate. Princeton: Princeton University Press.

O'Farrell, Clare. 1989. *Foucault: Historian or Philosopher?* New York: St. Martin's Press.

Peacock, James L. 1975. *Consciousness and Change.* New York: John Wiley.

Roth, Michael S. 1992. Foucault on Discourse and History: A Style of Delegitimation. In *The Philosophy of Discourse: The Rhetorical Turn in Twentieth-Century Thought.* 2 vols., ed. Chip Sills and George H. Jensen, 2: 102–21. Portsmouth: Heinemann.

Rowe, John Carlos. 1976. *Henry James and Henry Adams.* Ithaca: Cornell University Press.

Rowe, John Carlos, ed. 1996. *New Essays on the Education of Henry Adams.* New York: Cambridge University Press.

Rueckert, William H. 1982. *Kenneth Burke and the Drama of Human Relations.* Berkeley: University of California Press.

Safranski, Rudiger. 1991. *Schopenhauer and the Wild Years of Philosophy.* Trans. E. Osers. Cambridge: Harvard University Press.

Samuels, Ernest. 1989. *Henry Adams.* Cambridge: Harvard University Press.

Sills, Chip, and George H. Jensen, ed. 1992. *The Philosophy of Discourse: The Rhetorical Turn in Twentieth-Century Thought.* 2 vols. Portsmouth: Heinemann.

Simpson, David. 1995. *The Academic Postmodern and the Rule of Literature: A Report on Half-Knowledge.* Chicago: University of Chicago Press.

Taussig, Michael. 1992. *The Nervous System.* New York: Routledge.

———. 1993a. *Mimesis and Alterity: A Particular History of the Senses.* New York: Routledge.

Webb, Stephen. 1995. The Rhetoric of and about Excess in William James's *The Varieties of Religious Experience. Religion and Literature* 27(2): 27–45.

Weber, Max. 1946. *From Max Weber.* Ed. H. H. Gerth and C. Wright Mills. New York: Oxford.

Weiner, Annette B., and Jane Schneider, eds. 1989. *Cloth and Human Experience.* Washington: Smithsonian Institution Press.

Žižek, Slavoj. 1993. *Tarrying with the Negative: Kant, Hegel, and the Critique of Ideology.* Durham: Duke University Press.

Chapter Six

Arnold Krupat —

An Apollonian Response

> O God, O Venus, O Mercury, patron of thieves,
> Lend me a little tobacco-shop,
>   or install me in any profession
> Save this damn'd profession of writing,
>   where one needs one's brains all the time.
>   Ezra Pound

Born only to die. Maturing but to decay. In one end and out the other. Some days even the velcro won't hold. Been down so long it looks like up to me. Irony is here and there, everywhere; then and now, always and forever, so let's all join in singing the "contingency blues" (Jay 1997). Not.

It's with some trepidation that I play straight man Apollo to the throng of Bacchites, "jewgreek"—in the term of yet another James (Joyce)—to the higher jesuitical Daedalians.[1] But I'll try to tell my story. In the very useful double sense of James Clifford, the story will be *partial;* but partisanship and incompleteness are in the nature of narrative. Nonetheless, I want the story to be persuasive and not merely as fiction; that's in the nature of an ongoing commitment to knowledge, philosophy, truth: as we shall see.

• • •

Socrates's distinctive persona, at least as Plato represented it, was that of the *eiron,* one who, when doing things with words, claimed to know less than he actually did. Most immediately, the verbal *eironeia* of the Socratic *eiron* sought to undo the unwarranted assurance of the *alazon,* one who—as the *eiron* neatly showed—when pressed to do things with words turned out to know less than

---

1. The references are to Joyce's *Ulysses* ([1922] 1992) and *A Portrait of the Artist as a Young Man* ([1916] 1982). The protagonist of the latter is young Stephen Daedalus, student at Clongowes Woods College, a Jesuit institution. Stephen's last name references Icarus's father, prototypical artificer or artist. Classical Stephen appears importantly in *Ulysses* as well, in relation to Leopold Bloom, a Jew.

he claimed to: Socrates 10, Thirsites 0. The victory of the Socratic *eiron* was not, however, merely tactical or strategic, the outsmarting of a clumsier antagonist; rather, it was philosophical, a triumph conceived as a gain for knowledge. As I understand it, Socrates' particular innovation was to deploy rhetoric in the service of truth.

Formerly, this is to say, rhetoric, that whole bag of verbal tricks—antanaclasis, paralipsis, syllepsis, zeugma, and more familiar figurations including metaphor, metonymy, synecdoche, or, indeed, irony itself—said to have been invented in the fifth century B.C.E. by Corax and Tisias in Sicily, had been devoted to the art of persuasion regardless of truth (Ducrot and Todorov 1979: 73–75). Prior to Socrates, philosophy—a discourse not merely concerned to persuade but to arrive at truth—could only be threatened by rhetoric. Socratic irony as a strategy in the interest of truth has a long consequent history, although as so many of the essays in this volume note, today that strategy as more than strategic is an embattled or, as some would say, a thoroughly misguided strategy: if it's a matter of rhetoric *or* truth, well, most of us can say what rhetoric is.

Socratic or philosophical irony finds its literary form in the genre called satire, a genre that includes among its postclassical masterpieces Erasmus' "Praise of Folly" ([1509] 1994), Voltaire's *Candide* ([1759] 1990), Jonathan Swift's "Modest Proposal" ([1729] 1995), Mark Twain's "War Prayer" ([1905/1923] 1984), George Orwell's *Animal Farm* (1946), and, perhaps most recently, Alan Sokal's *Social Text* essay, "Transgressing the Boundaries: Toward a Transformative Hermeneutics of Quantum Gravity" (1996). "Satire," as Northrop Frye—an author largely unattended to by the essays in this volume—stated some forty years ago, "demands at least a token fantasy, a content which the reader recognizes as grotesque, and"—consistent with the story I am telling—"at least an implicit moral standard" (Frye 1957: 224).[2] Texts of this genre

2. Hereafter abbreviated AC. I follow Frye, here, rather than White (1973). Frye (1957: 223) explicitly states that "whenever a reader is not sure what the author's attitude is or what his own is supposed to be we have irony with relatively little satire," satire requiring, as I have quoted Frye, "at least an implicit moral standard." That might be called the modernist or, indeed, Apollonian view. White's (1973: 10) more nearly postmodern, or Dionysian, view is that "Satire views the hopes, possibilities, and truths of human existence revealed in Romance, Comedy, and Tragedy respectively. . . . Ironically, in the atmosphere generated by the apprehension of the ultimate inadequacy of consciousness to live in the world happily or to comprehend it fully."

But I think White is unnecessarily ironic, engaging, here, in a Foucauldian excess that he criticizes elsewhere (1987). I refer to a phrase like "the apprehension of the *ultimate* inadequacy of consciousness to live in the world happily or to comprehend it fully" (my emphasis). As Frye outlines it in relation to Menippean satire and to Voltaire's famous conclusion to *Candide* ("That's all very well, but we must cultivate our garden"), one important strand of satire is the "position" that practice is to be preferred to theory (1957: 230–31), and thus that "the ultimate inadequacy of consciousness" need not be the reference point for happiness or comprehension.

privileged a rationality thought to be capable of correcting error, even of arriving at universal, human truths. Of course, we recognize, now, that the truths supposed to be universally human were not that at all, but, rather, quite culturally and temporally specific Western, male, Christian partialities—"Eurocentric hegemony *posing* as universalism," as K. Anthony Appiah has written (in Lazarus, et. al. 1995: 78). Yet Appiah, as we shall see further, and others, acknowledge this in the interest of recuperating a genuine universalism and humanism consistent with what I and others prefer to call cosmopolitanism.[3] I mention this because the values of such a "radicalized" new humanism, universalism, and cosmopolitanism seem of considerable interest to some of the authors of these essays. I will return to this matter at the end of my remarks.

But let me bring the story I have been telling so partially up to date in just a bit more detail (most of it is, to be sure, quite well known). It is the rhetorician's, rather than the philosopher's, irony that animates work by Macchiavelli, and, later—and more germane to our purposes—by Friedrich Nietszche. Participating fully in what has been referred to as the epistemological crisis of the late nineteenth-century, Nietszche does not so much seek to persuade regardless of the truth, as to persuade that truth itself is a mask for the rhetorician's will, a radically ironic stance. Nietszche's tone and manner neither derive from nor are they productive of that sort of humility Fernandez properly sees in Erasmus (or Clifford Geertz or Albert Hirschman) or that Boon finds in Kenneth Burke (or Flaubert or Thomas Mann or William James).

After Nietszche comes the work of poststructuralist, postmodernist, or neopragmatic ironic anti-philosophers like Michel Foucault, Jacques Derrida, and Richard Rorty. Their rhetorical success has been such that any who wish to offer their own discourse—be it philosophical, literary, historical, or social scientific—as more than a "persuasive fiction" has an uphill battle to fight. Thus histories, according to Paul Veyne, are best thought of as "true novels" (quoted in Geertz 1990: 321), or, as Greg Dening (1988: 2) has put it, "the texted past for which we have a cultural poetic." Ethnographies are also texts, as George Marcus and Dick Cushman (1982) reminded us some time ago, and inasmuch as they tend to be narrative texts—explicitly or implicitly they tell a story— what Hayden White (1973) brilliantly demonstrated for histories would hold for ethnographies as well: that it was their "emplotment" rather than their data or "facts" which carried their "explanatory affect," and so their "truth-effect."

Although Thomas Kuhn had made us aware, in the early 1960s, "of the role of human communities in deciding just what ideas about nature shall count as

3. See, for example, Lazarus, et. al. 1995; Nussbaum 1995; Robbins 1995; Siebers 1993; Appiah 1992, and Said 1993. See also Rabinow 1986 and Krupat 1989, chap. 5: "Local, National, Cosmopolitan Literature"; 1996, chap. 5: "A Nice Jewish Boy Among the Indians."

scientific knowledge" (quoted in Hollinger 1995: 10), it was Michel Foucault's influence, only a little later, that spread the news most powerfully that even the truths of science had first to fall *dans le vrai*—to meet, as I would gloss this, prevailing discursive conditions for truthfulness—before their truth claims could be evaluated. Thus, for example, when Galileo requested the Church fathers to look for themselves through his telescope to see whether there were or were not sunspots, what could they do but refuse? Surely the doubtful evidence of one's poor senses could not outweigh the accumulated authority of generations of learned men! What Galileo told his examiners he had seen was, of course, true; but its truth, at that moment in time, could not be accepted as truth because it did not fall *dans le vrai*. For the human community authorized to judge, Galileo's device could have no authority.

How ironic!, we might say. But we would say that only because current usage has extended the term "irony" in ordinary speech to refer to any disparity between a reality and an appearance, an appearance and a reality: Here I am with my umbrella and the sun has kept on shining all through the day! How ironic! Such extensions of the term are sure to increase and multiply in common parlance, and there is no reason to bemoan that fact. Nonetheless, if the term irony in professional discourse—ethnographic writing, literary analysis, and the like—is still to have some use, I think it is important that it be somewhat more precisely delimited.

Of a different turn of mind, it would seem, Phyllis Chock begins her paper by writing that, "Irony is a pervasive condition of social life," which is to say— is it not?—that irony is a pervasive condition of life itself. Diane Losche quotes D. K. Muecke, who says exactly that. According to Muecke, "we may find nothing on earth and quite certainly nothing in heaven that is not ironic." I would be very interested in seeing the field notes that allowed Muecke to conclude "quite certainly" that everything is ironic even in heaven. But once everything is ironic, then nothing in particular is ironic (cf., if everything is explained by culture then "culture" explains nothing much) and we have lost a historically useful concept term.

State institutions have the authority to determine what sorts of speech fall within *le vrai,* and those who serve such institutions enforce the boundaries of *vraisembla*bility by taking seriously certain utterances while ignoring or misunderstanding others. This makes it difficult, as Phyllis Chock shows, for a Congressional witness who finds it necessary to break with or step outside the bounds of the Congressional *vrai* to get his alternative or countertruth recognized as potentially a truth at all. But although, in the examples Chock provides, members of Congress and certain witnesses sometimes claim to know less than they do, acting in the manner of the *eiron,* I fail to see why any and all deviations on the part of a witness from the expectations of the Congresspersons are to be taken as *ironic*. We know pretty well, that is, the moral or political "standard" upheld by each.

The lame jokes Senators and Representatives exchange may be seen as instances of the "phatic" function of language in Malinowski's sense, as cited by Roman Jakobson (1960: 355): a "set for CONTACT," a "profuse exchange of ritualized formulas . . . entire dialogues with the mere purport of prolonging communication." Some witnesses may offer slightly variant witticisms for their own purposes, but, again, where is the irony?

Granting that disparate visions exist—"visions of disparity," in the phrase Chock takes from Alan Wilde—it is only in the slackened, ordinary use of the term that these could be called ironic. Although the Church briefly prevailed over Galileo and his telescope, eventually the disparity was resolved in Galileo's favor. In much the same way, confronted with the disparity between the vision of the MOVE witness and that of the Congresspersons, it does not seem to me that we are caught impossibly between them—is the glass half empty or half full? what is the author's attitude or our own to be?—but, rather, called upon to choose between them. Congress, of course, does not really have such a choice. For a member of Congress to choose the vision of MOVE would be to expand the boundaries of veridical discourse so far that one would likely be re-MOVEd from Congress in the next election.

Mr. Fierro's statement that illegal immigrants are good for the United States is very much the kind of reversal that signifies irony, for it specifically seeks to subvert the premises of the members of Congress in the interest—let us grant Mr. Fierro the benefit of any possible doubts—of a truth superior to theirs. A similar irony would be at work were I to respond to the question, How can capitalism solve the problem of poverty? by saying that it can't, because poverty is what capitalism by its very nature creates. But neither of these particular ironies, Mr. Fierro's or mine, has any chance of persuading the Congress of its truth, because the Congress requires for its continued existence that such "truths" be ruled outside *le vrai*. Unfortunately, it may not be possible to do more than be *phatic* here.

Diane Losche's sense of having discovered irony in another place bases itself upon the extrapolation of a linguistic observation to a cultural interpretation. Linguistically, Losche locates irony in the fact that words are potentially ambiguous and/or polysemic. Metaphorically, "words can be, and often are, like a skin or surface," hiding an interior.

Losche goes on to say that the Abelam

> masculine cult circulates around one word, which can signify many particular pieces of information but always refers to one *central* concept—*maira*—which I would translate, at its simplest, most powerful and embracing, as "secret." (Emphasis added.)

Maira, Losche continues,

> can be used as a noun or an adjective and it always *encapsulates* the notion
> that beneath the surface there is another reality that may or may not become
> known. (My emphasis.)

But Losche does not only rely on metaphors of surface/subsurface (depth, "layers"), for she also introduces—as though they were the same thing—metaphors of circumference/center (circulation, encapsulation). "Thus from one
point of view a *maira* is a taboo . . . ," and a taboo is the "membrane dividing
two spaces." Later, Losche speaks of what may be "buried skillfully in the heart
of the structure," and also says that "at its center, the *maira* has no secret." This,
she, "the outsider, the audience in this theater, [calls] tragic irony."

The only irony I can see is an uncertainty as to whether one is dealing, metaphorically, with an onion ("the play of Samukundi language . . . reaches its
peak of articulation in this onion-like structuring of space and time . . .") or an
artichoke ("the spatial structure of the *korombo* is a series of nested secrets")—
like the painted wooden eggs which open to reveal a smaller egg nested within,
which opens to reveal . . . until we reach the smallest egg at the center. The
irony, not necessarily tragic, is that—apparently—neither the Abelam nor the
anthropologist knows whether she or he is dealing with onions or artichokes.

Then there is Felicité and her parrot. The ending of Flaubert's story seems to
me to fall within Frye's (1957) "fourth phase" of irony, a tragic irony "in which
irony is at a minimum" and "the sense of gentle and dignified pathos, often
symbolized by music" predominates (236).[4] Felicité, so ironically named, dies
deluded. She is granted no particular insight as recompense for her pain. In light
of James Boon's citation of Burke's recollection of Flaubert's observation—
"Madame Bovary, c'est moi"—perhaps we may read Flaubert's own sense,
quoted by Losche, that "This is not at all ironical [but] very serious and very
sad," not so much as a refutation of the story's irony but as a description of
its ironical *type,* in Frye's terms, "the 'all too human,' as distinct from the
heroic" (237).

Michael Herzfeld's witty account of Greek self- and social-construction

---

4. This is very different from the earlier ironies that saturate *Madame Bovary* and which I will
represent metonymically in a couple of sentences from the narrator's description of Emma Bovary's suitor, Rodolphe, at the Agricultural Fair: ". . . his broad-striped trousers disclosed at the
ankle nankeen boots with patent leather gaiters. These were so polished that they reflected the
grass. He trampled on horse's dung" (Flaubert [1857] 1965: 99). Born only to die, when we put on
those polished gaiters we're sure to step in shit. Flaubert's attitude here seems close to what Frye
(1957: 230) calls the sort of "cynicism" which is neither philosophical nor anti-philosophical, but
an expression of the hypothetical form of art. Satire on ideas is only the special kind of art that de-
fends its own creative detachment (231). This "cynicism," which even at the time of writing *Madame Bovary,* was tempered by Flaubert's awareness that "Madame Bovary, c'est moi," has, by the
end of his life, softened considerably.

reveals a great number of paradoxical beliefs that involve a range of ironies. I will go out on the limb of paraphrase here: Herzfeld's paper tells us that Greeks deny the possibility in general of knowing another's thoughts while confidently attributing motives in specific cases. They believe that another's language, higher or lower, like or unlike their own, can yet be shown up as inferior to their own. Greeks believe that all women except for those of a man's own family are less than admirable persons, and that one can always find a way safely and cannily to abjure one's oaths or gossip (I'm thinking of the bean-eating remark). Greeks live a highly bureaucratized life while thoroughly distrusting authority. Greeks attribute to the Turks and more recently the West, the cause of all their national problems and failings.[5]

These are indeed ironies—ironies, as it seems to me, once more, of the philosophic, satiric, or stable kind. Operative, here, in social performance or discourse, they function to affirm culturally agreed upon truth—more or less. Many Greeks, I take it, believe and behave these ways, and even if they don't, all Greeks—along with sophisticated, linguistically competent ethnographers like Herzfeld—understand what is going on when it comes to matters like these. So do we, I suppose, when we note that, He who hesitates is lost! while affirming as well, Look before you leap! Things get more complicated when we get to Cavafy's text—but because I do not read Greek and know Cavafy but little, I will defer to the interpretation by Jusdanis and Herzfeld.

James Fernandez's paper uses the ironies of the Development Project and some of the discourse surrounding it, to raise the important question of whether some "stability" may yet be found in our contemporary "culture of irony"— very much what James Boon is thinking about as he composes and meditates upon what may turn in to "nonstop" glosses on Kenneth Burke. Boon says, near the end of his paper, that Burke's theoretical goal—arguably Boon's as well— is to seek the motives of "ironic-dialectic." This I take as analogous to what I have called Socratic or philosophical or (with Frye) satiric irony, and what Fernandez, taking the phrase from Wayne Booth, as we have noted, calls "stable irony." (What Fernandez calls complicitous irony, if I may transpose his phrase, bears resemblance to what I have referred to as rhetorical irony.)[6]

In "the context of the discussion of development," Fernandez suggests, irony

5. These attributions, I think, may be considered as "weapons of the weak," in the phrase from James Scott that Chock also cites. Somewhat different but worth consideration is Vaclav Havel's (1985) exposition of "the power of the powerless."

6. And as well to what Linda Hutcheon calls "complicitous critique." Hutcheon describes this *ironic* postmodern strategy as "a deliberate refusal to resolve contradictions" (1988: x), a refusal that makes postmodernism "politically ambivalent, doubly encoded as both complicity and critique" (1989: 168). For those committed to a more philosophical irony, the problem is determining the degree of complicity and the degree of critique in any postmodern ironic performance—a task Hutcheon and most postmodernists would not, of course, countenance.

might be stabilized "by resting on an overriding commitment to [the alleviation of] poverty, sickness and hunger in the world." This leads him to raise
the possibility, via Erasmus—and also via the quotation from the early Clifford Geertz, who, as Boon points out, much later acknowledges a debt to Kenneth Burke—to raise the possibility of recuperating what he properly calls
humanism.

This resonates for me with a powerful account by Kwame Anthony Appiah
of what he calls the two stages of the postcolonial African novel. The first
stage, as Appiah outlines it, is marked by nationalism marshaled as a force
against colonialism. The second stage—I am summarizing and inevitably sim-
plifying—is marked by a certain disenchantment with the less-than-felicitous
consequences of nationalism's triumph. Appiah illustrates this complex second stage by an analysis of a "postrealist," apparently postmodernist novel by
Yambo Ouologuem called *Le Devoir de Violence* (1968), in English, *Bound
to Violence* (1968). Here, Appiah (1992: 155) writes, "If we are to identify
with anyone . . . it is with 'la negraille'—the niggertrash, who have no nation-
ality," and so find "one republic as good—which is to say as bad—as any
other." Here, "postcoloniality has become . . . a condition of pessimism," a
"kind of *post*optimism."

Yet Ouloguem's novel, Appiah continues, postmodern though it may appear,
is not, in Appiah's view, "an ally for Western postmodernism but an agonist
from which [Western] postmodernism may have something to learn." That is
because this particular sort of African postmodernism turns out to resonate
with what Appiah also calls humanism—a humanism—and here is the resonance with Fernandez's account—that is "grounded in an appeal to an ethical
universal . . . a certain simple respect for human suffering" (ibid.).

The humility that Fernandez, Erasmus, Booth, Boon, Burke, and I find in
philosophical, stable, satiric, or "true irony," may here ground its "truth" in
Appiah's "ethical universal" of "respect for human suffering"—a respect entirely consistent with commitment to "the alleviation of poverty, sickness, and
hunger" that still underlies aspects of the development project. It is this truth
that may unfashionably be instantiated against Strathern's (1990) retreat to
"persuasive fiction." Strathern's conclusion—that "there are still significant relationships to be studied"—is not quite consistent with Fernandez's own "conclusion"—that perhaps "functioning anthropologists"—and, I would again
add, literary critics, historians, and even philosophers—"do have something
relevant to say."[7] As Burke read both Marx and Carlyle, as Boon reads both

7. Cf. A. S. Byatt: "However initially attractive, even apparently 'true' the idea might be that all
our narratives are partial fictions, the wholesale enthusiastic acceptance of that way of thought re-
moves both interest and power, in the end, from both art and the moral life" (quoted in Whiteley
1998: n.p.).

Burke and the Balinese, so, too, may we try to read "cultures, histories, and critiques," in Boon's phrase, in such a way that our ironic recognition that there is
no complete escape from folly, no insight wholly free of an accompany
ing blindness is not incapacitating but indeed liberatory—at least relatively
so.[8] And this is where I will, perhaps ironically, stop if not adequately conclude.

References

Appiah, K. Anthony. 1992. *In My Father's House: Africa in the Philosophy of Culture.*
    New York: Oxford University Press.
Dening, Greg. 1988. *History's Anthropology: The Death of William Gooch.* Lanham,
    MD: University Press of America.
Ducrot, Oswald, and Tzvetan Todorov. 1979. *Encyclopedic Dictionary of the Sciences
    of Language.* Trans. Catherine Porter. Baltimore: Johns Hopkins University Press.
Erasmus, Desiderius. [1509] 1994. *The Praise of Folly.* Trans. John Wilson. Reprint,
    Amherst, Mass.: Prometheus Books.
Flaubert, Gustave. [1857] 1965. *Madame Bovary.* Ed. with a substantially new transla-
    tion by Paul de Man. New York: Norton.
Frye, Northrop. 1957. *Anatomy of Criticism.* Princeton: Princeton University Press.
Geertz, Clifford. 1990. History and Anthropology. *New Literary History* 21: 321–35.
Havel, Vaclav, et. al. 1985. *The Power of the Powerless.* Armonk, NY: M.E. Sharpe.
Hollinger, David. 1995. *Beyond Multiculturalism: Postethnic America.* New York: Ba-
    sic Books.
Hutcheon, Linda. 1988. *A Poetics of Postmodernism: History, Theory, Fiction.* New
    York: Routledge.
———. 1989. *The Politics of Postmodernism.* New York: Routledge.
Jakobson, Roman. 1960. Concluding Statement: Linguistics and Poetics. In *Style in
    Language,* ed. Thomas A. Sebeok, 350–77. Cambridge, Mass.: The MIT Press.
Jameson, Fredric. 1988. *The Ideology of Theory: Essays, 1971–86,* vol. 2, *Syntax and
    History.* Minneapolis: University of Minnesota Press.
Jay, Paul. 1997. *Contingency Blues: The Search for Foundations in American Criticism.*
    Madison: University of Wisconsin Press.
Joyce, James. [1916] 1982. *A Portrait of the Artist as a Young Man.* New York: Viking.
———. [1922] 1992. *Ulysses.* New York: Modern Library.
Krupat, Arnold. 1989. *The Voice in the Margin: Native American Literature and the
    Canon.* Berkeley: University of California Press.
———. 1996. *The Turn to the Native: Studies in Criticism and Culture.* Lincoln: Uni-
    versity of Nebraska Press.

8. It may be useful here to mention Fredric Jameson's insistence that the very fact of difference,
whether of form or content, is not in itself indicative of resistance or "critique." In a discussion of
"the social functionality of culture," Jameson (1988: 195–96) remarks that although both modernist and postmodernist art works were equivalently perceived as shocking and obnoxious at the
time of their appearance, modernist art functioned in a manner that was oppositional to the cultural
dominant whereas postmodernist art functioned in a manner quite consistent with the cultural dominant. For our present purposes, this is to say that the mere fact of irony cannot be taken as *either*
complicitous *or* critical in itself.

Kuhn, Thomas. 1962. *The Structure of Scientific Revolutions.* Chicago: University of Chicago Press.

Lazarus, Neil, Steven Evans, Anthony Arnove, and Anne Menke. 1995. The Necessity of Universalism. *differences: A Journal of Feminist Cultural Studies* 7: 75–145.

Marcus, George, and Dick Cushman. 1982. Ethnographies as Texts. *Annual Review of Anthropology* 11: 25–69.

Nussbaum, Martha. 1995. Patriotism and Cosmopolitanism. *Boston Review* 19: 3–6.

Orwell, George. 1946. *Animal Farm.* New York: Harcourt.

Rabinow, Paul. 1986. Representations are Social Facts: Modernity and Postmodernity in Anthropology. In *Writing Culture: The Poetics and Politics of Ethnography,* ed. James Clifford and George Marcus, 234–61. Berkeley: University of California Press.

Robbins, Bruce. 1995. The Weird Heights: On Cosmopolitanism, Feeling and Power. *differences: A Journal of Feminist Cultural Studies* 7: 165–87.

Said, Edward. 1993. *Culture and Imperialism.* New York: Knopf.

Siebers, Tobin. 1993. The Ethics of Anti-Ethnocentrism. *Michigan Quarterly Review* 32: 41–70.

Sokal, Alan. 1996. Transgressing the Boundaries: Toward a Transformative Hermeneutics of Quantum Gravity. *Social Text* 46/47: 217–52.

Strathern, Marilyn. 1990. Out of Context: The Persuasive Fictions of Anthropology. In *Modernist Anthropology: From Fieldwork to Text,* ed. Marc Manganaro, 80–122. Princeton: Princeton University Press.

Swift, Jonathan. [1729] 1995. *A Modest Proposal and Other Satires.* Amherst, Mass.: Prometheus Books.

Twain, Mark. [1905/1923] 1984. *The War Prayer.* New York: Harper.

Voltaire, François-Marie Arouet. [1759] 1990. *Candide.* Trans. John Butt. New York: Penguin.

White, Hayden. 1973. *Metahistory: The Historical Imagination in Nineteenth-Century Europe.* Baltimore: Johns Hopkins University Press.

———. 1987. *The Content of the Form: Narrative Discourse and Historical Representation.* Baltimore: Johns Hopkins University Press.

Whiteley, Peter. 1998. *Rethinking Hopi Ethnography.* Washington: Smithsonian Institution Press.

Part Two

Chapter Seven

MARY SCOGGIN

Wine in the Writing, Truth in the Rhetoric: Three Levels of Irony in a Chinese Essay Genre

Director Hu is a slightly stiff middle-aged administrator. . . . He tried to sound magnanimous as he told everyone around the table, "There is no hierarchy here; at the wine-banquet we are all friends equally." [A young woman] at the table was asserting her position as the real master of ceremonies, filling everyone's wine glass and making sure we all drank. She mocked her boss with sure-footed irony, "So be it [or "Yes, sir!"], Friend Hu." (Fieldnotes, January 1994)

This entry from my fieldnotes is a microcosm, containing the elements of irony I analyze below with reference to a particular type of essay writing in China. My intention in this paper is to investigate more generally the many elements of irony that contribute to this and other exchanges in verbal repartee, including the use of drinking ("wine") as a symbolic facilitator for challenge, the moral necessity of challenging individual power and social hierarchy in general, and finally the relations between a literary act and social identity in political protest essays (*zawen,* or "miscellaneous essays"). The features shared by the well-spoken joke above and the zawen discussed below are, I argue, important in understanding not only irony, but also conventions for expressing moral outrage, and political communication in Chinese culture.

I recorded this joke after a "wine-banquet," as the Chinese idiom refers to a formal dinner, in which several members of a large bureaucracy were saying good-bye to a visitor. The wine-server was an up-and-coming manager, and her joke was repeated around the table with much amusement, partially because of her quick use of a pun. "Friend Hu" *(Hu pengyou)* sounds like the phrase "fox and dog friends" *(hupeng gouyou),* meaning bad characters who hang around together. "Fox and dog friends" is a familiar set expression, but "Friend" is an inappropriate substitute for a proper title such as "Director." The young manager demonstrated the improbability of her boss's proposal to dismiss hierarchy by answering "Yes, sir!" but she still managed to achieve the social leveling he had asked for through joking at his expense. The assembled colleagues groaned in the laughing way puns require, and the merry mood was set for the evening; even the reserved guest of honor drank that night.

I posit three levels of irony, each involving the interchange between language and culture (Scoggin 1997). The first level of irony is *rhetorical*. This is similar to what Wayne Booth (1974) calls "verbal irony." It is relatively simple, involving mutual agreement between the speaker and listener about the message of an utterance, even though the words seem to point elsewhere. Sarcasm is the readiest example of first-level irony, clearly evident in the above example in the mocking sound of "Yes, sir!," the ludicrous title of "Friend Hu," and in the insulting suggestion of "fox and dog friends." Limiting this level of irony to the surface level of language itself does not deny its cultural construction, which is located in the conventions that make jokes possible. "Friend" is contrasted with parallel substitutions like "Director/Boss/Teacher" and, until recently, "Comrade" ("Comrade" having now moved firmly to the realm of sarcasm, subsequent to its short-lived ascendancy as a generic title for Mr./Ms. etc.), all of which can appear with a surname like "Hu" for a proper title.[1] But friends don't use titles between themselves. Supplemented by the suggestion of bad ("fox/dog") character, the appellation allows the manager to successfully insult her boss with conventional images of degradation. By sure-footed "success" here, I mean that the speaker, listeners, and readers agree upon what she has accomplished.

Interpreters of rhetorical irony do not always agree, however. The second level irony is its frequent *intractable ambiguity*. In the illustration above, the listener/reader may be left to wonder, has she complied with or rebuffed her boss in her response? Is she boldly honest, exposing hypocrisy, or merely clever, enjoying the opportunity to belittle the director? It is at this level that the morality of irony becomes a key issue. A range of critics from quite disparate intellectual backgrounds have argued that irony is not just double-edged, but "two-faced"—even cruel. To whatever extent it is deliberate, irony needs, in noted ironologist D. C. Muecke's terms, an "innocent victim." On the active side of the double structure of irony, "the very act of being ironical implies an assumption of superiority" (Muecke 1969: 31). While many philosophers of irony, including Muecke, Kierkegaard, and others, also note that this sort of superiority is impermanent and vulnerable to reversal (via God, for example), recent scholars have increasingly portrayed irony as a particular development of the modern/postmodern sensibility, in which producers of irony deploy clever,

1. Conforming with conventions of English I have put the title before the name, but it should be noted that in Chinese the name comes first, then the title.

elite, and evasive techniques, requiring the cultivation of rarified wit, but allowing its users to avoid real vulnerability (see, e.g., Behler 1990, Haiman 1998, and Dane 1991). Chinese criticism of the concept of "pure talk" *(qing tan)*, markedly anti-establishment commentary by gentry and officials of a certain status, captures a similar criticism of the ironic perspective by noting how it can easily careen into nihilism in political contexts.[2]

Still, irony is a perspective richly represented in Chinese aphorisms, folk sayings, and historical tales as well as a staple technique in literary miscellany. Kierkegaard's (1989: 256) characterization of irony as "the unerring eye for what is crooked, wrong, and vain in existence" resonates most tellingly with traditional Chinese views that castigate rhetorical strategies of indirectness and evasiveness, but ultimately accept the double-edged, intractable ambiguity of irony with a sense of resignation and grudging admiration.[3] Irony is a reflection of the imperfection of the human world, the practical recognition of contradiction between, as Kierkegaard would have it, essence and phenomenon, and irony can even be prized as a path to reflection, demonstrating the human capacity for learning virtue. Similarly, the essay writers I discuss below, from the midst of a pervasive atmosphere of suspicion against techniques of irony in China, must struggle to present the ironic position as vulnerable and moral, rather than permanently, evasively, ambiguous and irresponsible.

They attempt to do so through the third aspect of irony, which I call *indexical irony* to underscore how the assignment of irony draws upon contextual channeling in local environments. Irony here is created by attaching the variable levels of "context" to the deployment and reception of irony in sociocultural space and time, perhaps only temporarily, but with real life and time consequences. On this third level, in contrast to the second, an at least provisional conclusion of the meaning of irony is forced. The "Friend Hu" joke above works exactly the way many successful zawen do, exploding the hypocrisy of social conventions (in this case the view that wine offers the opportunity to dispense with ceremony), and simultaneously expressing the more effective function of language. In the scenario above, we had just sat down to a rather formal banquet, with no intention of using the wine to excuse boisterous behavior.

2. For an excellent comparison of the "moral" versus "nihilistic" portrait of *qingtan* in Chinese commentary, see Etienne Balazs 1964: 226–54.

3. Comparing Chinese and Western "great tradition" views on irony would take me far from the ethnographic material upon which I focus here, but it is interesting to note that while recent, particularly American, treatments tend to focus upon a special relationship between irony and modernity, thus emphasizing its most rarified or "elite" qualities, Chinese views often place the emergence of irony-related strategies and recognition back so far in history, so deeply within the conventions of communication, that every level of irony turns out to be pervasive and broadly based in human society. The same tension can be found in the present volume, with Paul Friedrich's essay strongly supporting the latter view.

Director Hu attempted to use the wine as a symbolic tool to break down the din-
ers' reserve, demonstrating his authority by providing us with a signal that we
were permitted to temporarily suspend the restrictions of hierarchy. As I, and I
think the others there, saw it, the wine-server briskly collapsed Director Hu's
fantasy that he could create a de-socialized realm by decree. She demonstrated
that she, conversely, was capable of collapsing social restraints through verbal
play, even as she also carefully appeared to uphold them.

The swift-moving oral process above, in which the presentation of wine as a
symbol fails and is met with the counterpresentation of an act of words, is writ
large below in the slower and less direct form of a literary event. Participants
and observers of the latter bring in literary history, politics, and entire "life stories" as context. I will show how these grander contextual fields are brought to
bear on the meaning that writers and interpreters themselves create through indexical irony. The role of "interpreter," potentially including any reader, is crucial; writers may attempt to define the context of a message in the course of social discourse, but recipient contextualizing (that is, deliberate "indexing")
may wrest control of the irony from its producer. The prevalent use of wine
tropes in the exchanges reported below signals awareness of this loss of control, but it is precisely because of this awareness that the writers can argue that
irony is not protective or evasive, as both Western and Chinese critics have
claimed, but rather the opposite, rendering a valuable social service while leaving the producer of irony vulnerable. The difference between a joke such as the
one above and at least some of the more obviously subversive essays below
is merely one of degree in social circumstances. The wine-pourer's control of
words, like her control of the wine, represents, at least for that moment, real
power over the discourse, and, often, susceptibility to backlash. Likewise, the
reflections on personal experience and historical reconstruction related by the
zawen writers I discuss below can serve as outlines of their own attempts to
control indexical irony.

Attention to personal/social and political context (among the many possible
elements of context upon which we might focus) in zawen is especially merited
because zawen writers have been irony specialists in a period when any expression of social detachment and ambiguity can be a political act. The Maoist
period is often presented by China specialists as a period of raw domination
and submission, and the writers I discuss here are among those that have been
explicitly castigated as "establishment intellectuals," people who live and work
within perimeters of Party newspapers and other state-organized literary organizations. I think that this accusation misunderstands the cultural nature
of power and its ruptures. Symbolic and discursive gestures of violence and
insurgence, like metaphor itself, cannot always be dismissed as "false" by

nature. I argue, with many students of Chinese culture, that a potent "paradox of power" is at work, constantly demanding that high status and authority will be challenged (Hsu 1989, Schoenhals 1993). For our purposes here, the most salient aspect of the paradox of power is that power holders, and the authority by which they hold it, are *expected* by Chinese cultural conventions to be subjected to fierce criticism, and that recognized power, while very real, is temporary and always vulnerable to displacement. This expectation is supported and reinforced with a battery of literary, philosophical and folkloric sources, complemented by modern, scientific, Marxist, capitalist, and other shifting inspirations. Partial concealment of this process in the tropes of wine, irony, or other disclaimers only serves to highlight the high stakes involved.

Drinking and Writing

Chinese zawen writers frequently note a parallel between drinking "wine" and writing zawen. To clarify some ethnoclassifications and connotations: the Chinese term *jiu* encompasses all alcoholic beverages, from wine or beer to spirits and cocktails. Some kinds of *jiu* have long elite pedigrees and rich cultural associations, many of them claiming that drinking may help you write good poetry, the traditional archetype of Chinese literary expression. Talking about drinking (e.g., an invitation to drink) is heavily loaded with social and cultural meaning. Drinking *jiu* is a powerful metaphor for a kind of saturation that has a strangely ambidextrous capacity either to whisk a person off into indifference or irrelevance, or, conversely, to help facilitate the delicious transgression of normal conventions and constraints in mutual understanding and insight.[4] I am abbreviating when I translate *jiu* as "wine," in order to capture its positive connotations and symbolic uses, at which the English word "wine" also hints. Wine, significantly, connotes not just sensual pleasures and affluence, but also ritual and social communion. *Jiu* in Chinese culture has a similar history, both as ritual instrument and secular, recreational drug.

Wine is specifically manipulated as a symbol by Chinese writers. It is discussed as a symbolic "truth tonic" through which people can balance a permanently hierarchical society with the constant, culturally recognized urge for social leveling. For zawen writers in particular, the properties of alcohol and drunkenness can operate symbolically as a mask, behind which the writer might find the courage to criticize particular relations of power and hierarchy. Sometimes foolish, wild, irresponsible, but also "true," and "deserved," these

4. Anthropological research on alcohol has consistently remarked on similar paradox, on both native and analytical levels: dependency versus self-reliance, power versus anxiety, ritual versus social deviation, etc. (Everett, Waddell, and Heath 1976; see also Eber 1995: 5–10).

criticisms are expected and highly valued by readers. That, at least, is the wine conceit encapsulated in the common saying: "after drinking, spit out the truth" (*jiu hou tu zhen yan*).[5]

But there is also a perverse process of cultural awareness wherein the mask of drinking can come to mark itself and thus fail as a social gesture. Instead of escaping the pressures of politic deference or hiding itself on the margins of social discourse, expectations about "things said while drunk," like repeated overuse of irony, may become too dependable. The overcultivation of wine impedes its utility as the channel of "true expression." Dwelling in drunkenness can eventually turn the truth to lies; but writers may turn to ironic zawen in an attempt to recuperate the symbolic effects of wine. Finally, the writers attempt to resolve this complex of reversible tropes as they individually reflect on their own constant motion. The writers themselves do not necessarily have the last word, of course. Living in a social world, no individual can rest permanently in any state, and pure drunkenness is no exception.[6] Willingly or not, drinkers are manipulated by the wine they drink, as writers are also manipulated by the irony they employ.

There are countless genealogies we could follow to trace the ways writers have connected wine to zawen, but one strand begins with zawen's inception as a new genre of literary and political expression, explicitly promoted by the writer Lu Xun (1882–1936) in the early years of the Chinese Republic. Cai Yuanpei (1876–1940), an erudite scholar, revolutionary, and the influential chancellor of China's premier Beijing University, in writing the preface to the first edition of *Lu Xun's Complete Works*, was faced with the difficulty of what kind of accolades to hang upon Lu Xun's contributions to literature and society, just as the definition of both was changing so radically that traditional accomplishments were both impossible and meaningless. Lu Xun had devoted a significant portion of his time to translating foreign works and to pioneering modern Chinese fiction on the model of the foreign "short story." Lu Xun later abandoned the foreign-inspired work for a puzzling new genre called the "miscellaneous essay," or zawen, combining fiction, poetic language, and polemic for newspapers. Cai Yuanpei concluded that the foreign work was "borrowing someone else's winecup to water [your] own 'pile of rocks'" ([1938] 1981: 225–26). Here, the "pile of rocks" is a sardonic reference to the "mountain" of Chinese culture. Water may be sufficient to nurture the verdant swells of other people's "mountains," but the impenetrable Chinese "rock" requires

---

5. The same word, *tu*, covers "spitting" and "vomiting."

6. I am responding here to James Clifford's comments on the presentation of the material at the 1996 panel that gave rise to this book, which suggest (in contrast to "coming to rest" in the consequences of the "morning after") that "drunk, singing, and blissfully delusional in the face of history" (Larry Taylor's expression) "was the place to be . . . forever."

stronger stuff. "Wine," then, is used as a magic tonic. The genre of zawen composed a gesture in which Lu Xun used his own winecup to water the Chinese
"mountain."

Cai Yuanpei's wine metaphor also makes use of a trope of place. It is in part
motivated by the fact that Lu Xun and he both come from Shaoxing, the land
of Shaoxing wine. In 1993, another Shaoxing native and zawen writer, Shao
Yanxiang, draws upon this same trope to define his own zawen mission in a personal collection of zawen. He takes *My Own Winecup* as his title, and explains:

> Whenever I hear the proverb "borrowing someone else's winecup to water
> your own pile of rocks," I think, why not use your own winecup? . . . Using it
> to water your own pile of rocks, perhaps it will be the medicine that can cor-
> rect the ailment?[7] Perhaps my "pile of rocks" does not belong solely to me,
> whoever shared the same ailment is someone who knows my music,[8] and will
> not go wrong in borrowing my winecup to water the "pile of rocks" that burns
> in their own chest, similar to mine; it can relieve the suffocation for a time.
> This winecup, that cup of wine, it does not matter whose it is, if it can water
> the rocks it is good.[9]
>
> This collection of zawen came about because of the "pile of rocks" in my
> breast, spitting it out feels satisfying. As for claiming that I am using my own
> wine to water my own rocks, we can see that the problem is not in the rock
> pile, but in the watering. Using wine to water worry is like "Greeting a shower
> of spring worry with a cup of wine to water it." Clearly, when you "slice a flow
> of water with a knife, you know the water will flow just the same," likewise
> we know when, "raising a cup to dispel the worry, it will strengthen the worry
> all the more." If you succeed in soothing the old worry, new worries will is-
> sue from the bottom of your cup. Raising the cup with a guest is nothing but
> "knowing that it cannot be done and doing it." (Shao 1993: 1–2)

Drinking (like writing zawen) is useless, so why do we do it? Shao Yanxiang
complains that the actual practices involved in social drinking—"prodding"
people to drink, pretending to be drunk, secretly pushing one's one agenda at
the drinking table—are all quite boorish in themselves ("On Drinking," Shao
1993: 48–51; this and subsequent quotes from Shao 1993 are translated in
Scoggin 1997). When something interesting happens while drinking, it is not
the wine but something else that is meaningful.

> True, the *untying the saddle at night by the riverbank* poet complained about
> *flowers with no one to pick them, wine with no one to prod [you] into drinking*

7. The term *kuai lei* is literally "rock pile." But it also means "indigestion," and is extended to
mean "gloominess," an abstract feeling of having an ailment of "blockage," a meaning that Shao
Yanxiang exploits here.

8. Reference to a folk tale about friendship and musical communion, see Scoggin 1997: chap. 1.

9. Returning to level-two irony, Shao Yanxiang presents us an eternal uncertainty; does it matter if the wine-cup is someone else's or not? His appeal to pragmatism parallels the white cat/black
cat analogy between capitalism and socialism that Deng Xiaoping made famous.

it, and being drunk with no one to scold [you] for it. But this poet's intention
was not in the wine. (Shao 1993: 49. I have added italics to show the quoted
allusions, whereas in the original grammar and meter alone indicate quoted
poetry.)

Where was the poet's intention?[10] The proper approach to reading zawen is
less about tracking down classical allusions and more about examining the
reader's own projection of the writer's intentions, that is, assigning the indexical irony of the writer's position. In this case, the Song Dynasty poet Huang
Gongshao is the writer, and Shao Yanxiang is the reader. The problem of the
"poet," in Shao Yanxiang's reading, is loneliness, the social alienation resulting
from banishment. It is a loneliness for all three different kinds of people, the
picker of flowers, the companion in drinking, and even the scold, in short, all
of the intimacy, good and bad, of human society. Drinking wine means nothing
without the company of the entire social spectrum, including its vanities and
evils. If we move one layer further out, then, with Shao Yanxiang as the writer
and ourselves as readers, there is an analogy between drinking and writing;
writing zawen might pull the crooked and ironic aspects of human society into
focus, even if drinking fails to do so.

Not in the Wine: A Zawen Event

Shao Yanxiang's zawen "On Drinking" first appeared, not in his own collection, but in *A Collection to Soothe Away Worries* (Wu 1988a), which includes
short essays and zawen by more than fifty writers. Most zawen appear first as
essays in newspapers or popular magazines, but the "zawen event" represented
by *Soothe Away Worries* was published in book format from the outset. The differences between the media are worth considering; a book of essays is pitched
for a more limited audience. These essays are more about writers, and less
about the total world of editors, readers, and immediate social problems. In this
case, however, disagreement over the purpose and audience of the publication
was divisive from the start.

The National Bureau of "Wine Culture" sought to capitalize, literally, on the
traditionally positive connotations of drinking when they asked Wu Zuguang,
a prominent playwright (and outspoken social critic and zawen writer) to col-
lect celebratory essays about drinking from his well-known writer-friends. In

10. Shao Yanxiang calls the writer a "Ci" (lyric-style) poet, providing the only hint, other than
the quoted lines, of the origin of this poem. In a process familiar not only to literature specialists
and sinologists but probably to most educated Chinese, I dutifully looked up "key phrases" in the
Song Ci-poetry concordances, to find the full poem, complete with musical score, attributed
(equivocally) to the late (thirteenth century) Song dynasty poet Huang Gongshao.

the conception of the Bureau, drinking was not supposed to represent trouble or ambiguity. If drinking does what it has been supposed to do through generations of Chinese poets, from ancient exiled ministers, to madcap Tang dynasty poets, to the confessional modernists, it will provoke insight for a solitary drinker, or facilitate delicious transgression of normal conventions and restraints in mutual understanding. Drinking is supposed to tear down the obstacles between humans. In the words of Wu Zuguang, introducing the collection, "from the very earliest times people have inseparably entangled their fate with *jiu* . . . she resonates joy, manifests sorrow, she can relieve loneliness and even provide happiness" (Wu 1988b: 1; Wu went out of his way to personify wine as feminine, presumably to highlight its exotic or nonstandard qualities).

Wu Zuguang came up with the organizing title *Soothe Away Worries (jie you)* from an ancient expression: "How can we soothe away worries? Du Kang [mythical inventor of wine] is the only answer" (in 1993–94, while I conducted fieldwork, this phrase was frequently plastered on the television screen in a commercial for liquor). He sent out a letter to several dozen of his acquaintances, all in different fields, from poets to novelists, cartoonists, actors, businessmen, and central Communist Party bureaucrats.

I do not know exactly what happened to change the final publishing plans. In two separately published versions, the initial invitation of the Bureau of Wine Culture remains in the preface, but it is as if it were merely a literary device, for it was never the Bureau that published these essays. The Publishing House of Inner Mongolia (often chosen to publish works through the "second channel," bypassing the New China Bookstore's distribution monopoly) put out the first 20,000 copies, which were snatched up eagerly in the small, secondary book shops and street stalls in 1988.

None of the essays in this volume were what anyone could call seditious political protest essays. Many of them, written mostly by men in their sixties and seventies, feature memories of the social warmth and richness of social encounters facilitated by wine, explicitly comparing this warmth with the bitterness and cold anger of conflict as experienced through the series of political events of the Mao era that is their own personal history. Still, this is a distinctly post-Mao work, marked in part by its collective refusal to engage directly with political issues. Some essays were written exactly as the Bureau must have imagined: light pieces of learned fluff, nostalgic memories, funny and stylish stories about famous people getting drunk together. Some deliver reverent hymns on the paraphernalia of wine types and contexts. Some include unlovely escapades of drunkenness and its embarrassing consequences, from expressing opinions imprudently to waking up in a strange bed.

However, within the collection there is a distinct subgroup of essays written mostly by a group of writers who are all known specifically as writers of the "Lu Xun" style of zawen. This "faction" had no praise for wine at all, only complaints. The original idea for this collection had been to use the high status of the zawen writers to publicize the charms of wine, but instead they wrote complaints against drinking. This initial contradiction in itself establishes only first-level, rhetorical irony; but to add to the irony brew, not only were these writers included, but ultimately, in mysterious publishing circumstances, they were actually featured. The writers declined to praise wine, and the Bureau declined to publish the work, but illustrations on the cover and dotting the volume were provided by one of the "dissenters," Fang Cheng, a *People's Daily* cartoonist (and therefore already an ironic culture critic by proper profession, in addition to the zawen side-line). Fang Cheng captured the ambivalence of the writer over his wine with a drawing on the cover of the book (fig. 1). This appears to be a rather colorless modern office bureaucrat, holding his writing brush modestly behind his back and looking with pensive lust at a jug of Shaoxing wine on the floor. The balance between desire for drink and drunkenness must be maintained, particularly for these writers whose interest is not in the wine, but in the potency of social criticism through writing about or like wine. The image shows only hesitation about wine, and thus we are left here on level-two irony: intractable ambiguity.

An attempt to disambiguate is made in a later Taiwan reprint of this collection. In this edition, Fang Cheng's cartoons are replaced throughout by cute little roly-poly Buddhas, in various postures of rip-roaring drunkenness (fig. 2). Even if the Bureau of Wine Culture had to bow out of this particular indirect advertising campaign, *Soothe Away Worries* turned out to be useful for selling wine, not only in the Taiwan publisher's conception but also in Mainland television commercials. But we will leave this particular small betrayal of Fang Cheng and the other zawen writers (which is also a movement to level three, demonstrating that the message of the collection remains vulnerable to *assignment* by others) to examine the process of the original publication. In this section I will concentrate primarily on level three, or how the writers tried to control the social and political context of writing.

The volume *A Collection to Soothe Away Worries* presented itself as a dialogic literary event. In addition to the invitation of the Wine Bureau, Wu Zuguang includes as front matter the letter he sent out to his friends, and discusses in particular one critical response he received from Yang Xianyi. Yang Xianyi, a literary translator, is a perfect model of the modern Chinese literati whose very public identity is associated closely with wine. According to Wu Zuguang in his preface to the volume, Yang Xianyi initially opposed the notion of *you*, "worry," in the title of this collection, saying "I drink for fun, how could this 'soothe' [the word also means "release" or "loosen"] any worry?" Wu Zuguang

Figure 1. Cover of *Jie You Ji* (Beijing, 1988),
designed by Fang Cheng, of *The People's Daily*

claims to have countered with a retort, which reads in part, "Today, in worrying about the people, worrying about the nation, can you find anything that does not warrant worry?" Yang Xianyi's essay within the volume includes a somewhat different account:

> Everyone knows I like to drink, that's why Wu Zuguang asked me to write this, but I sent him a flippant poem in response, including some nasty comments about certain people I won't repeat here. But he still wanted me to write, so I'll just throw some casual thoughts together. (Yang 1988: 72–73)

Figure 2. Back cover of *Jie You Ji* (Taipei, 1989), designed by Chen Wenzang.

The kind of disclaimer in which Yang Xianyi "throws thoughts together" is a "framing device" so common in Chinese writing that it has already occurred in two essays I have quoted above, Cai Yuanpei's preface for Lu Xun, and Shao Yanxiang's introduction to his own essays. It is a technique particularly suited for zawen, the self-styled "throw-away" genre; but make no mistake, it represents not carelessness but recognition of the impossibility of the goal at hand. Wu Zuguang also used it himself in his preface to *Soothe Away Worries,* claiming he had set out to recruit writers for this collection "in order to oblige a friend." Like a game that requires you to drink as a penalty, writing only when your friends, unforeseeable events, or national crises force you to write disguises the desire to be read. Everybody "knows," at least if they think about it from Yang Xianyi's worldly/cynical perspective, that however you may wish to express yourself and contribute to political and moral discourse, delivering even your most obedient and correct thoughts through language is impossible, often misunderstood, and only gives you something to worry about. Yang

Xianyi proceeds to take Cao Cao, the villain of the Three Kingdoms story, which begins nearly two thousand years ago, at the end of the Han Dynasty (ca. 184), as an example of the problem with drinking as a verbal conceit. Poised at the outset of an ambitious battle that will prove disastrous to him, the renegade statesman Cao Cao gathers his generals at a banquet on the Yangtze River where he composes some poetry, beginning with these famous words from which Wu Zuguang had taken his title: "How can we soothe away worries? Wine is the only answer" *(heyi jie you? wei you Du Kang).* Yang Xianyi remarks:

> If these are indeed Cao Cao's original words, it is a piece of dirty lying work that cannot be taken sincerely. Cao Cao wanted to hear his supporters comfort and praise him. (Ibid.)

In the Ming Dynasty novel version of the Three Kingdoms story, which first appeared around 1494, directly after Cao Cao's recitation of this poem, one of his loyal followers points out evil omens within it, and Cao Cao, being rather drunk, promptly murders him in a rage. This, of course, prefigures his own imminent defeat in battle, in which he barely escapes death. Yang Xianyi concludes:

> Cao Cao is a man of consuming ambition . . . how could he believe that wine could solve anything? Whether it is soothing worries or [simply] forgetting worries, neither is appropriate for him. . . . We, too, dare not forget to worry about the nation . . . there is only worry and more worry. We will have to let Cao Cao blame himself for what the words he wrote did.

On the one hand, Cao Cao, cynically or accidentally, we will never know, tricked his followers into saying things that would betray them and get them murdered. On the other hand, Cao Cao's own poem carried evil omens, seeds of his own destruction. Rhetorical (first level) and dramatic (indexed in hindsight—third level) irony are brought together in a terrible double-bind of irony on the second level, irresolvable ambiguity of the kind that may make a publisher back off. Invoking wine makes use of a trope that suggests the expression of "genuine" thoughts and more direct interpersonal communication. But drinking does not allow you to make the gesture you want in just the way you might hope. The Wine Bureau, too, anticipated only praise, but, like Cao Cao, got more than it asked for. Yang Xianyi's parallel, if it is indeed intentional, probably has little to do with the poor Wine Bureau. Yang was shooting for a bigger and more obvious target, which modern zawen history helps to illuminate.

Irony in a Post-Mao Era

"Post-Mao" is not a label that the people experiencing it use, but one that "outsiders" have attached to the period since Mao Zedong's death in 1976. The label is meant to signal contrast to the thirty years previous. In contemporary Chinese parlance, the significance of the Maoist era does exert a strong presence, mostly through commentary on contemporary contrast to it. Especially in this period of what often appears to be a process of deliberate erasing and forgetting Mao in China, the term "post-Mao," used outside of China where the contrast is not so apparent, is helpful to mark the resilient presence of that past, as well as its contrast to the present. In order to understand zawen writers' contemporary political postures, it is essential to understand them as quite actively responding to events that stem from the time of Mao Zedong. Mao had some specific things to say about both zawen and irony. I reproduce here a passage from the speech most frequently presented as the ideological foundation for national policies on literature and art for the first forty years of the People's Republic of China:

> Living under the rule of the dark forces and deprived of freedom of speech, Lu Xun used burning satire and freezing irony, cast in the form of essays, to do battle; and he was entirely right. We, too, must hold up to sharp ridicule the fascists, the Chinese reactionaries and everything that harms the people . . . [but] here, where democracy and freedom are granted in full to the revolutionary writers and artists and withheld only from the counter-revolutionaries, the style of the essay should not simply be like Lu Xun's. Here we can shout at the top of our voices and have no need for veiled and roundabout expressions. (Mao [1942] 1967: 92)

Note that assumptions about the positive and constant role of criticism are built into this view; expectations for social criticism are constant. This passage also reveals a problem: written language seems like it should be an effective and straightforward instrument for the social communication (including criticism) to which it is in service, but in its most important actual practices it is more often circuitous and veiled than not. In happy political circumstances, Mao claims, we should be able to communicate, complain, and challenge in a straightforward way, and have no need for irony. This, indeed, is the sentiment that some of my non-zawen-writing (avowedly "apolitical," and certainly not Maoist) interviewees expressed when they described to me how and why they hated zawen or were embarrassed by its very success as a genre in China. The zawenists argue in contrast that when all the social and cultural conventions and constraints of communication are taken together, Mao or no Mao, language is inadequate for expressing what is meant, even "here, where democracy and freedom are granted in full." There will always be room for zawen, they say; human nature will never allow straight shouting.

Mao's own proposal of dispensing with "veiled expressions" may be interpreted as crushingly ironic, especially when we make the parallel between Cao Cao's call for poetry and subsequent murder of his critic and Mao Zedong's many calls for frank and rigorous criticism, followed by punishing campaigns of revenge against critics. But even if we granted Mao Zedong the benefit of doubt that "democracy and freedom" are ever fully granted anywhere, we note that irony has not at all deteriorated in a post-Mao era, and the veiled genre of zawen flourishes. Shouting at the top of "our" voices (which is, indeed, how some have characterized much Maoist prose, see Huters 1990) turns out to be not merely dangerous, but also dull and ineffective.

On the other hand, writing in veiled and roundabout expressions can be, in itself, a condemnation of society and political circumstances. When Mao issued his invitation to "let a hundred flowers bloom, let a hundred schools of thought contend," again and again, the zawen writers in particular voiced opposition and criticism of the policies and the moral legitimacy of the new government. With the help of editors, newspaper bureaus, and other social institutions, they published these zawen in the daily newspaper for everyone to read. Over and over again, many of them suffered direct and dire consequences for writing what they "really" thought. Why did they do it? Were they crazy, or just drunk? This is a question often asked in China.

Claiming Drunkenness

Another writer in the *Soothe Away Worries* collection, Huang Shang, claimed that maybe it did help to be a little drunk. Just after liberation in 1949, as Mao Zedong's policy was being transformed from Communist base-camp discipline to national policy, Huang Shang wrote an essay lamenting what appeared to be the demise—very temporary, as it turned out—of the Lu Xun–style zawen. As a pointed rhetorical technique, he repeated passages in the wording of Mao's "Talks at the Yenan Forum on Literature and Art," from which I have quoted above. His point, in contrast to Mao's purported intention, was that the new formulation of policy on art and literature had choked off one of the most common and effective forms of Chinese social criticism (Huang 1950). Since the form in which he wrote was zawen (throw-away miscellany, now carefully preserved in several collections), Huang Shang made no footnotes or citations; the repeated Mao rhetoric was sufficient to achieve first-level irony, pointing to Mao and criticising Mao. Even if some of Huang Shang's casual readers might not have caught the alluded references, the critics who cared and could punish him did understand him correctly. What is the difference between this "irony" and "shouting at the top of [his] lungs?" Only the adventure of discovery, functions as an extra flourish of audacity to intensify the critical effect. This technique is similar to what ironologists call "dramatic irony," presenting by its very existence and self-knowledge the larger implications of his complaint in that particular social and political context.

Forty years later, in the *Soothe Away Worries* collection, Huang Shang wrote another essay to explain what he had been doing years ago. He said that while in the Nationalist capital in Sichuan Province during the war against Japan in the 1940s he learned to write with the help of famous Sichuan hard liquor, the same liquor, it is said, that aided such literary sage-spirits as Tang dynasty poet Li Bai. On occasion this wine-muse revisited him when returned to Shanghai in 1949 to work for one of the biggest newspapers in the newly victorious People's Republic of China. "One day [someone's] mother brought some of that essence back from Sichuan, and . . . under its influence I even wrote some short critical essays" (Huang 1988).

Huang Shang claims to have been drunk when he wrote the kind of criticism that Mao Zedong invited, and, at the same time, precisely the kind of essay Mao warned against. By the time he wrote the oblique 1988 essay, Huang Shang had secured his social and political position, and had nothing to fear. Writing ironically here is not a direct reflection of fear or evasiveness, but an act of protest through pure poetic manipulation, an indexical gesture that points to something that was or could be, not what is now. Huang Shang, like so many others in this collection of essays, was trying to do something with zawen literature because wine had ceased to be effective.

Mu Hui's Irony

The meaning of "irony" is difficult enough to capture in English; it would be a strange accident if we were to find a term just matching it in Chinese. Yet most would agree that Chinese verbal art of any era, particularly in literary form, is indeed a cup overflowing with irony. *Fan-hua*, "counter" or "back-speech," is a common modern suggestion for a term to translate the English word "irony," though this will often mean something like "sarcasm," and may even be a translation of that Western term.[11] "Counter-speech" might imply that one means the opposite of what one says, but we might also think of it something said or done in response, like a counterquestion, a countermove in a game of chess, or a "counter-essay," a written response. Still better as a solution to the translation of "irony" is a term used by Mu Hui, one of my informants, whose contribution to the *Soothe Away Worries* collection was entitled "In Counter-tone to Wine" *(Jiu de fandiao)*. I think Mu Hui's musical term "counter-tone" is a fitting candidate to catch the deeper sense of ironic paradox and simultaneously carry a resonance of Chinese poetic writing practices, which, in a sense, these kinds of essays have replaced. Mu Hui begins his essay by making reference to a series

11. This is the term Lu Xun used when he referred to the "irony" of the term "Free Talk," a newspaper column to which he contributed. Elsewhere he also claimed he was fond of *fanyu*, or "counter-language."

of frightful episodes of drunkenness and its horrible consequences from traditional Chinese ghost stories and historical fiction. Then he pulls up abruptly:

> Here I've been going on and on, and suddenly I realize, everything I've written is singing in direct counter-tone to what [Wu] Zuguang asked for in his invitation. But only Zuguang himself is to blame for seeking out the wrong postulant. While it is true enough that I "crawl on manuscript paper" [with my pen] for a living, this humble servant is not in any sense . . . a "giant officer of the wine forum" [military metaphor for a big drinker]. (Mu 1988: 37–41)

Mu Hui thus contrasts himself to a famous drinker like Yang Xianyi. He explains that the one time in his youth when he did get drunk was during civil war. He then woke to find himself AWOL on the enemy battle line. After that, amazingly, he still became a high-level Communist official and was often asked to travel and make formal inspections. In this position Mu Hui frequently found himself an honored guest, socially required to drink. Mu Hui admits that he often lied to cover up the fact that he could not bear to drink.

> From this, we can see that I am imperfect in that I lie. The common proverb says the wine makes it possible to tell the truth, so maybe it is something I should learn. . . . But though I am not good at drinking, and though I have lied on occasion, I still think I am rather accomplished at telling the truth. (Ibid.)

Though Mu Hui is a central cadre in the Communist elite, he is also an outspoken social critic. As literary editor of the Communist Party journal, *Red Flag,* he tirelessly attempted to make this central theoretical journal into an open, dialogic arena for meaningful ideological debate, on occasion nearly closing down *Red Flag* with his efforts. At the same time, throughout his career, Mu Hui has been a writer on the side himself, contributing critical essays to other journals and newspapers that point out the most unsayable and politically unwelcome contradictions, unprintable in his own journal. Mu Hui is very much a cultural warrior who devotes his spare time to writing, which represents for him a superior choice to deploying the mythical effects of drinking.

Indexing the Self: from Wine to Zawen

Many scholars in the "emergent" tradition of anthropology favor the term "life story" over "life history" in a theoretical move intended to "allow one to see how an actor makes culturally meaningful history, how history is produced in action and in the actor's retrospective reflections on that action" (Behar 1995: 150). I think this idea of self-conscious effort is successful for describing the process as a deliberate retrieval of contextual positioning that gives these events meaning. This framing is indispensable in establishing indexical irony. In Mu Hui's life story we have already seen how sensitive he is to the effects of his own interpretation of history. Asked to reflect upon the beauty of wine in his own life, Mu Hui "inadvertently" reveals its ugliness and inadequacies. This circumlocution, however, is only a twist on the road to describing the beauty of writing, and telling "the truth," that wine is supposed to help facilitate, but, he argues, at least for himself, writing zawen actually does facilitate.

We know that Mu Hui does not drink wine, he writes zawen instead. In this last section I will present Mu Hui's explanation of how and why he traded in his wine for zawen, and demonstrate that this is his answer to the problem of "worrying about the nation, worrying about the people." I am shifting genre only a little to present Mu Hui the story-teller as opposed to Mu Hui the zawen-writer. Mu Hui knew that I was conducting a study on zawen, and that I had read his essays. Face-to-face conversation in the context of an interview, where the subject is specifically explaining himself and his motivations, is generally slower-paced and more direct than the lightning-swift shifts and turns of written zawen. But as the stretches of transcript that follow will show, Mu Hui's conversation is crafted and powerful, full of zawen-like flavor.

Mu Hui considers himself an ironic writer, not only because of his sarcastic bent and quick tongue, but also because he himself embodies a tremendously ironic moral position. As a high-ranking Communist official editing the central literary instrument of state "propaganda," he sees his own position as profoundly ambiguous, and devotes much of his energy and talents to indexing his own meaning. I have selected portions of his story that reconstruct his explanation in his own words because his presentation is particularly revealing of the individual moral and political desires behind zawen. During interviews in Beijing he described details that give a "been there" quality to the extraordinary range of his experiences, from pig farmer to the center of delicate high-level political battles. He describes the back-breaking minutiae of plowing tea fields out of steep hills with the same gusto he describes sitting down with a political enemy to edit an attack essay against his own friend and ally.

We sat down to talk about zawen, not over wine, but over tea and cigarettes. My interview tapes are full of the sounds of tea and cigarette paraphernalia, which Mu Hui exchanges in alternating infusions. Smoking and tea are social acts; in China people often offer a cigarette or a drink of tea as an invitation to chat. The busy work of both filled our occasional silences with comfortable noises, like the click of the lighter and the tap-tap-tap of his knocking tea leaves down from the side of his little tea pot, a gnarly, dark brown, squatting "melon"-style vessel, followed by the sound of water pouring from the thermos bottle into the pot. The project of zawen is not only, or even mainly, the task of brave mavericks who take on a faceless bureaucratic political system, but an important side-line of the highly textured individuals that actually populate government organs, even "Party mouthpieces" like *Red Flag*. Mu Hui loves to describe the reactions of people unsettled by the inherent contradictions of his position:

One time I went to a conference. It was a conference on the classical novel, *The Golden Lotus*. There was one "woman warrior" there, a Sichuan woman, she was a real straight-shooting speaker. Because I was the head of an important literary department, something of an "official," they asked me to sit up at the front table with the panel. This woman, she was sitting down in front. She saw that I was sitting at the chair's table, and she cursed out loud, saying "What kind of deviltry is this! Who invited the spy to our conference!" [Mu Hui chuckled in delight] "Invited a spy to our conference!" She was very unhappy. After a couple of days we happened to be together eating (banquet style) she said to me "Do you know how afraid of you I was a couple of days ago?" (Mu Hui 1994)

"Fear" *(pa)* operates as a euphemism here, because it can directly mean a cowed sort of fear, but in Chinese it can also mean lightly veiled disgust and condescension; you may "fear" someone who merely annoys you or "ruins your day" as well as fearing someone who can truly hurt you. In this case the meaning of "fear" is deliberately kept ambiguous, as she presumably would like to display both points about Mu Hui: real fear is masked with condescending disgust. But in having revealed this ambiguity, she also puts both kinds of fear in the past. Mu Hui celebrates the "woman warrior's" eventual collaboration of his own self-indexing:

I asked her, "Well, what do you think now? Are you still afraid?" She said, "Look what work unit you're from, how can I not be afraid?!" "So why do you tell me this now?" She admitted, "Well, because I see now that you're not so bad" and we went on to speak of many other things . . . we remain friendly. (Ibid.)

Not everyone will collaborate, however. After the events in Tiananmen in 1989, Mu Hui left Beijing declaring he would never come back, in a classic gesture of protest. But in the end he returned, he said, because he could not live without his readers. Mu Hui's commitment to his "readers" is surely earnest, but it is also a "disclaimer," a modest cover for his consistent political commitment, the scent of which is distinctly threatening in his own environment. He returned to Beijing, to face immediate criticism by the other cadres at his old work unit, changed in name now, from *Red Flag* to *Seeking Truth*. Although he had officially retired in 1988, he still collected his pension from the magazine bureau, still attended policy meetings on occasion, and was still subject to criticism from them, now for his outspoken condemnation of the June Fourth incident, and even more vigorously for his subsequent published attack against another conservative party publication in 1992.[12]

They say to me, "Are you still having a problem with the old Cultural Revolution? So you suffered a little, nothing worse than a little criticism came your

12. A microstudy in the "ethnography of writing" itself, entitled "Why Did *Central Current* Quote Yan Yuanshu?" (Mu 1992).

way, do you still have personal resentment about that? So you felt offended, can't you get over that? Why are you continually harping on problems like this?" I told them, "That is not the way it is! The Cultural Revolution didn't do anything at all to me, but it toppled the Communist Party!"

Mu Hui scoffs at frequently heard warnings about a second coming of another Cultural Revolution. He says it's like worrying about the end of the world:

> If the Cultural Revolution happened again it would not be just me, I would be finished, but China would be finished. We took a trip to the brink of extinction, we know how it would feel to fall off completely. It's still not clear to me that we won't.

Mu Hui's ready criticism of Chinese society and culture, once again, is an indication of his own identification with the evolution of the Party, for better or worse. Indeed, for most of his life he was a model of socialist youth and socialist construction, a small icon of Communist victory. Many celebratory accounts attribute the Communists' success in the 1940s to moral legitimacy, in part because they could recruit bright young people like Mu Hui into the party.

> We used to say that the Chinese are hard-working and brave. I still think that's right, it truly is. Hard-working and brave. Take my own experience as a child. We really worked hard, with everything we had. If you didn't work you couldn't live! Right? Especially someone like me, we were pretty poor. My father died very early. I watched my mother doing various kinds of labor to make a living for us. So, of course, just as soon as I was done with classes I would do everything I could to help.
>
> How I came down this particular road was part arbitrary, but also part inevitable. When I was small I was good at composition. My essays were often pasted up on the board as a model, I don't know if you do it that way, but then our teachers would paste up the model compositions, mine were always up there. In a competition I won a provincial prize for the best composition. So I started writing essays quite young. In 1942 I started publishing, I was only 13 or 14. So I took the exams for the Chinese department to go to university.

Mu Hui joined the Party while in college.

> When I joined the revolution, I was a very good, really a very good and devoted party member. That is to say I was an earnest and obedient "bolt" [in reference to both Lenin and Mao]. Whatever the party wanted me to do, I did. But . . . I really got bored. After all, I'd had some education. I'd been in college, I felt quite lonely. So I asked for a transfer. I said I wanted to be in contact with the masses. My leader was quite unhappy. He criticized me as having an intellectual's stench [arrogance]. So he sent me to an army division to be a little soldier with the old comrades. This was an army unit, but it actually did involve contact with the masses. I was there until our area was liberated. They had me supervise the cadres study program in Xi'an. In order to do this I had to produce a very small publication. . . .
>
> Later, it was in 1958 that they decided they wanted to start a magazine. Every province was to establish a party magazine like *Seeking Truth,* like *Red*

Flag. Our province was to have one too. So I, along with several others [he named a string of people who are currently in top positions of the Cantonese provincial government] we got together to do this. We were a bunch of young people at the time, and we were to establish the magazine. This was a move into a different world, having to do with all the media such as newspapers, magazines, all that. They wanted us to write, and we wrote everything, literary prose essays, zawen, novels, I wrote all of those. But most of it was "singing praises" kind of thing. How could you have a different point of view? That would be too destructive. If someone said something was good, you just went along and said it was good. That was the way it was. Moreover . . . but see the thing of it was, at that time we didn't really see any problem with all this. It's not that we were hammered out, forced, deflated, anything like that, it was just that we really were that stupid. I was the most obedient party member. When the CCP said "Great Leap Forward!" we need to criticize and struggle intellectuals, accordingly I then said, "Intellectuals are rotten, stinky, rotten through!" Everything I wrote was like that. Even from THOSE kind of articles they could find a way to say that you are against the party, against socialism, what can you do?

But going along in this way, doing whatever they wanted you to do, writing anything they wanted you to write, I'd written maybe two hundred works big and small by the time the Cultural Revolution came along. Then, in a big rush out of no where, suddenly there came the "big character posters," saying a person (me) was [Mu Hui stood up to deliver this] "against the party, against socialism, against Mao Zedong Thought, a Big Bad Egg!" They "stir-fried" up pieces of my essays, saying this passage was insinuating something, that one was instigating something else. I was absolutely flabbergasted! I hadn't thought of any of it myself!

There was a comfortable clank of tea cups, as Mu Hui sat back down. In this segment of his story, Mu Hui has demonstrated his moral purity and conviction through the trope of "stupidity" (once again, common in zawen theorizing; see Scoggin 1997, chapter two). Originally a poor "street urchin" with a germ of intellectual promise, moving his way through the ranks of the Army, he had every motivation to be a model of correct ideology, and he was "stupid" enough to do it willingly and wholeheartedly. It was "they," the Communist establishment, who ruined their own best ideological capital. They did it by converting ambiguity (even where Mu Hui insists it did not exist) into an index of infidelity.

It just didn't exist! They just said it was there [in the text], though. They analyzed you to death until you felt that you were really rotten to the bone. You'd try to say what you meant subjectively differed from what came out objectively, it was subconscious, all of that was still no good. In the end you had to say that thoroughly, from the depths of your heart, "I hate Chairman Mao, hate the Communist Party, and meant to destroy it all!" It went back and forth, on and on.

It went on like that until we all went off to the Cadre's School. That was when they sent you off to farms for "reeducation." On the one hand you'd

farm, and raise pigs, all that labor we were not good at, and then on the other
we were to be "struggled," all that. But by that time the masses were tired of
it! They weren't comfortable doing it either. You had to find all kinds of ex-
cuses, and run back to Beijing. But us, "cow tails and snake gallbladders," we
couldn't go back to Beijing, and we didn't know how to sow the land. What do
you do with a bunch of people like this on the farm? That was when our thinking started to loosen up. Our unit representatives were also progressively more
lenient towards us.

I used this time to read some books. In these two years I read more than I
had read since college, since the time I joined the revolution. I read a great
deal, and with such close attention. Every night after eating I'd read, and read,
every night. I like to read history, classic novels, what is it that's so compelling
about reading that sort of thing? On the one hand it allows you to apply the
past to the present, think of it as old maladies flaring up again. I would write
some notes, just some thoughts, that sort of thing. At that time I never thought
I'd later write something like this [the zawen]. I never thought I'd ever write
anything again.

Any particular indexical representation, fixed in a particular time and space,
may be reworked and overturned later. Here, an indignant Mu Hui is represented against his will and belief in the role of "stinking intellectual" who had
"masqueraded" as a pure Communist. But Mu Hui did write again, and it was
the maliciously false "charges" of the Cultural Revolution that became supremely ironic in Mu Hui's self-indexing process.

But later these notes became useful. When I was thoroughly exonerated in
1980, everything was overturned, there was not a charge that stuck. So I was
"normalized" and returned to my job. Right at that time the big wave of consciousness liberation came along, sweeping up people like me. The amazing
thing is that for the great magnitude of this change in consciousness, the liberation of thought after the Cultural Revolution, it took me no time at all to
adjust to it. I remember when it started, for me this happened rather late. I
heard my driver curse Mao in front of me. I was really afraid! This is what
happened, didn't I tell you that I returned to Guangdong in 1977? They were
simply sending me back to Guangdong, where I came from, "We can't keep
this kind of person in Beijing." So I returned. While back in Guangdong, I
went back to the place where I had been in the guerrilla outfit during the war.
This driver took me everywhere. This driver, his awakening happened faster
than mine! He—shit!—he said, "if he [Mao Zedong] had just gone and died
ten years earlier then everything would have been ok! Then we wouldn't necessarily be in such a godawful mess!" He dared to say things as reactionary as
that! [Mu Hui supplied his own appreciative laughter] At that time that was
the low level of my own awakening.

But in that sort of situation, and this kind of talk had a lot of power for me.
And when I saw the conditions things were in my own rural area it taught me
a lot. For example, didn't I tell you I was fighting with the guerrillas? At that
time I established a relationship with someone who became my godmother.
She was a local woman, she became my godmother. So I especially went back
to see this Mama of mine. Mama was already about 70 then, and when I

arrived she was just feeding the pigs. When she saw me she was terribly happy, it had been thirty years since we saw each other. She was happy to see me, I was happy to see her. So, I said, "Ma, let's take a picture of the two of us!" I had brought another person along with me, so our picture could be taken together. She agreed, "good, let's do that. It's a very rare occasion to have you here." So she went to change her clothes, you know, she'd been feeding the pigs and her clothes were filthy, so she said she'd change her clothes for this, for me.

Mu Hui is a particularly talented orchestrator of his own irony, but no one can completely index himself. Here, his environment and I contributed. This passage of his story impressed me particularly, but I did not remember all the details of the telling while I listened to his story in person. As I transcribed my recording of this passage, I noticed there had been various noises in the background, including some kind of machine, some children playing, a motorcycle somewhere, but now all background noise had stopped in serendipitous cooperation with Mu Hui's dramatic point, and the whole room was full of the emotion in his voice. Reviewing this tape, I wondered, how did Mu Hui manage to manipulate even the environment outside his living room window and bring it into his own narrative? He spoke very quietly, leaning towards me.

When she'd changed, I looked and saw that it was still old tattered clothing with patches upon patches! And her son, standing there in front of me, began telling me how awful the last few years had been. He said, "It was right then, when you were here, those were our best times!"

Mu Hui paused to let the (second-level) ambiguity sink in before firmly assigning a meaning to it; "You tell me, was this praise of me or criticism of me!?" Mu Hui sat back throwing his head up as his eyes filled with tears. He tapped the tea leaves down from the inside walls of his teacup and lit another cigarette.

At the time, I could not stop the tears from coming. I felt that the ten years of suffering I had gone through was nothing compared to this Mama of mine, and it was all for nothing.

His tear-shaken voice recovered quickly as he tapped out his ashtray and delivered the moral with gruff (first-level) irony.

They protected us with their lives. Did they do that in order that they could live more miserably? So the whole way back, I wept. I let myself weep out loud. I said to my companion, see how I have mistreated my godmother? As a Communist Party member, I am ashamed! This was the biggest inspiration to my awakening and conversion. After that I felt that there was a need to take control of this Cultural Revolution. This was not a matter of my own personal anger or problems.

  Even now, some people say to me, they complain against me. For example, I could be said to be a person with political "problems" stemming from June Fourth [1989]. But there was no single act that ruined the Party's credibility.

Suddenly the hawkers are back, winding their way through the tangled alley
ways outside Mu Hui's window, charming me from a pleasant distance with
calls that must have changed little since before Liberation, "old furniture!,"
"swap your beer bottles!" These sociable sounds dovetail with Mu Hui's return
from his personal story to a more public recital of his position.

> I tell them, "You all are so left its hard to say where you're going. But if it
> weren't for the Cultural Revolution at least we wouldn't be so corrupt. Be-
> cause that's when the corruption started. From then." Of course you can't say
> that before that the party was perfectly pure, without any corruption, but the
> army really did bring the corruption to the country. It all comes down to every
> little thing people [in power] did that made the people suffer. The rape of
> women, the educated youth who were separated from their families, you know
> all that.

At the beginning of the Cultural Revolution kids were sometimes sent off to
farm villages independently rather than in groups, as they were later when the
process was routinized. Without their family networks they were vulnerable.
Rape, accounts of which abound in the stories and "scar" literature that marked
the emergence of a general disavowal of the Cultural Revolution, is a good example of that vulnerability, since it also works so clearly as a symbol of the
perpetrator's power and moral offense, and creates a chain of moral decay, jus-
tifying it, covering up, encouraging others, until an entire morally decrepit atmosphere is created. Rape, then, as a symbol of moral offense, stands for the
Cultural Revolution in general, and for a crime in which Mu Hui felt he himself had been implicated. For Mu Hui, the knowledge that he had left his Mama
to grow old in her rags crushed suddenly down upon him after thirty years of
doing what he had thought was right on her behalf. Writing ironic zawen and
subjecting himself to the indexical contextualizing of ferociously critical others is his penance. He presents it, however, as his privilege:

> So when people criticize me I say, this is not a personal grievance. It's not per-
> sonal at all. They destroyed the Communist Party! This is the kind of feeling,
> outrage, I am bringing to my work. To express it, my best weapon is the za-
> wen. That's what gives me the right to write zawen, those ten years for every-
> one else, not my ten years. Before this, I did a little of everything, here and
> there, all kinds of writing. After that, I still did my job, but mostly I write
> zawen.

•   •   •

Mu Hui's life journey from ineffective drunken soldier to pen-wielding cultural
warrior, as he describes it in his narratives and enacts it in his writings, is an
allegory on the story of zawen. He has styled it that way, because he himself
seeks to understand and also justify who he is and why this funny genre called

zawen, the "bonsai" of literary art, as he calls it, came to be such a big part of what he is and does. Hearing his story requires not just cooperation but "participant imagination" (Friedrich 1986: 3). I, for example, could never have even talked to Mu Hui without spending the years it took to understand even the very rough outlines of zawen practice and his role in the contemporary zawen phenomenon. During the brief minutes it took him to recount the climax of his post-Mao "conversion" story, it was I who heard the silence of the children and hawkers (the fact that I caught this cosmic cooperation on tape notwithstanding).

Even under direct tutelage, with my ears inclined to appreciation of Mu Hui's story, I cannot say I understand the contour of Mu Hui's every symbolic mountain and river, like the ancient eavesdropping friend Zhong Ziqi could when Yu Boya played his zither. In fact, those who can hear the meaning better than I are as likely to be Mu Hui's enemies and critics as his friends. In between the jokes and silly twists of zawen it is still impossible to forget that the point of it all is precisely a reminder that the interaction that happens through even the most uncooperative style of language is serious business.

Perhaps that is what makes even the wine tropes work, at least sometimes, no matter how tired the symbol of wine of the expression "in vino veritas" and its Chinese counterpart "after drinking, spit out the truth" may be. Uses of wine tropes are often ironic; that is, they mask the desire to engage with the various problems people seem to want to escape with wine, or with frivolous writing styles. In my files from fieldwork I have several unrelated articles and poems all titled roughly "writers and wine" *(wenren yu jiu)*. There seems to be a "natural" relationship between them. If I may personify for a moment, I think essentially Chinese writers and wine have the same problem; they both "want" to cultivate themselves, to improve and refine themselves, to stand apart in cultured richness and moral quality, but on the other hand, they both also want to be "drunk." Like Huang Gongshao's solitary drinker, they long to be consumed in the thick of the muddiness, imperfection and "miscellany" of life. The desire to be read has to involve a willingness to engage creatively and imaginatively in communicative processes over which participants have very little control.

The kinds of irony we find in zawen writing, however light and irresponsible in appearance, are ultimately intended to bring the most worrisome human problems into better focus, discussing, changing, if not actually resolving, problems such as hierarchy, moral censure, political struggle, and loneliness. Irony is a mask that in many ways does not hide or protect, but may emphasize, or accent an expression instead of hiding it. And yet irony, like wine, may also offer the opportunity to dismiss what is said as arrogant, foolish, or simply crazy. When these zawen-writers speak of hating wine, they truly hate the idea that it might make them socially and politically impotent. Drinking, like writing, is a risky business, and we cannot predict exactly when it might do the magic it promises, or bring the tragedy it threatens. Like drinking at a banquet, the publication of writing is an imperfect vehicle for the interpersonal engagement to which it is in service. And yet, like words that cannot be uttered until the speaker is drunk, something happens in the imaginations of all participants when pungent little bites of writing are dished up and sent out to the world to be devoured by friends and enemies alike.

References

Balazs, Etienne. 1964. *Chinese Civilization and Bureaucracy.* New Haven: Yale University Press.

Behar, Ruth. 1995. Rage and Redemption: Reading the Life Story of a Mexican Marketing Woman. In *The Dialogic Emergence of Culture,* ed. Dennis Tedlock and Bruce Mannheim, 148–78. Urbana: University of Illinois Press.

Behler, Ernst. 1990. *Irony and the Discourse of Modernity.* Seattle: University of Washington Press.

Booth, Wayne C. 1974. *A Rhetoric of Irony.* Chicago: University of Chicago Press.

Cai Yuanpei. [1938] 1981. Lu Xun xiansheng chuanji xu [Preface to the Complete Works of Mr. Lu Xun]. In *[Sixty Years of Lu Xun Research],* ed. Li Zongying and Zhang Mengyang, 1: 225–26. 2 vols. Beijing: Zhongguo Shehuikexue Chubanshe.

Dane, Joseph A. 1991. *The Critical Mythology of Irony.* Athens: University of Georgia Press.

Eber, Christine. 1995. *Women & Alcohol in a Highland Maya Town.* Austin: University of Texas Press.

Everett, Michael W., Jack O. Waddell, and Dwight B. Heath. 1976. *Cross-Cultural Approaches to the Study of Alcohol: An Interdisciplinary Perspective.* The Hague: Mouton Publishers.

Haiman, Hohn. 1998. *Talk Is Cheap: Sarcasm, Alienation, and the Evolution of Language.* Oxford: Oxford University Press.

Hsu, Helen F. 1989. *Agents and Victims in South China: Accomplices in Rural Revolution.* New Haven: Yale University Press.

Huang Shang. 1950. Zawen fuxing [Zawen Renaissance]. In *Zhongguo zawen daguan,* ed. Lan Ling, 3: 27–29. Tianjin: Baihua Wenyi Chubanshe.

———. 1988. Jiu hua [Wine Talk]. In *Jieyou ji* [A Collection to Soothe Away Worries], ed. Wu Zuguang, 42–44. Beijing: Neimongguzizhichu Zhongguo Wenhua Xinhua Shudian.

Huters, Theodore. 1990. *Reading the Modern Chinese Short Story.* Armonk, NY: M.E. Sharpe.

Kierkegaard, Søren. 1965. *The Concept of Irony.* New York: Harper and Row.

———. 1989. "In Vino Veritas." In *Stages on Life's Way.* Princeton: Princeton University Press.

Mao Tse-Tung. 1967. *Selected Works of Mao Tse-Tung.* Peking: Foreign Languages Press.

Mu Hui. 1988. Jiu de fandiao [The Counter-tone of Wine]. In *Jieyou ji* [A Collection to Soothe Away Worries], ed. Wu Zuguang, 37–41. Beijing: Neimenggu Zizhichu Zhongguo Wenhua Chubanshe.

————. 1992. Weishenme zhongliu yinjin ge yan yuanshu [Why Did Central Current Introduce This Yan Yuanshu?]. *In Memorandum of Anti-Left Writings,* ed. Zhao Shilin, 226–36. Taiyuan: Shuhai Chubanshe.

Muecke, D. C. 1969. *The Compass of Irony.* London: Methuen and Co.

Schoenhals, Martin. 1993. *The Paradox of Power in a People's Republic of China Middle School.* Armonk, NY: M.E. Sharpe.

Scoggin, Mary. 1997. Ethnography of a Chinese Essay: Zawen in Contemporary China. Ph.D. dissertation, University of Chicago.

Shao Yanxiang. 1993. *Ziji de jiubei* [My Own Winecup]. Hunan: Qunzhong Chubanshe.

Wu Zuguang, ed. 1988a. *Jieyou ji* [A Collection to Soothe Away Worries] Beijing: Neimenggu Zizhichu Zhongguo Wenhua Xinhua Shudian.

————. 1988b. Preface to *Jieyou ji,* ed. Wu Zuguang, 1–10. Beijing: Neimonggu Zizhichu Zhongguo Wenhua Chubanshe.

Yang Xianyi. 1988. Foreword to *Jieyou ji,* ed. Wu Zuguang, 72–73. Beijing: Neimonggu Zizhichu Zhongguo Wenhua Chubanshe.

Chapter Eight

LAWRENCE J. TAYLOR

Paddy's Pig: Irony and Self-Irony
in Irish Culture

An American from Iowa, a member of the Scientific Pig Farmers Association, embarks on a world tour to gather information on scientific pig farming techniques. His first stop is in Ireland, and he soon finds himself wandering along a country road in the wilds of Donegal. Seeing no obvious pig farms, he finally approaches a small cottage and knocks on the door.

The American—armed with a clipboard—informs the Irishman, in the loud and flat tones of the American Midwest, "I'm here for the SPFA—the Scientific Pig Farmers Association—to observe pig farming techniques. Do you have any pigs?"

"I do indeed," the Irishman answers, "I'm just off to feed them at the moment if you'd like to come along."

"That's swell," says the American, who follows him around the back of the house to the small sty. The Irishman wades out among the porkers and, bending over, grabs one of them around the waist, and with a colossal effort hoists the pig up into the air before him, staggers over to a low apple tree and, finding an apple, pushes the pig up toward it. The pig gobbles the apple and the Irishman staggers around the tree, pig in arms, until he finds another apple and again pushes the pig up to eat. He then puts the pig back on the ground and is about to lift a second one when the astounded Iowan interrupts him, "Hold on, hold on there! You can't tell me that this is how you feed your pigs?"

"Aye" Paddy responds.

"Why that's the most unscientific procedure I have ever heard of."

"How's that?" the Irishman inquires.

"Well, just for a start," says the American, looking at the data on his clipboard, "it's incredibly time-consuming . . ."

"Sure," the Irishman expostulates, smiling, "What's time to a pig?"

● ● ●

That joke,[1] or satiric narrative, is one of my favorite examples of a genre of "American joke" that has had some currency in Ireland for several decades now. I use it as a point of departure and return in this chapter, which considers the roles irony and self-irony have played, and continue to play in the Irish construction of a national self in historically changing contexts. In so doing, I hope to contribute to our understanding of "social and cultural poetics" (Fernandez and Herzfeld 1998) by examining some of the distinctive features of the self-ironic trope as it is used in the continuing negotiation of personal and national identity. In the course of this admittedly speculative survey of cultural fragments, I hope also to explore some of the ways that anthropology can contribute to cultural studies in Ireland, from which it has been conspicuous by its absence.

The treatment of texts as expressions and constructors of national identity is, of course, central to recent literary analyses in the "postcolonial" mode, including for Ireland works by Eagleton, Jameson, and Said (1990) and Kiberd (1996), to name only a few of the most prominent practitioners. They, in turn, have taken their theoretical models from social theorists of nationalism that include Fanon (1952), Benedict Anderson (1983), Gellner (1997), and the "subalternists" (see Spivak 1996), or from cultural studies à la Raymond Williams. In their search for subversive narratives and popular consciousness, literary analysts are finding themselves drifting further and further from the classic canon of Irish (and of course, other) literatures, and further into cultural realms that have long been the field of anthropological inquiry. Anthropologists, for their part, have freely borrowed from literary theories to interpret the sort of texts they encounter "in the field" rather than the library, and a variety of approaches to a socially situated "poetics" have been developing (see Fernandez and Herzfeld 1998 for a useful overview). This should be a natural meeting ground. That such a meeting has been slow to materialize in Ireland is a function of a variety of circumstances, I think. Rather than lament, however, I want to move ahead in a small way, adding another piece to an ongoing exploration of the boundaries between literature and anthropology in the Irish context (Taylor 1996, 1999). In one of those pieces (Taylor 1996), I argued there that anthropologists working in Ireland—and literary theorists as well—could well pay more attention to humor. Not only because it is a feature of Irish life, but because its existence—or better, performance—is an aspect of Irish identity, of the national self-image. As for irony (and more so, self-irony) that particular form of humor has been of particular anthropological interest possibly because its

1. I first heard this joke from Ciaran Carson, to whom I am grateful for the original inspiration for this piece. Carson soon after wrote a poem entitled, "What Is Time to a Pig?" (1986). As with other folk and popular oral traditions, this joke has a far wider distribution. An editor notes, "I first read this joke as a child, in an American anthology published—I think—in the 1940s; one party to the joke was a lost traveler, and the farmer's punchline was 'What's time to a durned hog?'"

tropic character leaves room for a fertile ambivalence. Considering that ambivalence is a key feature of the postcolonial condition, according to Fanon and
his followers, there may be here an interesting possibility for interdisciplinary
exploration. I will return to the joke at the end, after encountering a fair few
pigs on the way, but suffice it to note for the moment that the ironic opposition
in this perhaps late postcolonial state is vis-à-vis the American. It is that opposition coupled with my field experience in southwest Donegal that pushes me
to consider the topic. There, ironic views of various Others, as well as of the
personal and national Self, were not rare and in fact are considered a verbal art
form. Within that discourse, there was at least as much concern with defining
Irishness in relation to Americans and American culture, as to England and
English.

●   ●   ●

However it is applied to current circumstances, Irish humor has long had what
we might call a political function. In his magisterial survey, *The Irish Comic
Tradition,* Vivian Mercier (1962) argues that combative humor is among the
central features of Irish literature and indeed culture:

> Three archaic attitudes which have remained imbedded in the popular beliefs
> of the Irish: first, that wisdom can be demonstrated by the propounding or an-
> swering of seemingly insoluble riddles; second, that the dexterous use of ver-
> bal ambiguity is inseparable from wit and wisdom; third, that truth can be ar-
> rived at by witty dialectic. (86)

In the realm of political humor, irony has deep historical roots. It is a crucial
element in satire, which was, for the ancient Irish, both an art form and a mor-
tal weapon. From pre-Christian through medieval times, kings and chieftans
employed poets or bards who composed poems that praised their patrons and
damned, through merciless satire, their patron's enemies. The standard form
this satire took was the personal lampoon based on either an exaggerated description of the subject's flaws, or, more subtly, "praise" of non-existent virtues.
For Mercier, the fact that the satire remains so "personal" is evidence of its origin as magic, as was "the persistent belief, still alive in the nineteenth century,
that satire had the power to inflict actual harm on its victim" (145). Actually, the
belief persisted longer yet, as revealed in the poet Patrick Kavanagh's ([1938]
1971: 326–27) story of the man who walked ten miles to ask him to compose
a damning satire on his neighbors, "I want ye to make a ballad on them, a good,
strong, poisonous ballad. I'll give you the facts, and you'll make the ballad."

But the specifically ironic element in satire, according to Mercier, develops
along with a certain level of sophistication, and self-satire, one might add, not
only requires greater sophistication, but also entails a greater risk. The risk lies

in the possibility that nobody will get the joke, and that it will be taken literally. In effect there must exist a "community of understanding." Unlike the more obvious invective satire, irony creates a dramatic situation of conspiracy between the ironist and the listener, at the expense of a third party. Which is to say that the use of irony relies on a shared world of meaning, and therefore, is either predicated on or helps forge a social relationship. In Mercier's words,

> Three elements are necessary for satisfactory response to irony. The reader's possession of norms, his ability to compare ironic statements with these norms, and the realization, based on certain hints let fall by the ironist, that the latter shares his norms. (1962: 2)

So the reader—or listener—joins the ironist in a community of opposition created by the joke. Apparently, the Irish bards were a sophisticated enough company to trust each other to hear the ironic note, and even to indulge in self-irony, such as when the bardic institution itself was the subject of satire in *Imtheacht na Tromdháimhe* (The Proceedings of the Burdensome Bardic Company 1860). But the ability to indulge in satire, let alone self-satire, according to Mercier, was much weakened by the horrors of Irish life in the eighteenth and nineteenth centuries. In that period, while an Anglo-Irishman like Swift could afford to be ironic, political satire was impossible for the Irish Catholics in view of "their deep emotional involvement in the miseries of their country." Mercier notes that:

> Even an Irish nationalist of English stock, John Mitchel, found irony impossible to sustain in face of the enormity of the Great Famine. Lacking the necessary detachment for satire, Irish nationalists vented their indignation in factual indictments of the British misgovernment of Ireland; the facts were never in short supply. (185–86)

In that same period, of course, the Irish were the butt of English comic identity politics, a tradition that stretches back as far as Geraldus Cambrensis—Gerald of Wales—a Norman cleric who visited and described Ireland in the twelfth century. It is perhaps a delicate issue to decide whether his view, like that of Herodotus and others in the classic "encountering the Other" literature, is of The Other (as in self-defining by opposition) or just an other. By Spencer's time (in the Age of Elizabeth), however, it is clear that the Irish had come to fill a very specific symbolic as well as any political or economic need for the English. European Romanticism would make such oppositions both more culturally central and, of course, 'weighted' differently, though that of course depended on who was using them. The earlier occidentalizing of the wild Celt in his picturesque landscape appealed to the Romantic sensibility, but increasingly gave way later in the century to a straightforward stigmatizing of the Irish as either dangerously savage, or comically barbarous. In the first case, in line with the general idiom of the time, he was rendered more and more simian-like. That nineteenth century return to the earlier "savage" trope certainly conforms to one of the two contemporary cultural projects of western Europe (and the United States): colonizing abroad. The comically barbarous character was perhaps more useful in the service of the other "project": civilizing or domesticating at home.

By Victorian times, the English could view the Irish as either distant savages or as caricatures of proper peasants. In the latter case, the comic rendition relied on a number of parodic targets, which might, in some measure, be read not only as attacks on the Irish, but on an earlier Romantic sensibility: an ironic picturesque. Thus, for example, the English traveler or Punch cartoonist encounters a landscape awesome only in its humidity, and home to stinking hovels within which are to be found not only filth and degradation, but a promiscuity of animal and human. Here is a reversal or confusion of basic Victorian categories: an image that summed up an unrepentant confusion of civilized domesticity: "the pig in the parlor." That picture embodied the central Victorian obsession with the separation of domestic spaces, with particular reference to the civilizing properties of the parlor. A proper parlor would make both children and the lower classes behave properly. But—the stereotype implied—nothing would work on the Irish. They slept with their pigs, and even if you gave them a house with a parlor, they would continue to do so. The Irishman thus found sharing his pig's home, was nearly always given something, usually too much, to say. He is in fact the embodiment of a hyperbolic oral culture whose ornamentation is not only extravagant, it is ridiculous, leading poor Paddy into a humor over which he has no control. In one typical version of this encounter, when the Englishman asks about this confused domestic arrangement, Paddy replies, "Sure, and doesn't he have every possible thing he could wish for here under the roof?"

Jeremiah Curtin (1940), an American visiting southwest Donegal in the 1880s, offers a wonderfully telling account of another version of this symbolic confrontation of English traveler and wild Gael (see Taylor 1995 for a portrait of the same place a hundred years later).

> That afternoon I went up the hill to Barror's to have the old man tell me another myth. On the way I rested for a few moments in a house where a pig that weighed at least two hundred pounds lay in the kitchen, stretched on his side in front of the peat fire. When I congratulated the woman on having such a fine, fat pig, her answer was "God be blessed, that's our rent." While I was talking to Barror two women English tourists who had been at Bun Glass [sic] halted at the door and stared at the family, much as though they were some new species of monkey."

Curtin clearly represents a new twist here, for the "pig in the parlor" had of course a different, but equally potent meaning for him. He was apparently delighted with what for him was a sign of the pre-civilized (rather than savage) folk. Pigs as myths were to be found by the same hearth.

That equation between authentic folk and their narratives would take on a more potent sense and mission a few decades later, when the revival of interest in the Gaelic language and culture found a central place in the self-definition of a cultural nationalism which eventually held sway in the newly independent Ireland. This seems an instance of what Ernest Gellner (1997) called "small nation nationalism," wherein the characterization of a subordinate national self is embraced, but sentimentalized and extolled. Hyperbolically, oral culture, and even the pig by the hearth, are seen as noble features of a tribal zone into which folklorist-nationalists could venture at will from their own Victorian parlors.

There were more critical, even potentially subversive voices, like Synge's, but the master narrative (as we now say) was decidedly unfunny. At this stage of self-invention, irony did not figure: as can be seen from the picture of Irishness enshrined in De Valera's famous 1943 speech on the ideal image of Irish life. In that same period, the newly established National Folklore Commission was hard at work filling an archive with stories collected from all over the country, but with a preponderant emphasis on the Gaelic-speaking west, clearly seen as a kind of tribal zone. Several of the more reflexive locals responded to this external interest their own "naive" Gaelic-language (Gaeltacht) autobiographies, depicting "the last days" of traditional life on the rain-soaked wind-battered isles and peninsulas of the western seaboard, from the Blaskets to Tory Island. These became instant classics in the original and in English translation, and probably to the detriment of future generations' ability to enjoy them, were enshrined as required secondary school reading. The welter of self-definition was no doubt deadly serious to some, but it presented features that could only be called ironic. The very consciousness of the "folkloric character" of these western people and texts showed the collector to be alienated from the very tradition in which he was seeking his own identity. While in the Irish case this was or could be ascribed to colonialism (particularly with reference to the loss of Gaelic), elsewhere (e.g., in France) class, geography, and modernizing forces created similar situations. In any case, for the collector of folklore, the local Irish speaker with the pig in the parlor was at once inner Irish self and tribal Other. This fact set the stage for an overwhelmingly symbolic interaction.

Bravely into this self-definitive whirl stepped the great satirist Flann O'Brien (alias Brian O'Nolan, alias Myles na Gopaleen), taking on the central icons in his 1941 Gaelic-language mock autobiography *An Béal Bocht*—"The Poor Mouth."

The form is a parody—perhaps not so much of the naive Gaeltacht autobiographies mentioned above as of the way they were read and sanctified. However, nobody involved in the dialectic fugue of self-definition escapes O'Brien. The role of the pig and the house in the success or failure of what Norbert Elias called the "civilizing process" is taken up as follows, in the voice of the reminiscing 'true Gael' who begins with a description of the sleeping arrangements:

> Our house was undivided, wisps of rushes above us on the roof and rushes also as bedding in the end of the house. At sundown rushes were spread over the whole floor and the household lay to rest on them. Yonder a bed with pigs upon it; here a bed with people; a bed there with an aged slim cow stretched out asleep on her flank and a gale of breath issuing from her capable of raising a tempest in the centre of the house; hens and chickens asleep in the shelter of her belly; another bed near the fire with me on it.

Civilization arrives in the form of a lost school-inspector who

> . . . let a long roar of amazement out of him and stood there on the threshold staring in. Says he: Isn't it a shameful, improper and very bad thing for ye to be stretched out with the brute beasts, all of ye stuck together in the one bed? And isn't it a shameful, bad and improper state that ye're in here tonight? 'Tis true for you, I replied to the gentleman, but sure we can't help the bad state you've mentioned. The weather is bitter and every one of us must be inside from it, whether he has two legs or four under him. If that's the way it is, says the gentleman, wouldn't it be easy for you to put up a little hut at the side of the yard and it a bit out from the house? Sure and 'twould be easy, says I. I was full of wonder at all he said because I never thought of the like nor of any other plan that would be handy to improve the bad state we were in — all of us stuck together in the end of the house. The next day I gathered the neighbours and explained exactly to the gentleman's advice. They praised that advice and within a week we had put up a fine hut adjacent to my house. But alas! things are not what they seem to be! When I, my grandmother and two of my brothers had spent two nights in the hut, we were so cold and drenched wet that it is a wonder we did not die straight away and we couldn't get any relief until we went back to the house and were comfortable again among the cattle. We've been that way ever since, just like every poor bit of a Gael in this side of the country. (O'Brien 1973: 18–20)

The pig is further used to satirize both friends and enemies of the local, still hyperbolically oral, culture—so that he paraded out in shorts as a literate English speaker for the Englishman, and is taken later on for the most authentic of Gaeilgeoirs by a folklorist. All this from a Gaelic speaker, born in rural Tyrone. The very fact of the book was ironic. By writing his tract in the same language as the Gaeltacht autobiographies, O'Brien established his own nationalist credentials and added his book to the short list of modern Gaelic classics along with the works he was parodying. Historian Gearóid Ó Tuaithaigh (pers. comm.) describes the historic context of this stinging treatise as follows:

> Imagine Gaelic Ireland as an Old Woman dying on her bed, surrounded by her loyal sons who are doing whatever little they can, with medicines and prayers, to keep her alive. Into the room bursts the drunken brother — O'Brien — who knocks over candles, medicines, everything and shakes the dying mother by the shoulders.

The real irony here, was indeed in the fact that, while wildly inventive and modern, the book is arguably far more rooted in actual Gaelic tradition than those of the revivalists.

But there was another, contemporaneous ironic reappropriation of the Victorian parlor Gael on the streets of Dublin, discussed by Kiberd (1996), as represented by Brendan Behan. When I first arrived in Ireland in 1973, that tradition was still very strong—as was the object of its irony, and one of its best versions was the song "The Sea around Us," penned by Brendan's brother, Dominic, and recorded by the Ludlows in 1970:

> They say that the lakes of Killarney are fair
> That no stream like the Liffey can ever compare
> If it's water you want you'll find nothing more rare
> Than the stuff they make down by the ocean.
>
> The sea oh the sea, gra geal mo chroi
> Long may it roll between England and me
> It's a sure guarantee that some hour we'll be free
> Thank God we're surrounded by water.

Irish listeners would immediately recognize it as a parody, first of all, of the standard local "anthems" very popular both in Ireland and, perhaps more so, abroad among immigrants and their descendants. These songs are another vital ingredient in a Victorian, sentimental, parlor Ireland—taken together they conjure the geography of that Imagined Ireland. Each extols the scenic virtues of regional landmarks, very often bodies of water: Galway Bay, Lough Rea, the Shannon, and in this case, that favorite romantic landscape trope (see Gibbons 1996) and perpetual tourist destination, the lakes of Killarney, and Dublin's River Liffey. Having tricked the listener into expecting the standard contest among local land and waterscapes, the song switches idioms from nineteenth-century Victorian rural sentimentality to Dublin street directness—"If it's water you want . . . the stuff they make down by the ocean." So it is not only the maudlin regional ballad that is being parodied here, but also the sentimental parlor nationalism that goes along with it. Forget the lakes and rivers, Dominic tells his audience, and look to that body of water that "rolls between England and me." The sea, of course, surrounds and demarcates the entire Island of Ireland, thus obviating not only local borders but also the big one that separates the Republic from Northern Ireland.

The song takes on the tone of acerbic sarcasm in the next two verses. The first victim is that favorite of Victorian Irish parlors, Thomas Moore.

> Tom Moore made his waters meet fame and renown
> A great lover of anything dressed in a crown
> In brandy the bandy old Saxon he'd drown
> But throw ne'er a one into the ocean.

The reference is perhaps to Moore's song, "The Meeting of the waters"—which paints a charming picture of a river valley in the southeast of Ireland. But the audience recognizes a more thorough parody aimed at a certain type of romantic nationalist for whom, like Moore, music might be a substitute for rebellion. A trade-off that has dire consequences is spelled out in the next verse:

> The Scots have their whiskey, the Welsh have their speech
> And their poets are paid about ten pence a week
> Provided no hard words on England they speak
> Oh Lord what a price for devotion.

Finally, Dominic turns his attention once more to the actual history of invasion and resistance—Irish history as "one damned thing after another"—making the point that only extreme measures have been effective.

> The Danes came to Ireland with nothing to do
> But dream of the plundered Old Irish they slew
> Ye will in your Vikings said Brian Boru
> And threw them back into the ocean.

> Two foreign old monarchs in battle did join
> Each wanting their head on the back of a coin
> If the Irish had sense, they'd drown both in the Boyne
> And partition throw into the ocean.

How is the song self-ironic? One is reminded of the poetic satire, "The Burdensome Bardic Company"—that assault on bardic techniques, pedantry, subject matter, and social behavior of centuries earlier, which might be viewed as the precursor of Dominic Behan's attack on his own predecessors. It is hard to believe that Behan was not considering his own position as the latest in a long line of Irishmen "singing" their way to freedom.

O'Brien and Behan both launch ironic attacks on the sentimental, Victorian parlor variety of Irish nationalism. But each in his own way is also self-ironic, and that is a higher art form. Higher, because self-irony preserves, even lays bare, the ambivalence at the core of the postcolonial experience. Further, by virtue of its intrinsic reflexivity, this same self-irony draws attention to the artist and art form. In so doing, it unmasks the genre in which it participates—deconstructing its own narrative. But at the same time it empowers itself through the performance. In the cases at hand, one might say that both authors—certainly O'Brien, perhaps Behan—are defining Irishness, not through the images and icons they deconstruct, but through the performance itself. They are reasserting a cultural temperament and comic tradition which never went away, but survived in attitudes and idioms in a city and country that never really conformed to the folkloric image. Indeed, it is worth noting that some of the most successful current Irish fiction and drama can be described as acerbically self-ironic, a reappropriation of the stereotypically rural self that is still so useful to foreign and some Irish audiences. Among these would be the novels of Roddy Doyle, beginning with *The Commitments* in 1988, portraying an alternative "real Ireland" in the council housing of peripheral Dublin, where every rural virtue is stood on its head. Then there is the brilliantly black humor of Patrick McCabe's *The Butcher Boy* (1993) wherein Irish boy as pig actually finds his way into a middle class parlor and takes a shit on the floor. Even the iconic West is back on stage—but perverted, and with critical references to on or off-stage Americans, in plays like Martin McDonough's "Beauty Queen of Lenane," and the wonderfully reflexive and deeply self-ironic "Stones in His Pockets," by Marie Jones.

•   •   •

Ironic performances are not confined to stage or text. As an anthropologist living in and visiting Donegal over the last twenty-five years I have always been impressed by the uses of irony and self-irony there, and elsewhere in Ireland. There are forms reminiscent of *An Beal Bocht,* like village fisherman John Phaddy's recitations as everyone sat in the rowboats waiting for a salmon to jump. In mock-heroic fashion he would give a satiric description of each crew as a bunch of *michusamhacht amaidan* (malformed idiots). He would thus "take the piss out" of all competitors, but of course draw artful attention to the gap between the heroic circumstances that should accompany such narrations and the paltry world in which they found themselves. By implication he was another poor excuse for a heroic age bard, but—at the same time—an able performer of just this sort of exercise. A performance of Irishness in its local mode, if you will.

But the comic forms that are most explicitly turned to the task of self-definition were the jokes that implicitly answer the question: Irish as opposed to what? These I encountered, and continue to hear, all over the country. There are of course, English versus Irish jokes, which tend to take the stereotype of the Irish and play with it.[2] There are also the dozens of Kerryman jokes, very popular in the '70s, which arguably take those same English Irishman jokes and project them on the inner tribal self in the West. And there are the American jokes. Like the one with which I began.

2. The current mode is an intriguing spin on the Irishman, Scotsman, Englishman jokes wherein the characters are called, "Paddy the Irishman, Paddy the Scotsman, and Paddy the Englishman." In my favorite of that genre the three find themselves stranded together in the Sahara. They stumble over a bottle containing a genie, who emerges and gives them each a wish. "I wish I was back in London," says Paddy the Englishman, who vanishes from site as he pronounces those words. "Well then," says Paddy the Scotsman, "I wish I was back in Edinburgh." And off he goes as well. Paddy the Irishman looks around him then and laments, "Christ, it's lonely here now, I wish they were back," thus proving who is the real Paddy.

In fact, most American jokes are simpler affairs playing especially on notions of size. The jokes always involve a battle of wits between a self-convinced American sophisticate, who brags about America, and an apparently simple Irishman. The Irishman gets the last word and that word is nearly always ironic. But the most sophisticated and, I would say, powerful versions are self-ironic— as we have seen, a form that preserves the ambivalence at the heart of the interaction and of self-definition. Like the pig joke with which I began, which in Flann O'Brienesque fashion, brilliantly appropriates the whole history of this coupling of pig/oral versus sophisticated written culture in a construction of self and world worthy of the late Wittgenstein.

In the joke, the American's scientific rationalism is satirized even as the rural Irishman is given a self-ironic gloss. If this is the self-irony of postcolonialism, it is interesting to note the following. Not only has the anecdotal English Other given way to the American: he figures, not as colonial exploiter, but as a combination of rational scientist and tourist (reminiscent, of course, of earlier English tourists—or the American anthropologist), who is regularly duped by what only appear to be simple natives. There is even a Gaelic-language novel by a local priest satirizing the ethnographers of the smallest of the Aran Islands (Standún 1993).

The identity ambivalence inherent in relation to Americans is of course different from that forged in a colonial context vis-à-vis the English. Americans were, in the first instance, actual relations and/or neighbors who had left the home place and had, to use the suggestive expression, "came back to us a Yank." That sort of transformation was clearly both a hope and a fear in a world in which emigration was long a central feature of local life. Although many went to England as well, it is interesting to note that there is no equivalent term, indicating perhaps that there was not the comparable sense of expected transformation. The person who went to England would remain Irish, for becoming "English"—a clear, essentialist ethnic category from both sides of the divide— was not an option.[3] But "American" is a far more ambiguous category, seen in some ways as a personality type and worldview attainable by and attachable to any ethnicity. People came back from America different—but the meaning of the difference was, and remains, unclear.

In fact, if anything, this ambiguity and ambivalence has increased in 2000. Now there is a widespread belief that Ireland as a whole might succumb to American culture and lose its national identity in that way. Thus, on both the personal and collective levels, the American, and particularly the Irish American, is always a challenge to an Irish person's sense of national identity and self.

---

3. A class full of Irish University students could only come up with the phrase "plastic paddy" for the descendants of Irish immigrants to England. They all acknowledged the ambiguously negative sense of the term, but were unable to say exactly what was meant or why.

The man or woman who comes back from America is always a potential self—realized or not, one that is believed, in a general way, to be making unfavorable comparisons between Ireland and America.

In the jokes, the function of the self-ironic trope is, of course, not only to expose the ambiguous notions of self, but to protect that self from the American visitor or investigator who is trying to "be," or somehow capture through description and/or analysis, the Irish. One theme of the ironic twist here is the escape from knowledge: "You are not us. You will never know us." Interestingly, young Irish abroad can also perform this sense of distance. In the words of an Irish University student who had returned from a visit to the United States, "I was with a group of Irish and we would tell Americans ridiculous lies and they would always believe them, about what was going on in Ireland. It got to be a joke among us, that Americans never got it when you where slagging them. They have no sense of irony." The notion that Americans have no sense of irony, or at least do not "get it" when the Irish are being ironic, is another, and probably far more frequently invoked version of this opposition. This is the Irish version of what Herzfeld (1997) has called "cultural intimacy." To make this point, the jokes and the "slagging," and of course the retelling of the incidents of slagging, all stress the very lack of that "shared world of meaning." To revert to Mercier's definition, the joke and the slagging demonstrate that the American and the Irishman do not share norms. A cultural distance is created where it may have been threatened.

But there is also a performance level to this joke, as with other works we have been considering, where another sort of interaction, and hence social relation, is being acted out or created. The fact that self-irony is or can be funny is not unimportant. The joke, we know, in the trope, is clearly at "someone's expense." But there is another sort of power relation involved in which the joke-teller, by making someone laugh, gets power over him or her, or in the slagging incident establishes an unrecognized, but possibly unsettling effect on the poor American who does not "get it." If pleasure is, or should be, involved then so is it in sex, and as with sex, in the joke the pleasure adds to rather than detracts from the power. It is the very fulcrum of domination.

Among these performances, the self-ironic joke is a particularly powerful move in Mercier's battle of wits. It taps into the very ambivalence that is an aspect of the postcolonial condition, and performs that ambivalence for the ironist as much as for the audience. Which leads us back to our song, "The Sea around Us." In that barroom ballad—as it became in performance—the bravado of the heroically resistant Irish was leavened by an ironic view of their own present and past. But if the words and performance of the song left any doubt as to this element, the knife was inevitably twisted by some wit who would alter the refrain, changing "T'ank God we're surrounded by water" to

"T'ank God we're surrounded by porter (as in beer)." Since the people singing
this were in a pub and would often hold up their pints at this point, the meaning could not be lost (though possibly obscured) by even the most theoretically
prepared anthropologist. The singer appropriates himself and his companions
as a metonym for Ireland: drunk, singing, and blissfully delusional in the face
of history. All this while the situation in the North was heating up and when the
very same crowd might be singing the Wolftones song, "The Men behind the
Wire"—a reference to political internees in Longkesh prison—at some other
point in the evening. But in adding another layer to Behan's parody of nationalist song, the crowd at once displays its collective verbal wit by "carnavaliz-
ing" (Coleman 1997) the work, and asserts its shared identity as the kind of
people who know such songs and know how to play with them. All of which
amounts to a self-conscious performance of Irishness.

• • •

In defining "irony," the *OED* refers both to a figure of speech and a condition.
According to Terry Eagleton, self-irony is a trait for which Irish nationalism
"has never been particularly notable: "Michael Collins never looked much like
a man intent on doing himself out of business, a task that as it happened was
left to others. And though irony may be a favored trope of the literary intellectual, it is hard to summon much of it when you have been blinded by a British
army rubber bullet" (Eagleton, Jameson, and Said 1990: 27)

Perhaps. Certainly Collins was no self-ironist, but perhaps the working-class
streets of Dublin, like the hills of Tyrone, were more fertile grounds for a self-
awareness born of the disjunction between idealized images and stubborn reality. Yet the happy conjunction of serious political goals and a strong sense of
irony certainly can be said to have characterized both the songwriter Dominic
Behan, and his more famous, playwright brother, Brendan. Although usually
blinded by something other than a rubber bullet, Brendan did, as a child, run
guns for the IRA, and pay for that in a British borstal home; he thus cannot easily be dismissed as only a "literary intellectual." (And should we, by the way,
account Eagleton's own evidently self-ironic dismissal of "literary intellectuals" to his own Irish side, I wonder?) Brendan, at any rate, had no trouble sum-
moning a collective and individual self-irony in response to that ever-troubling
question of Irish identity. "Now Ireland," he famously remarked, "is a country
that combines Catholicism with revolution. Now that may confuse you, but
don't worry, it confuses us even more."

In fact, irony, and more particularly self-irony, seems a well-developed Irish
trait, and perhaps especially so in the neverending quest that is nationalism: a
search not only for political autonomy, but also for self-definition. This is to say

that the trope may have a role to play in both personal and collective politics, and that the Irish may have something to teach anthropology about the relation between "plays on words" and "power plays." An exploration of some elements of Irish self-irony suggests the special role such a trope may play in colonial and postcolonial contexts, where—in the Irish case—the "self" being treated to ironic definition may be not only Irish, but (in some measure) British and, laterally, American.

It may be hard to be an ironic nationalist, but rather than disappearing under the weight of colonial and postcolonial experience, self-irony is a figure of speech particularly suited for that condition.

While ironic satire makes perfect sense as a weapon of those either in power or at least in a culturally dominant position—like that most renowned of Irish satirists, Swift—self-satire is not a terrible risk for those on the bottom.[4] They are already the butts, not only of jokes, but also of reality. Thus, while irony is often the tool of the powerful, self-irony can be nearly irresistible for those who find themselves at the opposite end of the stick and who have the wit to use it— as a manner of seizing the situation, if not in one way, than in another.

It is commonplace to note the profound ambivalence in the colonial or post-colonial sense of self. While not disputing the importance of this debilitating effect of a long and oppressive relation with the English, there is also a kind of potential power in that Irish experience. The ambivalence in question can be a philosophic asset, a potential awareness of a basic truth about self and other that operates everywhere, but perhaps more subtly than in the colonial context. Further, that ambivalence is an emotionally powerful state, so that when it is directly tapped by self-irony, the results are perhaps more powerful than among those for whom the truth about themselves seems clear. Finally, to return to the specifically Irish case, it might be that now the ambiguous sense of self is more developed vis-à-vis Americans than vis-à-vis the English.

No matter at whom the self-irony is really directed, the speech—whether in the form of joke or song—is a recognition of the performer's condition, in effect acted out in the performance itself. It is a preemptive strike, beating the enemy to the punchline. The power of the self-irony is in the message of the performance: "in making this joke of myself, or ourselves, I manifestly have more power over myself than you do. I am the "Paddy" in the story, but the fact that it is me telling the story is a warning: "I can do a better job on myself than you or any so-called sophisticated outsider could do (so don't bother), and I could easily do a job on you."

4. Jewish humor—famously self-deprecating or worse—certainly can be interpreted along these lines. I would suggest that in such cases, like the Irish one, the function of an ideology and practice of "cultural intimacy" of the kind Herzfeld (1997) discusses, is particularly pointed and quite self-conscious.

Acknowledgments

This paper has greatly benefited from the suggestions and comments of Gearóid Ó Tuathaigh, Antony Farrell, and student/faculty audiences at Queen's University Belfast, NUI Galway, and NUI Maynooth.

References

Anderson, Benedict. 1983. *Imagined Communities: Reflections on the Origin and Spread of Nationalism.* London: Verso.
Behan, Dominic. N.d. "The Sea around Us." Song recorded by The Ludlows, ca. 1970.
Coleman, Steve. 1997. Joe Heaney and Style in Sean-nós Singing. In *Blas: the Local Accent in Irish Traditional Music,* ed, Thérèse M. Smith and Mícheál Súilleabháin, 31–52. Limerick: Irish World Music Centre, University of Limerick.
Curtin, Jeremiah. 1940. *Memoirs of Jeremiah Curtin.* Ed. Joseph Schafer. Madison: The State Historical Society of Wisconsin.
Doyle, Roddy. 1988. *The Commitments.* London: Heinemann. Reprinted in *The Barrytown Trilogy.* New York: Penguin, 1995.
Eagleton, Terry, Frederic Jameson, and Edward Said. 1990. *Nationalism, Colonialism, and Literature.* Minneapolis: University of Minnesota Press.
Fanon, Frantz. 1952. *Peau noire, masques blancs.* Paris: Editions du Seuil.
Fernandez, James, and Michael Herzfeld. 1998. In Search of Meaningful Methods. In *Handbook of Methods in Cultural Anthropology,* ed. H. Russell Bernard, 89–129. Walnut Creek, CA: AltaMira Press.
Gellner, Ernest. 1997. *Nationalism.* Washington Square, NY: New York University Press.
Gibbons, Luke. 1996. Topographies of Terror: Killarney and the Politics of the Sublime. Special Issue, *Ireland and Irish Cultural Studies,* ed. John Paul Waters. *South Atlantic Quarterly* 95(1): 23–44.
Herzfeld, Michael. 1997. *Cultural Intimacy: Social Poetics in the Nation-State.* Routledge: New York, London.
Imtheacht na Tromdháimhe [The Proceedings of the Burdensome Bardic Company]. Transactions of the Ossianic Society. Dublin, 1860.
Kavanagh, Patrick. [1938] 1971. *The Green Fool.* London: Martin Brian and O'Keeffe.
Kiberd, Declan. 1996. *Inventing Ireland.* Cambridge: Harvard University Press.
McCabe, Patrick. 1993. *The Butcher Boy.* New York: Fromm.
Mercier, Vivian. 1962. *The Irish Comic Tradition.* Oxford: Oxford University Press.
O'Brien, Flann. 1973. *The Poor Mouth.* London: Picador. Translation of *An Béal Bocht.* Dublin: National Press, 1941.
Spivak, Gayatri C. 1996. *The Spivak reader: Selected works of Gayatri Chakravorty Spivak.* Ed. Donna Landry and Gerald MacLean. New York: Routledge.
Standún, Pádraig. 1993. *Na hAntraipeologicals.* Indreabhán, Conamara: Cló Iar-Chonnachta
Taylor, Lawrence J. 1995. *Occasions of Faith: An Anthropology of Irish Catholics.* Philadelphia: University of Pennsylvania Press; Dublin: Lilliput.
———. 1996. "There Are Two Things People Don't Like to Read about Themselves": The Anthropology of Ireland and the Irish View of Anthropology. Special Issue,

Ireland and Irish Cultural Studies, ed. John Paul Waters. *South Atlantic Quarterly* 95 (1): 213–25.

————. 1999. Re-entering the West Room: On the Power of Domestic Spaces. In *House Life: Space, Place and Family in Europe,* ed. Donna Birdwell-Pheasant and Denise Lawrence-Zúñiga, 223–37. Oxford: Berg.

Chapter Nine

MARY TAYLOR HUBER

Irony and Paradox in the "Contact Zone": Missionary Discourse in Northern Papua New Guinea

> "Modern man does not proclaim; he speaks. That is,
> he speaks with reservations. . . . Irony (to varying degrees)
> [is] the equivocal language of modern times."
> Bakhtin (1986: 132)

When Mikhail Bakhtin called irony "the equivocal language of modern times," he had in mind the novel's way of parodying hierarchic forms of speech, and the general secularization of modern European languages through a "lengthy and complex process of expunging . . . the sacred and authoritarian word." Of course, Bakhtin's association of irony, equivocation, and modernity was not unique. In *The Great War and Modern Memory,* for example, Paul Fussell (1975: 326, 335) explored how poets, novelists, and even ordinary soldiers used irony to memorialize their experience of trench warfare's "absurd remove from the usages of the normal world" and to question not only the war, but also the innocence the Great War had savaged, the civilization the war seemed to belie.

At about the same time, Europe's colonial territories were providing another zone in which savagery and civilization were perceived to meet and clash.[1] Less

1. Mary Louise Pratt (1992: 6–7) proposes the term "contact zone" to refer to "the space of colonial encounters, the space in which peoples geographically and historically separated come into contact with each other and establish ongoing relations, usually involving conditions of coercion, radical inequality, and intractable conflict." She prefers the term "contact zone" to "colonial frontier" because "the latter term is grounded within a European expansionist perspective" (ibid.). Linda Hutcheon (1994: 93) has adopted Pratt's concept of the "contact zone," seeing its volatile mix of cultures and power as a place where irony "comes into being." I continue to use the term "colonial frontier" as a way to foreground how the "contact zone" was perceived by expatriates in the colonies, but agree with Pratt's insistence on keeping the context in sight. As James Clifford (1992: 4) noted in a review of Pratt's *Imperial Eyes: Travel Writing and Transculturation,* "to speak

extreme than life in the trenches, life in the colonies was still far enough removed from the normal—or at least the normative—to "guarantee," as Fussell puts it, "that a structure of irony sufficient for ready narrative recall" would be attached (326). Europeans in the colonies laced their conversation, letters, memoirs, and reports with wry vignettes about native ineptitude; arch comments about the corruption of fellow expatriates; and bemused accounts of their own accommodations to frontier conditions. Through irony, they not only invited their audiences to see the colony as inimical to civilization, but also to regard with some equivocation the civilizing mission itself.

I say "some equivocation" because few denied that a greater good justified the imperial enterprise. Greg Dening (1996: 215) has observed that scholars have long seen early European encounters in the Pacific Islands "as a Romantic moment in which Europe comprehended the artificiality of its own civilisation before the simplicity of native lives." Yet Dening rightly warns against exaggerating "the effect of this experience of the primitive as any more that the exotic experience of the few." For colonists who came later, island life continued to reinforce a sense of cultural superiority. But there can be no doubt that for many expatriates, the experience was dissonant enough to invite an attitude of reservation about certain *aspects* of Western ways, and to use irony to make the point.

Within this general tendency of colonial discourse, colonists varied considerably among themselves in regard to which pieties they questioned, how they attempted to control the interpretation of their comments, and how far they meant their equivocations to go. In this chapter, I look at how colonials with a variety of affiliations represented their experience along the north coast of Papua New Guinea, but focus especially on Catholic missionaries, and argue that one must understand their use of irony within the context of narrative traditions specific to the missionary community itself. In particular I suggest that these missionaries' irony was tempered by its evocation of religious paradox, in which a seemingly contradictory statement conveys a sacred truth. Other colonists might juxtapose local realities and cosmopolitan expectations to the distinct disadvantage of one or the other or both. But when these missionaries used irony to question the applicability of distant standards to their New Guinea mission, their aim was not really to criticize the Church or the locale. Rather, they evoked biblical paradox to blur the line between piety and equivocation in order to suggest that in out-of-the-way places, God may work in unusual ways.

---

of travel in contact zones shifts the focus away from the traveler's experience of discovery and towards his (or, less frequently, her) dependency on established routes and relationships, indigenous and colonial."

As sister tropes of indirection, irony and paradox bear so close a family resemblance that it is hard to keep them apart, suggesting an ease of passage between them which is, of course, precisely the point. For the purposes of this discussion, Chris Baldick's definitions in *The Concise Oxford Dictionary of
Literary Terms* are a good starting point, highlighting, as they do, the games
these tropes play with context and contradiction. For Baldick (1990: 114),
irony is "a subtly humorous perception of inconsistency in which an apparently
straightforward statement or event is undermined by its context so as to give it
a very different significance." Paradox, in contrast, is "a statement or expression so surprisingly self-contradictory as to provoke us into seeing another
sense or context in which it would be true" (159). Both irony and paradox use
context to question straightforward meanings or interpretations. But while
ironies show apparent truths to be contradictory, paradoxes show seeming contradictions to be true.[2]

In colonial discourse, irony was often used to establish that the special world
of the colonist is not the world of ordinary experience that their friends, relatives, colleagues, and countrymen take for granted at "home."[3] Paradox, on the
other hand, could take the very disparities that irony disparaged, and give them
a positive—even transcendent—twist. It is important to note, however, that
both irony and paradox depended upon and preserved the oppositions they
played on—between colony and metropole, primitive and civilized, colonized
and colonizer, us and them. As Gyan Prakash (1995: 3), writing about Western
representations of colonial realities, has noted:

2. The relationship between irony and paradox has been represented in different ways by different writers. For example, in his article, "Irony in Anthropology: The Work of Franz Boas,"
Arnold Krupat (1990) sees paradox or oxymoron as one of four types of irony that have characterized modernism in literature and social thought. The other three are antiphrasis (negation), aporia
(doubt), and catachresis (misuse). Still, Krupat agrees that the basic distinction between paradox
(or oxymoron) and other kinds of irony is that the contradiction it embodies is only apparent, not
real: "The figure of the oxymoron presents apparently absurd or incongruous linkages, but oxy-
moronic figures may be distinguished from catachrestical figures in that the absurdity or incongruity of the oxymoron is only apparent, not real; however paradoxical the statement on the face of
it may be, a fully coherent, rational point may be extracted—e.g., in such phrases as 'coarse gentleman,' or 'noble savage'" (136).

3. "Home" is a powerful figure in colonial discourse. As I say in my discussion of gender practice within a Catholic mission in Papua New Guinea, ". . . an idealized concept of "home"—where
things were done right—was frequently used to legitimate the subjugation of places "abroad,"
where it was not possible for things to be "properly arranged" (Huber 1999: 181). In that same article (201, n. 2), I note that Edward Said (1993: 79) makes a similar argument for literature, arguing that Jane Austen uses the beauty and order of Mansfield Park to validate its extension to Sir
Thomas Bertram's overseas properties in the Caribbean. Said has been criticized for his reading of
Austen on this issue by Susan Fraiman, who also notes that he does not address the argument made
by his student Suvendrini Perera (1991), "whose book on empire and the English novel . . . [argues]
that 'home' was a construct policing British women as well as colonial 'others'" (Fraiman 1995:
810, 816).

Paradoxes and ironies abounded, as did the justification of the gap between rhetoric and practice on the grounds of expediency and the exceptional circumstances of the colonies. These contortions of the discourse were endemic to colonialism not because of the colonizer's bad faith but due to the functioning of colonial power as a form of transaction and translation between incommensurable cultures and positions.

The study of colonial discourse raises vexing questions of method. In the following discussion, I examine the colonial situation as it was represented by different kinds of expatriates in a variety of literary genres. It may be true, as Pels (1990: 102) argues, that the only way to analyze expatriate discourse without reproducing the juxtaposition between self and [native] other upon which it depends, is to interrogate that discourse from the perspective of expatriates' interaction with indigenous people. This should not, however, make it either impolitic or unproductive to examine colonial discourse from several perspectives with different questions in mind. It is certainly important to "deconstruct [expatriate] representations for their orientalism" (Ortner 1999: 21), but it is also worth asking how expatriate rhetorics served expatriate projects by encoding relations—often of competition and conflict—between or within colonial communities and institutions themselves.

Irony and Colonial Experience in Northern New Guinea

The Sepik region of northwest Papua New Guinea was long a colonial backwater that few Europeans much loved.[4] The centers of the struggling German colony of Kaiser Wilhelmsland, established in 1884, were to the east and north, and it appears that the first relatively permanent European resident in the Sepik was a coconut trader who set up shop on a small offshore island in 1894. A German Catholic missionary order, the Society of the Divine Word, arrived in 1896, building their headquarters on a little island nearby. The Neu Guinea Compagnie followed with a string of coconut-trading stations along the north coast.[5] Then came the German colonial government and a few planters, recruiters, scientists and explorers. Through their several efforts, a semblance of

4. The modern-day country of Papua New Guinea comprises two former colonial entities: Papua in the South, and New Guinea in the north. The north was annexed by Germany in 1884 and administered by the Neu Guinea Compagnie for ten years before the German government finally took over in 1899. Australia took over at the beginning of World War I and then ruled the colony as a League of Nations Mandate until the Japanese invaded during World War II. After that war, New Guinea and Papua were combined as a single United Nations Trust Territory under Australian rule until the granting of self-government in 1974 and independence in 1975.

5. The German coconut trader was a man named Ludwig Kaernbach, and it was he who suggested to the Catholic mission that they build their first station near his own. When he died six months later, the Neu Guinea Compagnie gained their toehold in the area by taking over Kaernbach's operation (Wiltgen 1969: 331–33).

colonial order began to take shape, before the Australians took over the colony in an uncontested military action during World War I. With the exception of the extraordinarily energetic and efficient Catholic mission, and of growing labor recruitment for more prosperous parts of the territory, the place more or less remained a colonial frontier until after the second world war.

What this meant from the perspective of the few Europeans working or traveling in the region was a situation that lacked much of the infrastructure that colonials elsewhere enjoyed. Transportation, commerce, and communications were at a minimum, enhancing the contradictory qualities of colonial life. Without the financial resources to support an adequate staff, field personnel often found it necessary to become generalists. Without adequate and dependable sources of supply, they had in addition to their own jobs to become masters of improvisation in the culinary, technical, medical, and procedural arts. As the first leader of the Catholic mission summed up the situation in the early 1900s: "No matter what kind of job comes up, the story is always the same: if we don't take care of it ourselves, no one else moves a finger" (quoted in Wiltgen 1969: 340).

Many Europeans in this period commented ironically on the myriad ways in which local circumstances belied metropolitan ideals. The reports, letters, and memoirs produced by Europeans in the area during that time all dwell on the region's singular character, the difficulties faced by the writers, and the lengths to which they had to go to adapt. In the clichéd words of a young American priest who joined the Catholic mission in 1935, New Guinea was "a land of the unexpected," a theme as frequently illustrated by the peculiarities of its European denizens as by the exotica of native life. No European was exempt, it seems, from the prevailing rusticities of life. Traveling in the Sepik during the 1920s and 1930s, for example, one might meet, according to travelers and memoirists: a Catholic bishop in shirtsleeves checking in the cargo from a coastal steamer (Marshall 1938: 221), a government officer on a tax raid outside his jurisdiction (Townsend 1968: 159), a planter who had left his coastal estate to roam the interior recruiting labor (Mead 1977: 103), or an illiterate drifter running the district's major store (McCarthy 1963: 137).

Perhaps nothing was used so frequently by memoirists to characterize the singularity of life in the region as such "standard" deviations from the proprieties of the division of labor that underlay contemporary ideas of the status quo. Romola McSwain (1977: 29) has pointed out that Europeans in New Guinea "saw the economic, political and religious systems as discrete entities," in which individuals were supposed to involve themselves "in only one aspect of the economy," and in which missions were supposed to restrict "their activities almost entirely to religious and educational change." It was precisely the lack of fit between these conventions and reality that made occupational confusions so useful to colonists as a rhetorical device for depicting the unusual and un-conventional aspects of life on the frontier.[6]

For field agents, subject to the logic and whims of a distant bureaucracy, the situation was structured—especially, in anecdotes and stories—something like a joke. On the one hand, agents had a pattern of formal distinctions and procedures that defined their place and role within a bureaucratically organized institution. On the other hand, these agents were in a local situation lacking most of the supports that make a rationally organized system rational. If the rules are characterized as an "order" and the local situation as its opposite, the balance of power was usually toward the local, whose eruption into the bounds of the former was all but inevitable. This subversion of institutional order—this "leveling of hierarchy, the triumph of intimacy over formality, of unofficial values over official values" matches exactly Mary Douglas's analysis of the form of a joke (1975: 98). It can also, not coincidentally, be called irony, when it invites evaluative comparison between the said and the unsaid; the official and the unofficial; the expected and the actual situation.

Consider the story of the founding of the town of Wewak in 1936, as related by G. W. L. Townsend (1968), then the district officer in charge. An inveterate institutional iconoclast, Townsend parodies an ossified bureaucratic order by juxtaposing it with a local situation calling for imagination and common sense:

> . . . the Lands section and I had locked horns early in my residence at Wewak. That part of the headland where I wished to build the station was about 17 acres in extent, but the surface was irregular, with two waterponds and several gullies. It was my idea to build on selected sites, taking into consideration the topography of the ground, the views and giving each building decent grounds.
>
> Lands, however, proceeded as though the headland were as flat as a billiard table. The Department carved it up into 20 town allotments without regard to

6. Most of the colonists who wrote memoirs gained their experience of New Guinea in the process of doing—or attempting to do—their jobs. It is not surprising, perhaps, that in a society where occupations formed the major elements of social classification, those without an identifiable occupation were represented as either regrettably disorderly or attractively free. J. K. McCarthy (1963) devotes a few pages in his memoirs to one such character who, significantly, "blew into" the isolated mission post of Marienberg one day in the 1930s:

> In the next few weeks I got to know Smythe better and I found that there was much more to him than appeared. He was an interesting and well-read man who lived with his own philosophy while he managed to do without the conventions that applied to his fellow men. Despite his dissolute and improvident ways he had a strange attraction for the natives. He was in fact a beachcomber but it takes a great deal more than a mere drunken loafer to achieve that status. For a start, a beachcomber must possess some sort of innate charm so that other men will bear with him; he must be prepared to refuse all work that might put him on their level and he must have sufficient education to let him expound on life—thereby guaranteeing drinks from his listeners. (70)

Writing in 1963 about the 1930s, McCarthy commented nostalgically, "Beachcombers have died out in New Guinea—a pity for they were interesting characters and they supplied a want in the isolated country" (ibid.).

humps, bumps, ponds or gullies. . . . When the Administrator did arrive with
an officer of the Lands Department he had a file six inches thick. [To Townsend's objections about the size of the allotments] he quoted a letter from the
Secretary of Lands which said in part: "These allotments are already larger
than one would find in towns in Australia." By this time I was getting hot under the collar and snapped back without thinking too much about it: "Australia! It's a pity the draftsman responsible hadn't lived in Texas!" (221)

The story continues two years later, Townsend having done nothing about lay-
ing out the town in the meantime:

> It remained up in the air until McNicoll succeeded Griffiths and, in 1938, vis-
> ited Wewak. He, too, came armed with the Lands Department file and lifting
> an eyebrow, rifled through it.
> "Where do we start" he asked.
> "Do you know the size of this District?" I asked him, on impulse.
> "No. Not exactly."
> "Well, it's 30,000 square miles."
> He remained silent.
> "Will you let me lay out 20 acres of it?" I asked at last.
> He burst out laughing, put the file back in the dispatch-box and told me to
> have the plans prepared and sent to Rabaul. Thus the danger of Wooloomooloo-
> size allotments being forced upon Wewak was averted—at least until the
> place was rebuilt after the war. (222)

In this anecdote, built upon the incongruity between abstract models and reality, "Lands" loses and Wewak wins (temporarily) thanks to Townsend's persistent insubordination. This is not an isolated instance, however, for Townsend
relates much of his career through episodes conforming to this pattern. Yet
while his stories bear his personal signature they also bear a family resemblance to the anecdotes in other officers' memoirs as well. The oppositions set
up between "six-inch files" and "humps, bumps, ponds, and gullies" are resolved by the field officer himself, who becomes an actor rather than a mere
agent blindly following the rules. The abstract is pitted against the concrete, the
proper against the practical, organization against the person, in stories that are
funny because they never truly subvert the aims of the colonial government, but
merely improvise (and presumably improve) upon means.

It was, of course, just a short step, to redirect irony's "edge" (Hutcheon 1994)
from the official order itself to its unfulfilled realization on the "frontier." Perhaps this is most evident in the comments of memoirists on the failure of colonial society to respect the ideology of separate domains. Indeed, competition
between Europeans during the period before World War II frequently involved
accusations that one group was poaching, so to speak, on the other's ground.
The British naturalist, A. J. Marshall (1938: 225), for example, felt that there
was really no need for the Catholic missionaries to conduct their wide range of

activities in the late 1930s, when the government, in his opinion, was finally firmly in control. He admired the efficiency with which missionaries ran their stations and plantations, but noted the incongruity of a religious institution that had "Ltd." following its name.

Margaret Mead's (1977) letters from the field were full of ironic observations on outpost civilization. For example, she once wrote with relief that she had avoided a trip from her Mountain Arapesh village to the coast, where, she said, all the whites "feel that the native should be reserved for their special varieties of exploitation" (124). Like other travelers of the time, Mead used a boat trip to sum up her impressions as she journeyed to the "bush" from the colonial capital at Rabaul:

> . . . we had five days on the [steamer] Montoro and our first touch of outstation life again. Rabaul is very civilized and full of cocktails these days. On the Montoro there were two sisters come to inspect their order, two Methodist missionaries who didn't drink anything, a huge Australian priest who looked like his German brethren and whose Queensland accent was like a blow in the face, so unexpected it was, a mob of miners who told one the names of imaginary public schools they had once attended and how their fathers refused to let them go out of Africa with Cecil Rhodes because it was 'like going into trade' and who solemnly discussed the charms, probably never seen, of Budapest, and an earnest-faced boy coming up to do two years at a lonely trading station in Papua. (219)

Although Mead's ironic tone keeps us from knowing what she felt about Rabaul's cocktail party "civilization," she leaves no doubt that she found outstation life a poor excuse for *real* civilization, a sham. In the capital, people, like the drinks, were mixed. But on the Montoro, the Methodists didn't even drink; the priest looked like his dignified German confreres but had an undignified Australian accent, the mob of miners only pretended to dignity, and the earnest-faced boy would not go far at his lonely trade post. In Marshall and Mead, we find few of those "robust nineteenth-century ideals of progress and civilization" that marked colonial discourse in Africa (Spurr 1993: 23), and indeed, even in New Guinea during the brief high point of the German imperial venture before the first World War. In Mead, especially, we find a "modernist sensibility" in regard to local colonial realities, one that views their pretense ironically, "in terms of impotence, anxiety, and loss" (Spurr 1993: 23).

Missionary Irony

Like other denizens and travelers along New Guinea's north coast, Catholic missionaries used irony to attack opponents, build community, and represent their project to supporters and authorities back home. The mission's first leader,

Eberhard Limbrock, appears to have been a master of the ironist's art. Perhaps this was necessary, because his situation was so ambiguous. After all, Limbrock's first big battles were to obtain land for his religious institution to establish a commercial plantation, and his first big opponent was the Neu Guinea Compagnie, the commercial firm that held the powers of government under a German charter. Limbrock had to explain to all and sundry players just why it was so important for the mission to obtain large parcels of land, and to expose just why it was that his requests were being opposed. When, for example, in 1899 he was offered land in Hansa Bay instead of in Potsdamhafen, his preferred location, Limbrock wrote:

> Whereas in Potsdamhafen the natives appear to be quiet and peaceful, the numerous inhabitants of Hansa Bay have a reputation for ferocity, bloodthirstiness, and some of them also for cannibalism. But since very much copra can be made there, the New Guinea Company would be pleased if we went to Hansa Bay first to transform the savage spirits of these people—I do not know by what kind of magical formula—into gentle lambs. On the other hand the Company wants to keep us at a distance from Potsdamhafen so that it can retain there its monopoly on everything. (In Wiltgen 1969: 335)

It was under Limbrock's direction that the mission eventually became the major economic force in the region through its string of coconut plantations and mission stations along the coast. It also became a leader in transportation, communications, and education too. But none of this was perceived as benign or neutral by his business competitors, and Limbrock used irony not only to defend his unusual requests for land but in arguing the case for conventional mission projects like education, as well. Indeed, he once made the following "modest proposal" to the German Governor in response to complaints about mission schools:

> If the envy of other business firms asserts that such educational establishments are of material advantage for the mission, it would be recommended that a public request be made, that all such business enterprises everywhere should found such and similar educational establishments. The more the better! And if they so desire, we shall be ready to put at their disposal any number of Sisters, Fathers and Brothers for the supervision and direction of those schools and for teaching in them. The only condition is that free board and lodging be provided for them, and that they be granted full freedom, time and opportunity to conduct their religious exercises and conduct the work that is proper to them as missionaries. . . . Whatever gain and profit there may be, we shall gladly leave to the business firm that undertakes the happy enterprise. (359)

If, to secular colonials, the mission's combination of "business" with "religion" rang untrue, the internal problem for the mission had less to do with such secular categories than with their theological cousins, "spiritual" and "material" work. In Catholic circles in the late nineteenth century, it was expected that "material" work, like building churches, planting gardens, and sewing clothes, would be necessary in some missions. It was, however, assumed that such activities could be contained within the conventional hierarchy of missionary means, in which "development work" and "charitable aims" remained subordinate to "direct" means such as prayer, example and sacrifice, preaching, and the catechumenate and baptism (Schmidlin 1931: 340–391).

It is important to note that this hierarchical model of missionary means created a missionary situation different from that of missionaries fielded by some evangelical groups at about the same time. Beidelman's (1982) historical ethnography of the Church Missionary Society in Tanzania, for example, places great emphasis on the contradictions that the technical requirements of frontier work caused for missionaries whose spiritual identity rested upon a rejection of the achievements of secular culture and science (99–126; see also Nemer 1981: 22). Unlike those ascetically inclined missionaries, the Catholic missionaries of the Society of the Divine Word were not embarrassed by the necessity of using modern technology and science in their work, nor of engaging in commercial activity to maintain themselves in the mission field. The internal problems caused by Eberhard Limbrock's plantations and industries in New Guinea resulted not from any contradiction between the work required and the Society's spiritual orientation, but from the fact that the work grew too large to be maintained within the Society's division of spiritual and material labor between priests and brothers—a division that embedded the theologically approved hierarchy of missionary means within the class structure of the European countries from which most of its missionaries were drawn.

Indeed, it was not long before complaints from some of the missionary priests found their way back to the mission's headquarters in Steyl, Holland. The work of establishing plantations, building new stations, running the boats, building a sawmill, and running experiments in tropical agriculture, was simply too much for the brothers alone to handle, and priests found themselves overseeing the material work, and having little time left for the spiritual work of evangelization (Wiltgen 1969: 70). Limbrock himself acknowledged that the spiritual and material aims of pioneer work were proving contradictory rather than complementary in the conditions that obtained, writing to the society's head:

> Someone might well object that we missionaries ought to withdraw ourselves more from material occupations. . . . Of course, we try to let the Brothers do as much of this work as possible, so as to keep ourselves free for divine services and evangelizing. But unfortunately up till now the good Brothers are just not numerous enough. . . . For better, then, or for worse, we have had to accommodate ourselves to what was unavoidable and to take over the work

ourselves. It pained us deeply, however, that in the meanwhile the mission
work had to suffer greatly. (352)

Expectations concerning the division of labor were not all that suffered in
this New Guinea mission. For example, the small size and limited political
scale of lowland societies, the many languages in this region, and the striking
differences in customs among neighboring villages all worked to limit the possibilities for brotherhood among the missionaries, not to mention for central-
ized policy, so close to the heart Roman Catholic ideas about the structure of
the church. As one official visitor to the mission in 1922 remarked: "this very
lack of any universal binding characteristic among the people . . . sets up real
barriers of difficulty between the Fathers and Brothers themselves. . . . What is
meant here is that each [station], being so entirely segregated from the others,
has its own distinct problems to such an extent as to be almost a distinct mission by itself" (Hagspiel 1926: 69).

Missionaries during this era clearly expressed awareness of the ironies of situations in which they so often found themselves. One young American priest,
for example, in trying to characterize his experience in New Guinea as strange,
focused on confusions in the hierarchical structure of the mission: "Plans seldom materialize in New Guinea," Father Angelus wrote, so instead of becoming a junior member of headquarters staff, he was suddenly left alone.

> When the schooner pulled out . . . I remained behind with a three-fold title,
> namely pastor of a flock that speaks pidgin, German, and the Tumleo lan-
> guages; newly appointed procurator of the Vicariate and the Rector of the
> Central station. *That's New Guinea all over.* It surely seemed strange to hear
> Father Blas on his return asking me for permission for certain articles and to
> arrange the order for confession, etc. he is ten years my senior and ordained
> six years before me. (1936; my emphasis)

Clearly, however, Angelus is not criticizing his order's habits of seniority, much
less the hierarchical structure of the Church. Indeed, as he says of his bishop's
self-sacrificing ways—giving his missionaries clothes from his wardrobe and
food from his table—conditions in New Guinea may demand a reversal of hierarchy's usual trappings, but not of its fundamental nature at all. The conventional designation of the bishop as "the father of the mission" was less appropriate, in Fr. Angelus's view, than what the bishop preferred to call himself,
"the servant of the servants of God" (ibid.).

Paradox and Politics

Like other expatriates in New Guinea, the Catholic missionaries along the
north coast used irony to convey the contrasts and disparities of the colonial

situation. The differences, however, should also be pointed out. As opposed to the clear thrust of Government Officer Townsend's irony, or to that, say, of the naturalist Marshall or the anthropologist Mead, much Catholic missionary irony over the years has had a blunted edge. Townsend took clear aim at the absurdities of misplaced bureaucratic ideals; Mead directed her critique at the pettiness and exploitation of unrestrained outpost civilization. But the missionaries could neither deny the validity of the Church they were trying to "plant" in New Guinea, nor could they see their attempt to create the church in New Guinea as a sham.[7] Missionaries may have expressed the nature of New Guinea (Fr. Angelus's "That's New Guinea all over") through its resistance to conventional models but, in general, missionary literature tries not to overstate the opposition. After all, if circumstances in New Guinea were truly opposed to the establishment of the Church, what would that say about the past and future of the missionary project?

The problem for missionary ironists, then, was not only to represent the distance between the two worlds of New Guinea and the Roman Catholic Church, but to deny that distance made a real difference at one and the same time. Indeed, one might note a family resemblance between this tendency in missionary literature and one of the "basic tropes which emerge from the Western colonial experience," identified by David Spurr (1993: 3). In discussing rhetorical appropriation, Spurr notes:

> The European role in colonial territories depends on the clear demarcation of cultural and moral difference between the civilized and the noncivilized. But the ultimate aim of colonial discourse is not to establish a radical opposition between colonizer and colonized. It seeks to dominate by inclusion and domestication rather than by a confrontation which recognizes the independent identity of the Other. (32)

To achieve this effect, missionaries had at hand in their own religious culture ready models, from hagiographical formulas to biblical verse. Wayne Booth has pointed out that ironic reversals are often used to express the inadequacy of our worldly expectations in the context of God's larger plan—as in Matthew 23: 11–12: ". . . he that is the greatest among you shall be your servant. And whosoever shall exalt himself shall be abased; and he that shall humble himself shall be exalted" (quoted in Booth 1974: 236–37). The topsy-turviness of missionary experience in New Guinea was certainly dignified for ironists and audiences attuned to the missionaries' implicit quotation of hagiographic and

---

7. "Planting the church" is not a simple metaphor, but a phrase evoking a whole missiology. In general, a mission oriented to "planting the church" was trying to build an institution, while other missions might be more oriented to saving individual souls. These positions map on to more general theological positions about the role of the church in salvation.

biblical forms. It is, after all, but a short step from Booth's "ironic reversals" to paradox, where the contradictions reveal something that is not false but true (Shaw 1994: 2).

Interpreting missionary irony, I suggest, requires sensitivity to narrative traditions within the religious community and thus to the politics and pieties of paradox in the biblical tradition.[8] As Frank Kermode has written of Jesus's teachings in Matthew, "The Law is transformed . . . with many consequences of paradox and excess" (1987: 390). Story after story about Jesus stress that the new world is to be "a world of paradox," a world "turned upside down."[9] Missionaries' depiction of New Guinea as a world where the church is somewhat skewed, if not exactly turned upside down, could suggest to religious readers that what the missionaries are doing there is not, in fact, inauthentic, but all the more deeply real. Roland Barthes put it well: "The singularity of a 'vocation' is never better displayed," he wrote, "than when it is contradicted—but not denied, far from it—by a prosaic incarnation" (1972: 31).

Whole genres of mission literature—written and oral—fit this general plan. For example, missionaries have long been fond of self-deprecating humor that evoked the paradox of God's transcendent purposes working through flawed human effort. I heard more than once of renowned missionary priests who were reputed to have ended their careers thinking they had made only one convert: themselves. Another priest told me about "the funniest confession story" he had ever heard, and it turned on a linguistic problem: a newly arrived priest without full command of New Guinea Pidgin, wondered what his colleagues were teaching about sin when a penitent told him in confession, "mi slip nating, pater." The new priest thought the poor fellow was worried about sleeping naked, when, in fact, the penitent was confessing to omitting his nightly prayers, of not remembering God.

Missionary biography and autobiography—both written and oral—make frequent use of the theme of personal humility, which has, of course, great religious resonance to Christians of all kinds (Huber 1998). In his aptly titled autobiographical essay, "The Short Story of a Long Life," Leo Arkfeld (1992), bishop and pilot in the region for over thirty years after the Second World War, tells how he found his vocation as a missionary priest—not through his own

8. *The New Princeton Encyclopedia of Poetry and Poetics* (s.v. "Paradox") states: "Paradoxes are especially suited to an expression of the unspeakable in religion, mysticism, and poetry. First discussed in its formal elements in Stoic philosophy and classical rhetoric, the paradox became more widely used after Sebastian Frank (*280 Paradoxa from the Holy Scriptures*, 1534) and has always retained an appeal for the Christian mode of expression" (Behler 1993: 876).

9. Kierkegaard ([1846] 1992) was especially attuned to the ironies and paradoxes of religious sensibility and expression. Indeed, he saw Jesus' modes of indirect speech to be essential to his message, which cannot in fact be taught in any straightforward, objective way. By destabilizing a person's normal assumptions, they create a space in which that person can seek subjective truth.

seeking, but after accidentally shooting his own foot on his family's Iowa farm (5–8). True to the symbolism of losing oneself in one's vocation, Arkfeld carefully absents himself from the story of his New Guinea years, focusing on collective accomplishments in the mission field. And this appears to be how Arkfeld composed his life in the field as well as on the page. Many missionaries who have known him for years regard him as a simple, straightforward character: as a seminary classmate of the bishop's told one visitor to the mission, "he may not be an interesting, fascinating personality, but he is abidable . . . you can live with him . . . because he has a profound respect for men. . . . [He is a] man of mercy. That means he knows himself . . . that he has an acquaintance with his own poverty, because these men are always compassionate." [10] It is worth noting that this paradox of humble power or the power of humility is integral to hagiography, in particular the technique that shows a saint's "self-emptying," and which serves rhetorically to make the saint available to be filled by a transcendent other or, for that matter, by other human beings (Heffernan 1988). [11]

Another genre of missionary literature involves airplane stories, common during the age of mission aviation from the late 1930s to the 1980s. These stories stressed the rough conditions for mission pilots—including Leo Arkfeld, who was a pilot as well as bishop, and responsible for seeing that most of the mission's many stations had airstrips, however perilous they had to be. It was necessary, during that era of mission flying, to play freely with the rules: the strips were often substandard, the weather unpredictable, no tower was around to guide in a plane at night. A mission pilot had to fly, as one publicity piece put it, "on a wing and a prayer. This formula has always brought him back home unscathed—even when the wing was flapping a bit" (Mihalic 1977). And that was the point. There were plenty of close calls that made for amusing stories to circulate within the mission and to mission supporters, but the underlying message was not that the rules were ridiculous (as a Townsend might have said) or that flying without them was reckless (as a Meadean perspective might suggest). From the mission's perspective, the message was that it was precisely through such risks that the future of the church would be secured (Huber 1988: 138–45; Ruiter 1976).

Missionary irony is perhaps most markedly and publicly encapsulated in the images of its bishops, who embodied both the Church and New Guinea through

10. Fr. Matthew Kelty, in an interview with Karol La Casse, 22 March 1982.

11. This paradoxical relationship of humility and power also fascinated Kierkegaard. George Steiner (1998: 11) remarks: "Once again, the logic of contradiction, of the paradox . . . is instrumental. Where it attains the requisite pitch of lived intensity, where it is fully analogous to that of Jesus, humility is total powerlessness, a finality of impotence. But it is precisely this impotence which constitutes, exactly in the sense of Jesus' revaluation of values, a greater power, very nearly an impotence of the absurd."

their combination of high spiritual office and critical practical skill. Fr. Limbrock, the embattled pioneer, became known as "The Man of Providence" because his controversial plantations and industries enabled the mission to survive the privations of World War I; Joseph Loerks, the mission's bishop between
the wars, was a boat captain; and Leo Arkfeld, bishop during the post-World
War II years, was the pilot, the "Flying Bishop," I mentioned before. By representing these bishop through traits that were not conventionally associated with
bishops but that were useful in the New Guinea situation, these images brought
the two worlds into productive contact, while respecting the sense of distance
that the figures ultimately mask. As Fredric Jameson (1982) has noted:

> in order to act on the real, [the literary or aesthetic gesture] cannot simply al-
> low reality to persevere in its being outside of itself, inertly, at distance; it
> must draw the real into its own texture. . . . The symbolic act therefore begins
> by producing its own context in the same moment of emergence in which it
> steps back over against it, measuring with an eye to its own active project. (74)

The argument of these images is doubly ironic—paradoxical, in fact. What
at first appears to be incompatible (irony 1), is ultimately not (irony 2). But this,
of course, is also religious paradox: what appears to be contradictory conveys
a sacred truth. Thus Eberhard Limbrock's "material upbuilding" was eventually presented by the missionaries not as a deflection from the mission's more
"spiritual" tasks, but rather as a condition and sign of the mission's capacity to
perform them. Joseph Loerks, the traveling boat captain of the interwar years,
was presented not as the negation but as the guarantee of the mission's capacity to maintain itself as a centered religious community. And during the postwar period leading to national independence, the mission's development work,
symbolized by Leo Arkfeld, was presented not as a deflection from, but a vital
addition to, the mission's more conventional spiritual ministry.

Clearly, some missionary irony—like Limbrock's political sallies—has
been of the "simple corrective" kind, aimed at exposing and thus negating an
opponent's "mistaken" or "absurd" position.[12] Other missionary irony, tending
toward paradox, opened up a world where coherence is less obviously assured.
Indeed, owing to their resonance with religious expression, many ironic stories
and images have a sliding scale of "truth revealed" (Booth 1974: 234). Although they call explicit attention to a local situation—a confusion of prece-
dence, language, or work—they implicitly place this situation in larger contexts, sliding all the way up to the most general condition of humankind. Yet
the questions remain of how far the missionaries have intended their ironies to
go and how far their intended audiences have taken them. My argument is that
going to the top, so to speak, was one of the principal ways that missionaries

---

12. Muecke (1969: 119) distinguishes between "simple corrective ironies and the ironies of
paradoxes, dilemmas, and other impossible situations.

attempted to control the discontinuities of colonial experience. It allowed the missionaries room for play with the rules, by arguing to their superiors and supporters around the world, that New Guinea—at least—was a place where the "good will out," as Archbishop Arkfeld liked to say. For the good of the Church, innovation—even irony—*had* to happen.

Conclusion

Representation has emerged as a major issue for discussion and debate concerning the legacy of imperialism. In scholarly arenas as well as in political forums, it has become increasingly clear that the imperial mission was carried on through representational practices, in addition to everything else it also involved. In recent years, especially, these practices have become subject to interpretation as varieties of "colonial discourse." But, as I have tried to suggest in this brief discussion of irony in colonial Papua New Guinea, "colonial discourse," is no more a seamless web than "colonialism" itself. As Nicholas Thomas (1994: ix) has observed, "it is becoming increasingly clear that only localized theories and historically specific accounts can provide much insight into the varied articulations of colonizing and counter-colonial representations and practices."

Irony, in particular, may be sensitive to the positions of various authors and audiences, because it can inscribe such a wide range of what Alan Wilde (1981) calls "horizons of assent." In northern New Guinea, expatriate writers from many walks of life wrote ironically, or equivocally (to return to Bakhtin's term), about the authority of distant standards by depicting their subversion in the "contact zone" or, from their own perspective, the "colonial frontier." The government officers and scientists mentioned here represent the situation as a failure in either the standards themselves (Townsend) or their application and enforcement (Marshall and Mead). To varying degrees, these authors all implied that the colonial world was one in which, through better policy, a more harmonious ideal might yet be attained.

The missionaries, no less than their fellow colonials, perceived Northern New Guinea as one in which distant standards were not always possible or appropriate to apply. For the missionaries, these disjunctions were particularly troublesome, because despite a temporal horizon that could accommodate detours on the road from mission to church, the difficulties they faced in New Guinea early on put in question the compatibility of New Guinea with their preferred model of the church. Missionary irony encoded this difficulty through its special appeal to the resources of religious language. This is one of those cases where, as Paul Fussell (1975: i) noted, "literary tradition and real life notably transect," and "life feeds materials to literature while literature returns the favor by conferring forms on life." Paradox allowed missionaries to leave the

contradictions unresolved, and to accept (or at least represent) the dishar-
monies of their worldly situation as a sign of higher harmony instead. This was
at once an affirmation of openness to displacement by the "local" and a denial
of any real displacement at the same time.

This affirmation of openness to displacement by the "local" was not, of
course, without its ambiguities. First, the "local" itself is a construct that was
experienced and understood by missionaries and other colonials in part in
terms of its very resistance to the projects they had come to pursue. Second,
"openness" does not mean openness to everything. Indeed, different missionary groups may be open to quite different things, and in this Catholic mission,
with its general tolerance of innovation among its missionaries, the priest at
one station might be "open" to things that the one next door might reject.[13]
Third, "displacement" itself is a relative term. In Papua New Guinea, missionaries hoping to establish a congregational form of church polity have found that
they could only pursue their goal if they set up a supralocal system of central-
ized offices and services, while missionaries from more centrally organized
polities, like the Catholics discussed here, have adjusted their practice to conditions that required more "localism" than appeared to be consistent with
official views of their church.

But despite all the ambiguities and reservations one could raise about the
Catholic missionaries' practice or the mission project itself, their affirmation of
openness to displacement by the local is not unimportant. Certainly everyone's
projects have been subject to displacement in the field. And many are those
who have soldiered on along their original path (or as close as they could stay
to it), whatever the cost to local people and themselves. In a remarkable essay
on the man who once embodied the idea of benevolence for many Europeans
and Americans, Fernandez (1964) observes of the "unalterably colonial" regime at the famous hospital in Lambarene:

> Schweitzer, like all colonials, whatever humanitarian motives inspired him,
> imposed a system upon a people according to which, in the end, he judged that
> people's behavior and in whose name he justified impersonal treatment how-
> ever mild. (557)

13. This was, in fact, a criticism that some priests directed at Bishop Arkfeld's general encouragement of priestly innovation during my fieldwork in the mid-1970s. However, as I mentioned
earlier, the mission had long bowed to the wisdom of the priest "on the spot," leading to some
strange juxtapositions. For example, Bryant Allen tells the story of two priests who were posted to
neighboring stations on the north coast in 1930, both of whom "made strenuous efforts to establish
mission influence in the villages south of the mountains." While following a similar pattern of establishing "camps, houses, chapels and school buildings," one to the east, and the other to the west,
their approach to evangelization differed—one was said by villagers to have raged against the local spirit cult, pulling down their secret objects and forcing women to look at them; while the other
was said to be far more concerned with sorcery, "a theme which found some sympathy with many
villagers." (Allen 1976: 82; see also Huber 1988: 90).

"In Schweitzer," Fernandez concludes, "we see the whole contradiction of colonization: the sacrifice of the natives for the greater good" (558). Indeed. But could Schweitzer have been more open to the local, seeing in the difficulties of establishing his hospital's routine the sign of deficiencies not in the people's character but in the routine itself?

Certainly colonialism, like other systems of structured inequity, made it very difficult for those caught up in them to see each other clearly. And even if they wished to do so, it was not within the power of most participants to change the macrosystem(s) which had created the contact zones in the first place. Still, these zones might have been more humane places if more colonials and post-colonials had seen the contradictions and incongruities of their work with a sense of self-irony. This is not that variety of irony—all too common among colonials—that Kenneth Burke (1969) calls "romantic" and which places ironists "outside of and superior to" those they rule or the roles they reject. What I have in mind is the kind of irony that Burke calls "classic" or "true," that is "not superior . . . [but] based on a sense of fundamental kinship with the [other], as one *needs* him, is *indebted*, is not merely outside him as an observer but contains him *within*, being consubstantial with him" (514). In other words, irony tempered by a sense of paradox may help open one's eyes to alternatives. As we know, the effort to act on this perception—to (say) run a medical service or a school or a church or a scientific project more in tune with local ways—has been accompanied by its own problems, but remains a worthy challenge for all of us caught up in a world system that appears all too willing to sacrifice everything local to someone or something else's "greater good."

Acknowledgments

This essay elaborates an argument that was published in 1988 in *The Bishops' Progress: An Historical Ethnography of Catholic Missionary Experience on the Sepik Frontier* (Smithsonian Institution Press). Since then, I have had the opportunity to explore further a variety of critical approaches to irony, as well as the burgeoning literature on colonial societies and colonial discourse. My ethnographic debts have also grown, in particular to Archbishop Leo Arkfeld (1912–1999). In 1989, Archbishop Arkfeld entrusted to me an archive of historical documents and interview transcripts which had been collected by Karol La Casse, who passed away before she could begin work on the biography of Leo Arkfeld that she had planned to write. Some of the material presented in this essay was from my own fieldwork in Wewak, Papua New Guinea in 1976–1977, and some is from the archive that I later received. Many thanks to Linda Layne and to the two scholars who reviewed the manuscript for the University of Chicago Press for comments on earlier drafts of this essay.

References

Allen, Bryant J. 1976. Information Flow and Innovation Diffusion in the East Sepik District, Papua New Guinea. Ph.D. diss., Australian National University, Canberra.

Angelus, Fr. 1936. Unpublished letter from Tumleo Island, 20 February 1936. Bishop's Office, Diocese of Wewak.

Arkfeld, Archbishop Leo. 1992. The Short Story of A Long Life. Manuscript.

Bakhtin, M. M. 1986. *Speech Genres and Other Late Essays.* Trans. Vern W. McGee; ed. Caryl Emerson and Michael Holquist. Austin: University of Texas Press.

Baldick, Chris. 1990. *The Concise Oxford Dictionary of Literary Terms.* New York: Oxford University Press.

Barthes, Roland. 1972. *Mythologies.* New York: Hill and Wang.

Behler, Ernst H. 1993. Paradox. *The New Princeton Encyclopedia of Poetry and Poetics.* Ed. Alex Preminger and T. V. F. Brogan. Princeton: Princeton University Press.

Beidelman, T. O. 1982. *Colonial Evangelism: A Socio-Historical Study of an East African Mission at the Grassroots.* Bloomington: Indiana University Press.

Booth, Wayne. 1974. *The Rhetoric of Irony.* Chicago: University of Chicago Press.

Burke, Kenneth. 1969. *A Grammar of Motives.* Berkeley: University of California Press.

Clifford, James. 1992. No Innocent eyes. Review of *Imperial Eyes,* by Mary Louise Pratt. *Times Literary Supplement,* 11 September 1992, pp. 3–4.

Dening, Greg. 1996. *Performances.* Chicago: University of Chicago Press.

Douglas, Mary. 1975. Jokes. In *Implicit Meanings: Essays in Anthropology.* London: Routledge & Kegan Paul.

Fernandez, James. 1964. The Sound of Bells in a Christian Country—in Quest of the Historical Schweitzer. *The Massachusetts Review* (spring): 537–62.

Fraiman, Susan. 1995. Jane Austen and Edward Said: Gender, Culture, and Imperialism. *Critical Inquiry* 21: 805–21.

Fussell, Paul. 1975. *The Great War and Modern Memory.* London: Oxford University Press.

Hagspiel, Bruno. 1926. *Along the Mission Trail.* Vol. 3, *In New Guinea.* Techny, IL: Mission Press, SVD.

Heffernan, Thomas J. 1988. *Sacred Biography: Saints and Their Biographers in the Middle Ages.* Oxford: Oxford University Press.

Huber, Mary Taylor. 1988. *The Bishops' Progress: A Historical Ethnography of Catholic Missionary Experience on the Sepik Frontier.* Washington, DC: Smithsonian Institution Press.

———. 1998. Pious Lives: Hagiography and History in Mission Biography. Paper presented at the American Anthropological Association Annual Meetings. Philadelphia, PA.

———. 1999. The Dangers of Immorality: Dignity and Disorder in Gender Relations in a Northern New Guinea Diocese. In *Gendered Missions: Women and Men in Missionary Discourse and Practice,* ed. Mary Taylor Huber and Nancy Lutkehaus, 179–206. Ann Arbor: University of Michigan Press.

Hutcheon, Linda. 1994. *Irony's Edge: The Theory and Politics of Irony.* London: Routledge.

Jameson, Fredric R. 1982. The Symbolic Inference; or, Kenneth Burke and Ideological Analysis. In *Representing Kenneth Burke,* ed. Hayden White and Margaret Brose, 68–91. Selected Papers from the English Institute, n.s. 6. Baltimore: Johns Hopkins University Press.

Kermode, Frank. 1987. Matthew. In *The Literary Guide to the Bible*, ed. Robert Alter and Frank Kermode, 387–401. Cambridge: Harvard University Press.

Kierkegaard, Søren. [1846] 1992. *Concluding Unscientific Postscript to Philosophical Fragments*. Ed. and trans. Howard V. Hong and Edna H. Hong. Princeton: Princeton University Press.

Krupat, Arnold. 1990. Irony in Anthropology: The Work of Franz Boas. In *Modernist Anthropology: From Fieldwork to Text*, ed. Marc Manganaro, 133–45. Princeton: Princeton University Press.

McCarthy, J. K. 1963. *Patrol into Yesterday: My New Guinea Years*. Melbourne: Cheshire Publishing Pty.

McSwain, Romola. 1977. *The Past and Future People: Tradition and Change on a New Guinea Island*. Melbourne: Oxford University Press.

Marshall, A. J. 1938. *The Men and Birds of Paradise: Journeys through Equatorial New Guinea*. London: William Heinemann.

Mihalic, Francis. 1977. On a Wing and a Prayer: Papua New Guinea's Flying Bishop. *Paradise* (In-flight magazine of Air Niugini), no. 3 (January 1977): 29–30.

Mead, Margaret. 1977. *Letters from the Field 1925–1975*. New York: Harper and Row.

Muecke, D. C. 1969. *The Compass of Irony*. London: Methuen.

Nemer, Lawrence. 1981. Anglican and Roman Catholic Attitudes on Missions: An Historical Study of Two English Missionary Societies in the Late Nineteenth Century (1865–1885). *Studia Instituti Missiologici Soeietatis Verbi Divini*, no. 29. St. Augustin: Steyler Verlag.

Ortner, Sherry B. 1999. *Life and Death on Mt. Everest: Sherpas and Himalayan Mountaineering*. Princeton: Princeton University Press.

Pels, Peter. 1990. How Did Bishop Arkfeld Get His Feathered Mitre: Contradiction and Irony in the Ethnography of Missions. Review Article. *Critique of Anthropology* 10(1): 103–112.

Perera, Suvendrini. 1991. *Reaches of Empire: The English Novel from Edgeworth to Dickens*. New York: Columbia University Press.

Prakash, Gyan. 1995. After Colonialism. Introduction to *After Colonialism: Imperial Histories and Postcolonial Developments*, ed. Gyan Prakash, 3–17. Princeton: Princeton University Press.

Pratt, Mary Louise. 1992. *Imperial Eyes: Travel Writing and Transculturation*. London: Routledge.

Ruiter, Ivo J. 1976. Wirui Services Story. Unpublished transcript. Reproduced in Huber (1988): appendix A.

Said, Edward. 1993. *Culture and Imperialism*. New York: Vintage Books.

Schmidlin, Joseph. 1931. *Catholic Mission Theory*. Techny, IL: Mission Press, SVD.

Shaw, W. David. 1994. *Elegy and Paradox: Testing the Conventions*. Baltimore: Johns Hopkins University Press.

Spurr, David. 1993. *The Rhetoric of Empire: Colonial Discourse in Journalism, Travel Writing, and Imperial Administration*. Durham, NC: Duke University Press.

Steiner, George. 1998. The Wound of Negativity: Two Kierkegaard Texts. In *Kierkegaard: A Critical Reader*, ed. Jonathan Ree and Jane Chamberlain, 103–13. Oxford: Blackwell.

Thomas, Nicholas. 1994. *Colonialism's Culture: Anthropology, Travel and Government*. Princeton: Princeton University Press.

Townsend, G. W. L. 1968. *District Officer: From Untamed New Guinea to Lake Success, 1921–46*. Sydney: Pacific Publications.

Wilde, Alan. 1981. *Horizons of Assent: Modernism, Postmodernism, and the Ironic Imagination.* Baltimore: Johns Hopkins University Press.

Wiltgen, Ralph M. 1969. Catholic Mission Plantations in Mainland New Guinea: Their Origin and Purpose. In *Research in Melanesia.* Proceedings of the second Waigani Seminar, Port Moresby, 329–362. Canberra: Australian National University Press.

Chapter Ten

— GEORGE E. MARCUS —

The Predicament of Irony and the Paranoid Style in Fin-de-Siècle Rationality

The uses of irony are legion and often very ideological. It is one of those banner concepts, plucked again and again over the past two decades from traditional literary analysis, to be deployed as the framing existential condition for one or another project of cultural analysis. The application of the notion of irony that I favor here derives from Hayden White's (1973) use of this trope to characterize the fin-de-siècle phase of historical imagination in nineteenth-century Europe in his now classic study *Metahistory*. White employed an elaborate apparatus of poetic tropes to understand the rhetoric of realism in European historical narrative and its fate. His sense of irony as defining a crisis of representation in historiography was an inspiration to Michael Fischer and me in our evocation of the 1980s as an experimental moment, not only in ethnography but across the human sciences (Marcus and Fischer [1986] 1999).

During the nineteenth century there was a sustained series of efforts to find a "realist" mode of description. All ended in irony because there were a number of equally comprehensive and plausible, yet apparently mutually exclusive conceptions of the same events. To quote White (1973: 37):

> The aim of the Ironic statement is to affirm tacitly the negative of what is on the literal level affirmed positively. . . . It presupposes that the reader or auditor already knows, or is capable of recognizing, the absurdity of the characterization of the thing designated . . . Irony thus represents a stage of consciousness in which the problematical nature of language itself has become recognized. It points to the potential foolishness of all linguistic characterizations of reality as much as to the absurdity of the beliefs it parodies.

White goes on to examine how it was Nietzsche and Croce who philosophically confronted and introduced this essentially modernist predicament—synonymous with ironic consciousness—to the twentieth-century European historical imagination.

As Fischer and I argued in *Anthropology As Cultural Critique,* ([1986] 1999) realist modes of description have oscillated with a tradition of ironic meta-commentary upon language since the latter's introduction at the end of the nineteenth century. The ironic tradition was powerfully reinforced during the 1970s and 80s by waves of critical thought that have inculcated a pervasive sus-pension of faith in the idea of grand covering theories and reigning paradigms of research in a number of fields. Thus we are left in the human sciences in this fin-de-siècle, like the last, in a supremely ironic mood along with a powerful ambivalence toward it. The situation now in U.S. academia seems to me to be one of impasse and frustrated desires to overcome it in the wake of the heavy dose of 1980s ironic imagination, in White's sense. There would be a certain nobility in living with irony—and the self-critical consciousness it entails—as part of the modern condition, were it not for the almost irresistible pressures to view such irony as a predicament that should be overcome. Such pressures are perhaps an inevitable function of participating in institutions, as academic in-tellectuals do, that demand the production of positive, instrumental forms of thought along trajectories of progress.

But indeed, academic postmodernism, so-called, would hardly have been worth the effort if postmodernity itself had not happened. Just as representa-tions are social facts, as Paul Rabinow asserted in the title to his contribution in *Writing Culture* (Rabinow 1986), so the crisis of representation, or the predicament of irony, keenly experienced in the sphere of academic intellectual life over the past decade, is a social fact. Thus complex versions, idioms, artic-ulations, and resemblances of the same academic crisis of representation have been a pervasive feature of the situated experiences of social change that we in the human sciences have often taken both as our object of study and as a legit-imating reference for much of our theoretical discourse in recent years. Yet, with the traditional forms of realism in disarray and under suspicion—the sense of impasse brought about by the predicament of irony—there is no con-ventional access to precisely those features of ironic consciousness exhibited in the locations of our research and inquiry that indeed define the distinctive quality of contemporary social transformations almost anywhere. Our own predicament of irony, in short, denies us the means of realist representation in the tradition of empiricist inquiry to address this very same and defining predicament among our diverse contemporary subjects. Thus, this problem of dealing with the ambivalences and impasses of irony's deep critique of ratio-nality and realism is not merely academic, but is a complex feature of contem-porary social life itself and should be a primary focus of contemporary re-search, if only the means existed in theory and method (see Marcus 1997 for a more elaborate argument).

Entering this breach following my participation in the 1980s critiques of representation specifically through my investments in the anthropological tradition of ethnography, energized by those very critiques, I have been involved since the early 1990s in the Late Editions project. This is the production of a temporally limited and marked series of annuals published by the University of Chicago Press through the year 2000 (Marcus, 1993, 1995, 1996, 1997, 1998, 1999, 2000a, and 2000b). The purpose of this effort has been to recognize, address, and probe through various topics and in diverse institutional and everyday locales precisely this embedded predicament of irony, mirroring or at least resembling through acts of translation in research, the academic preoccupation of this era. With the uncertainty about realist forms of representation, our project has wagered on working with the situated "conversation," the genre that the French call the *entretien,* as a means of access to the exposure of the ironic in the various subjects and settings that the volumes of the series have presented. Before discussing further the circumstances of Late Editions conversations, both as fieldwork and discursive form in lieu of standard analytic and descriptive exposition, I want to clarify a little more the theoretical underpinnings and rationale of the project.

What are the social conditions and what is the expression of the related crisis of representation, so self-consciously reflected upon and so theoretically elaborated in academia, as a dimension of contemporary locations, ethnograpically explored? It seems to me that there are practices, anxieties, and ambivalences present in any location that are specifically keyed as a response to the intimate functioning of nonlocal agencies and causes, and for which there are no convincing commonsense understandings. The basic condition that stimulates this widespread predicament of irony is an awareness of existential doubleness, deriving from a sense of being *here* with major present transformations ongoing that are intimately tied to things happening simultaneously *elsewhere* but without certainty or authoritative representations of what the connections are. Indeed, there are so many plausible explanations for the changes, no one of which inspires more authority than another, that the individual subject is left to account for the connections—the behind-the-scenes structure—to read into his or her own biography the locally felt agency and effects of knowledge of great and little events happening elsewhere.

In short, past and conventional ideas of the "social" and how it functions no longer work, or rather no longer have authority, and social actors are confronted with the same kind of impasses that academics these days uncomfortably experience. But the impasses are quite pragmatic problems requiring responses, for everyday life to proceed at all, that range from evasions, displacements, to halfhearted investments in old theories or exotic constructions and idiosyncratic theories of the way the world works. The Late Editions volumes probe these varieties of ad hoc and embedded responses in different locations to massive changes in the world for which there is no one authoritative macro narrative.

Yet, ethnography can only go so far as the sole means of documenting these diverse embedded understandings of agency out of a predicament of ambivalence and irony as the distinguishing social fact, in many locations, of this fin-de-siècle. Its documentary function in complex engagement with the inadequacy of traditional genres of the real is the limit of the Late Editions project. Exposing embedded crises of representation is indeed a radical challenge to the assumptions and cognitive style of classic social theory, and the sorts of theory which developed the critique of representation—largely theories of culture explored in textual analysis—were never concerned with the social except as a general (and often nostalgic) referent. Ethnography could try to reflect these essentially high-literati ideas as enacted by people "on the ground," but it could not do so convincingly without a complementary social theory, and it is precisely a complex theorization of the social in the classic sense that was lost in the thrust of 1970s and 80s critiques. Until recently, that is. . .

A fascinating set of debates focused on the work of Ulrich Beck and, swirling around the notion of "reflexive modernization" (see Beck, Giddens, and Lash 1994), offer the sort of theoretical and markedly sociological discussions that suggest a systematic frame for the pieces of the Late Editions project, which itself has been inspired by the practices of ethnography. Reflexive modernization is a social-theoretical construct raised in response to the long intellectual trend of the late 70s through the present of speaking in terms of postmodernism and the positing of a present era of postmodernity, but without a grounded sociological interest or perspective. In a powerful way, it returns the social to theoretical discussions that have been weak on it—that had no way, except through ethnography to reground its ideas systematically in contemporary social change. While incorporating the critical power of postmodernist discourse to disrupt the existing establishment of narratives of social thought, it nonetheless attempts to ground and systematize these critical initiatives in more sociological and empirical terms.

The construct of reflexive modernization proposes that the modernity characteristic of industrial society is succeeded by a modernity which involves living with constant risk, as much a production of economic activity as wealth, with irreducible contingency, and in a more complex, less controllable world. Ulrich Beck's key construct, risk society (Beck 1992), alters the assumptions by which modern societies have been theorized. To quote Beck (1994: 6, 11–12):

> In the sense of a social theory and a diagnosis of culture, the concept of risk
> society designates a stage of modernity in which the threats produced so far
> on the path of industrial society begin to predominate. This raises the issue of

the self-limitation of that development as well as the task of redetermining the standards (of responsibility, safety, monitoring, and damage limitation) attained so far with attention to potential threats. The problem here is, however, that the latter not only escape sensory perception and exceed our imaginative abilities: they also cannot be determined by science. The definition of danger is always a *cognitive* and *social* construct. Modern societies are thus confronted with the bases and limits of their own model to precisely the degree they do not change, do not reflect on their effects and continue a policy of more of the same. . . . In a political and existential sense, the fundamental question and decision that opens up is, will the new manufactured incalculability and disorder be opposed according to the pattern of instrumental rational control, that is, by recourse to the old offerings of industrial society (more technology, market, government and so on)? Or is a rethinking and a new way of acting beginning here, which accepts and affirms the ambivalence—but then with far-reaching consequences for all areas of social action?

Reflexivity as self-monitoring both on the level of institutions and of individual persons becomes not only a pervasive activity of society, but also a key focus of social thought itself. One of the most valuable dimensions of the debates over reflexive modernization and risk society is precisely their detailed theoretical examination of the idea of reflexivity itself as socially situated activity—a dimension which of course closely aligns this theoretical project with the project of Late Editions, derived from ethnography. In these debates, the sense of reflexivity as critical self-reflection is interestingly distinguished from reflexivity as mere feedback-monitoring, and, most importantly, as self-confrontation. But, in any of its senses, reflexivity is pervasive in modern rationalist organizations and institutions. The question for Late Editions is, how post-modern (how critically reflexive?, how open?, how shaken-up in rationalist cognition?, how frustrated by a sense of impasse?, finally, how ironic?) are the conditions of reflexivity within the operations of various institutions and formal organizations affected by the same predicament of irony that has affected so emblematically academic thought over the past two decades?

Beside the complex notion of reflexivity, the other core assumption developed within the construct of reflexive modernization that is particularly relevant to understanding the social circumstances in which de facto crises of representation occur, out there, so to speak, that the Late Editions project documents, is the progressive freeing of agency from structure or the emergence of individualization as a prominent social form. Individualization is not classic methodological individualism, but a condition in which the loss of authority of paradigms and metanarratives to explain contemporary risks, dangers, and uncertainties leaves individuals to put things together. From this reweighting upon the individual to make sense of large matters very personally, new sorts of politics and political movements arise out of intimacies—responses to risk in the most personal aspects of life, that cannot even be organized and encompassed by the now familiar kinds of social movement tied to identity issues. Not to be mistaken for a return to mass society theory or liberal individualism associated with market regimes, discussions of reflexive modernization require new theories of the social, as yet only partly worked out. To quote Ulrich Beck again (1994: 15): "Put in plain terms, 'individualization' means the disintegration of the certainties of industrial society as well as the compulsion to find and invent new certainties for oneself and others without them. But it also means new interdependencies. Even global ones. Individualization and globalization are in fact two sides of the same process of reflexive modernization." The circumstance of individualization defines precisely the kind of subject position, or structure of feeling, in relation to which Late Editions tries to conduct its interviews.

The Late Editions Conversation

Each year, as editor of the series, I commissioned a set of contributions for a particular volume, by asking experienced scholars (often anthropologists, but also others representing a mix of disciplinary trainings) to return to sites of knowledge and expertise to conduct strategic conversations and interviews as the raw material for pieces that would be edited and molded from it. The constant pressure in producing pieces for the volumes was to develop strategically edited interview material at the expense of authorial exposition and overvoice. Each piece thus reflects a struggle between the conventional tendency of scholarship to enunciate, if not objectively then authoritatively, and the insistence of the project to make arguments, express positions and points of view through the *entretien*. The results have been predictably mixed, but we hope they are always interesting even when the enunciatory desire overtakes editorial indirection.

The inspiration and reflective model for the Late Editions project is of course the ethnographic interview/conversation/dialogue in the context of fieldwork, more than the journalistic interview that the series might also evoke for some. But there are important differences between the ethnographic encounter in fieldwork and the Late Editions mise-en-scène that go to the heart of the bigger difference defining contemporary society to which the Late Editions project is designed to provide access. In effect, the mise-en-scène of anthropological fieldwork, as conceived in informal disciplinary culture, misses the sort of embedded perspective that Late Editions fieldwork most wants to expose. Anthropologists have always understood themselves as being both inside and outside the sites in which they are participant observers. That is, they have never naively thought they go native, and in fact are critical of those among themselves who are so naive, but understand that they always remain marginal, fictive natives at best. Still, they have always operated on the faith, necessary for the kind of knowledge they produce, that they could be more insiders than outsiders if only by skills of translation, rapport, sensitivity, and learned cultural competencies.

In contrast, while starting from the same inside-outside boundary positioning, the ideal Late Edition piece does not have the same faith in being able to probe the "inside" of a culture, nor does it presuppose that the subject is on the "inside" of a culture, given that local knowledge reflecting a crisis or representation or a predicament of irony is never about being local. The Late Editions bias is thus toward the recognition of its authors as always present markers of "outsideness," never stirring from the boundary, a presence that makes possible certain kinds of access that a faith in being able to get inside does not. It is only in an interview situation where the outsideness is never elided and is the basis of an affinity between author and subject that the ironies of being caught in the impasse of a crisis of representation, albeit with different expressions and interests, are made accessible. The resolute outsideness of the interviewer in relation to a subject sensitive to the outside makes possible the elicitation of the variety of ways that the anxiety within the local situation about a specific predicament of irony manifests itself. These forms of anxiety are the essence of reflexive modernization as enacted.[1] They are what the Late Editions project is interested in making accessible through modifications of the classic vision of the ethnographic encounter.[2]

Late Editions is trying to get at a form of local knowledge which is all about the kind of difference that is not accessible by working out internal cultural logics—it is about difference that arises from the anxieties of knowing that one is somehow tied into what is happening elsewhere but without the relationships being clear or precisely articulated. Subjects are participating in discourses that are localized but are not their own. Douglas Holmes (1993) has called these "illicit discourses," and the Late Editions project is concerned with such illicit

1. The notion of reflexive modernization is distilled from key theoretical notions of what constitutes postmodernity (e.g. the much vaunted time-space compression, see Harvey 1989), but that has been virtually inaccessible to ethnography.

2. The bias in anthropology is that the insider's account is possible even though there is a clear recognition of the insider/outsider boundary from which any ethnographic investigation operates. The different assumption of the Late Edition project, and thus the different context of elicitation it establishes, always creates the conditions for the expression of ambivalence in the subject, deriving from the affinity of the predicament of irony between the ethnographer and subject. What Late Editions ethnographers want from subjects is not so much local knowledge as their forms of anxiety generated by their awareness of being affected by what is elsewhere but without a narrative of what the connections are, or rather with too many narratives about what the connections might be. The Late Editions ethnographer in this sense makes that elsewhere present. It is not that this is unrecognized in anthropology, but it is always referenced in terms of ethical discourse, and this frame does not get at what the Late Editions project seeks to document.

discourses in this sense: fragments of local discourses have origins elsewhere without the relationship to that elsewhere being clear. This uncertainty creates anxiety, wonder, and insecurity, in different registers both in the ethnographer and her subject. This recognition of a common predicament of irony is the primary basis for defining the complicity that is at the center of Late Editions interview relationships. Complicity is the highlighting of this external determination of local discourses, marked and set off by the Late Editions author's presence as fieldworker but free of the old ideology of rapport or collaboration that traditionally has evoked the ethnographic process. Free of this mise-en-scène, the Late Editions encounter seeks to materialize dimensions of others which the interview in traditional fieldwork cannot get at as well.

As a metaphor for the knowledge-producing relationship, complicity, rather than rapport or collaboration, works here, not as an ethical matter only, but as a cognitive one as well (see Marcus 1999 for elaboration). In a sense, it is because there is so much inquiry and desire to document in the contemporary world—so much competition for the ethnographer—the task of "passing" has become much harder, even to contemplate as a satisfying ideology of fieldwork. Thus, ethnographers in the mode of Late Editions attempt to make the most of the recognition that they are always markers of the outside locally, and this identity, if ideologically valorized, will make accessible interesting dimensions in particular about the shared crisis of representation that the Late Editions author looks for in her interlocutors.

The Paranoid Style in Fin-de-Siècle Rationality

The volumes of Late Editions have probed the embedded responses to the contemporary impasse resulting from this fin-de-siècle's predicament of irony across a variety of settings and among a range of subjects.[3] We intend that cumulatively the materials exposed in these volumes will constitute an assemblage for a certain constituency who come to follow the series and its rationale and who will treat the assemblage itself as a corpus for internal comparisons

---

3. Late Editions 1, *Perilous States,* on life amid the ruins of civil societies in transformed political orders; Late Editions 2, *Technoscientific Imaginaries,* on the present conditions of doing science; Late Editions 3 and 4, *Connected* and *Cultural Producers,* on the changes in communication media and how they affect representation; Late Editions 5 on the transformation of the corporation in the name of its new interest in culture; Late Editions 6 on paranoia as a reasonable expression of rationality in a number of settings; Late Editions 7, *Para-sites,* on the projects of reflexive critique of those positioned within or alongside (but *not* emblematically against) powerful institutions and engines of contemporary change; and Late Editions 8, *Zeroing In on the Year 2000,* on the immense value of zero symbolically, cognitively, and technologically in the practices of contemporary scientists and experts.

and associations across its diverse materials, but tied to very specific and detailed exposures of many local predicaments of irony.

Paranoia within Reason: A Casebook on Conspiracy as Explanation, Late Editions 6, captures most cogently one variety of response to the impasse resulting from a pervasive and embedded crisis of representation that the Late Editions project is designed to explore. Late Editions 6 probes a mobile style of thinking that the historian Richard Hofstadter labeled and analyzed so well in the atmosphere of the 1950s United States as the "paranoid style," with its associated production of conspiracy theories. This formation has never been absent from most societies, at most times, in most places (after all, in anthropology, Evans-Pritchard's *Witchcraft, Oracles, and Magic Among the Azande* [1937] could be considered the classic text on this subject) and has been particularly prominent in U.S. life through the Cold War (for which the Hofstadter piece is the classic statement along with the novels of Don DeLillo, e.g., 1978, 1982, 1988, 1997, for the later Cold War). Still, there is something distinctive about the paranoid style at the end of the century in the post–Cold War world no longer organized by empires and the clash of ideologies, or for that matter civilizations, as some old cold warriors (Samuel Huntington [1996], for example) would like to recreate. While indeed there are plenty of instances that perpetuate the Cold War style of paranoia and conspiracy theories and reflect its legacies, this complex is also increasingly found at the heart of rationalist activity and processes which were either immune to or the open enemies of such irrationalism—that is, within the pillars of rationality of law, science, and economics. The paranoid style is not all a fringe phenomenon but is at the very heart of certain controversies in which these hyper-rationalist spheres are engaged.

To quote Hofstadter ([1952] 1967):

> What distinguishes the paranoid's style is not then the absence of verifiable facts (though it is occasionally true that in his extravagant passion for facts the paranoid occasionally manufactures them), but rather the curious leap in imagination that is always made at some critical point in the recital of events. (37)

> The typical procedures of the higher paranoid scholarship is to start with such defensible assumptions and with a careful accumulation of facts, or at least what appear to be facts, and to marshal these facts toward an overwhelming "proof" of the particular conspiracy that is to be established. It is nothing if not coherent; in fact, the paranoid mentality is far more coherent than the real word since it leaves no room for mistakes, failures, or ambiguities. (36)

Not always as intentional as Hofstadter indicates, conspiracy theories emerge in the realm of the rational as a response with a vengeance, a sort of blind fury, a once-and-for-all response to the sense of impasse and ambivalence amid an excruciating predicament of irony. They emerge at the limits of, or as an alternative to, self-deception.

From where does this paranoid style come within the regimes of the rational? Not from the Cold War effect, I would argue, but rather as a response to the predicament of irony itself, as one kind of dramatic response to the experienced crisis of representation where it has blocked knowledge functions dependent on an authoritative hierarchy of plausible metanarratives. And it is most likely to arise within the regimes of the rational at those points where the uncertainties of risk society, as theorized by Beck, are most apparent, most likely in the sphere of environmental issues, dangers, and disasters.

As was noted, conspiracy theories combine plausibility, deep knowledge of certain facts, and often seamless fictional connection between persons, events, and processes, assigning (often secret, disguised) agencies within structures that seem to be coming apart or about which authoritative understandings have diminished. These are precisely the characteristics that define an option for operating as a scientist, a jurist, or economist in a world of reflexive modernization, of high irony, where there is little faith in metanarratives as such or where ambivalence is insurmountable. This is a paranoia that is a direct function of the predicament of irony, and deserves to be differentiated from the conspiracy theories and paranoia attributed so obviously to irrational margins, fringes, cults, militias, and old Cold Warriors. As will be seen, though, in the context of the politics of particular controversies, there are often blurrings and alliances between conspiracy theories within the rational and irrational—a joining together of Cold War paranoia and that created in response to a loss of authority in paradigms of knowledge.

Briefly, I want to explore just such a case developed by Myanna Lahsen (1999) as one contribution to Late Editions 6—this is her study of the global warming debate since the late 1980s and its complex constituencies and alignments. Climate change is the kind of issue that has been labeled as transscientific, namely, the situation in which science is being asked questions it is not in a position to answer. This is the kind of arena, then, that is appropriate to Beck's concept of the risk society in which scientists and others must operate in a condition of maximum irony, uncertainty, and ambivalence. It is thus a condition where otherwise rational experts might engage in paranoid politics and its mode of conspiracy theory.

Climate models, supercomputer simulations of the interaction of the atmosphere, oceans, and land in the presence of increasing levels of carbon dioxide and other greenhouse gases, are central supports for the view that humans are altering the climate system, with at least possible regionally disastrous effects. But the models are imperfect and involve uncertainties, and critics point to disparities between climate records based on observations and the modeled simulations of past climate systems. Uncertainty in the science of climate-change enables different actors and groups to draw different conclusions concerning the seriousness of the future threat. Remedial action to significantly minimize projected future climate changes would require fundamental changes in current socioeconomic structures at a global level. Given these stakes, and considering that the computer models' ability to simulate climate dynamics is still crude, it is hardly surprising that the scientific debate concerning climate change is highly charged politically.

Lahsen's work provides a fascinating, intricate map of how old conspiracy theorists of the extreme right, perpetuating after the Cold War the cause of free enterprise against communism, now, in the replacement guise of environmentalism, connect with the paranoid tendencies of scientists in good standing who have been skeptics of the disorderly world-out-of-control visions of the global warming trend, marking one case of a crisis of representation being fought out over the limits of knowledge in a trans-science space.

As Lahsen says,

> The success of influential mainstream scientists in creating concern about [global warming] soon created a backlash among some scientists, politicians, and socioeconomic forces in U.S. society. The backlash comprises accusations concerning the motives of scientists and environmentalists stirring up public concern, and it has provoked a wealth of equally acrimonious counter-accusations, rendering the scientific controversy . . . bitter and rife with conspiracy theories. (111)

Lahsen represents here (although her work is more balanced and comprehensive in its coverage of positions) only one side of this paranoid crossfire—the one that challenges the environmentalist claim that there is such a human-made crisis. She shows how the discourse of a few high-profile scientists skeptical of the theory largely endorsed by international scientific establishments connect with interests, views, and values of industries and right-wing groups in U.S. society. Among all positions to the controversy, there is a trading of accusations of conspiracy, the paranoid style thus blanketing the field of controversy itself. Both the skeptical side and the certainty side are proposing conspiratorial metanarratives to escape the impasse of ironic uncertainty and the absence of authoritative answers. Each tries to overcome the impasse in trans-science space and join older more manichean political interests that define each side—conspiracies of the left and right, and paranoid styles that crosscut both. This is then a passion play of the crisis of representation as a challenge to instrumental rationalities. It stands for a considerable trend in one decisive and worrying response to the moment of heightened irony that we are living through in this fin-de-siècle.

A Concluding Note

As a general issue in contemporary cultural studies, the predicament of irony, identified here as the broad condition of knowledge of this era, has been most frequently expressed as the concern with the indeterminacy of interpretation. A source of liberation and possibility for some, but of deep frustration for others, the tendency for contemporary cultural analyses to assert that things are always simultaneously "both . . . and," or "neither . . . nor" signals the ideological commitment of culture theory to crosscutting multiplicity, flexibility, and open-endedness as the most effective modes of resistance to often subtle forces of domination coming from the cold, hard, and systemic processes of capitalist political economy. While neither innocent nor romantic about the possibilities of opposition in the cultural sphere, so much scholarship these days is satisfied to elide or avoid the singular, fixed definition of whatever it makes an object of study. Indeed, keeping the subject open—in the state of irony—is the means by which scholarship expresses and enacts a form of resistance. This is nowhere more apparent than in the development of the theoretical interest in subjectivity toward a trend of identity politics and scholarship pervading such arenas as feminism, postcolonial studies, and new formations of ethnic studies. In this trend, the writings of theorists such as Judith Butler and Homi Bhaba have been of central influence, through the wide and often imprecise proliferation of such concepts as hybridity and performativity, and through such existential constructs as living in exile or diaspora, being marginal, or crossing borders as a way of life.

"Emergence" is the temporality associated with these states of subjectivity in cultural studies literature in which identities are not fixed or describable in determinate ways, but are unfolding (with open possibility) as they are being studied (Marcus 1994). Such a temporality guarantees a felicitous and liberating indeterminacy. Studying something emergent does not place the onus of prediction upon the scholar, nor does it imply futurism associated with strong utopic or dystopic visions, nor does it embed perspective in an historical metanarrative in which the terms of description are largely given. In effect, emergence is precisely the temporal dimension that "hedges bets," so to speak, that guarantees the qualified, contingent hopefulness that the cautious, critical moralism of work in cultural studies favors.

The typical subject, then, of contemporary critical cultural analysis is caught in webs of irony, betwixt and between, in the throes of agonies (ambivalent accommodations) and ecstasies (small, but clearcut resistances). The dissatisfaction with this pervasive construction is based on the discomforts of the ironic condition as White defined one kind of climax for an era of intellectual activity. Here, irony is an expression of a sustained, pervasive, and seemingly inescapable condition, and not just an effect, a tropological gloss, or a mere strategy or rhetoric of interpretation. For many, it is the sort of condition that is unsustainable for long, even excruciating, driving the rationalist, the expert, or the professional, in some cases, to the reasonableness of paranoid explanation, as described above. Not that such paranoia is absent from academic debate during and in the wake of an era of ironic predicament, but strong opposition has grown to the hard-won successes of cultural studies scholarship in reestablishing an informed respect and even authority for the toleration of difference in social and cultural life without any of the previous too-easy solutions for such tolerance in the models of liberal pluralism. Beyond the highly partisan assaults on the political correctness, the interpretive excesses, and indeterminacies of cultural studies theory and scholarship in the ironic mode, official institutions of state and economy have demonstrated the desire and habit of even appropriating the principles respecting difference established by this intellectual trend on cultural issues, but in terms that generate fixed, determinate categories that close off possibility to suit certain instrumental purposes and the conduct of policymaking. This official appropriation of strict forms of multiculturalism has provided perhaps the strongest justification for the continuing style of cultural studies scholarship in the ironic mode, committed precisely to resisting constructions of the determinate subject or fixed identity. The history of multicultural debate and its appropriation and rigidification in public discourse, state policy, and private institutional practices exemplifies this general fate of the heady indulgence of ironic predicament in academia during the 1970s and 1980s—and the continuing need to pursue this indulgence.

Thus, challenge to the assimilation of its own best insights and principles remains an oppositional task of ongoing critique for cultural studies scholarship, for which the ironic mode of indeterminacy is still a powerful strategy and style of argument, description, and interpretation. But precisely because this mode of scholarship remains a residue of a major and far more general period of irony in the rhetorics of explanation, which in reaction, is easily characterized as malaise, leading to undecidable conflicts of interpretation in intellectual work and the consequent paralysis of positive knowledge production, it is especially vulnerable at a moment when there are many who would like to see the pendulum of academic fashion move in a direction that wants distance from the lures and excitements along with the discomforts and insecurities of an era of ironic predicament. Paranoid explanation aside, well into this fin-de-siècle many in the humanities and social sciences look desiringly for new larger theoretical frames to restart inquiry on a more certain course (even entertaining old Victorian hopes for "consilience" [Wilson 1998] and the universality of the laws of evolutionary process). Perhaps too much taken by my own development in the questions and styles posed by the ironic predicament stirring more than a decade ago, and thoroughly immersed in the ethnographic probes and conversations of the Late Editions project, I personally can still only see irony in these latest efforts to get beyond it.

References

Beck, Ulrich. 1992. *Risk Society: Towards a New Modernity.* Trans. Mark Ritter. London: Sage.

———. 1994. The Reinfection of Politics: Towards a Theory of Reflexive Modernization. In *Reflexive Modernization,* ed. Ulrich Beck, Anthony Giddens, and Scott Lash, 1–55. Stanford: Stanford University Press.

Beck, Ulrich, Anthony Giddens, and Scott Lash. 1994. *Reflexive Modernization: Politics, Tradition and Aesthetics in the Modern Social Order.* Stanford: Stanford University Press.

Clifford, James, and George E. Marcus, eds. 1986. *Writing Culture: The Poetics and Politics of Ethnography.* Berkeley: University of California Press

DeLillo, Don. 1978. *Running Dog.* New York: Scribner.

———. 1982. *The Names.* New York: Scribner.

———. 1988. *Libra.* New York: Scribner.

———. 1997. *Underworld.* New York: Scribner.

Evans-Pritchard, E. E. 1937. *Witchcraft, Oracles, and Magic among the Azande.* Oxford: Oxford University Press.

Harvey, David. 1989. *The Condition of Postmodernity.* Oxford: Blackwell.

Hofstadter, Richard. [1952] 1967. *The Paranoid Style in American Politics and Other Essays.* New York: Random House.

Holmes, Douglas. 1993. Illicit Discourse. In *Perilous States.* Late Editions 1, ed. George E. Marcus, 255–82. Chicago: University of Chicago Press.

Huntington, Samuel. 1996. *The Clash of Civilizations and the Remaking of the World Order.* New York: Simon & Schuster.

Lahsen, Myanna. 1999. The Detection and Attribution of Conspiracies: The Controversy Over Chapter 8. In *Paranoia Within Reason,* Late Editions 6, ed. George E. Marcus, 111–36. Chicago: University of Chicago Press.

Marcus, George E. 1994. General Comments. In *Further Inflections: Toward Ethnographies of the Future,* ed. Susan Harding and Fred Myers. Special issue of *Cultural Anthropology* 9(3): 423–28.

———. 1997. Critical Cultural Studies as One Power/Knowledge Like, Among, and In Engagement With Others. In *From Sociology to Cultural Studies: New Perspectives,* ed. Elizabeth Long, 399–425. Oxford: Blackwell.

———.1999. *Ethnography Through Thick and Thin.* Princeton: Princeton University Press.

Marcus, George E., ed. 1993. *Perilous States: Conversations on Culture, Politics, and Nation.* Late Editions 1, Cultural Studies for the End of the Century. Chicago: University of Chicago Press.

———. 1995. *Technoscientific Imaginaries: Conversations, Profiles, and Memoirs.* Late Editions 2, Cultural Studies for the End of the Century. Chicago: University of Chicago Press.

————. 1996. *Connected: Engagements with Media.* Late Editions 3, Cultural Studies for the End of the Century. Chicago: University of Chicago Press.

————. 1997. *Cultural Producers in Perilous States: Editing Events, Documenting Change.* Late Editions 4, Cultural Studies for the End of the Century. Chicago: University of Chicago Press.

————. 1998. *Corporate Futures: The Diffusion of the Culturally Sensitive Corporate Form.* Late Editions 5, Cultural Studies for the End of the Century. Chicago: University of Chicago Press.

————. 1999a. *Paranoia within Reason: A Casebook on Conspiracy as Explanation.* Late Editions 6, Cultural Studies for the End of the Century. Chicago: University of Chicago Press.

————. 2000a. *Para-sites: A Casebook against Cynical Reason.* Late Editions 7, Cultural Studies for the End of the Century. Chicago: University of Chicago Press.

————. 2000b. *Zeroing In on the Year 2000: The Final Edition.* Late Editions 8, Cultural Studies for the End of the Century. Chicago: University of Chicago Press.

Marcus, George E. and Michael Fischer. [1986] 1999. *Anthropology as Cultural Critique: An Experimental Moment in the Human Sciences.* 2d edition. Chicago: University of Chicago Press.

Rabinow, Paul. 1986. Representations Are Social Facts: Modernity and Post-Modernity in Anthropology. In *Writing Culture: The Poetics and Politics of Ethnography,* ed. James Clifford and George E. Marcus, 234–61. Berkeley: University of California Press.

White, Hayden. 1973. *Metahistory: The Historical Imagination in Nineteenth Century Europe.* Baltimore: Johns Hopkins University Press.

Wilson, E. O. 1998. *Consilience.* New York: Knopf.

Chapter Eleven

—— PAUL FRIEDRICH ——

Ironic Irony

Introduction (1), Method: Triangulation and Focus

In what follows I want to argue about irony and its relations to such maximal forces as time and power, to more specific things like culture and language, and to tropes such as the simile, and the genre and the life experience of tragedy. The argument will be illustrated by data and ideas from texts that I have chosen in part, because, I happen to be intimately familiar with them and so in a position to practice what (in his lectures) anthropologist Ralph Linton used to call "the method of triangulation." By this he meant comparing a small number of systems that one knows well that are culturally and psychologically distanced from each other. Triangulation contrasts, on the one hand, with focusing on one system in great depth, typically using qualitative methods, and, on the other, with using a wide sample of a dozen or thirty or more languages or cultures, in which latter case some quantification naturally suggests itself. The primarily qualitative method of triangulation felicitously combines microsystemic intensity of insight with the balance of a comparative perspective—as I have found in teaching comparative poetry and poetics through Tang Chinese, and nineteenth- and twentieth-century American and Russian texts. In this chapter, triangulation will be used to look into the role of irony in many aspects of life and culture—interpersonal (e.g., marital) relations, clan and ethnicity, political factionalism, and religious symbolism from both the uniquely individual and the social and cultural points of view. Triangulation will be used to explore subtypes of irony and other, intersecting phenomena: sarcasm, mendacity, ambiguity, and figure, notably, the simile.

Within this model of triangulation, the *Odyssey* is the most important corner. Less important are the Russian novel *Anna Karenina* and an ethnography, *The Princes of Naranja,* two works that afford insights into many subtypes of irony—despite the acute noncomparability of their writing. The first of these is by a high aristocrat about and mainly for other aristocrats (fewer than 2 percent of Russians in the late nineteenth century). The second is written by an American scholar about a village of Tarascan Indians in the cool green mountains of southwestern Mexico for audiences of anthropologists and Mexicanists, or at least persons interested in those fields. Presumably whatever holds for social princess Anna Karenina and the peasant "Princes of Naranja" will also hold for many of the myriad phenomena that lie between them and, to a limited extent, for some of what lies beyond.

These remarks on method suggest critical questions about how anthropology and literature can and should be integrated. At one extreme, only mad poets and some dotty critics (Arnold [1887] 1970) think that literature *is* life, that the contents of literature is essentially equal to the contents of life outside literature. At the other extreme, mad poets, again, cervantine readers,[1] and critics who are decadent in a technical sense, think that life *is* literature, that we live in a continuum of being on stage, on set, in the pages of romance, and so forth. Between these extremes, and recognizing that *de músico, poeta, y loco, todo tenemos un poco*,[2] there is the vast intermediate gray zone of the most diverse, subtle, extenuated, and fuzzy interconnections between literature and anthropology— obviously with mimetic or realistic prose, but just as critically with magic realism, surrealist poetry, and even the (totally ironic) theater of the absurd. One strong example of such interpenetration is where protagonists Anna Karenina and Odysseus are felt to be "like someone I've known," or even more real than someone known in "real life." On the other hand, an intensely lived experience can seem more like a poem or novel than most poems or novels. In this essay, the interconnection has been exploited as a heuristic matter of rhetoric and exposition. For example: to illustrate how a unique individual defines himself ironically or how an ironic process may color an event, the definition of himself as a "Gypsy" by the young rake Vronsky and the multiple, interacting duplicities of Odysseus and Penelope serve as well as any "real life" examples and *differ in no relevant way* from "real life" examples. They have the additional, heuristic value that many readers are familiar with the "data" and do not have to be clued in and given all sorts of ethnographic background: "redundancy" does not have to be built in for the example to sink home (if they have not read *Anna Karenina* they will soon see analogies to Rhett Butler or some other exemplar of the libertine archetype in question). Otherwise, literature used judiciously and "with all due circumspection" can only enrich and deepen anthropology as the study of man and woman—particularly in the case of irony.

1. A reader like Don Quixote, who saw "reality" (e.g., windmills) in terms of picaresque romances.
2. "We all have a bit of the musician, the poet, and the madman" (Spanish proverb).

Outside our immediate tradition, Eskimo lyric poetry and the Mayan Popol Vu in the New World, and Basho's haiku and *The Dream of the Red Chamber* in the Orient, have become classics of world literature because they contain hundreds of metaphors of a human condition that is beyond time, place, and culture—Anna of the adulteress (or sexual betrayer), Odysseus of someone trying to get home—metaphors and images that an appropriately humanistic anthropology focused on irony can ignore only at its methodological and conceptual peril.

Introduction (2): Multivocalism and Reflexivity

Let's shift to other abstractions. Irony may merely adorn the material reality of a fatal auto crash, or the hard skeletal structure of a kinship diagram. But, as we will see with the *Odyssey,* irony may form the core of human experience, even *be* that core. Irony, in other words, may constitute an aspect, perhaps comic, of a situation, or be the deepest ascertainable significance of a personal trauma or a cultural event (Steedly 1993: 236–40). In these comprehensive terms, then, irony may be defined provisionally as the infinite lacks of fit between what is intended to be felt and understood and what is actually understood and felt in speaker versus addressee, word versus deed, or theory versus practice (this is obviously a pragmatic [e.g., Peircean—and/or Confucian!] definition). In what follows, two of the leading *questions* about irony are: (1) what are its generative and originating roles?, and (2) what are its relatively secondary roles—for example, as a figure of speech equal or superior to metaphor in power? The overall argument, as will be detailed below, rests on the multivocalism of the word "irony" itself. The main *objective* in the argument that follows is to adumbrate a theory of "ironic irony," by which I mean, again provisionally, that irony should be seen as a galaxy of interacting, synergistic, cumulative, encapsulating and encapsulated levels, aspects, and dimensions of ironies about ironies—the most intense and intriguing of which is when the speaker or author doubles back on himself to be ironic about something already multiply so. Let us take up our major categories of analysis, starting with the most powerful: time. But first let us turn away from abstractions to an opening key and a heuristic bracket: some intratextual workings in the irony-drenched and irony-structured pages of Homer's *Odyssey* (e.g., Winkler 1990: 129–61).

Proem: Odyssey (1)

Homer's *Odyssey* has been read as a revenge saga, a romance, a comic opera, an epic, and the world's first novel, but no matter what genre the critic chooses, the dominant and organizing trope from start to finish is irony (e.g., Segal

1983). It begins with "... him alone, longing for his wife and his homecoming, does Calypso, bright among goddesses, hold back in her hollow caves, yearning for him to be her husband" (1.13–14). Yet Odysseus's nightly love "of necessity" is soon ironized by the fact that the main audience at the next point in the text is none other than womanizer maximus Zeus. The relation between Odysseus and the island-dwelling goddess is ironized many times later on—in book 5 by, for example, her anger at the gods' jealousy at her passionate attachment, followed by the subtleties of mutual tenderness and understanding during the couple's last supper and night of love. What had come to be a nocturnal "necessity" is given further ironic depth by the eventual recounting of how hungered-for her warm, woman's love had been to the exhausted traveler when he first landed. Numerous passages allude to Odysseus's sojourn with Calypso from diverse points of view and attitude—including his mention of it when he recounts his adventures to his wife during their first night of reunion near the end of the epic. An ironic texture to the relation is created by the scores of passages that variously echo, parallel, contradict, complement, and holograph each other within a complex orchestration of meanings where different levels and varieties of irony enrich each other.

Categories (1): Irony and Time

As the Calypso sequences in the *Odyssey* suggest, irony, unless seen through time, is an illusion, an illusory freezing of the last twist in a continuous twisting. Partly because irony is a mood or a syndrome of moods, it can never be fixed or constant but, on the contrary, must shift, rotate, and metamorphose from one split second to the next. The many clichés and formulas of irony—such as an "ironic situation"—which imply that irony is a fixed thing, or a "terminal synchrony" are only conceptual prefabs, misconceptions, figments of ordinary discourse and even more ordinary imaginations. The very popular idea of moments of time without expectation or intention is almost entirely a culturally defined illusion—be it most sudden illuminations of the American or Japanese Zen Buddhist or "moments of truth" in the bullfight or the boudoir. Let us illustrate this from another one of our systems.

The necessarily temporal essence of irony is witnessed by any shift in the personal relations between two people. Anna Karenina had been wont to worry if her husband came to bed five minutes late, but, on alighting from the train after her conversion-like fall for another man, the first thing she sees in that husband is his oversized, gristly ears pushing up his hat. Either these ears had been a source of irritation all along and had now grown more irritating, or she had never noticed them before but now did so because of her inflamed and altered perception. Whichever the reading, this of the ears and hat is ironic because it compels the reader, through "indirect infectiousness" (Eide 1995), to follow Anna through her recoding of what had been, superficially at least, a not unhappy marriage (Morson 1988)—through, that is, to her new consciousness of—or unconscious mindset toward—the duplicity and two-facedness of what she had been saying for seven years of an ostensibly happy marriage.

The continuously protean, shape-changing essence of irony is entangled with vast ranges of experience, be it the nuances of a glance by Anna Karenina, or the grinding tragedy of a family's life, or the national tragedies of the Chechens or the Palestinian Arabs. Potential, multitemporal tragedy lurks beneath the "humor" in a bric-a-brac of senses: ranging from the elegant and glittering surfaces of neoclassical comedy, to German "gallows humor," and the sardonic "Indian humor" of the Tarascans of Mexico and many other Native Americans who smile, without much joy, as a piglet run over and partly disemboweled by a truck races around the plaza squealing insanely and dragging its entrails in the dust. No matter what the social and political context—here a slowly dying porker as a metaphor of the human condition and the ambivalent humor it provokes—time and process always imply irony, often about preexisting ironies of a situation. The complexly temporal nature of irony includes all kinds of sequences and quantities, that is, all kinds of time, be they linear or nonlinear, durative or punctual, potential or future, hypothetical or imagined. All of these instances and many others, given the dialogic situation of all communication, involve some slippage or lack of fit between the intended meaning and what was understood, between what was anticipated and what actually happened.

Irony is also vividly witnessed in local-level politics. Let us recur to the Mexican-ethnographic corner of our triangle, a village of about a thousand souls in the early decades of this century—one of several dozen Tarascan Indian communities with a total population amounting to 5 percent of the state of Michoacán. By 1926, a united Indian faction had won back the village's ancestral lands from Spanish landlords and their non-Indian peons, but by 1937 the same faction had split apart over "a question of skirts," climaxed by a public confrontation between the wives of the two main leaders. These men were first cousins and long-time collaborators, the one specializing in village matters, the other in the region and state (the latter of these, incidentally, was notoriously given to womanizing, as captured by the Tarascan *thya-*, "to want," plus the "guts, innards" suffix *-ni-*, *thyani-*, "to lust after"; such epithets in the allegations of his enemies gave an ironic seasoning to the high agrarian ideals of his speeches). Each of the resulting factions that resulted from the schism within "one family" then allied itself with non-Indian peons whom they had formerly fought in what became, as one renowned "fighter" put it, no longer a struggle for the land, but "pure politics that brought widows and orphans" (quoted in Friedrich 1986: 132). Political relations, like conjugal ones, alter from second to second, are constantly ironizing.

Categories (2): Irony and Power

Irony involves differences, not just of time, but of power. The falsifying lenses of the pure aesthete or the idealist often block out or at least distort the role of power in irony, thereby reducing it to a figure of speech or a pervasive mood or a mere integument on the surface of a structure. But, as noted, irony is also a matter of human relations and human feelings as they shift through time and, since these feelings and relations can never be completely coordinate and symmetrical, to say nothing of egalitarian, irony always involves and implies— when it does not advertise—power (defined tentatively as a differentiated control over material resources and over human relations and minds). When men and women, be it dissolute kings and their mistresses or "normal" parents and children, do not understand each other, particularly when they are conscious or even self-conscious of this slippage—when they are fully aware of the Tannenesque phenomenon of "you-just-don't-understand"—it is always in part because one side or the other of the dialogue controls what the other wants or needs—without necessarily understanding what is wanted or needed (Tannen 1990). Often the needy side, as, for example, the Russian Gypsies, use irony to grasp back the needed power. In general, irony is always somehow political and, conversely, differences of power, whether or not realized by dialogue, are always at least implicitly ironic.

The way power and most importantly economic or political-economic power always necessarily implies irony can, to begin with, be a relatively individual affair between two persons. Let us return to one of our corners of evidence on irony: *Anna Karenina*. At the start of the novel, Anna depends financially on the husband, whom she scandalously and remorselessly cuckolds. Later she gets gifts and other material support from her lover. Consciousness of this material dependence would seem to feed her mounting guilt, jealousy, and insane anxieties. Yet the crucial "Marxist" economic facts are alluded to only twice in 760 pages by Tolstoy (who might have felt that such allusions would recall stereotypical scenarios of eighteenth- and nineteenth-century novels and ought to be kept to a minimum as both out-moded and belaboring the obvious). Tolstoy's ironic treatment (through understatement) of a situation that is already ironic and is talked about ironically, illustrates a most intense variety of the ironic irony being developed here.

What matters more than whether something is ironic or not is the *degree* to which it is—from minimal or zero irony to maximal or total irony. Zero irony, as was already suggested above, is exemplified in the pure subjectivity of a person perceiving his or her own inner state when either alone or where the audience does not matter. Such zero irony occurs in the moments of some mothers' consciousness-obliterating pain while giving birth or in the joy or ecstasy of some mothers after (natural) childbirth (L. Friedrich 1939), and in shared ecstasy. But there are also dyadic situations with zero irony, as in some "life-changing dialogue" (Attinasi and Friedrich 1995). There are even mass ("mob psychological") situations where the "moment of truth" is felt nonironically by many individuals in a crowd with respect to something experienced more or less collectively—Victor Turner's *communitas* (1969): the half-insane spectators watching the end of a great *faena* and then the *gran estocada* (stabbing home) of a bullfight in a small Spanish town (where many save all year for their tickets). Or, to take a radically different event, many of the listeners at the first reading of "Howl" by Allen Ginsberg. . . . Such moments, to the participants, are outside power and time.

The inevitable irony, be it finely nuanced or fiercely withering, that is implied by any power differential, be it between two people or of international scope, can be illustrated by the politics of two conjoined albeit mutually contradictory facts of recent local Mexican history. On the one hand, Mexico's hegemonic ideology as it was lived-out in village and city in the 1930s gave the appearance of collusion, or at least some agreement, with Communist principles and tactics, ranging from the vandalizing of churches to diplomatic support of the Spanish Loyalists. Over the same time span, on the other hand, local leaders and their fighting men effectively opposed and not infrequently assassinated their Communist rivals. Politics, the art of power, is predicated on not saying what you really think, on word and deed being continuously out of kilter. Irony is always a fact of politics, as when it becomes a component in a critical, antigovernmental, even anarchist ideology.

Ironies of Power: Odyssey (2)

That differences of power always generate irony is illustrated vividly by connected but noncontiguous scenes in the *Odyssey*. In book 2, Odysseus's only son, Telemachus, summons the "long-haired Achaians" to a meeting and then squares off in courageous debate against his mother's suitors and their kinsmen for wasting his household's wine and livestock and for dishonoring his parents. His hot tears and dashing of the scepter to the ground are countered by accusations by one suitor that his mother is carrying on with them or holding out promises to all of them that she has no intention of keeping; he describes her delay tactics. The entire scene is replete with irony since his outraged appeal to virtue is repeatedly undercut by the suitors' arguments and the raw fact of their greater power. Later on they try to detain him and, in book 4, after learning of his clandestine departure on a quest for news of his father, make plans to assassinate him. Still later, at points in books 16 and 19, Telemachus' renewed assertions of his rights over his household are matched by the suitors' assurances that they will withdraw their claims to his property when she marries one of them. At times they even profess affection for Telemachus, and one promises to defend him with his life. Any polity—from a dyad, to the members of a powerful manor, to the complexities of a modern nation-state—necessarily implies massive and intersecting ironies which prevent anything within its bounds from being totally non-ironic (except in the purely subjective sense of absolute non-irony introduced above). The ubiquity and omnipresence of political irony does not diminish its significance, any more than the universal mortality of man lessens the import of death, or the sexual connotations of actions and objects reduce the significance of their sexuality.

Categories (3): Irony, Culture, and Pan-Culture

The relations of power just dealt with are a primary source for the symbolic processes in terms of which culture is defined by many anthropologists. It follows that culture always includes irony and that irony is always to a large degree a matter of culture, specific to individual cultures in all their uniquenesses and idiosyncracies. One would not gather this reality of cultural relativism from the universalizing discussions in literary criticism where ironies that are diagnostically Ancient Greek or Modern American are presented as though they were quintessential truths for all times and in all places. Let's look at some extreme examples.

A good dictionary is an excellent repository of cultural specifics. In a first-rate Russian one we find irony defined in a familiar way as using words in the opposite of their "literal meanings' (Volin and Ushakov 1945: 1: 1224–25); this is captured in Krylov's fable when the fox says to the donkey, "But whence, oh wise one, do you wander?" An author such as Leo Tolstoy may be well-grounded in Russian folk meanings as well as the French model on whom Krylov drew (Jean de la Fontaine) but can elaborate, articulate, and stretch the modes of irony in many different directions.

The dynamics of Anna Karenina's predicament plus her character plus the linguaculture of irony can generate an unusual density of expression. On one page we find the word used three times by Anna in contrasting but culturally acceptable and intelligible ways: (1) "'But how, Alexei, teach me how,' she said with pathetic irony at the inevitability of her position"; (2) "'Oh, but not through my husband,' she said with natural irony"; and (3) "'What would you have me do?' she asked with the same light irony" (Tolstoy 1995: 172). This extraordinary density of irony—"pathetic, natural, light"—instances Tolstoy's favored formal figure of repetition. It is also profoundly meaningful because it occurs at the critical point when Anna is disclosing her pregnancy to her lover—with some ambiguity as to their respective feelings and even who the father may be. When a writer enlarges the scope of a trope such as irony he creates a space full of nuances that, while not in most people's active vocabularies, would be understood instantly and hence are natural. Tolstoy's proliferation of ironic nuance here is part of the meta-irony of his discourse, that is, of his being ironic about irony (particularly if we include the French subtexts that run through much of his "classic" period). To a lesser extent, and less consistently, these processes hold for all speakers of any language and illustrate how an ironic predicament, while ensconced in the symbolism of a specific culture, can also reflect what used to be called "the psychic unity of mankind" and universal processes of that unity—here expanding the scope of a trope.

Inferable universal or pan-cultural processes are also part of irony. The human experience that people never fully mean what they say and that nobody fully understands anybody is reflected in the discourse patterns and the actual talk of all peoples in all cultures. Life without a considerable consciousness of the ironic, irrespective of how that consciousness is coded linguistically, would be about as psychotic as belief in the literal reality of absolute love. This partial universality of irony bears on many things, including the colonial, the proselyte, and the anthropological-comparativist situations. A long and lamentable succession of colonial administrators, missionaries, and anthropologists has concluded that the lack of an overt expression entailed the lack of a sense of irony among primitive and "savage" peoples; yet the lack of a word or idiom that corresponds to our American English "irony" does not by itself demonstrate an absence of irony, of a feeling or sense of irony, in a given linguaculture (by which is meant, here and elsewhere, a combination of both the cultural-semantic aspects of language and the linguistic aspects of culture; Friedrich 1989: 306–7). On the contrary, whether or not they have a well-developed terminology, politically and economically subordinate groups like Gypsies, Native Americans, and the Scheduled Castes in India, are often particularly sensitive to irony. Both existential irony on the part of primitives and peasants and a naive obliviousness to irony on the part of colonial administrators are integral components of a more general situation. I cannot think of anything more generically and genuinely human than the sense of and need for irony.

Culture, whether unique and individual or universal, has already been described above as a product of unequal power (the reverse also holds). Culture is instantiated by any unique actor who, for example, draws on symbols from the cultural reservoir to profit himself or profit from someone else—or just to define himself ironically. Thus Anna's future husband responds to a suggestion that he should marry by alluding to his own past and then to the reputation for promiscuity, extraordinary in its degree, even in his social set, of all his close friends and relatives, including his mother, his brother, his best friend, and his salient mistress (e.g., Thérèse). Referring to one of the Russian and, indeed, European stereotypes of the Gypsy as wayward and wanton, even lascivious, footloose, and free to roam (Lemon 1995), he says, "I was born a Gypsy and I will remain a Gypsy." This self-characterization is ironized yet further by Anna's later obsessive concern with the possibility of his cheating on her—or worse, marrying a young and wealthy beauty. The cultural and structural facts of irony are balanced by the nonlinguistic ironies inherent in situations, and by the idiosyncratic personal ironies of the characters or of the author who, in either case, may be constrained by irony or exploit it as a resource.

Culturally specific irony informs, not just the unique individual, but, of course, events and organizations in society, particularly politics. Returning to the Mexican corner of our triangulation, in 1923 the Indian agrarians of the village of Naranja were desperately short of funds—and also of signatures for a petition seeking restitution of land previously seized by Spanish entrepreneurs in cahoots with the government. They were guided by Primo Tapia, their egregiously ironic leader, a swarthy trilingual anarchist. Under his leadership they collected 109 signatures, many of them from conservative pro-Catholic villagers, because "many children were being born but not baptized, people were marrying outside the church and dying without last rites." These same signatures were then tacked onto the petition as the results of a "census of persons originally petitioning for lands": the very restitution of the land that the conservative villagers opposed (Friedrich 1977: 91–92). Tapia's tactic was in tune with the "Indian humor' that, as illustrated earlier with the dying porker, arises in answer to unexpected accidents, notably violent ones, and practical jokes. Three years later this same deceitful and ironic leader was captured and lynched—as Mayan Indian leaders are being destroyed in 2000—but, within a year, he had been mythologized into a Christ-like martyr whose entry into the pearly gates was accompanied by a choir of "little angels" (*angelitos*, the souls of infants who die before being baptized). As a mood shared by those who remember such events, irony interpenetrates the ebb and flow of conflict and oppression, of ambiguity and paradox in a given society.

Ironic Tall Tales Structured by Culture: Odyssey (3)

Equally illuminating representations show how irony, especially its mendacious variety, or where it intersects with mendacity, is always defined in partly cultural terms. The *Odyssey*'s chief protagonist, the wily and indomitable Odysseus—but just as much his long-abandoned wife, the yet more wily and subtle Penelope—are created for us in a context of mirroring ironies that encompass all the actors from Zeus down to a simple agricultural worker. In book 13, Odysseus, having met his patron goddess Athena disguised as a "delicate shepherd," and having been assured by her that he is indeed in Ithaca (we are supposed to believe that he did not know), spins a lengthy yarn about how he is in flight after murdering the son of the King of Crete. The additional, embedded irony here is that an accomplished fabricator of falsehoods describes himself, falsely, as hailing from what even three millennia ago was reputed to be a country of liars—the triple negative yielding an ironic one, or at least a paradox. Revealing herself then, Athena rebukes him, albeit with affection, as a man "insatiable in deceit," who cannot get along without tricks even in his native land. Later on, in books 14 and 19, Odysseus spins out yarns with yet more stretching, first to the foreman of his crew of four (or twenty?) swineherds, and then to queen Penelope herself. In these tall tales he not only includes himself with diagnostic and hence "true" details, such as his wearing a golden brooch on which a dog throttles a fawn, but even creates a fiction about himself contriving a credible falsehood. Such embedding of mendacity, like the embedding of the dream interpreter within the dream in book 19 is peculiar to, but not unique to, the *Odyssey*. Equally peculiar, and probably indeed unique, is the swineherd's pun whereby wanderers *(aletés)* don't ever tell the truth *(alétes)* because they depend on the goodwill of their hosts.

These episodes suggest that all mendacity is logically a subset of irony, although the reverse—that all irony is mendacious—is not the case. The anecdotes show why Odysseus, taken as a specifically Greek culture hero, which he always was anyway, has been admired on his native soil for the aptitude, adaptability, and "cunning intelligence" (Detienne and Vernant [1978] 1989) which he displays in overcoming obstacles. These qualities are indeed so persuasively presented that they and the positive take on them have spread, ironically enough, to cultures in the Western World, notably England and Germany, where mendacity is generally condemned—or given a radically different role. In a similar way Homer emerges as the great pioneer in the grand philosophical tradition that leads to the sophists and that most sophisticated anti-sophist, Socrates, above all of *Cratylus,* the master of an irony so diagnostic and lucidly characterized that it has become one of the primary and essential subtypes of the phenomenon in any realistic, world comparative, anthropological sense.

Categories (4): Irony in Language (1)

The most ubiquitous and the most powerful part of culture—in terms of symbolic processes—is the natural language with which it is associated. Irony is embedded in all levels and components of language—particularly in what was designated above as linguaculture. Again, one would hardly expect the near ubiquitousness of irony in the discussions of grammarians who conceive of language as sets of rules for decontextualized and dehumanized forms, who worry about the sigmatic aorists that describe Clytemnestra's actions (Sapir 1924). Nor would one suspect the near ubiquitousness of irony from what is said by the logicians and language philosophers who are concerned with certain kinds of "truth values" and the primacy of "reference." And yet even these syntacticians and grammarians make the latent roles of irony the latent subject of their learned disquisitions, and irony has been the overt and explicit subject of much modern syntax—the ironic properties of certain kinds of sentences—and of much cultural linguistics—the pragmatic meanings of speech forms as they are actually used in cultural contexts. Indirect discourse and most reported speech is ironic because multiple embedding implies multiple slippage (Tannen 1984, 1990): when, for example, in book 17 of the *Odyssey,* Telemachus tells his mother Penelope what Menelaus says the Old Man of the Sea says that he heard from yet another source. On the other hand, much other reported speech is so minimally ironic as to be practically non-ironic: "We had just sat down to supper and she said, 'Please pass the salt.' " But whether the non-ironic contextualizes the ironic, or vice versa, it is part of the overall system of meanings we are talking about here.

The interpenetratedness of irony reflects the truth, stated earlier, that nothing close to perfect communication is possible; that, to phrase it otherwise, language, in both performance and structure, is always figurative and symbolic. Add to this that language is necessarily intentional and goal-oriented, and that the linguistic means are never adequate to the intended goals or ends, and it follows that language and speech reduce and falsify even when mendacity is out of the question or downright irrelevant. Language and speech imply or enable irony, and in many cases the ironic implications are as important and profound as any other—particularly because of the way any level of irony is embedded in a more inclusive level or itself contains another level—one version of our "ironic irony." The irony always inherent in language is aptly illustrated by the fascinating meanings of the word itself, ranging from the etymological (specifically, Greek) *eirein,* "to speak the opposite of what one means," to the loose and comprehensive usages current in America today (many of them illustrated by this anthology). Close to the Greek original is a Russian usage, as in "the Gypsies are an ironic people," that is, a people who hide what they are, who put on a public front that is the opposite of domestic reality. Some Russians contrast the often disheveled and indigent beggars and their sick-looking children on the city streets with the spotlessly clean homes of the wealthy extended families from which they supposedly sally forth although, obviously, "Gypsy Kings" and mendicant alms-seekers live in different places (Lemon 1995).

The irony inherent in language is equally well illustrated by the pervasive if not ubiquitous French-Russian bilingualism or bilingual subtextuality in *Anna*

Karenina. Hundreds of pages of Russian text depend to a significant degree for their meaning on the underlying French that is being alluded to. This is particularly instanced by the alternation, be it voluntary or involuntary, between the formal pronoun *vy* and the informal *ty,* which alternation is subtly calibrated with frequent switching between the native Russian language and the second native (i.e., second natural) but still alien French language into which protagonists and antagonists often break—at times for long stretches (Lyons 1980). Russian aristocrats in Anna's position would normally use either French, with its formal *vous,* or the informal Russian *ty* when speaking to a lover. Some of the bitterest ironies during the last days and final arguments of her life are symbolized by these alternations when, for example, her lover switches to the French *vous* to avoid the intimacy of the Russian *ty.* Tolstoy's "pathetic," "light," and "natural" ironies, all on one page, as discussed earlier, betray the French subtext in question and so manage to be interlingually ironic about irony, another type of "ironic irony." *Anna Karenina,* then, partly exemplifies a whole universe of ironies involving implicitly bilingual, sublingual, and interlingual texts—a universe that extends from the outright copying or at least reworking of Odyssean formulas in Virgil's *Aeneid* to the Irish English subtexts in Beckett's *Waiting for Godot* to the speech of refugees, migrants, and immigrants everywhere struggling with the hegemonic language(s) of their new homelands.

Irony in Language (2): "Honor" in (Indian) Mexico

At the level of society and politics—shifting, again, to Mexico—there is a constant irony in the uses, abuses, and even the avoidance of the word for "honor" in Mexico. On the one hand, in the Spanish of the great bulk of the population one often witnesses a mind-boggling hypocrisy where exaggerated professions of honor and respect walk hand-in-hand with an equally overgrown political corruption and ethnic discrimination. "She honors us," said an arrogant Mexican trucker (in a Mickey Mouse T-shirt) to his Indian interlocutor in Naranja while ogling a barefoot Tarascan woman shuffling past wrapped to her eyes with her shawl. Her black skirt, trailing in the dust, covered her ankles and feet down to her toes and the edges of her soles. In the county seat, as I have seen, men like this feel no compunction about jostling such a woman off the sidewalk. Primo Tapia, the ironic Tarascan regional leader introduced above, gained his just goals of land and educational reform by resorting to mendacious ruses and sudden violence, and his achievements were not talked about in terms of honor; "He never thought of honor. He thought of the land and his people," exclaimed another leader at a town meeting thirty years later apropos of two villagers who had been appealing to this exotic virtue (Friedrich 1986: 25). In the Tarascan language there is no word or idiom that corresponds well with

Spanish and mestizo "honor" (Pitt-Rivers 1966), although the root for "shame" *(khura-),* often with attached "body-part suffixes," is frequent and psychologically important. Incidentally, the snippets on Tarascan body-part suffixes that are given in this essay work in political or family discourse as threads in a vast network of what could be called "linguistically channeled corporeal irony" that is to some extent shared by all natural languages. The Tarascans, as this anecdote illustrates, may pursue goals that we would call honorable—regaining ancestral lands—while denying the value and lacking the word, whereas the Mexican mestizo often invokes honor precisely when, again by our standards, he is acting dishonorably. Irony is clearly and invariably integral to any and all questions of ethnic identity and conflict.

A partly literary variation on the theme of honor was played out by a Tarascan leader called "Flatface" because of the flattened nose in his pockmarked face. His biography and character combined contradictory facts. To begin with he had posed as "an original revolutionary without blemish, a comrade-in-arms of Primo Tapia" (Friedrich 1986), although this mix of local and hegemonic-elite ideologies was hardly credible and almost totally untrue. Furthermore, during his acquisitive and ruthless control over village and region, Flatface had nursed grudges as long as was needed to settle them by assassination or violent intimidation (Tarascan *hata-yari-ni,* "to nurse a grudge" with the "face" suffix *-yari-*); incidentally, in private life he was a virtuous father to his sons and a faithful, indeed uxorious, husband to his politically ambitious wife. But whether or not this paradoxical leader was exploiting ideologies or resorting to violence in a style reminiscent of Machiavelli, the idea of honor was absent from his speeches or the words of his contemporaries—except in the sort of ironic double-talk illustrated above by the T-shirted truck driver. The Machiavellian side of his life was curiously nuanced: one of his nephews, his chief political supporter, had, along with three other village leaders, read *The Prince* to the point of quoting the immortal Florentine to their local anthropologist ("Haven't you read Machiavelli, Pablo?"). The literal and metaphorical texture of an ironic local politics was thus interwoven with a living literary text of classical political theory—yet another type of ironic irony.

Irony in Language (3): What's Ironic in a Name? Odyssey (4)

One complex and illustrious example of irony being embedded deeply in language is the name *Odysseus.* Late, in book 19, we learn that Odysseus's mother's father Autolycus ("Lone Wolf"), when asked to name his infant grandson, had responded with the name Odysseus because he himself had been angered or damaged by many—playing here on the equivocal root *oud-* that can mean "anger, damage, hurt" and so forth *either* as active agent *or* as the passive patient. Eventually young man Odysseus goes on a boar hunt with his Lone-Wolf

mother's father and her brothers in a classic case of the "benevolent avuncu-
late" in a patrilineal society. In any case, the eponymous hero's name suggests
myriad ironic ambiguities with a scope over many sections of the epic: Odysseus the destroyer or the sufferer, or both (Dimock 1956; Peradotto 1990).

Odysseus earlier on in the text had overcome the "anger, damage, and hurt"
implied by his name through the exercise of what turn out to be some of its additional linguistic meanings, as follows. In book 9 he first tells the Cyclops that
his name is *ou-tis* or "No One" or "Nobody." This word, an ordinary pronoun
in Greek as it is in English, also pans on Odysseus's most essential trait, that is,
his "cunning intelligence" for which the Greek word is *metis* (totally unrelated
to the Greek pronoun etymologically). But note the additional delicacy that the
homonymous *me*, taken by itself, is the negative imperative corresponding to
the *ou* that is embedded in the pseudonym that dupes the Cyclops. The speaker,
Odysseus, thus exhibits and exemplifies his character by the form and the ref-
erence(s) of the name with which he dubs himself. The structure of irony patterns out as in the following graph:

Mood	Pronoun	Pseudonym	Proper Name	Quality
Indicative *ou*	*outis*	*Outis*	Odysseus	"Nobody"
Subjunctive *me*			Metis[3]	Cunning Intelligence

A bit later in the same book 9, after he has been blinded by Odysseus, the Cyclops calls out to the neighboring cyclops. They convene around the cave and
ask him, "What is the matter? who is trying to kill you?" He answers that "Nobody" is trying to kill him. "So why are you waking us up in the middle of the
night?" is their intensely ironic—to us—reaction. The several planes of irony
that are interacting by this time are in a sense resolved at the end of book 9
when Odysseus, succumbing to his own Iliadic hubris, shouts back at the Cyclops vaunting with what I am calling zero-irony *from his point of view,* that he
is "Odysseus, Sacker of Cities, Son of Laertes, having his home in Ithaca."
Thus the paranomastic play in this book 9 becomes the background for the onomastic episode in book 19 that was analyzed above.

Irony in Language (4): The "Speech Event" Model

What has been said so far about the linguistic matrix of irony leads us toward
the more inclusive truth that what I've been calling ironic slippage potentially
involves all the variables in the so-called speech situation, or, more generally
the "act" of communication (see e.g., Jakobson [1960] 1987). Minimally

3. In later sources, such as Hesiod, Metis was a goddess of wisdom and chief consort of Zeus,
who swallowed her; their eventual offspring, Athena (patroness of Odysseus), sprang from the head
of her father.

speaking, these variables, with Odyssean examples, are: (1) the *addresser* (e.g., Calypso) and (2) the *addressee* (e.g., Odysseus) in the parting scene described above; (3) the *code,* in this case both the spoken Greek of the Archaic Period and the contemporaneous *art language* with its many archaisms and dialect mixtures, and (4) the *message,* such as Calypso's formal address to Odysseus or her (less formal) invitation to sleep together their last night; (5) the *topic,* such as the raft he builds with her help or, at another level, these two protagonists as presented by Homer, and (6) the *context:* Calypso's cave—or the Cyclops's. Although other variables have been proposed, these six remain as the most basic. The six variables obviously fall into three pairs in terms of dialogic, linguistic, and referential dimensions.

Let us illustrate them briefly. Much of this essay is concerned with slippages in the comprehension of messages between addresser and addressee, as in the protracted recognition scenes between Odysseus and Penelope (Murnahan 1987). But the other variables in their interactions also generate fascinating ironies. Take, for example, the above-mentioned onomastic ironies of the name Odysseus, involving the message ("Nobody") and the code (Homeric Greek), in particular. Or take the two ironically contrasting scenes in *Anna Karenina,* both of them creating *contexts* for the *topic* of adulterous love: Anna and her lover are depicted vividly as dancing through the steps of a mutual seduction in the glow of a Moscow ballroom; later (in a bedroom?), after a physical consummation, shuddering with what Tolstoy calls "shame, horror, and joy" (Tolstoy 1995: 135). Irony, then, is generated by the interaction *between* the six basic variables of the speech situation (especially between the members of each of the sets of pairs: message and code, and so forth). Irony is also generated by the interaction *among* subsets *within* any one of the six variables (for example, conflicting dialects or idiolects within the variable of the code). It is also generated, finally, by interaction between any one of the subsets in one variable and any subset in any other variable—particularly the "magisterial" ironies of the relation between the writer, or other addresser, and his or her protagonists, or between any writer or speaker and the person he or she represents or speaks about: Homer and Odysseus, Tolstoy and Anna, Everyman and whatever So-and-So is reported to have said. All indirect and reported discourse is, by definition, at least potentially and implicitly ironic. As we get into these exponentially expanded scopes of irony we are confronted by a practical infinitude that is suggested by the sociolinguistic idea of "the speech event." At a more philosophical level, since all language (and all knowledge) is dialogic, involving at least intended or potential intercommunication between two or more persons (Tedlock and Mannheim 1995: 1–3), it follows that all language and use of language are significantly ironic (with certain exceptions as noted).

Irony in Language (5) and Beyond:
Intimations of a Taxonomy or Typology

I have waded ambitiously into the subject and it is now clear that irony comprises far more than figures of language. But this fact of the breadth of its scope enhances rather than diminishes its importance as a progressively encapsulating trope—just as the relative absence of irony may itself work to intensify irony. One's first mental association to irony may be to a time-honored list of subtypes such as the *verbal irony,* where, as already noted, what is stated is antithetical to or at least significantly different from what was intended, or the irony of naiveté, a pose of innocence or simplicity (Preminger, Warnke, and Hardison 1974: 407–8). The devices of *dramatic irony* that align the author with his audience and some of his characters in opposition to the (tragic) hero. In *Socratic* irony and its close cousins in (Zen) Buddhist and Confucian irony, the master shares information with his reader or some of his listeners and often with some of his interlocutors. In a related situation, the author "teases" his readers by keeping an ironic distance between himself and his protagonists, or ironically plays one of his texts against the other as seems to have been done by the author(s) of the *Iliad* and the *Odyssey.* In *Romantic irony,* exemplified by Heinrich Heine, a sudden shift near the end of the work catastrophically restructures the reader's perspective, whereas in the closely allied *comic irony* of madcap Buddhism or the *Barber of Seville* or the TV sitcoms, the participants fail to understand and communicate over time, with mounting laughability. There is the *structuralist irony* of Jakobson and Lévi-Strauss turning a sonnet by Baudelaire inside-out in an attempt to show how certain interactions between small finite sets give intimations of metaphysical problems beyond any set theory. There is the *Marxist irony* of Berthold Brecht where the arbitrariness of a political economy replaces, from the sufferer's point of view, the capricious and often vindictive humor of the gods. The generic idea of irony subsumes the over two dozen varieties in classical and medieval rhetoric such as sarcasm, exaggeration and understatement, mockery, even the sneer, or the moral-cum-cruel indignation of Juvenal, Jonathan Swift, and other satirists, and each variety has subtypes. How to interweave and systematize them within one theoretical scheme, or at least a taxonomy or typology?

All these figures and yet other variations on the theme of irony are, on the one hand, only subsets of one subset, that is, irony, of the generic set of all tropes that can be labeled *modal.* Modal tropes include "expressions of mood that run from emphatic assertion to passivity to outrage to joy to command to sarcasm to threat to pathos to assertion to question to perhaps the most intriguing of all, irony" (Friedrich 1991: 30). These modal tropes or figures are coordinate with at least four other great sets of tropes that will be defined and illustrated later in the essay: imagistic tropes, formal tropes, and tropes of contiguity, notably the metonym, and tropes of analogy, notably the metaphor: the great, doublebacked bow in the *Odyssey* is both similar to Odysseus and a part of him, both a metaphor and a metonym. On the other hand, this same irony, because of its formal variations and its connection to the emotions, is arguably the most powerful and widespread of all the tropes and figures of any kind— at least equal to the metaphor, that darling of Western critics.

Metaphor contributes to irony yes, but is certainly outdone by it as a trope in dramatic and epic poetry, and may rival it in lyric—witness most of Thomas Hardy and his famous poem "The Village Maid," riding, as it does, on the ironic meanings of the word "ain't," used by a farm girl turned gentleman's mistress. Witness Robert Browning's "My Last Duchess," built on conceitful allusions to previous duchesses who also had been poisoned or otherwise destroyed. Yet the pervasive and deep power of irony in high literature is but a specific, aesthetically precisioned and refined instance of the ironic tropology of everyday life. Since all tropes, as Peircean signs, are interconnected and mutually implicatory, it follows that all tropes of language, culture, and even of raw, simian behavior, individually and in their multifarious interactions, always and necessarily, if indirectly, imply some degree of irony, notably ironic irony.

Irony, as already noted, figures in the tropology, not only of language but of deed and behavior. As has recently been proven (Meyer 1995), the novel *Anna Karenina* was an enormously complex, competitive, and of course, creative response to *Madame Bovary:* hundreds of details, symbols, and stylistic turns in the latter are adapted in the former, although, while he praised the novel in contrast to other works by Flaubert, Tolstoy denied any major influence and hardly mentioned his model in the course of a long life. For the reader aware of these intertextual relations or intuiting them, the experience of Anna and her tragedy becomes subtly ironic, particularly if that reader compares Tolstoy's view of Anna's intense but discreetly alluded to sexuality with the more openly depicted sexuality of her Gallic prototype, or, yet more specifically, if the reader compares peasant Emma's erotic dreams of princes and castles with their metamorphosed and formally commuted counterparts when aristocratic Anna and her lover dream of an ominous little peasant who mutters in French. Irony is integral and crucial in all such intertextual matters, particularly when they involve gender, be it gender identity, gender reversal, gender conflicts, or gender symbolism in general.

The issues of deed, behavior, and act were raised above because part of the problem of irony is that we tend to drift into a poorly oriented nominalism, or at least dependence on words: we all know the word "irony," so it must mean *something*—what? The fact is that the word "irony" denotes and refers to a great many things: (1) literarily, to critical factors in genres such as tragedy or to totally ironic genres like the theater of the absurd; (2) linguistically, to a trope contrasting with other tropes of mood and of course the many other sets discussed above; (3) practically and pragmatically, to a quality or essential component of many kinds of situation and event, even culture and history—the ironies of the united fronts that link agrarian socialists and urban communists, or diehard monarchists and lower-middle-class fascists; and (4) philosophically, irony takes in a wide variety of basic points of view, including several metaphysical ones (notably of Søren Kierkegaard and Albert Camus). In addition to this, the myriad subsets of irony, as noted, partially subcategorize each other or variously intersect with each other, but the total set of ironies (even if we ignore that the total set is open-ended) does not fall into a taxonomic tree, a well-ordered typology, or, in fact, any other kind of formal representation. The subsets of irony are, to put it mildly, fuzzy. In light of this *nomina confusa* situation, it could and probably would be argued that irony is so vague and culture-bound that any attempt at discussion or definition will veer into essentialism of a heinous sort.

Categories (5): Polytropy—Odysseus (5)

Since irony is only one kind of modal trope, and since modal tropes are in turn matched by four other large sets of tropes, it is striking how, like metaphor among analogical tropes, irony can dominate and organize an entire work or history, even a long one, with all the other figures playing subordinate and supporting roles. The pervasive mood that dominates the *Odyssey,* from the Archaic point of view, is the longing or urge of a man to get home to wife and (home)stead, and the coordinate need for revenge against anyone who threatens these things. Yet, even within the *Odyssey* and within its own tradition, this straightforward nostalgia was ironized by the fact that Penelope's ruse of weaving a shroud by day and unraveling it by night, while it postponed remarriage, also kept the suitors on the premises. It was also ironized by Odysseus's lack of fidelity to his wife and indications that he will leave her again for further adventures; a heroism that calls for survival challenges the main conception of the hero in the *Iliad* (Ames 2000). Some two millennia later the Archaic teleology was further ironized by its interplay with the view of Dante that Odysseus was primarily a searcher for understanding and knowledge.

Within the overall ironic and modal framework just pointed to we find countless tropes of other kinds. The tropes of images include Penelope descending the stairs. The olivewood stake sizzling into Polyphemus's eye, no matter what it connotes to Freudians and their cohorts, has, *as image,* haunted the Western imagination for some three millennia. We find countless *formal* tropes:

in the syntactic disjunctions in Agamemnon's description (in Hades) of his own murder (Fitzgerald 1963: 470–72), in the play with proper names like "Nobody" or "No One" and Odysseus, and also in the phenomenon of "lyric breakout" (Friedrich 2000), where at an emotional and narrative high point of intensity there emerges what is formally like a lyric poem—as in the recognition scene between Odysseus and his son. We find countless *analogical* tropes, notably the "reverse similes" (Foley 1978) where something is persuasively likened to what it is least like, often with a cross-over in gender or a similar category—as when Odysseus, the Sacker of Cities, weeps like a captive woman being dragged from her sacked city for rape and captivity, and the brilliant metaphors implied by single words or phrases as when Odysseus disguised as a beggar reports to Penelope that he has seen himself, her husband Odysseus, surrounded by women who admire his clothes, which, he hints, are layered like a (phallic) onion. We find brilliant tropes of contiguity in time and place or space—inventories, anatomies, and metaphorized synecdoches, as when Penelope's veil is part of her image but also stands for chastity (or is it flirtatiousness?) before the suitors. All of these figures feed into the dominant mood of Odysseus's longing to return to his wife and home, and to exact vengeance. The way these subordinate tropes contribute to the thrust and orchestration of the dominant one is a small scale model, as we shall see, of the way any case of irony contributes to the thrust and orchestration of larger universes of the same phenomenon. The interaction of irony and other modes and moods with other tropes is yet another, more comprehensive aspect of "ironic irony."

Categories (6): Irony and Tragedy

The nature of irony is not sufficiently explored by placing it within a framework of other tropes, categories, and ideas as has been done above. It must also be experienced and conceptualized practically and pragmatically—that is, as it is realized in the courses of action and as it affects and infects real, unique individuals. The flux of misfittings and misunderstandings that is the stuff of irony can play out humorously, notably in the humor of the unexpected and unpredictable—situation comedy, practical jokes, or tragicomedy. And, as already intimated, not everything ironic is immediately or obviously tragic, although potentially anything can be seen that way. But the fact is that the most insight-yielding outcomes of irony are often starkly tragic ones. A working definition of tragedy is: whatever leads to suicide or homicide, whether literal or figurative, with consciousness on the victim's part of the moral, the aesthetic, or the psychiatric implications, or, in plainer English, of the evil, the ugly, and/or the mad. In these gross and reduced terms most tragedy involves and implies irony. One obvious example is Eugene O'Neill's *Anna Christie* where an acute awareness of fate ("that old devil sea") is spliced with a raw sailor's gradual disillusionment over what turns out to have been an idealized prostitute. Another obvious example is Ovid's *Pyramus and Thisbe* where, as so often in "real life," tragic consequences—here successive suicides—result from miscommunication (misreading the "material evidence" of blood-stained clothes). A more subtle irony arises when such tragic stories are parodied, as in Shakespeare's use of the same Ovidian tale in *A Midsummer Night's Dream.* There is little misunderstanding, true, between main characters Achilles versus Agamemnon in the *Iliad* because they share and act by the same code of honor, but a strongly ironic cast to the whole stems from misunderstandings between other participants. As convincing as these literary examples are the myriad "normal situations" (of marriage, sibling ties, and parent-child bonds) that are pregnant with tragedy when, to paraphrase Emily Dickinson, the brains have been running evenly and true within their grooves but then "one splinter swerves." The catastrophic outcomes of these deviant swervings of cerebral splinters mean that, to go further, tragedy always implies irony, that the tragic is neither possible or meaningful without a substantial admixture—often pre-mixture—of irony.

Tragedy at one level is a type of mood, a modal figure that, as already argued, may become the dominant or controlling element in a segment of life, or a work of art. Anna Karenina, as a unique individual, is essentialized as strongly sensuous and sexual, but the power of this fundamental trait is made intensely ironic by the way aspersions are cast on her as a loose, wanton, or fallen woman both by herself and by Tolstoy's moral commentary—no matter how devious and indirect it is at times. Much of what Anna says or means about lust, loathing, and shame condemns not only her acts but her eventual lifestyle and even fault lines of her life (Friedrich 1998). By the end of the story, the synergism between her deep shame, her defensiveness, and defiance about it, and the nuanced, ironic and sarcastic shaming on the part of others reduces her to the condition of a victim of shame poetry in an archaic Slavic or Greek society, where, at some times, suicide was the best available escape. When the unique actor is eloquently ironic about an essentially ironic situation in which he or she has been trapped we have yet another kind of ironic irony.

In the ethnography of social and political experience, as in literature, the tragedies of irony are often predicated on the pros and cons of kinship. A set of cousins in our patrilineal Mexican village, men who were linked through female relatives (the sons of sisters in most cases), stood together for a just cause, agrarian reform, in 1926. A decade later they broke into rival factions invoking fraternal and quasi-fraternal loyalty to justify allegiance *(pherá-para-ni* "to support," plus the "back suffix" *para)* while at the same time invoking flagrant cases of kinship betrayal to motivate and justify retaliatory vendettas. Fraternal and extended fraternal loyalty, and even more, brotherly love, is where irony and tragedy, in some of their most extreme forms, merge. The ironies of kinship, which are always culturally specific to a high degree, have been the prime materials for much tragedy, from Aeschylus to Tolstoy, from the political histories and ethnographies of Herodotus to the political history of towns in Mexico, and many points between and beyond these extremes.

Retrospective Tragedy: Odyssey (6)

That irony is both a prerequisite for and consequence of tragedy is strikingly illustrated by conflicts between the dark emotions of envy and jealousy and the more positive and compassion-arousing ones of longing or yearning both of which, as already noted, infuse the *Odyssey*. This binary modality leads to a happy ending of sorts—if we ignore the 108 corpses of young men, the cream of Ithaca's youth, and the prophecy, which later so inspired Dante, that our hero will sooner or later set off for distant shores and inevitable adventure. The conventionally happy ending is, moreover, counterpointed by an acute sense of what might be called *retrospective tragedy:* husband and wife are keenly aware that they have lost twenty of what might have been the best years of their marriage: ". . . For indeed nothing is greater or better than this, that a man and a woman maintain their household in likemindedness of spirit" (6.182–84). Yet despite the fact that these famous lines were spoken earlier as part of Odysseus's winning the support of an attractive young woman on a beach; and despite the unforgettable Circe and Calypso adventures, and the sack of Ismarus with the rape of its women; and despite Odysseus's future departure as foretold by Tireseus, these lines and hundreds of other details suggest significant likemindedness and a retrospective sense of loss. That acute sense within the context of their joyful reunion, which comes at the end of the work (book 23), is anticipated with Homeric orchestration in book 16, where recognition by the son, and then the joyful reunion of son and father after twenty years, is deepened and made poignant by a sense of what the son had lacked while growing up and what the father lacked by not having helped to raise him. In this variant of tragic irony, a sense of irreparable loss is embedded in a context that deepens the meanings in many ways and converts the whole scene into what above was called a metaphor of the human condition: any encounter that leads or gets us back to a great love may be fused with a haunting sense of what was lost by not meeting—or not meeting again—sooner. The "miracle of recognition" (Reinhart 1996) goes hand in hand with recognition of irretrievability. Tragedy involves such ironic irony: layerings of contrasting and contradictory feelings which dialectically reinforce each other by deepening the meanings of the event—recognition and reunion.

Conclusions (1)

The following sketchy review of how irony may be connected with the broad categories of time and power, culture and language, and also with trope and the genre and experience of tragedy, should also suggest its enormous richness and interpretive power. Irony is so powerful, albeit often insidiously so, that much of cultural anthropology and sociocultural linguistics—to name only two relevant fields—centers on it or is organized in its terms. It arguably dominates or controls the respective oeuvres of master ethnographer Lila Abu-Lughod and master cultural sociolinguist Deborah Tannen: witness how both turn standard analytical categories inside-out to write a feminist texture interwoven with an ironic critique of that texture, how both are aware of the theory and nuances of irony. Yet the idea of irony, or, rather, the constellation of the many subcategories, aspects, and elements of irony often remains covert or latent for both the scientific (or scientist) ethnographer and the antipositivist (or humanistic) one. Frequently such ethnographers or sociocultural linguists seem to be insensitive to irony and fail to employ it, if not as an explicit conceptual tool, then at least as an artful device and organizing principle. In what verges on a parody of this whole situation, pace-setting "postmodernist" anthropological critics George Marcus and Michael Fischer (1986) have concluded, after a survey, that the ethnographies in their sample either failed to convey the irony in the cultures studied, or failed to comment on it: while the latter may be true, the former is not. One ironic background here is that such anthropological critics have typically skirted or avoided works that are particularly rich in irony, such as those by Abu-Lughod (1986, 1993) and Tannen (1984, 1990). A second is that many masters of ethnographic practice are more sophisticated theoretically than the pace-setting and often enough supercilious postmodernist critics for whom their output has been input. But the most immediate irony is that the ethnographies sampled contained so much irony that the critics could not see. The lack of a widespread, self-conscious and even self-reflexive theory of irony stands out as one of the salient problems in many areas of anthropology and linguistics over the decades. Heraclitus said, "All is flux," a (metaphysical) postulate that rings true and remains theoretically relevant down to the present day. In a similar vein, I am claiming, provisionally, that "All is irony." This claim is in some ways less powerful than the one by Heraclitus; for one thing, as noted, linguacultures vary in their constraints and tendencies when it comes to irony. On the other hand, the statement can be made or paraphrased in any language, be it Ancient Greek, modern American English, or some universal language. The statement holds in terms of the partly linguistic relativism and indeterminacy of all knowledge, notably those of physics and other bastions of objectivity in the material world that Heraclitus was mainly thinking of.[4]

Conclusions (2)

The ultimate fallacy when it comes to irony is to think about it piecemeal in terms of isolated cases and events—as has been done in the majority of studies, both literary and anthropological. This *conceptual atomism* has obscured the more fundamental reality that all cases, texts, and examples are always encapsulated by larger and larger ironies, and also encapsulate smaller and smaller ones. The variously intersecting and encompassing or encompassed levels are well illustrated by intratextual and intertextual relations in comparative literature. The text of *Anna Karenina* includes numerous points where the author is ironizing about an instance of irony (hence the perilous way he often comes near to but, I feel, blocks a parodic reading). Of course, one of Tolstoy's inspirations was the consumately ironic Pushkin, but, as noted, the text also interplays frequently with the equally inspiring *Madame Bovary* (Radulescu 2000). Since Tolstoy never explicitly alludes to this sub- or intertextuality, there is the pervasive irony of the author saying one thing, the classic tragedy of *Anna Karenina,* but meaning another, his no-holds-barred duel with Gustav Flaubert. Similar to this is the relation between the *Iliad* and the *Odyssey.* Gregory Nagy (1979) and others have demonstrated with brilliance that there were two epic traditions, or, anthropologically speaking, co-traditions, such that the two bards who finally synthesized something like the monumental texts we have today, or, if you prefer, the younger and the older Homer, are constantly quoting each other; in Pietro Pucci's (1987) anthropomorphizing trope, the two texts are "jealous" of each other and "tease" each other. An epic formula like Odysseus's full title in direct address ("Odysseus, son of Laertes, Sacker of Cities"), used by Calypso to address him on their last night, is given

4. Of the several examples above of "zero irony," the one regarding the pain of parturition and then postpartal ecstasy has been repeatedly questioned by readers. To begin, while a man cannot obviously speak firsthand of giving birth, the vicarious experience of it can be considerable—in my case discussions with closely associated women including my mother, participation in birth as a father, considerable reading in the natural childbirth literature, and so forth. Second, anthropologists should be the last to question the validity of experience which crosses the lines of gender, ethnicity, age, and so forth; in some ways, it's our job to cross those lines. Because of cognitive focus and sheer empathy and compassion, a person can often understand something in or about another better than that other does, and better than he or she understands many things about himself or herself. Some of the best writings about men are by women, and vice versa; some of the best writings about war are by persons who have never experienced it physically, empirically (e.g., Stephen Crane), et cetera.

connotational depth by the way it presumably alludes to a use of the same formula at a key point in the earlier *Iliad*. Such intertextuality is but one instance of innumerable ways levels of irony interact: we begin, for example, with two auguries of a hawk as an omen, followed by the interplay between these two and the multiple responses of the audience(s), and then the allusive interplay between all this and other readings of other ominous birds and other omens (Friedrich 1998), and then the ironizing author ironizing about himself. . . The ever more comprehensive and intercomprehensive ironies are themselves comprehended by the authors, from Homer and Flaubert to this day, who ironize not only about their ironies but about the language of those ironies.

The realities of ironic encapsulation and interdependence that have just been described, or at least pointed at, inform all ethnographies but particularly the more interesting ones, ranging from the Latin rhetorical subtexts in Lewis Henry Morgan's studies of Iroquois rhetoric and politics, to E. E. Evans-Pritchard's Latin historical subtexts in analyses of African political organization, from the orchestrating lyric theme in James Fernandez's (1982) *Bwiti* (Coleridge's "Kubla Khan" among the Fang) to the organizing role of an Old Testament theme in Carol Delaney's (1991) *The Seed and the Soil* ("Genesis 22" in rural Anatolia). Such ironic and ironizing totalities may also involve deeper, completely personal things: some aspect of the author's life, implicit and hidden, may yet orchestrate and control the subtext in an ethnography or ethnohistory even where the author is conspicuously absent or nearly so (except in the introduction). One could infer that Margaret Trawick's *Notes on Love in a Tamil Family* is one such case, as might well be Lila Abu-Lughod's *Writing Women's Worlds* and *Veiled Sentiments* (in the latter case the author's own, personal mythology is apparently masked by her overt ideology of following in the footsteps of her father). My own work in *Agrarian Revolt* and *The Princes* is driven and structured by two personal and private mythologies which, to my knowledge, have never been suspected. These anthropological and literary examples illustrate Pasternak's (1990: 213) contention that all creative work (including Chopin's *Etudes*) is basically autobiographical. They could be multiplied without end as concise and dramatic instantiations of the more general phenomenological fact that all irony, from a glance by Anna Karenina to ideologically contradictory political assassinations in Mexico, is always part of a larger universe of the interlocking and overlapping ironies of which much of life is constituted. Thus, to improve on "Conclusions (1)" above, it is not that irony, like flux, "is all," but that any segment, level, or aspect of irony is only fully meaningful in terms of its relations to other segments, levels, or aspects of irony, be they smaller or larger, within a cosmos where *all partakes of irony.*

Coda (1): Irony and Lucidity

The foregoing raises additional problems, to one of which I now turn as a synecdoche and suggestion of what lies ahead. In the face of "all partakes of irony," there stands the long and cogent tradition, notably the French humanist tradition in the spirit of Montaigne to Camus, of the possibility, indeed, the human need, for something called "lucidity." Lucidity is actually a complex syndrome that combines clarity, coherence, consistency, and, as it were, a rigorous mental luminosity. Lucidity is one ultimate criterion of intellectual courage and integrity in the face of a beastly world: when everyone is turning into rhinoceroses (or the fascists they are metaphors of) Ionesco's courageous protagonist calls out "I will maintain my lucidity." Emerging mainly from the models of music and plane geometry in Ancient Greece and from the model of mathematics so central in French education, these assumptions of a possible lucidity, without fuzz or residue, when they enter the worlds of words and politics, immediately become diversely nuanced, chaotic and—ironic. Lucidity in any clean-cut, mathematical sense turns out, in these realms, to have been a culturally specific illusion. But not a total illusion, just a compromised one, because a high level of semimathematical lucidity is still possible. Generic lucidity is combined with high levels of irony in great writing, be it Homer and many High T'ang poets, or some of the works of Flaubert and Tolstoy, or thinkers like Plato and Peirce, or playwrights like Beckett and Ionesco, or, at the (lower) level of anthropology, the work of Abu-Lughod, Fernandez, and others.

Coda (2): Zero Irony versus All-Is-Irony

The second paradox is created by the phenomenological fact that, from the experiencer's point of view, *and that only,* a certain kind of experience—the pain of childbirth, the ecstasies of love, or artistic creation, or victory in athletics, or a bullfight—can, for a second of time or somewhat more, totally eliminate any qualifying ambiguities, mendacities, ambivalences, slippages and all the rest we have been grouping under "irony."[5] The *Odyssey,* our main source here, contains three such instants: not only the catastrophic self-identification to the Cyclops that was noted for book 9, but Odysseus's contemplations of suicide

---

5. Another connection between Greek and modern thought is shown by the so-called Epimenides paradox, or Cretan Liar paradox. Epimenides was a Cretan who said, "All Cretans are liars"—obviously a problem in irony. The Epimenides paradox and the related paradoxes of Zeno were crucial in the construction of Gödel's (1931) Theorem which in "normal English" runs: "All consistent axiomatic formulations of number theory include undecidable propositions" (Hofstadter 1980). Gödel's Theorem would seem to hark back to Odysseus's ironic yarns in books 13 and 14 of the *Odyssey.*

in book 4 and his eruption of anger about his olive-tree bed in book 23. But all all such moments of zero irony, including the Odyssean ones, are empowered and given meaning by the larger contexts of the ironies of text and life which precede and follow them, out of which they emerge and into which they sink again. The non-ironic moments of recognition between father and son, between man and woman, that were told above, are meaningful in the context of one of the more ironic texts in world literature: the *Odyssey*.

The twinned concepts of totalizing and zero irony lead, each in its way, in different directions. Both point toward ever-greater distancing between subject and object, between addresser and addressee, author and protagonist, speaker and society—in short, toward alienation (zero irony being totally subjective and proprioceptive). Yet to limit the import of irony to alienation and the like is a great flaw of many ironists, including Benjamin Constant and other Romantics, Søren Kierkegaard and subsequent existentialists, and many, perhaps most, modernists—because both zero irony and total irony also may point toward ever greater integration and conceptual/emotional enrichment, be it through the interplay of ironic nuance in the dialogue of lovers or the moments of non-ironic truth with which these nuances alternate. On the one hand, then, we have an ironic space where Everyman is No-man in a world of dangers, frustrations, inadequacies, and alienation; on the other hand, a space where a totally non-ironic experience is transiently possible and where, otherwise, frequent understanding is a matter of degree and improved understanding is possible and pleasurable: where, in short, "the gentle king" and "the wise queen" can live together in (relative) likemindedness.

Acknowledgments

For their careful critiques at an early stage and for their pervasive critique of later stages I stand indebted, respectively, to Alaina Lemon and Dale Pesmen, and to Kevin Crotty, Domnica Radulescu, and Josephine Reed. I am also grateful to James Fernandez and Mary Huber for input at various points. The translations from Homer above are my own.

References

Abu-Lughod, Lila. 1986. *Veiled Sentiments: Honor and Poetry in a Bedouin Society.* Berkeley: University of California Press.
———. 1993. *Writing Women's Worlds: Bedouin Stories.* Berkeley: University of California Press.
Ames, Keri. 2000. The Endurance of Heroism in Homer's *Odyssey* and Joyce's *Ulysses.* Ph.D. dissertation, University of Chicago.
Arnold, Matthew. [1887] 1970. Count Leo Tolstoy. Selections reprinted as: *Anna Kar-*

enina as Life, not Literature. In *The Dialogic Emergence of Culture,* ed. Dennis Tedlock and Bruce Mannheim. Ann Arbor: University of Michigan Press.

Attinasi, John and Paul Friedrich. 1995. Dialogic Breakthrough: Catalysis and Synthesis in Life-changing Dialogue. In *The Dialogic Emergence of Culture,* ed. Dennis Tedlock and Bruce Mannheim. Ann Arbor: University of Michigan Press.

Dekker, Annie. 1956. *Ironie in der Odysee.* Leiden.

Delaney, Carol. 1991. *The Seed and the Soil.* Berkeley: University of California Press.

Detienne, M. and J.-P. Vernant. [1978] 1989. *Cunning Intelligence in Greek Society and Culture.* Trans. J. Lloyd. Highland, NJ: Sussex and Atlantic.

Dimock, George E. 1956. The Name of *Odysseus. The Hudson Review* 9: 52–70.

Eide, Brock. 1995. Indirect Infectiousness in *Anna Karenina.* Manuscript.

Fernandez, James W. 1982. *Bwiti: An Ethnography of the Religious Imagination in Africa.* Princeton: Princeton University Press.

———. 1986. *Persuasion and Performance: The Play of Tropes in Culture.* Bloomington: Indiana University Press.

Fitzgerald, Robert, trans. 1963. Postscript to Homer, *The Odyssey.* New York: Doubleday Anchor.

Foley, Helen. 1978. Reverse Similes and Sex roles in the Odyssey. *Arethusa* 2(1–2): 7–26.

Friedrich, Lenore. 1939. I Had a Baby. *Atlantic Monthly* 163: 461–69.

Friedrich, Paul. 2000. Lyric Epiphany. *Language in Society,* in press.

———. 1998. The Tragedy of Shame: Anna Karenina. *Peirce Seminar Papers. Essays in Semiotic Analysis* 3. In press.

———. 1997. An Avian and Aphrodisian Reading of the *Odyssey. American Anthropologist* 99(2): 306–20.

———. 1991. Polytropy. In *Beyond Metaphor: The Theory of Tropes in Anthropology,* ed. James Fernandez, 17–56. Stanford: Stanford University Press.

———. 1989. Language, Ideology, and Political Economy. *American Anthropologist.* 91: 295–312.

———. 1986. *The Princes of Naranja.* Austin: University of Texas Press.

———. [1970] 1977. *Agrarian Revolt in a Mexican Village.* Chicago: University of Chicago Press.

Hofstadter, Douglas R. 1980. *Gödel, Escher, Bach: An Eternal Golden Braid.* New York: Vintage Books.

Jakobson, Roman. [1960] 1987. Concluding Statement: Linguistics and Poetics. In *Language and Literature,* ed. Krystyna Pomorska and Stephen Rudy, 62–95. Cambridge: Harvard University Press.

Lemon, Alaina. 1995. *Sincere Ironies, Performed Authenticities: Romani Cultures in Soviet and Post-Soviet Russia.* Ph.D. diss., the University of Chicago.

Lyons, John. 1980. The Pronouns of Address in *Anna Karenina:* The Stylistics of Bilingualism and the Impossibilities of Translation. In *Studies in English Linguistics for Randolph Quirk,* ed. Sidney Greenbaum, Geoffrey N. Lerch and Jan Svartvik, 235–49. New York: Longman.

Marcus, George E., and Michael M. Fischer. 1986. *Anthropology as Cultural Critique: An Experimental Moment in the Human Sciences.* Chicago: University of Chicago Press.

Meyer, Pamela. 1995. *Anna Karenina:* Tolstoy's Polemic with *Madame Bovary. The Russian Review* 54(2): 244–59.

Morson, Gary Saul. 1988. Prosaics and *Anna Karenina. Tolstoy Studies Journal* 1: 1–12.

Murnahan, S. 1987. *Disguise and Recognition in the "Odyssey."* Princeton: Princeton University Press.

Nagy, Gregory. 1979. *The Best of the Achaeans: Concepts of the Hero in Archaic Greek Poetry.* Baltimore: Johns Hopkins Press.

Pasternak, Boris. 1990. Chopin. In *Selected Writings and Letters,* Trans. Catherine Judelson, 213–19. Moscow: Progress Publishers.

Peradotto, J. 1990. *Man in the Middle Voice: Name and Narration in the Odyssey.* Princeton: Princeton University Press.

Pitt-Rivers, Julian. 1966. Honor and Social Status. In *Honor and Shame: The Values of a Mediterranean Society,* ed. John G. Peristiany. Chicago: University of Chicago Press.

Preminger, Alex, Frank J. Warnke, and O. B. Hardison, eds. 1974. *The Princeton Encyclopedia of Poetry and Poetics.* Princeton: Princeton University Press.

Pucci, Pietro. 1987. *Odysseus Polytropos: Intertextual Readings in the "Odyssey" and the "Iliad."* Ithaca: Cornell University Press.

Radulescu, Domnica. 2000. Emma's Mouth: The Tragedy of Language in Flaubert's *Madame Bovary.* Manuscript.

Reinhardt, Karl. 1996. The Adventures in the *Odyssey. Reading the Odyssey,* ed. Seth L. Schein, 13–133. Princeton: Princeton University Press.

Sapir, Edward. 1924. The Grammarian and His Language. *American Mercury* 1: 149–55.

Segal, Charles. 1983. *Kleos* and Its Ironies in the *Odyssey. L'Antiquité classique* 52: 22–47.

Stanford, W. B. 1968. *The Ulysses Theme.* Ann Arbor: University of Michigan Press.

Steedly, Mary Margaret. 1993. *Hanging Without a Rope: Narrative Experience in Colonial and Postcolonial Karoland.* Princeton: Princeton University Press.

Tannen, Deborah. 1990. *You Just Don't Understand: Men and Women in Conversation.* New York: William Morrow.

———. 1984. *Conversational Style: Analysis of Talk Among Friends.* Norwood, NJ: Ablex.

Tedlock, Dennis, trans. 1985. *Popol vuh: The Definitive Edition of the Mayan Book of the Dawn of Life and the Glories of Gods and Kings.* New York: Simon and Schuster.

Tedlock, Dennis, and Bruce Mannheim, eds. 1995. *The Dialogic Emergence of Culture.* Ann Arbor: University of Michigan Press.

Tolstoy, Leo. [1973–76] 1995. *Anna Karenina.* Trans. Louise and Aylmer Maude; rev. and ed. George Gibian. New York: W.W. Norton.

———. 1959. *Anna Karenina. Roman v Vos'mi Chastyakh.* Moscow: Gos. Iz. Khud. Lit.

Trawick, Margaret. 1992. *Notes on Love in a Tamil Family.* Berkeley: University of California Press.

Turner, Victor. 1969. *The Ritual Process: Structure and Anti-Structure.* Chicago: Aldine.

Volin, B. M., and D. N. Ushakov. 1945. *Tolkovyy slovar' russkogo yazyka.* Moscow: Gos. Iz. Inost. Nats. Slovarey.

Winkler, J. J. 1990. Penelope's Cunning and Homer's. In *The Constraints of Desire,* pp. 129–61. New York and London: Routledge.

Chapter Twelve

—————————— JAMES CLIFFORD ——————————

The Last Discussant

It's the last session of the American Anthropological Association. In a random room, somewhere in the San Francisco Hilton, people gather amid sliding walls, electric chandeliers, and stackable chairs. Sunday afternoon: last day, last speaker, last gasp of the session on irony.

The "discussant" waits for his moment, watching the audience thin out. Some words from a tune keep running through his mind, "Talkin' Hard Luck" sung by John Cohen of the New Lost City Ramblers: "I was born in the last month in the year, in the last week in the month, in the last day of the week, in the last hour of the day, in the last minute of the hour, in the last second of the minute. . ."

Audience members, with suitcases beside them and overcoats on their laps, shuffle their feet.

And at the song's end: "You know I've been balled out and balled up, and held down and held up, and bulldozed and blackjacked, and walked on and cheated, squeezed, and mooched . . . Well I been cussed and discussed, boycotted, talked to and talked about, lied to and lied about, held up and hung up and doggone near murdered. And the only reason I'm stickin' around now, folks, is to see what in the heck is gonna happen next!"

And the last discussant—his time running out—knows pretty well what's going to happen next. Everyone scatters for the airport, for the freeway. *A pretty good image for the next century,* he thinks on his way to the podium: *people in cars and airplanes, scrambling to get home.*

• • •

My remarks begin and end with Paul Friedrich's phrase, the "necessarily temporal essence of irony." Things alter. Irony is a perpetual loss of fit, and thus a process of moving on. Friedrich's reading of the Calypso section of the

Odyssey hopes to resist any disengaged last word: "an illusory freezing of the last twist in a continuous twisting." Irony, like time, keeps on going. Stop and go. Odysseus the commuter—waiting in departure lounges, lost in urban sprawl. Bumper to bumper he glares at the billboard: "IF YOU LIVED HERE YOU'D BE HOME ALREADY." Stop and go: where we start again.

George Marcus stops time with a historical moment, mapping a fin-de-millenarian hyperconsciousness of irony. He does so without much benefit of hindsight or any teleological narrative. Thus he works, inside Western chronology, by retrospective analogy, connecting, via Hayden White, with Nietzsche's late-nineteenth-century awareness of problematical language and the artificial, political nature of claims for the real. With this revived endgame as his "moment," Marcus eschews nostalgia or prophecy, entertaining only contemporary ways to live in, to think with, irony. He invokes the Late Editions series he edited, its receptive, open-ended ethnographic probing of an "embedded predicament of irony" in everyday and institutional locales. Irony is a condition of the given conjuncture rather than an "impasse that should be overcome." Marcus sees a "complex, less controllable world," no longer seeming to move along clear tracks of progress, rationalism, Enlightenment, technological development, or nation-building. The West frays as it becomes more "global." Formerly discrete places and identities overlap and mix in confusing ways. As people struggle to relate near and far, to make sense of an interconnected but irregular, risky world, they blend paranoid and rational explanations. In his acceptance of ironic displacement as a fact of life, not a pathology to suppress or cure, Marcus seconds Friedrich, for whom any escape from the ironies of temporality, power, and language is a flight from reality. They differ in that Friedrich offers a general human condition and Marcus a historical conjuncture.

A dose of Friedrich's universalism might give Marcus pause in his focusing of intensified ironic awareness at the end of certain (peoples') centuries. And a bit more historical reflexivity might have tempered Friedrich's apparently unironic assertion that he has uncovered deep forms of human social and political experience: the ironic essence of temporal, political, and communicative relations. Why are these truths, triangulating Homer, Tolstoy, and Friedrich, especially urgent today? What is the political and historical condition for their rediscovery? And why have they remained hidden to so many intelligent people?

Friedrich has little to say about the current conjuncture for his discoveries, offering only a vague slap at "postmodern" critics. He gives a single example which "verges on a parody of this whole situation" of insensitivity to irony: Marcus and Fischer's *Anthropology as Cultural Critique*. For the record, I cannot find the position he attributes to Marcus and Fischer in their book. And it would have been more helpful if, in citing several works, "rich in irony," that "supercilious Post-Modernist critics" have supposedly neglected, Friedrich did not limit himself to work which appeared only after Marcus and Fischer. Like many critics of "postmodernism" these days, Friedrich's vehemence is an index of closeness, not distance. For the temporal relativism Friedrich takes seriously in Heraclitus' "All is flux" rivals the most radical arguments of a Derrida or a DeMan. Moreover, it is surely arguable that his sweeping claims for irony belong to a pervasive historical condition of the "West"—a state of universalized instability. Indeed the current volume taken as a whole makes sense, finds its audiences, in this context of negotiated, conjunctural, contested and unfinished visions of the (historical, the human) real.

But irony only gets the last, never the final, word. We can be sure, at least, of more surprises. History keeps dissolving into histories. Who, fifty years ago, would have predicted the current dynamism of "indigenous" politics? The local inflections of "capitalism?" We stick around to see what in the heck is going to happen next.

In the meantime, the time of everyday lives, people make the best of their situations. Mary Taylor Huber, Mary Scoggin, and Lawrence Taylor show people dealing ironically with power structures they can't control. Irony is a means of getting some purchase on slippery power—whether it be Papua New Guinea missionaries finding that conversion is a messy process, or Chinese writers adopting the masks of humor and drunkenness as they negotiate a repressive regime, or Irish tricksters using self-mockery against powerful foreigners. Ironic comprehension here serves a double function. On the one hand, it helps people contain, perform, step partly outside a situation, thus gaining some control. On the other hand, by highlighting the artificial, the tactical nature of such containments, irony recognizes historical conjuctures as uncontrollable, in process, with unpredictable outcomes.

The two functions are visible in Mary Taylor Huber's very interesting analysis of Catholic Missionaries' uses of irony and paradox as they wrestle with the dissonance and disorder of the colonial contact-situations in which they find themselves. Most prominent, of course, is the ideological function of irony, expressing and containing complexity, innovation, and deviance. All sorts of civilizing expectations are questioned by the very messy translation work and fraught political encounters of evangelism. Missionaries often confront (and some accept) that their expectations do not fit practical reality. Syncretic compromises, making things up as one goes along, are the order—or disorder—of the day. Can this makeshift work really be "sowing the gospel?" How much dissonance is okay? When does Melanesian Christianity stop being Christianity?

In response to this sense of being in an "experimental moment" (with a vengeance), in danger of losing the ability to control one's work and its meanings, many have adopted a scapegoating, paranoid style that cuts through all the ambiguities and representation problems to assert a clear truth. Many evangelists

have doggedly sustained this kind of simplistic vision of good and evil, of be-
fore/after transformations, of struggles with the devil, passages from darkness
into light. But Huber's more liberal evangelists take a different route. They are
pragmatists, open to a considerable degree of paradox and dissonance. Their
way of accommodating themselves to a situation they can only partly control
is to accept that God works in strange ways. Biblical paradox can always be
mobilized, making it more acceptable to leave contradictions between rules
and realities unresolved. Huber's analysis shows, however, that this ability to
sustain a considerable degree of pragmatic play and receptivity depends on the
absolute nonquestioning of an ultimate horizon of order (albeit an inscrutable
one): that of Divine purpose.

Perhaps we can derive a general point about irony as an ideology of order,
or perhaps of acceptable disorder. Complex, nonreductive, experimental, "predicaments of irony" can be tolerated and managed—thereby avoiding paranoid
reductions and literalist simplifications—but only by not questioning some
horizon of order, some ultimate sense that things are ultimately translatable or
will come out all right in the end. It would be interesting to explore a bit further what these unquestioned horizons might be for the ironic ethnographer and
colonial officer whose tolerance for dissonance is contrasted by Huber with that
of the evangelists. What order, what management of disorder, is being accomplished in their deployment of irony? (I've argued, in *The Predicament of Culture,* discussing the case of Marcel Griaule, that "ethnographic liberalism"
functions within colonial situations—and also national and neocolonial contexts—by embracing an ironic, outsider/insider role and style.)

But for missionaries in places like New Guinea, the open-endedness of
divine purpose in the scattering and hybridizing of God's Word may not be
simply a way of managing dissonance. Indeed, in some cases (I think of Maurice Leenhardt in New Caledonia) it can permit a critical, humanly impressive,
acceptance of partial understanding and historical change. When evangelical
legacies are suddenly rearticulated by anticolonial, national, and indigenous
"kastom" movements, an ironic attitude permits openness to the unexpected.
I think of a veteran Anglican missionary watching the New Hebrides transformed into Vanuatu. He speaks of mission-trained priests assuming leadership
roles in the independence movement. With a guiding movement of his hands:
"We told them: 'Follow the Holy Spirit, Follow the Holy Spirit.' . . . [the hands
suddenly veer off at right angles] 'So they followed the Holy Spirit!'"

An appeal to Divine intention here allows the veteran to accept fully the
historical legitimacy of decolonization, and the limited perspective of his
own many years of experience. This is no small achievement of historical self-
location and openness. Irony, here, encodes a certain "negative capability" in
the face of Friedrich's relentless temporal shifts of perspective. To say that what

has shifted—as the diverse peoples of the former New Hebrides become the diverse peoples of an emerging Vanuatu—is part of an epochal decolonization is perhaps only to say that "History" (like the inscrutable Holy Spirit) can be counted on to veer off, but not to point in a clear direction. For "decolonization" is not, in practice, guaranteed by any "postcolonial" teleology. What the future holds for newly "sovereign" places like Vanuatu, in the messy world of global, regional, national, and local interconnections, time will tell. If the Holy Spirit (or the Historical Order) you believe in is enough of a *trickster*. . . well, almost anything can happen.

Same goes, maybe, if you get drunk enough! Mary Scoggin subtly brings out the ways hope and defeat are mingled in Chinese discourses on wine. Ironic belatedness and control usually favors one aspect of this mixture, the sense of defeat—in the sense, that is, of seeing through everything, of knowing every meaning is coopted, every hope for change naive. And yet, when Huang Shang writes a barbed critique of Mao's "Talks at the Yenan Forum on Literature and Art," and pays the price for his impertinence, he says later "I was drunk when I wrote certain things." Wine is equally about present recklessness and the morning after. Like irony, drinking is a matter of unleashed desire mixed up with thinking better of it later. But do we have to come to rest in the latter position, the morning after. . . ? Hegel's Owl of Minerva, with a historical hangover?

I prefer the night before. Lawrence Taylor gives us a song whose singer is, like Ireland, "drunk, singing, and blissfully delusional in the face of history." A kind of inebriated hope, in which we glimpse, intertwined, the method and the madness of subaltern irony. Taylor's serious joke about the colonized trickster (who deploys the dominator's stereotype so well that, for a moment, the power game is reversed) nicely evokes a contemporary *neo*colonial moment. It's an anti-*American,* not anti-British, joke. But is this mordant irony a transformative strategy or just self-defense in a context of global dominance? Without a coherent narrative of historical transformation (can we speak of world revolution, without irony?) subversive tactics of this kind will always be ambiguous. Indeed, the same can be said of all "postcolonial" hybridities, localisms, resistances, and transgressions—making the best of bad situations. But these often seem to be all we have, beginning again to imagine a more democratic, egalitarian global future.

In ironic predicaments things never lead quite where we want them to, and our last word quickly becomes part of another story, the butt of someone else's joke. Is there a positive (by which I mean more socially just) transformative dimension to this perpetual displacement? Drunk, singing, and blissfully delusional in the face of history, we act as if there were. Otherwise all we have is the sour taste of the morning after, its hard-nosed and moralistic confrontations with "reality."

I keep coming back to Paul Friedrich's ambivalently hyperironic paper in this light. What to make of its extremism, its "torrent of anecdotes and arguments?" He finds irony virtually everywhere—not merely a rhetorical style, but a pervasive structuring principle of human (even "simian"!) existence. Because situations and perspectives change, because power differentiates and is duplicitous, because communication entails embedded contexts and gaps between speakers and listeners, irony is inescapable and constitutive of subjects and societies. The stress on temporality cuts deepest, at least for those of us struggling within and against what might be called "late historical consciousness." People and societies always change. They get older and grapple with things differently. A political or social arrangement will inevitably, a decade later, mean something else. To see orders and meanings as temporally contingent, as historical articulations, assumes that they will eventually be disarticulated and rearticulated, for better and worse.

It cannot be clear where this leads us, or points. What divinatory, if not exactly prophetic, process is immanent here? Friedrich's ultimate "ironic irony" trumps all other tropes of experience. Is this celebration a kind of dissipation, by excess? Is Friedrich drunk on irony? And if so, why? Is the point simply to lay bare a human condition that others have missed, or repressed? Is this a song of growing older, seeing things change, and oneself changing? It is surely all that. But I can't help thinking that in this recurring urge to go off the deep end there's more than a superior knowingness, more than can be contained by the happy ending Friedrich belatedly attaches, where "zero irony" (momentary ecstasy) dialogues lovingly with "totalizing irony" (the tragic structure of human existence).

Is there any way out of irony? No, argues Friedrich, nor should there be. Moments free of irony are evanescent, quickly given meaning and power in their surrounding cultural, linguistic, political contexts. Irony is human life itself: a structuring and displacing process manifested as human time, power, culture, language and, the ultimate expression of it all, "tragedy." It is a provocative extremism, particularly now at the end of our long, excessive twentieth-century session with irony at its cruelest and most exuberant. In Friedrich's vision, undomesticated irony seems to be a poetical and political force for perpetual displacement, for metamorphosis. Am I wrong to sense here, a subversive energy, a dissolute (Dionysian) argument for and from process, an approach which places again on the agenda the *question* of temporality (and thus the fraying of linear History)? Friedrich helps us confront the necessity of disintegration: death as a transformative source for more life.

In our belated fin-de-millénaire, too late and too early, what help can we get from a displacing, reopening, processual irony—for imagining futures, for an alertness to alteration? Hung over, the morning of January 1, 2000, we keep

keep on living, changing, stumbling, veering off. Ironic hope? Hopeful irony? Such oxymorons need to start making sense. . .

• • •

But how long, he wonders, before all this seems like "a late twentieth-century thing"? Delusional in the face of History, the last discussant heads for his car.

Coda

—————— JAMES W. FERNANDEZ AND MARY TAYLOR HUBER ——————

Irony, Practice,
and the Moral Imagination

It would open us to ironic observation if we were to pretend that this collection has cleared a straight and secure path through the complexities of irony in anthropology and in social life more generally. A capacious literature testifies to the difficulties of tying down this irregular register in human affairs. Irony resists capture by crisp definition because its scale of reference slides so quickly from a play on words to a war of worlds. At this far end, irony, like its poor relation cynicism, signals "lost belief" (Chaloupka 1999). It is a potential consequence of all practice, arising as it does in the space between the world as planned or promised and the world as achieved or received. Yet the problematic of unrequitement in which irony flourishes has a positive as well as negative pole. Belief may be lost for good as well as bad reasons. And the loss, whether justified or not, may excite the moral imagination to explore routes to a better way of life.

Certainly many recent debates in anthropology and neighboring fields have been provocative of irony. Universalist judgments are regularly challenged by relativist arguments accompanied by ironic overtones and imputations. Claims to cultural authenticity are accosted ironically by awareness of the recurrent invention of tradition. General observations on character and culture (the natural calling of the human sciences) are subject to ironic criticism, for acquiescent and anesthetized essentializing, and for the concealment of the inevitable partiality of judgment. These debates not only challenge our capacity to manage our subject matter, but also contribute to our sense that these are ironic times for our discipline. They make a predicament (Clifford 1988), to echo the word now widely used, of treating any subject in the anthropological spectrum of interests with any entirety and sense of unambiguous engagement.

It is, however, precisely because of this predicament, and in the interest of giving ourselves tools for addressing and managing it with greater wisdom and

understanding, that a collection of essays on irony in anthropology has perti-
nence. The literature on irony is full of typologies: dramatic, historic, philosophic, or Socratic. And indeed, Clifford Geertz (1968) introduced the notion
of Anthropological Irony to the classic list some decades ago. The essays in this
volume open up new meanings of Geertz's "irony of rapport"—the relations
between anthropologist and subject—by treating it from the perspective of
"true" and "self-" irony. But we also find in these essays new and interesting
ways of conceptualizing irony by considering the predicaments of others, for
example, indexical irony (Scoggin), inclusive-exclusive irony (Fernandez),
constrained irony (Chock), insubordinate irony (Herzfeld), paradox (Huber),
paranoid irony (Marcus), and ironic irony (Friedrich). It is not only anthropologists, it seems, but anthropologists' subjects, who live in ironic times.

Yet there is danger lurking here. Are we projecting our own condition of lost
belief onto others? Are we succumbing—like so many contemporary media
and cultural critics—to a tendency to see irony everywhere and in everything?
If everything is ironic, what virtue lies in treating irony as a distinct topic in anthropology or other field? If everything is ironic, how can we know to what degree irony is a local resource, under what particular conditions irony is used by
others, or even by the anthropologist, as a consequence of the peculiarities of
the ethnographic enterprise? How can we know irony as something useful to
pay attention to in our own or others' practice? This is a problem of the limits
of irony: if all is irony what is the use of the concept itself?

Paul Friedrich, in this volume, points out that irony is always with us, inevitably implicated in the nature of time and power, culture and language,
tropes and tragedy. However, our own view—and, we suspect, that of most of
our contributors—is that all is only *potentially* ironic. The task of the anthropologist is to explore the circumstances in which that potential is recognized,
mobilized, moralized, or politicized. And that is what these essays have tried
to do in their various ways. They have indicated that there are certain times,
places, and situations which seem to invite irony and where people use it for
better or for worse. As we said in the introduction, "All of our authors would
probably agree with Paul Friedrich that situations inviting irony are inherent in
the nature of language, the passage of time, and the structure of social life. But
most would probably also agree with George Marcus that irony flourishes in
certain historical conditions, and that these conditions are now especially intense and widespread." Yesterday, we might argue, colonialism provided precisely such conditions; today globalization has taken over this task and brought
it back home.

And this brings us to the final issue we want to address in this coda, the
relation between the four main terms of the collection's title: irony, practice,
the moral imagination, and anthropology. We have argued that irony arises in

practice and excites the moral imagination by its identification of a gap, contradiction, inconsistency, or incongruity. But one could ask whether irony is just as likely to undercut than serve moral thought and practical action, as contemporary critics of today's culture of irony suggest (see, e.g., Purdy 1999, but also see Scott 2000).[1] And indeed a number of essays in this collection indicate that irony can be an evasion of focused reasoning on moral issues and an alternative to action—a form of inaction, as one of our contributors has said. The possibility that irony could be a detour from, rather than a route to, responsibility is particularly troubling for scholars in the humanities and social sciences, where an ironic sensibility has been so well developed in recent years.

While the moral imagination may not be much easier to define than irony itself, we would like to suggest a simple enough definition relevant to those who work in the human sciences: the creating of as clear an image, or set of images, as possible of existing social conditions in their positive and negative aspects, along with an image or set of images of one's own obligations for achieving through practical action better conditions for all concerned. In other words scholars, like professionals more generally, have a set of responsibilities in the world, and not just to their own fields. Reflection on the ironies of scholarly practice—in anthropology or any of its neighboring disciplines—need not be handmaiden to irresponsibility, but can instead aid self-awareness and disarm some of the hazards that inevitably accompany action.

Irony—including self-irony—can be an aid to responsibility in even more direct ways. For the world is full of powerful persons and projects that take themselves and their responsibilities so seriously as to be repressive (whether intentionally or not) in minor or major degree. Here irony can perform an important and, in the end, responsible task of parodying the absolutist impulse and mocking master narratives held militantly. We agree that when metanarratives are questioned, people are often at sea. But that is precisely the point. The

1. As we write, Jedediah Purdy's *For Common Things: Irony, Trust, and Commitment in America Today* (1999) is being reviewed in virtually all our important cultural forums—the *New York Review of Books, Harpers, The New Yorker, Time, Salon, Slate,* NPR, CNN, *The New York Times Magazine.* It is especially interesting to us that "irony" is sharing these minutes of fame with Purdy who, in the preface to *For Common Things,* establishes his claim to serious social criticism by embracing commitment and denouncing irony as a tired, defeatist, and immoral stance. Some of Purdy's reviewers, Benjamin De Mott in the *New York Review of Books* and Roger Hodge in *Harper's,* for example—have pointed out that this is a fairly one-sided view of a complicated trope. As De Mott (2000: 18) says, "He seems unaware of irony as a means of holding dim outlooks and wilted language in precise, sustained focus, for perusal and edification." Some commentators are asking whether irony's days as a sign of sophistication are numbered, whether young writers today are questioning irony and exploring attitudes of sincerity instead (e.g., Scott 2000: 40). Some critics are questioning the adequacy of the contrast between irony and sincerity itself (Harris 2000). In brief, it would seem that the collection we offer here participates in a cultural moment of considerable resonance.

task of the anthropologist is to find out what people do in these situations, how they sort it all out, and to modestly—recognizing in Burkean fashion that we are all tossing in the same boat—provide what help we can. We note that even those philosophers most highly attuned to irony—those who are often seen as our main "metanarrative busters"—are themselves searching for some sort of ground for moral action (see, e.g., Rorty 1999). It would be Pollyanna-ish to think there is not much work to be done in the world to make it a better place, and Candidean to assume that irony is the best of all possible registers with which to do it. However, in an age in which irony is so highly profiled, reflections on the role of irony in social and professional life are, we would argue, of the greatest relevance.

References

Chaloupka, William. 1999. *Everybody Knows: Cynicism in America*. Minneapolis: University of Minnesota Press.
Clifford, James. 1988. *The Predicament of Culture: Twentieth Century Ethnography, Literature, and Art*. Cambridge: Harvard University Press.
DeMott, Benjamin. 2000. The West Virginian. Review of *For Common Things*, by Jedediah Purdy. *The New York Review of Books*, 9 March 9, pp. 17–18.
Geertz, Clifford. 1968. Thinking as a Moral Act: Ethical Dimensions of Anthropological Fieldwork in the New States. *The Antioch Review* 28(3): 139–58.
Harris, Elise. 2000. Infinite Jest. Review of *A Heartbreaking Work of Staggering Genius*, by Dave Eggers. *The Nation* (20 March): 45–48.
Hodge, Roger D. 1999. Thus Spoke Jedediah. Review of *For Common Things*, by Jedediah Purdy. *Harper's Magazine* 299 (September): 84–85.
Purdy, Jedediah. 1999. *For Common Things: Irony, Trust, and Commitment in America Today*. New York: Alfred A. Knopf.
Rorty, Richard. 1999. *Philosophy and Social Hope*. London: Penguin Books.
Scott, A. O. 2000. The Panic of Influence. Review of *Brief Interviews with Hideous Men*, by David Foster Wallace. *New York Review of Books*, 10 February, pp. 39–43.

Contributors

James A. Boon is professor of anthropology at Princeton University. His latest book is *Verging on Extra-Vagance: Anthropology, History, Religion, Literature, Arts . . . Showbiz.* His current research addresses intersensory aestheticisms in the checkered past of cross-cultural description.

Phyllis Pease Chock is professor of anthropology at Catholic University of America, Washington, DC. She is the author of numerous articles on aspects of ethnicity, gender, and immigration in the United States, especially as issues of federal legislative and policy debate, and the co-editor (with June R. Wyman) of *Discourse and the Social Life of Meaning.* She also serves as the editor of *Anthropological Quarterly.*

James Clifford is professor in the History of Consciousness Department, University of California, Santa Cruz. He is author of *The Predicament of Culture* and *Routes: Travel and Translation in the Late Twentieth Century.* His current research explores issues of globalization, intercultural process, and indigeneity.

James W. Fernandez is professor of anthropology at the University of Chicago. He is author or editor of numerous works treating the dynamic role played by the various tropes in communicative interaction, including *Persuasions and Performances: The Play of Tropes in Culture,* and *Beyond Metaphor: The Theory of Tropes in Anthropology.*

Paul Friedrich is professor in the departments of anthropology and linguistics, and in the Committee on Social Thought at the University of Chicago. He has worked in Mexico, India, and with Russian exiles. His main works include *Agrarian Revolt in a Mexican Village, Proto-Indo-European Trees, The Meaning of Aphrodite,* and *Music in Russian Poetry.*

Michael Herzfeld is professor of anthropology at Harvard University. Although he has hitherto conducted all his fieldwork in Greece, he is now working on a new project on the uses of the past in Rome, Italy, and is also planning new research in Thailand. His works include *The Social Production of Indifference: Exploring the Symbolism of Western Bureaucracy, Cultural Intimacy: Social Poetics in the Nation-State,* and *Portrait of a Greek Imagination: An Ethnographic Biography of Andreas Nendakis.*

Mary Taylor Huber is a senior scholar at the Carnegie Foundation for the Advancement of Teaching, where she is exploring "Cultures of Teaching and Learning in Higher Education." Her work on colonial cultures includes *The Bishops' Progress: A Historical Ethnography of Catholic Missionary Experience on the Sepik Frontier,* and *Gendered Missions: Women and Men in Missionary Discourse and Practice,* co-edited with Nancy Lutkehaus.

Arnold Krupat is a member of the Division of Global Studies at Sarah Lawrence College in which he has several times team-taught (with Peter Whiteley) a course entitled "Ethnography and Literature." His most recent books are *Here First: Autobiographical Essays by Native American Writers* (edited with Brian Swann), *The Turn to the Native: Studies in Criticism and Culture,* and *Ethnocriticism: Ethnography, History, Literature.* He has also published a novel called, *Woodsmen, or Thoreau and the Indians.*

Diane Losche is an anthropologist who teaches in the School of Art History and Theory, College of Fine Arts, University of New South Wales in Sydney, Australia. She has done research on the art and culture of the Sepik region of Papua New Guinea. The focus of her research is both anthropology and contemporary art. Her most recent publication is *Double Vision: Art Histories and Colonial Histories in the Pacific,* which she edited with Nicholas Thomas.

George E. Marcus is professor and chair of the anthropology department at Rice University. He has just completed editing the eighth and final volume of the fin-de-siècle series of annuals, Late Editions, published by the University of Chicago Press. He is co-author (with Michael Fischer) of *Anthropology as Cultural Critique,* and co-editor (with James Clifford) of *Writing Culture.* His most recent book is *Ethnography Through Thick and Thin.* He is currently engaged in a study of the contemporary Portuguese nobility at the invitation of the Marquis of Fronteira and Alorna.

Mary Scoggin is assistant professor of anthropology and Chinese studies at Humboldt State University. Her work on Chinese literature and contemporary media in the People's Republic of China concerns issues such as censorship, literary community and theories of expressive culture.

Lawrence J. Taylor is professor and head of the Department of Anthropology at the National University of Ireland, Maynooth. His main areas of research have been in Ireland and on the United States/Mexico border. He is the author of *Dutchmen on the Bay, Occasions of Faith: An Anthropology of Irish Catholics* and, with photographer Maeve Hickey, *The Road to Mexico, Tunnel Kids: Lives on and under the US/Mexico Border,* and *Ambos Nogales: Intimate Portraits of the Border!*

Index

————————— • • • —————————